Terrorism in the Twenty-First Century

Terrorism in the Twenty-First Century

FOURTH EDITION

Cindy C. Combs
University of North Carolina at Charlotte

PEARSON

Prentice
Hall

Upper Saddle River, New Jersey 07458

Library of Congress Cataloging-in-Publication Data

Combs, Cindy C.
 Terrorism in the twenty-first century / Cindy C. Combs.—4th ed.
    p. cm.
 Includes bibliographical references and index.
 ISBN 0-13-193063-X
 1. Terrorism.   2. Terrorism—Forecasting.   I. Title: Terrorism in the 21st century.   II. Title.

 HV6431.C472 2006
 303.6'25—dc22

                                                                        2005018659

Editorial Director: Charlyce Jones Owen
Editorial Assistant: Suzanne Remore
Director of Marketing: Heather Shelstad
Senior Managing Editor: Lisa Iarkowski
Production Liaison: Fran Russello
Manufacturing Buyer: Sherry Lewis
Cover Design: Bruce Kenselaar
Composition/Full-Service Project Management:
  Donna Leik: TechBooks/GTS York, PA

This book was set in Times New Roman by TechBooks/GTS York, PA. It was printed and bound by
Courier companies, Inc. The cover was printed by Courier companies, Inc.

Pearson Education LTD. London
Pearson Education Singapore, Pte. Ltd
Pearson Education, Canada, Ltd
Pearson Education—Japan
Pearson Education Australia PTY, Limited

Pearson Education North Asia Ltd
Pearson Educación de Mexico, S.A. de C.V.
Pearson Education Malaysia, Pte. Ltd
Pearson Education, Upper Saddle River,
  New Jersey

10 9 8 7 6 5 4 3 2 1
ISBN: 0-13-193063-X

Contents

PART III   HOW DO THEY OPERATE?

7 Terrorist Training   123

8 The Media: A Weapon for Both Sides?   153

9 Domestic Terrorism in the United States   174

PART IV   RESPONSES TO TERRORISM

Preface

The events of September 11, 2001, and the subsequent U.S. and international response, clearly demonstrated the need to understand the phenomenon of terrorism, which has dramatically impacted the peace and stability of our world. This fourth edition, which reflects much of the aftermath of this dramatic event, includes a more in-depth analysis of the type of terrorism generated by religious zealotry and explores the use of weapons of mass destruction by terrorists. As in previous editions, I examine the legal and political responses of individual nations and of the international community, through the instrument of the United Nations, to terrorist attacks as they become increasingly lethal, indiscriminate, and widely dispersed. The transformation of terrorism into a form of "netwar" and the ability of nations to deal with this asymmetric threat is also explored.

It has always been important that this text be easy for both students and professors to use, with material organized clearly and concisely and presented without prejudice. To prevent as far as possible a pejorative use of the material, the examination of the concept of "terrorism" emphasizes a legal, operational definition applicable to terrorist *acts,* rather than to the individuals, groups, or states who carry out such acts. This makes the term much less likely to be applied with prejudice; if the term is applied in the legally correct fashion, it can be done objectively rather than subjectively. This also facilitates the use of the book by a wider audience, since each individual, group, and state can be evaluated in the context of the nature of the actions taken.

To keep this new edition "user-friendly" for students, I have retained the original structure, expanding the chapter on terrorism within the United States and the section on weapons of mass destruction, including a brief examination of the threat of terror networks, and offering a more comprehensive list of suggested readings at the end of each chapter for future research. I have also updated the data concerning the trends in terrorism, adjusting it to explore the data provided by the U.S. Department of State with other data sources.

This edition still begins with an updated chronology of recent terrorist incidents, designed to make the reader aware of the dimensions of the problem, followed by a brief look at terrorism in historical perspective, with emphasis given to understanding the cyclical nature of these acts of violence. Evaluation sections at the end of each chapter, designed to challenge readers to apply their understanding to current events, has been useful in provoking excellent student discussion of the concepts. The historical analysis is particularly useful, because many of the "new" terrorist events have historical roots that contribute significantly to an understanding of the phenomenon.

In addition to building an interest in the study of terrorism, I have highlighted criteria useful in studying the types of modern terrorism. Applying such criteria to individuals, groups, and states makes it possible to differentiate to some degree between such terms as *crusaders* and *criminals,* between state-sponsored and state-tolerated terrorism, and between separatist and nationalist groups. Familiarity with operationalized terms makes it easier to apply such terms without prejudice and, more significantly, to evaluate the response options for each type.

The text is organized in a style intended to be quite comfortable for course use in a lecture or a seminar-style class. Lists of key concepts, case studies, evaluation sections, significant endnotes, and lists of suggested readings are designed to allow people with a variety of learning styles and reading approaches to master the content easily. Faculty can readily accentuate, elaborate, or co-relate examples that are similar, parallel, or contrary, with a sound framework for student understanding. With this format, I hope to engage readers with various preparatory backgrounds and academic experiences, in this vital subject of terrorism. This is a subject we certainly can no longer afford to comfortably ignore, nor can we safely build effective policy without a firm understanding of this phenomena.

ACKNOWLEDGMENTS

The Center for Homeland Security established at The University of North Carolina two years ago facilitated opportunities to research as well as to teach in this vital field. Charlotte has a strong commitment toward the integration of research and teaching, encouraging faculty to generate materials that are of use in the classroom.

Because our Master in Public Administration program developed a concentration in disaster management with a focus on homeland security, I owe thanks in this edition to its director, David Swindell, for offering me the opportunity to teach about terrorism and homeland security and to work on grants in this field. Special thanks also to my daughter, Elizabeth, who not only survived my courses but also helped me edit and index this edition.

My husband, Lee, was again my strongest critic and best researcher, downloading all types of information in the wake of the attacks on America and the development of America's response, including the "war on terror." Our daughters, Sara, Elizabeth, and Katherine, with their assessments of the inherent "dullness" of social science from a student's perspective, kept me focused on making this fourth edition interesting and exciting to the students who will be its primary consumers.

Terrorism
in the Twenty-First
Century

Introduction

The terrorist of yesterday is the hero of today, and the hero of yesterday becomes the terrorist of today. In a constantly changing world of images, we have to keep our heads straight to know what terrorism is and what it is not. Even more importantly, we need to know what causes terrorism and how to stop it.

Eqbal Ahmad

Eqbal Ahmad, an activist scholar born in India and trekking with his brothers to the newly formed state of Pakistan in 1947, died in 1998, before the attacks in the United States in September of 2001. But his insights into the phenomenon of terrorism are poignantly relevant as the world seeks to come to grips with this escalating asymmetrical threat. We are still groping to find a working definition of terrorism and an organized method of applying the term that does not make the hero of today the terrorist of tomorrow.

In the wake of the September 11, 2001, attacks in New York City and Washington, DC, remarks by al-Qaeda spokesman Suliman Abu Geith, that the perpetrators of the attacks had "destroyed America with their airplanes," evoked an image of terrorists at war with a country. Geith's comment that these individuals had "moved the battle into the heart of America" was reflected in the response of the U.S. government, which issued a declaration of "war" on terrorism in the wake of these attacks. The subsequent war in Afghanistan and the war initiated by the United States in Iraq were premised on the threat of terrorism and the need of the state, individually or collectively, to respond. The early years of the twenty-first century are clearly demonstrating the changing nature of terrorism and its challenge to international

1

peace and security. This challenge is one that the international communities, as well as individual nation-states, are in many respects ill-prepared to meet.

The last decade of the twentieth century, although it offered positive changes with the end of the cold war and the capture of the world's most notorious terrorist-for-hire, did not mark the end of terrorism. Instead, terrorism began to become a larger, not a smaller, player in international politics, as states stepped back from open warfare but left many national groups angry and determined to seek justice by violent means. September 11 was, in that sense, a "wake-up call" not only for the United States but also for the world that terrorism continues to constitute a clear and present danger, a weapon evolving often faster than are the world community's responses to it.

The ruthless declaration, "To get anywhere, you have to walk over the corpses," made by Ilyich Ramirez Sanchez in 1975 while holding 11 OPEC ministers hostage, evoked the image of terrorists as they menaced so many lives during the latter part of the twentieth century. When Sanchez, known to the public as Carlos the Jackal, was taken from his home in the Sudan by French police in the summer of 1994, it seemed to many that this capture might mark the beginning of the end of terrorism. The end of the cold war made governments less willing or able to engage in state-sponsored or state-protected terrorism, and many hoped that the capture of Carlos was symbolic of a growing willingness between states to cooperate to end the decades of bloody terrorist acts.

However, in 1994 less than one month after Carlos' capture, the international community reeled from the alarm of weapons-grade plutonium "on sale" from former Soviet arsenals. During the spring and summer of that same year, German police uncovered four attempts to sell smuggled nuclear material that could actually be used to make an atomic bomb. On August 10, Lufthansa Flight 3369 from Moscow to Munich was found to contain 350 grams of atomic fuel aboard in a lead-lined suitcase carrying MOX. A Colombian and two Spaniards were arrested. A 35-year-old German man was arrested two days later trying to sell an extremely pure sample of plutonium to a police informant.

None of the recovered materials were sufficient to produce even a small, crude atom bomb. But the fact that weapons-grade plutonium was on the market acted as a red alert for many terrorist experts in Western governments. Frightening questions have been raised about the possibilities of nuclear terrorism, a potential threat largely written off during the past few decades as too expensive, too heavily safeguarded, and too politically costly to be an attractive option for most groups engaged in terrorist activities. Now many of those who study terrorism wonder if, with bomb-grade plutonium finally "on sale," a rogue state or group might try to buy enough to build a bomb. The potential threat of a "dirty bomb" in the hands of a group waging terrorism has also become a part of "homeland security" planning in the United States today.

The threat of biological and chemical terror has also grown more substantive, particularly after the attack in the Tokyo subway using sarin gas. In the wake of the September 11 attacks, the discovery of anthrax in the mail system in the United States raised the possibility that individuals or groups might engage openly in biological terrorism. Countries and their citizens began to feel increasingly vulnerable to attacks in the mail, on the water systems, even through the air ventilation of buildings. Awareness of terrorism has never been stronger, while understanding of the phenomena continues to grow as the world seeks answers and options to cope with the threat.

Terrorism in the twenty-first century may well be quite different from that experienced in the twentieth. The wave of terror that Carlos the Jackal embodied apparently is fading, although the "holy wars" invoked by individuals like Osama bin Laden gain strength and credibility. In the 1980s, we witnessed the beginning of the shift in contemporary terrorism from ideologies of the extreme left toward fundamentalism from the extreme right. Both types of terror continue to play an important role in international politics, but the pattern for the twenty-first century is less clear. The willingness of groups in the twenty-first century to use, or attempt to use, weapons of mass destruction offer an indication of disturbing new trends in contemporary terrorism. Moreover, terrorism taking the form of "netwar" offers a new asymmetry to this threat.

To understand what terrorism may likely be in the twenty-first century, it is important to first examine what is known about terrorism in the twentieth century. Political science is founded upon a need to *explain* and to *predict* actions in the political realm. For that purpose, this text examines the known facets of contemporary terrorism, attempting to explain the primary characteristics of *what, who, why,* and *how*. Predictions about forthcoming patterns of terrorism can then be based on an understanding of previous and present patterns of behavior.

Terrorism, whether leaders like bin Laden or Saddam Hussein are captured or killed, will not end. It will continue to exist, but it does appear to be changing. Evaluating present conditions and attempting to predict future trends can offer useful insights for policymakers and for citizens in this new century.

CHAPTER 1

An Idea Whose Time Has Come?

Key Concepts

terrorism

mass terror

dynastic assassination

random terror

focused random terror

tactical terror

The terrorist of yesterday is the hero of today, and the hero of yesterday becomes the terrorist of today. In a constantly changing world of images, we have to keep our heads straight to know what terrorism is and what it is not.

Eqbal Ahmad

Selective Chronology of Recent Terror

1993	February 26	*United States:* Seven dead, 1,000 injured (some seriously) in car bomb explosion in World Trade Center, New York.
	March 12	*India:* Three hundred dead, over 1,300 injured by coordinated series of bombings in heart of Bombay.
	September 22	*South Africa:* "Day of terror" as 31 die on day Parliament debates formation of Transitional Council.
	December 9	*Egypt:* One person killed and six injured when members of Al-Gama'a al-Islamiyya opened fire on two movie houses that were showing foreign films. The group stated that the attack was in retaliation for the screening of "immoral" films.
	December 14	*Algeria:* A large group of armed terrorists attack a work camp of a hydroelectric project in Tamezguida. Fourteen Croatian citizens were taken out of the camp. Twelve were murdered by having their throats slit; two escaped with injuries. The Armed Islamic Group claimed responsibility, stating that the attack was part of an ongoing campaign to rid Algeria of all foreigners and to avenge Muslims killed in Bosnia.
1994	April 6	*Rwanda:* Assassination of presidents of Rwanda and Bururndi in missile attack on their plane. Genocidal war in Rwanda erupts.

	April 24	*South Africa:* Nine dead, 90 injured in a car bomb explosion near African National Congress (ANC) headquarters in central Johannesburg. White separatists opposed to South Africa's first multiracial elections believed responsible.
	July 18	*Argentina:* A car bomb explodes at the Israeli-Argentine Mutual Association (AMIA), killing nearly 100 persons and wounding more than 200 others.
	July 19	*Panama:* A commuter plane explodes in flight over the Santa Rita mountains, killing 21.
	December 24	*Algeria:* Members of the Armed Islamic Group hijack an Air France flight in Algeria. The plane arrives in Marseille, France, on December 26. A French antiterrorist unit storms the plane, ending the 54-hour siege in which three hostages were killed by the terrorists. All four terrorists killed during the rescue.
1995	March 20	*Japan:* Members of Aum Supreme Truth carried six packages onto Tokyo subway trains and punctured the packages with umbrella tips, releasing deadly sarin gas that killed 12 persons and injured more than 5,000.
	April 19	*United States:* Car bomb blows up Oklahoma City federal building. One hundred sixty-eight dead, hundreds more injured.
	July 25	*France:* A bomb detonated aboard a Paris subway train as it arrived at St. Michel station kills 7 commuters, and injures 86.
	November 4	*Israel:* Prime Minister Yitzhak Rabin assassinated by Jewish extremist at peace rally.
	November 19	*Pakistan:* A suicide bomber drove a vehicle into the Egyptian Embassy compound in Islamabad, killing at least 16 persons and injuring about 60 others. The Japanese and Indonesian embassies, the Canadian High Commission, and the UK housing compound were among the damaged buildings. Al-Gama'a al-Islamiyya, the Jihad Group, and the International Justice Group all claimed responsibility.
	December 16	*Spain:* Several bombs detonated in different areas of a department store in Valencia, killing one person and wounding eight others. Basque Fatherland and Liberty (ETA) claimed responsibility.
1996	January 31	*Sri Lanka:* Suspected members of the Liberation Tigers of Tamil Eelam (LTTE) rammed an explosives-laden truck into the Central Bank in the heart of downtown Colombo, killing 90 civilians and injuring more than 1,400 others.
	March 4	*Israel:* A suicide bomber detonated an explosive device outside the Dizengoff Center, Tel Aviv's largest shopping mall, killing 20 persons and injuring 75 others. HAMAS and the Palestine Islamic Jihad both claimed responsibility.
	April 18	*Egypt:* Four al-Gama'a al-Islamiyya (IG) militants opened fire on a group of Greek tourists in front of the Europa Hotel in Cairo, killing 18 Greeks and injuring 12 Greeks and 2 Egyptians. The IG claimed that they intended to attack a group of Israeli tourists they believed were staying at the hotel.
	June 25	*Saudi Arabia:* A fuel truck carrying a bomb exploded outside the U.S. military's Khubar Towers housing facility in Dhahran, killing 19 and wounding 515 persons. Several groups claimed responsibility.
	December 17	*Peru:* Fourteen members of the Tupac Amaru Revolutionary Movement (MRTA) took over the Japanese ambassador's residence in Lima, holding 72 persons hostage for four months.

1997	April 11–12	*Bosnia-Herzegovina:* Police discovered and defused 23 land mines under a bridge that was part of Pope John Paul II's motorcade route in Sarajevo, several hours before the Pope's arrival.
	April 27	*Cambodia:* Khmer Rouge guerrillas attacked Vietnamese fishermen and woodcutters in the Barkeo district of Ratanakkiri, killing nine persons and wounding ten others.
	July 30	*Israel:* Two bombs detonated in the Mahane Yehuda market in Jerusalem, killing 15 persons and wounding 168 others. The Izz-el-Din al-Qassam Brigades, the military wing of the Islamic Resistance Movement, claimed responsibility.
	October 15	*Sri Lanka:* LTTE guerrillas detonate a massive truck bomb in the parking lot of a major hotel next to the new World Trade Center in Colombo, killing 18 persons and injuring at least 110 others.
	November 17	*Egypt:* Six gunmen enter the Hatshepsut Temple in Luxor and for 30 minutes methodically shoot and kill tourists trapped inside the temple's alcoves. Fifty-eight foreign tourists are killed, along with three Egyptian police officers and one Egyptian tour guide. Al-Gama'a claimed responsibility for this attack.
1998	August 7	*Kenya and Nairobi:* U.S. embassies in Nairobi and Dar es-Sala'am are bombed, killing 224 persons and wounding about 5,000. The attacks were believed to be carried out by Osama bin Laden's organization al-Qaeda.
	August 20	*Afghanistan and Sudan:* U.S. missiles are launched to strike five camps belonging to bin Laden's organization in Afghanistan and a factory for the manufacturing of chemicals in Sudan. These attacks were made in retaliation for the bombing of the U.S. embassies.
1999	February 15	*Austria:* Kurdish protestors stormed and occupied the Greek Embassy in Vienna, taking the Greek ambassador and six other persons hostage. Several hours later the protestors released the hostages and left the embassy. The attack followed the Turkish government's announcement of the successful capture of the Kurdistan Workers' Party (PKK) leader Abdullah Ocalan.
	March 1	*Uganda:* According to French diplomatic reports, 150 armed Hutu rebels attacked three tourist camps, killed four Ugandans, and abducted three U.S. citizens, six Britons, three New Zealanders, two Danish citizens, one Australian, and one Canadian. On March 2, U.S. Embassy officials reported the Hutu rebels killed two U.S. citizens, four Britons, and two New Zealanders. The remaining hostages were released.
	July 6	*Angola:* Local press reported National Total Union for the Total Independence of Angola (UNITA) rebels ambushed a German humanitarian convoy, killing 15 persons and injuring 23 others. The convoy was transporting goods for Catholic Relief Service.
	December 24	*Nepal:* Five heavily armed militants hijacked an Indian Airlines Airbus carrying 189 passengers and 11 crew en route from Katmandu to New Delhi. After refueling in Pakistan, the plane was diverted to Dubai, United Arab Emirates, where the hijackers released 27 hostages along with the body of a hostage they had murdered. The hijackers then flew to Qandahar, Afghanistan, and demanded the release of 36 militants imprisoned in India. On December 31 the Indian government agreed to release three imprisoned militants in exchange for the hostages' safe return. Within less than three months of his release, one of the militants formed a new group, and began terrorist attacks on India.

2000	March 21	*India:* Armed militants kill 35 Sikhs in Chadisinghpoora Village. Members of two groups, the Lashkar-e-Tayyiba and the Hizb-ul-Mujahideen, militant Muslim groups in Kashmir, arrested.
	May 5	*Sierra Leone:* Revolutionary United Front (RUF) militants kidnap 300 United Nations Assistance Mission in Sierra Leone (UNAMSIL) peacekeepers. By May 28, the last of the peacekeepers were released unharmed.
	July 27	*Colombia:* In Bogota, suspected Guevarist Revolutionary Army (ARG) militants kidnap a French aid worker affiliated with Doctors Without Borders.
	October 12	*Yemen:* In Aden, a small dinghy carrying explosives rams the U.S. destroyer, USS *Cole,* killing 17 sailors and injuring 39 others. Supporters of Osama bin Laden are suspected in this attack.
2001	June 1	*Israel:* HAMAS claims responsibility for the bombing of a popular nightclub in Tel Aviv that caused over 140 casualties.
	September 11	*United States:* Two hijacked airliners crashed into the twin towers of the World Trade Center in New York City. Soon thereafter, the Pentagon was struck by a third hijacked plane. A fourth hijacked plane, suspected to be headed for a high-profile target in Washington, crashed into a field in southern Pennsylvania. More than 3,000 people were killed in these attacks. U.S. intelligence information indicated that Osama bin Laden, based in Afghanistan, was responsible for coordinating the attacks.

Were the 1990s an exceptionally violent decade? Perhaps. Is this violence diminishing in the early part of the twenty-first century? Given the events of September 11, 2001, and the subsequent "war on terrorism," this is probably not the case. But the preceding decade was clearly less violent than those decades during which the world experienced the trauma of global war. There was certainly less loss of life than during the years in which the Indochina conflict raged. Fewer lives were claimed by political violence during the 1990s than by traffic accidents on U.S. highways annually.

So why is so much attention directed toward developing policies to cope with terrorist violence in recent years? It has, as experts like Walter Laqueur note, attracted what could be considered an inordinate amount of attention, compared to other major problems of our times, such as global debt and world hunger. Terrorism has been the subject of countless speeches by political leaders throughout the world, and the impetus for numerous initiatives and conferences by foreign policy experts. The drama of terrorist-directed events such as those outlined in the beginning of this chapter attracts enormous attention in the press and on television worldwide. Terror-violence did, in many respects, become an accepted method of warfare during the latter part of the twentieth century. In the twenty-first century, terrorism itself has become a target of "war" on the part of the international community, clearly increasing the level of violence and the number of victims.

Indeed, in the wake of the events of September 2001, a global "war on terrorism" has begun to be waged, led by the United States and sanctioned by the United Nations. While the initial context of the "war" took place in Afghanistan, neither the toppling of the Taliban leadership nor the destruction of the al-Qaeda network in

Afghanistan sufficed to "win" this new war. Terrorism is an ancient "enemy" with roots in many cultures and followers in many creeds. A "war" against such an enemy will not be quickly brought to a successful conclusion.

Certainly terrorism has been waged by a wide variety of individuals and groups. It has been a favorite tactic of national and religious groups, by individuals whose ideologies fall on both the left and the right of the political spectrum, by nationalist and internationalist movements. It has been used as an instrument of state policy. It has been directed against autocratic as well as democratic regimes, although political democracies have been the most frequent target. At times it has been an instrument of last resort for movements of national liberation whose political attempts to change the system have failed; at other times, it has been deliberately chosen by such movements *before* other such political options have been attempted.

States have sponsored terrorism outside their own frontiers and have used terrorism as a weapon against their own citizens. Terrorism remains, paradoxically, both an instrument designed to force radical social and political changes and an instrument of oppression in seeking to prevent such changes.

Even with the increased use of terrorist violence, or perhaps because of its proliferation, there remains a great deal of confusion as to what the term *terrorism* really encompasses. Many definitions of terrorism are, in fact, encoded political statements. Too often the term is used in a pejorative sense, attached as a label to those groups whose political objectives one finds objectionable. To study this phenomenon, we must first establish a workable and useful definition—workable in that it has sufficient precision to allow us to identify the phenomenon when it occurs, and useful in that it is acceptable to a fairly broad range of political persuasions. Terrorism is a politicized term, just as terrorism is a political crime. Its definition must therefore be politically acceptable.

MODERN DEFINITIONS OF AN OLD CONCEPT

Terrorism is a phenomenon that is becoming a pervasive, often dominant influence in our lives. It affects the manner in which governments conduct their foreign policy and the way corporations transact their business. It causes alterations in the role and even the structure of our security forces. It forces us to spend huge amounts of time and money to protect our public figures, vital installations, citizens, and even our system of government. It influences the way we travel and the places we travel to see. It even affects the manner in which we live our daily lives. Our newspapers, radios, and televisions inundate our every waking moment with vivid details of terrorist spectaculars from all corners of the globe.

But what *is* terrorism—this "it" to which we attribute so much influence today? Before we can assess just how great a threat "it" poses and exactly whom "it" threatens, we need to determine what "terrorism" is. And it is precisely this problem of definition that has caused political, legal, and military leaders to throw up their hands, metaphorically, in discouragement and dismay.

Because terrorism is a political as well as legal and a military issue, its definition in modern terms has been slow to evolve. Not that there are not numerous definitions available—there are hundreds. But few of them are of sufficient legal scholarship to be useful in international law, and most of those that are legally useful lack the necessary ambiguity for political acceptance. As Eqbal Ahmad noted, "Officials don't define terrorism because definitions involve a commitment to analysis, comprehension, and adherence to norms of consistency."[1]

Thus, the problem of defining terrorism is not insuperable, but it must be handled with caution in order for subsequent use of the term to have meaning. To say that the number of terrorist incidents is rising annually would have little meaning unless it is clear precisely what such an incident *is* and *is not*.

Moreover, it helps to put the term into an historical perspective. Terrorism is not a modern phenomenon. The admixture of religion and politics fomenting terrorism in many areas today has a counterpart in the Hashashin of the Middle Ages. Incidents such as the *Achille Lauro* hijacking have precedents dating back many centuries. The statement that "one man's terrorist is another man's patriot" illustrates the historical continuum of conflict under which terrorism is operationally defined.

Ideology has always had an ambiguous relationship with terrorism—at one point justifying and at another condemning the same act. Theorists (and practitioners) of both the left and the right have advocated the use of what has been termed "terrorist" violence. Understanding the context of the ideological debate helps to deal with the justifications offered in contemporary times for terrorist acts.

It also helps to assess the ideological commitment of the perpetrators of terrorism. Profiling modern terrorists is one way of assessing what terrorism is committed for today. An understanding of the impact of group dynamics is also useful in critiquing the rationale behind such acts. Patterns in the type of recruiting done among groups committing terrorist acts lend substance to these profiles of modern terrorists.

While the official definition of terrorism adopted by many countries, including the United States, today limits application of the term to nonstate actors, terrorism is not strictly a phenomenon committed by individuals or groups. In fact, *terrorism* as a political term derived from *state* terror. So analysis of ways in which states use terrorism as an instrument of foreign and domestic policy offers vital insights, particularly when a war, such as the one initiated by the United States in Iraq in 2003, is premised to some degree on the commission of state terrorism by the leader deposed in the ensuing conflict.

Some states are even involved in the network emerging among individuals and groups involved in the commission of terrorist acts. Opinions differ as to the extent, cohesiveness, and ideological commitment of this network, but evidence of its existence is beyond reasonable dispute. Nations such as Iraq, Syria, and Iran have repeatedly been accused of involvement in state-sponsored terrorism. The linkage between these states and terrorism will be explored in depth later, focusing on questions such as: How is the terrorism financed? What are its targets? The emergence of what is termed *netwar* as a pattern for some modern terrorist groups and the creative use of money transfer systems like *hawala* offer opportunities to plumb the murky depths of the "terror network."

Understanding of *why* and *who* leads to questions of *how*. Profiles of terrorist events offer thumbnail sketches and disturbing insights into the *how* of terrorism. The depth of media involvement in the making of a "terrorist spectacular," for instance, can provide useful clues to understanding why this is so sensitive an area of democratic policymaking. Analysis of potential targets and weapons raises crucial and frightening questions for democratic systems.

The responses of the systems—legal, military, and political—to the threat and reality of terrorism is, of course, crucial to any understanding of the problem of terrorism today. The willingness as well as the capacity of the international community, and of an individual nation, to respond to this form of "warfare" is critical to any assessment of the role of terrorism in shaping our world. The difference between the responses to domestic, as opposed to international, terrorism may also be critical as democratic nations seek ways to respond to terrorism without sacrificing fundamental principles of democracy.

Democracies, throughout history, have been the effective targets of terrorist attacks, because democratic systems must "play by the rules" and thus cannot respond in comparable fashion to terrorist attacks. Autocracies and totalitarian systems are able to respond more easily to terrorist acts *with* terrorist acts, which sometimes serve as an effective deterrent, but democracies cannot make such responses. A quick look at terrorism in a democratic system such as the United States, with its enactment of the PATRIOT Act and efforts to create a functional Homeland Security system, offer insights into the patterns of terrorism and response characteristic of many democracies today.

Ultimately, the question may not be how nations can eliminate terrorism—if it is indeed a centuries-old practice and well entrenched as a useful tool in warfare—but rather how much terrorism a state can tolerate. New laws and new technology are changing the face of terrorism, but since it is not vanishing, then new thresholds for "acceptable" violence may well be emerging. With the development of effective and accessible chemical and biological as well as nuclear weapons, these thresholds may determine the survival of humanity.

This discussion in no sense covers *all* that could be said about terrorism. This is a contemporary review of current acts of terrorism. Definitions of terrorism, like the act itself, continue to undergo changes. The definition suggested in the following section highlights certain important facets of the issue, answering some questions while raising a multitude of others. Such a study can only provide a frame of reference from which it should be possible to analyze this phenomenon—the instrument and the nemesis of rulers, governments, and citizens.

CRUCIAL COMPONENTS OF TERRORISM

While it has not been possible, yet, to create a universally acceptable definition of terrorism, it is both possible and necessary to specify certain features common to the phenomenon. This in turn makes it feasible to create an operational definition of this term. Acts possessing *all* of these attributes could then be identified as terrorist acts with some consistency. Without falling into the political quagmire of attempting to label individuals or groups as terrorist, certain types of *actions* could be identified as terrorism, regardless of who commits them, for however noble a cause.

Let us consider a loose definition of contemporary terrorism. It must of necessity be "loose," because its elements tend to form a variety of compounds, which today fall within the rubric of terrorism. For the purposes of this investigation, **terrorism** will be defined as *a synthesis of war and theater, a dramatization of the most proscribed kind of violence—that which is perpetrated on innocent victims—played before an audience in the hope of creating a mood of fear, for political purposes.*

This description of terrorism has a number of crucial components. Terrorism, by this definition, involves an act of violence, an audience in which a mood of fear is created, innocent victims, and political motives or goals. Each of these elements is contained in the definitions currently in use by national and international agencies today. For example, the U.S. Department of State uses the definition incorporated in Title 22 of the United States Code, Section 2656f(d):

> premeditated, politically motivated violence perpetrated against noncombatant targets by subnational groups or clandestine agents, usually intended to influence an audience.

The Federal Bureau of Investigation (FBI) also includes these key elements in its definition of terrorism:

> The unlawful use of force or violence against persons or property to intimidate or coerce a government, the civilian population, or any segment thereof, in furtherance of political or social objectives.

All of these criteria are incorporated into many modern definitions of terrorism in use today. Each term deserves some clarification in order to formulate a clear set of parameters for this frequently misunderstood and misused concept.

Violence, Audience, and a Mood of Fear

First, note that terrorism is fundamentally a violent act. Sit-ins, picket lines, walkouts, and other similar forms of protest, no matter how disruptive, are *not* terrorist acts. Violence—the threat of violence where the capacity and the willingness to commit violence are displayed—is endemic to terrorism. The violence need not be fully perpetrated—that is, the bomb need not be detonated or all of the passengers aboard an airliner killed—in order for it to be considered a terrorist act. But the capacity and the willingness to commit a violent act *must* be present.

This violence need not be lethal to human targets to meet these definitional criteria. Violence is destructive, but the destruction need not necessarily take lives; it may instead disrupt lives without destroying them. For instance, the modern phenomenon known as cyber attacks, discussed in a subsequent chapter, could be called a form of terrorism, because it is certainly potentially disruptive, although clearly not lethal to human targets. The violence is against a system, rather than a physical human body, but the disruption and the mood of fear induced are potentially devastating.

This means, then, that it is the *perception* of the audience of that violent potential that is crucial to classifying an act as terrorism. Terrorism is, as Brian Jenkins noted two decades ago, essentially theater, an act played before an audience, designed to call the attention of millions, even hundreds of millions, to an often unrelated situation through shock—producing situations of outrage and horror, doing the unthinkable without apology or remorse. Unlike similar acts of murder or warfare, acts of terrorism are neither ends in themselves, nor are they often more than tangentially related to the ends sought. They are simply crafted to create a mood of fear or terror in that audience.

This mood is not the result, moreover, of the numbers of casualties caused by the act of violence. Automobile accidents cause greater numbers of injuries and deaths each year in the United States, without necessarily invoking a mood of terror among other drivers (or pedestrians). Nor is it the deliberate nature of the death inflicted that causes the audience response. Individuals are murdered in nonpolitical, nonterrorist acts throughout the world each year, without provoking widespread fear.

Victims: The Right Place—But the Wrong Time

Instead, the creation of this mood of intense anxiety seems specifically linked to the nature of the victim of terrorist acts. As one scholar notes:

> To qualify as an appropriate victim of a terrorist today, we need not be tyrants or their sympathizers; we need not be connected in anyway with the evils the terrorist perceives; we need not belong to a particular group. We need only be in the wrong place at the wrong time.[2]

Terrorism is thus distinguished from guerilla warfare by deliberate attacks upon innocent persons and the separation of its victims from the ultimate goal—the "playing to an audience" aspect of a terrorist act. Terrorism can be distinguished from legal acts of warfare and ordinary crimes of murder. As David Fromkin points out:

> Unlike the soldier, the guerilla fighter, or the revolutionist, the terrorist . . . is always in the paradoxical position of undertaking actions the immediate physical consequences of which are not particularly desired by him. An ordinary murderer will kill someone because he wants the person to be dead, but a terrorist will shoot somebody even though it is a matter of complete indifference to him whether that person lives or dies.[3]

Put more simply, the difference between a terrorist act and a similar crime or war activity is that terrorist acts are perpetrated *deliberately* upon innocent third parties in an effort to coerce the opposing party or persons into some desired political course of action. Victims are chosen, not primarily because of their personal guilt (in terms of membership in an opposing military or governmental group), but because their deaths or injuries, the disruption of their lives, will so shock the opposition that concession can be forced to prevent a recurrence of the incident or will focus attention on a particular political cause. Terrorist acts, in other words, are constructed to deliberately "make war" on innocent persons not involved in combat situations.

This distinction will need some explanation. The laws of war permit waging war between national armies, within certain humanitarian limits. Even for the enemy in a violent protracted conflict, some types of behavior (such as genocide and torture) are expressly forbidden, and certain basic amenities are required to be preserved (regarding such issues as the treatment of prisoners of war).[4] "War" as waged by terrorist acts violates these rules in that those deliberately destroyed are not principally armed military opponents, but the hapless civilians. Rules of international behavior, particularly those that pertain to political responsibility and military obligations, offer maximum protection to the civilian noncombatant, regarded as innocent persons even in time of war. Terrorism makes a practice of persistent, deliberate harm to precisely that type of person.

The distinction between a terrorist act and a legitimate act of guerrilla warfare is not always clear. General George Grivas, founder and head of the Cypriot EOKA, asserted in his memoirs: "We did not strike, like a bomber, at random. We shot only British servicemen who would have killed us if they could have fired first, and civilians who were traitors or intelligence agents."[5] The French Resistance, the Polish Underground, and the Greek Guerillas were called terrorists by the Nazi Occupation; yet they, like the EOKA, attacked primarily military personnel, government officials, and local collaborators.

During World War II, the Polish-Jewish Underground planted explosives at the Cafe Cyganeria in Kraków, a meeting place for Nazi officers, which no doubt resulted in injury to Polish waiters as well as to the desired military targets.[6] The point here is that the terrorist deliberately chooses to invoke injury on the innocent in an effort to shock the "guilty" political or military audience. Injury to the innocent thus is not an undesirable accident or by-product, but the carefully sought consequence of a terrorist act.

A terrorist act is committed, not against a military target necessarily—as the individual or group perpetrating the act does not seek to overthrow by military force—nor against the person in direct opposition to the perpetrators, as the ultimate goal is not usually the death of one leader. Unlike the terrorism practiced by nineteenth-century anarchists, twentieth-century terrorist acts are deliberately aimed against innocent persons, third parties whose loss of well-being can be expected to evoke a desired response from the opposition and/or the audience watching the event throughout the world.

It is important to note here that the terms *civilian* and *noncombatant* are not used in this working definition of terrorism. There are two critical reasons for this omission. The first is that the term *civilian* is not easily applied in low-level guerrilla warfare, where many who engage in such conflict are never formally enrolled in any army nor are they issued any materials that would identify them as soldiers (uniforms, identification tags, and the like). Therefore, their status as "civilians" will always be called into question, making application of the term *terrorism* to the acts against them always somewhat subjective.

The reason for omitting the term *noncombatant* is similarly rooted in a desire to prevent subjective use of the term *terrorism*. Many of the world's military are engaged today in what are termed *peacekeeping* activities, which in theory at least should be a noncombat status. Unfortunately, the term *peacekeeping* itself does not appear in the United Nations Charter, so there is a lack of clarity as to what peacekeeping really is and what the rules for such activity should be. Thus, the soldiers engaged in this type of activity could be regarded as combatants or noncombatants, depending on the political view of the group or government reacting to their activities. This confusion as to definition, and hence to status, would make the application of the term *terrorism* to attacks on such military units too pejorative and legally vulnerable to be useful. When clarity of definition for peacekeeping makes it possible to determine whether or not military engaged in such activity are combatants or noncombatants, it would be unwise to use this term in a working definition.

Until recently, although most of the victims of terrorism were innocent of any crime, they were also relatively few in number. In those terrorist incidents recorded in the 1950s and 1960s, the actual number of casualties was relatively small. Experts speculated that perhaps the terrorists felt a need to avoid alienating certain groups of people or portions of society. Perhaps it was also true that terrorists ". . . want a lot of people watching, not a lot of people dead."[7]

But the attacks in 2001 that took place in New York and Washington, using fully loaded passenger airplanes to crash into crowded centers of commerce and government, appear to herald a loosening of the threads constraining terrorists in their search for victims. As the craving for a worldwide audience increases among groups utilizing terrorism, the increasing tolerance of that audience for violence may actually be pushing terrorists to widen their target range, to create a more spectacular event for their audience.

Thus, as the violence becomes more randomized, it is being directed against a wider range of innocent persons. Children are becoming targets, as the massacres at the Rome and Vienna airports demonstrated. Ironically, this increase in innocent targets may well be a direct result of a viewing audience who is no longer as interested in attacks on military attachés or political figures.

Political Quicksand

Terrorism, then, is an act of violence perpetrated on an innocent person in order to evoke fear in an audience. One further component, however, is necessary for this definition. As it stands, such a definition could reasonably be applied to actions taken by professional athletes on the playing field!

The addition of a "political purpose" to the concept of terrorism continues to create enormous legal problems. Although establishing parameters for this concept of political purpose is crucial, particularly in light of the fact that political crimes and criminals have enjoyed special status under international law for centuries, the concept remains largely undefined.

Much of the confusion today results from a misperception that the presence of political *motivation* is sufficient to establish the political character of an action. An extradition case in 1980 clearly stated that, "An offense is not of a political character simply because it was politically motivated."[8] The prevailing Anglo-American rule of law, derived from *in re Castroni,* contains two basic criteria for determining the "political" quality of an action. These requirements, simply stated, were that (1) the act at issue must have occurred during a political revolt or disturbance, and (2) the act at issue must have been incidental to and have formed part of that same revolution or disturbance.[9]

A political motive thus may be termed *necessary* but it is not sufficient to earn for an action a "political offense" status under international law. Nicholas Kittrie suggested that a "pure political offense" would consist of acts "which challenge the State but affect no private rights of innocent parties."[10] By this definition, a political revolution or disturbance is an essential ingredient, in which the political offense plays only a part. Moreover, the offense must bring harm *only* to the State, while protecting innocent parties from harm through reasonable precautions. This has the effect of narrowing the classes of acceptable victims and eliminating random acts of lone assassins or revolutionaries.

Political assassination by organized revolutionaries careful to cause as little harm as possible to innocent persons remains protected to some extent within the political offense provisions of international law. Hence, the assassination of the Grand Duke Sergius might qualify for political offense status, while the mob violence of the Paris Commune would clearly not.

Obviously, the political element of an act of terrorism adds considerable confusion, both in the legal and the political realms. Although it is a necessary component to a definition of terrorism, it is so ambiguous a concept that it is often a two-edged sword, offering insights into the causes of an act while providing gaping loopholes in the law through which perpetrators of heinous acts continue to slither.

One legal expert has described the problem in this manner:

> In order to maintain a proper balance between human rights and world order, it is imperative that the world community in rejecting the proposition that all forms of violence are justified if supported by political goals, avoid the trap of supporting the other extreme, that violent opposition to an established regime is never permissible by international standards. Consequently, the principles of self-defense and the requirement of proportionality need to be re-examined, refined and injected more vigorously into this area.[11]

What distinguishes terrorism, then, from purely political actions may be the illegality of the violence employed, primarily in terms of the victims of the offenses. As noted earlier, many activities, including some sports and many movies, have as a goal the instilling of fear in an audience or opponent. What distinguishes the terrorist of today from the football player, the political assassin, and the revolutionary engaged in regular or irregular warfare may be the *lack* of legitimacy that his or her actions enjoy under international norms. By its very nature, terrorism involves the deliberate disruption of norms, the violation of generally accepted standards of decency, including the laws of war as they apply to the innocent and helpless.[12]

Because this is a confusing and contradictory area in the definition of terrorism, it is useful to review the issue once more. What is it, then, which distinguishes the terrorist act from other acts of war, as well as from other political or common crimes? Few would argue that wars, whether between or within states, could or should occur without violence, without the inflicting of injury and death. As individuals we may deplore the violence, but as nations we have recognized its inevitability, and have accorded it a limited legitimacy.

But international rules have been created and accepted that govern the acceptable types of violence, even in war. The international community does not forbid the use of *all* violence; it does, however, suggest basic rules for the use of violence. Many of these rules are directed toward the protection of innocent persons. Even in the life-and-death struggles between nations, these laws focus on minimizing of danger of injury or death to noncombatants, civilians with neither military or political rank nor involvement in the conflict.[13]

Political motivation, then, is *not* a lever by which acts of terrorism can be justified under international law. On the contrary, international law makes it clear that, regardless of the motive, some acts of political violence are never acceptable.

TYPOLOGIES OF TERRORISM: USEFUL TOOLS

At this point let us look at some typologies of terrorism that may serve to help us distinguish between types of terrorism as they pertain to revolutionary and guerrilla movements. Feliks Gross, a leading authority on revolutionary terror, has suggested that at least five types of terror-violence exist:

1. **Mass terror** is *terror by a state, where the regime coerces the opposition in the population, whether organized or unorganized, sometimes in an institutionalized manner.*
2. **Dynastic assassination** is *an attack upon a head of state or a ruling elite,* precisely the kind of terrorism that the international community tried to criminalize in the mid-nineteenth century.
3. **Random terror** involves *the placing of explosives where people gather (such as post offices, railroads, and cafes) to destroy whoever happens to be there.* "Algerian revolutionaries left bombs in public places," one scholar notes, "in Paris, apparently convinced that one Frenchman blown to bits was pretty much like any other."[14]
4. **Focused random terror** *restricts the placing of explosives, for example, to where significant agents of oppression are likely to gather* (as in the aforementioned case of the Polish-Jewish Underground).
5. Finally, **tactical terror** is *directed solely against the ruling government as a part of a "broad revolutionary strategic plan."*[15]

Such a typology leaves some guerrilla activity enmeshed in the terrorist label. Although similar difficulties afflict other such typologies, several important points can be derived concerning the phenomenon of terrorism by examining some of them. J. Boyer Bell's excellent study of terrorist types yields many insights into the kinds of terrorism prevalent today, thus contributing to an understanding of what is encompassed by the modern meaning of the term.[16]

Although numerous other typologies of terrorism have been offered by various scholars, review of them in detail would not significantly contribute to the development of a workable definition of contemporary terrorism. However, a few important points of interest can be made about these typologies. One is that most typologies developed today include some form of state terrorism as well as individual and group terrorism. What Gross terms "mass" terrorism is described by U.S. State Department analyst Thomas Thornton as "enforcement" terror,[17] and by political scientist Paul Wilkinson as "repressive" terror.[18] Whatever the label applied to this particular type of terror, it is obvious that some consensus exists on the propriety of including some repressive state tactics in the classification of terrorist acts.

The typologies also suggest that a wide variety of acts have been encompassed under the rubric of terrorism, including many engaged in by revolutionary groups, and composed of both internal activities and activities that cross state lines, but all of which are politically motivated and directed toward some end other than the immediate act of violence. These observations serve both to fortify the conclusions already drawn concerning the distinctive nature of terrorist acts and to highlight certain points of dissension that may contribute to cloud our understanding of this term.

Table 1.1 summarizes some of the types of terrorism in use today. Although not all of the possible categories of terrorism are included, it is useful to compare the tactics, targets, and perpetrators of such types of terrorism.

TABLE 1.1   Types of Terrorism

Type	Committed by	Target	Tactics
Mass terror endemic authorized enforcement repressive	Political leaders (e.g., Idi Amin's rule in Uganda)	General population	Coercion organized or unorganized
Dynastic assassination	Individuals or groups (e.g., Russian anarchists)	Head of state or ruling elite	Very selective violence
Random terror	Individuals or groups (e.g., airline attacks on the World Trade Center in New York)	Anyone in "the wrong place at the wrong time"	Bombs in cafes, markets, and similar places
Focused random terror	Individuals or groups (e.g., PIRA and UDF bombings in Northern Ireland)	Members of the "opposition"	Bombs in specific cafes and markets
Tactical terror (revolutionary)	Revolutionary movements (e.g., M-19's attacks on Colombian justices)	The government	Attacks on politically attractive targets

USING TACTICS AS LABELS

Before summarizing the conclusions concerning a working definition of terrorism, one further point needs to be emphasized. Both the typologies of terrorism and the working definition of terrorism being offered treat terrorism as a *tactic*, not as a *goal*. This is important to remember, if the term *terrorism* is not to be used or misused by governments unsympathetic to a group's cause. To describe a particular action as a terrorist action does not, and should not, in any sense define either the group or the cause for which it uses that tactic as terrorist.

It is true that if an individual, group, or government chooses to use this particular tactic repeatedly, there is every chance that those observing the actions will associate the tactic with those individuals. Continued or prolonged use of such a tactic by any group or government contributes to the perception of that group or government as terrorist by the audience for whom the crime is committed. This is not necessarily accurate, nor is it inaccurate: it is simply a natural phenomenon. A congressman who repeatedly supports war efforts and defense buildups may well expect to be labeled a "hawk" both by those who agree with his position and by those who disagree with it. This is simply a recognition of his patterns of action.

The same is true to some extent of groups that repeatedly engage in terrorist acts. The frequency with which they engage in such actions, and to some degree the openness with which they do so, will certainly have an effect on whether their audience views them as terrorists. This does not mean that the ends toward which they strive are bad, somehow tainted with the opprobrium of terrorism. It simply means that the audience for whom the terrorist acts are generally staged have mentally associated the actors with the actions taken in pursuit of the cause.

This is, of course, a very narrow line of reasoning, one not clearly understood by the general public, which is often the audience for terrorist events. That same public frequently attaches a terrorist label to individuals and even to groups who engage on a fairly regular basis in terrorist acts. But in terms acceptable in the legal and political community, it is only the *act* that can accurately be labeled as terrorist, not the individual or the group, and certainly not the cause for which the tactic is employed.

Members of a group cannot engage in questionable or even blatantly illegal actions on a regular basis and not be tainted with the negative labels associated with such actions. Members of Mafia families, although they may themselves be several steps removed from the actual commission of organized crimes, are nevertheless viewed by both the general public and by law enforcement agencies as being linked to, and part of, those deplorable actions.

So it is with terrorism. Those who commit it, and those whose groups or governments have chosen to use it as a tactic, cannot escape the label of terrorist given them, not by governments, but by the very audience toward which such acts are directed. The justice of a cause rarely is sufficient, in that audience's view, to excuse the use of such a tactic. Although politicians and ideologues may accept the rationale, covertly or openly, that the ends for which they struggle justify the means that they choose to employ, most of the civilized world remains unwilling to accept this rationale. Certain acts can be described by definition as terrorist acts whether they are carried out by democratic governments in pursuit of reasonable policy goals or by armed revolutionaries fighting for freedom against tyranny.

Conclusions

Terrorism, then, is an act composed of at least four crucial elements: (1) It is an act of violence, (2) it has a political motive or goal, (3) it is perpetrated against innocent persons, and (4) it is staged to be played before an audience whose reaction of fear and terror is the desired result. This definition eliminates football players, lunatics on a killing spree, and the assassin who tries to kill a bad ruler, from the label of terrorist. All acts of violence are not terrorist acts, however heinous the acts may be.

Unfortunately, the line between acceptable types of violence and unacceptable types is not always clear. Violence by revolutionaries and by the state is sometimes difficult to categorize clearly as terrorist, even given the working definition evolved here. Further study of the history, ideology, and individuals involved in terrorist acts may increase our understanding of this important but confusing term.

Evaluation

Using the definition in a practical application is one method of increasing one's understanding of the usefulness and limitation of the definition. Listed below are two brief sketches of what were termed by some observers to be terrorist acts. Use the four criteria in the definition of terrorism suggested in this chapter to decide whether these incidents were, in fact, terrorist acts. Try also to decide which type of terrorism, if any, was involved, using any one of the typologies mentioned.

1. In November of 2003, a U.S. transport plane carrying soldiers engaged in peacekeeping and nation building in postwar Iraq was shot down by a surface-to-air missile. Sixteen of these soldiers, who were being carried to planes to take them on the first stage of their journey home for a brief leave, were killed. Iraqi groups seeking to force the United States out of their country claimed responsibility for the attack.

2. At 2:30 p.m. on March 30, 1981, President Ronald Reagan was shot in the chest by a gunman. The would-be assassin, John W. Hinckley, Jr., shot the president as he walked to his limousine after addressing the American Federation of Labor–Congress of Industrial Organizations (AFL-CIO) meeting at the Washington Hilton Hotel. Shooting from a distance of about 10 feet, Hinckley shot Reagan, Press Secretary James Brady, Secret Service Agent Timothy J. McCarthy, and Washington policeman Thomas K. Delahanty. Evidence at the subsequent trial indicated that Hinckley was motivated by a desire to impress actress Jodie Foster.

3. Just before dawn on October 23, 1983, a suicide vehicle laden with about 2,500 tons of TNT blew up the U.S. Marine headquarters near Beirut, Lebanon, airport. Around 230 persons were reported killed, most of them as they slept. The Free Islamic Revolutionary Movement claimed responsibility for the action.

4. In April 1999, an attack by two students at Columbine High School in a suburb of Denver, Colorado, resulted in the deaths of 15, while more than 20 people were wounded, some of them critically. The attackers, identified as Eric Harris, 18, and Dylan Klebold, 17, both juniors at the school, reportedly laughed and hooted as they opened fire on classmates after they had booby-trapped the school with pipe bombs. Harris and Klebold were members of a group calling itself the Trenchcoat Mafia, outcasts who bragged about guns and bombs, and hated Blacks, Hispanics, and student athletes.

SUGGESTED READINGS

Friedlander, Robert. *Terrorism: Documents of National and International Control,* Vol. 1. Dobbs Ferry, NY: Oceana, 1979.
Howard, Russell D., and Reid Sawyer, ed. *Terrorism and Counterterrorism: Understanding the New Security Environment.* Guilford, CT: Dushkin/McGraw-Hill, 2002.
Jenkins, Brian, and Janera Johnson. *International Terrorism: A Chronology, 1968–1974.* A report prepared for the Department of State and the Defense Advances Research Projects Agency, R-1587-DOSIARPA (March 1975). Santa Monica, CA: Rand, 1975.
Laqueur, Walter. *The New Terrorism: Fanaticism and the Arms of Mass Destruction.* Oxford: Oxford University Press, 1999.
Leeman, Richard W. "Terrorism." In *Morality and Conviction in American Politics: A Reader,* ed. Martin Slann and Susan Duffy. Upper Saddle River, NJ: Prentice Hall, 1990.
Schmid, Alex. *Political Terrorism.* New Brunswick, NJ: Transaction Books, 1983.
Sederberg, Peter. "Explaining Terrorism." In *Terrorism: Contending Themes in Contemporary Research,* ed. Peter Sederberg. Boston: Houghton-Mifflin, 1993.
Wilcox, Ambassador Philip, Jr. "Terrorism Remains a Global Issue." *USIA Electronic Journal* (February 1997).
Wilkinson, Paul. *Terrorism and the Liberal State.* New York: New York University Press, 1979.

NOTES

1. Eqbal Ahmad, "Terrorism: Theirs and Ours." In *Terrorism and Counterterrorism: Understanding the New Security Environment,* ed. Russell D. Howard and Reid Sawyer (Guilford, CT: Dushkin/McGraw-Hill, 2002), 47.
2. Irving Howe, "The Ultimate Price of Random Terror," *Skeptic: The Forum for Contemporary History* 11, no. 58 (January–February 1976): 14.
3. David Fromkin, "The Strategy of Terror," *Foreign Affairs* 53 (July 1975): 689.
4. See Treaty and International Agreements Series no. 3365.
5. Robert A. Friedlander, *Terrorism: Documents of National and International Control* (Dobbs Ferry, NY: Oceana, 1979), vol. 1, 40.
6. Howe, "The Ultimate Price of Random Terror," 14–15.
7. Brian M. Jenkins, *International Terrorism: A New Kind of Warfare* (Rand: June 1974): P-5261, 4.
8. *Escabedo v. United States,* 633 F2d. 1098, 1104 (5th Cir. 1980).
9. *In re Castroni* 1 Q.B. 149, 156, 166 (1891).
10. Nicholas N. Kittrie, "Patriots and Terrorists: Reconciling Human Rights with World Order," *Case Western Reserve Journal of International Law,* 13, no. 2 (Spring 1981): 300.
11. Kittrie, "Patriots and Terrorists," 304.
12. Friedlander, *Terrorism,* 286.

13. *Principles of the Nuremberg Charter and Judgment,* formulated by the International Law Commission, 1950 (UN General Assembly Records, 5th Session, Supp. 12 A/1315).

14. Howe, "The Ultimate Price of Random Terror," 15.

15. Feliks Gross, *Political Violence and Terror in Nineteenth and Twentieth Century Russia and Eastern Europe* (New York: Cambridge University Press, 1990), 8.

16. J. Bowyer Bell, *Transnational Terror* (Washington, DC: American Institute for Public Policy Research; and Stanford, CA: Hoover Institution on War, Revolution and Peace, 1975), 10–25.

17. Thomas Thornton, "Terror as a Weapon of Political Agitation," in *Internal War* ed. H. Eckstein (London: International Institute for Strategic Studies, 1964), 77–78.

18. Paul Wilkinson, *Political Terrorism* (Cambridge, MA: Harvard University Press, 1974), 38–44.

CHAPTER 2

Not a Modern Phenomenon

Key Concepts

assassination

hashashin

narcoterrorism

fedayeen

tyrannicide

jihad

divine right of kings

political asylum

state terrorism

privateers

guerrilla warfare

cycle of violence

netwar

Ironically, perhaps, terrorism in its original context was also closely associated with the ideals of virtue and democracy. The revolutionary leader Maximillien Robespierre firmly believed that virtue was the mainspring of a popular government at peace, but that during the time of revolution must be allied with terror in order for democracy to triumph.

Bruce Hoffman

Even though the word *terrorism* originated during the French Revolution and the Jacobin Reign of Terror (1792–1794), individual acts of terror-violence can be traced back at least to the ancient Greek and Roman republics. By some definitions, the assassination of Julius Caesar in 44 B.C. was an act of terrorism, at least to the extent to which a modern political assassination is defined as terrorism. Modern political science, at any rate, tends to treat **assassination,** *the murder of a head of state,* as a terrorist act.[1]

Group terrorism became more common as early as the Middle Ages. In fact, the word *assassin* comes from an Arabic term **hashashin,** which literally means "hashish-eater," or "one addicted to hashish."[2] It was used to describe *a sectarian group of Muslims who were employed by their spiritual and political leader, Hassan I Sabah, to spread terror in the form of murder and destruction among religious enemies, including women and children.*

Accounts of Marco Polo's travels include lurid tales of murder committed by these assassins, acting, it was supposed, under the influence of hashish or other such drugs. It was reported that these early terrorists were motivated not only by religious promises of eternal reward, but also by promises of unlimited access to hashish. Even the Crusaders, who killed not only fighting men but also women and children in their effort to take Jerusalem from Muslim hands, made mention of this group of fanatics and the terror they inspired.[3] The potent combination of religious and political fanaticism with intoxicating drugs made the legacy of the "Brotherhood of the Assassins" formidable. It is still evident to some extent in the unrest that plagues the Middle East today. **Narcoterrorism,** as the *linkage between drugs and terrorism* is often termed today, will be described in more depth in a later chapter. The impact of religion in stimulating terrorism must also be examined further, as it has become once again a potent force in the modern world, as the events of September 11 demonstrated.

Another Brotherhood of Assassins emerged from a combination of religion and politics in the 1890s. The Hur Brotherhood, whose roots were in the Sind region of British India, resembled the earlier Islamic Brotherhood of Assassins. Although this later brotherhood was suppressed, after considerable bloodshed, another Hur rebellion occurred in Pakistan in the mid-twentieth century. Indeed, much of modern Pakistan's terrorism from its Sikh minority derives from that group's religious and political dissatisfaction with Muslim Pakistan's leaders. Religion and politics continue to take innocent lives in this turbulent region of the world, as India and Pakistan, both nuclear powers, stand poised on the brink of war over Kashmir, a land divided by both religion and politics.

Islam is not, in any sense, a violent religion. Neither is Christianity, Judaism, or any of the other religions in whose name violence has been carried out. However, the mixture of religion and politics has too often resulted in violence, frequently against innocent victims, which makes it, according to the definition suggested in the preceding chapter, terrorism. The Middle East, as the home of three major world religions, has been plagued by a variety of violent sects. Today, nations such as Iran have witnessed, and perhaps fostered, the creation of several violent sects, whose blending of religion and politics resembles that of the Brotherhood of Assassins. Table 2.1 offers a brief insight into a few of the larger of these radical groups, their location, and their violent activities.

The **fedayeen,** *the Islamic "self-sacrificers,"* perceive themselves as engaged in a "holy war" against threats to their religion and culture. This type of war—being waged by more militant sects such as the Taliban in Afghanistan, and Osama bin Laden's al-Qaeda network, which claimed responsibility for the attack on September 11, 2001, on the World Trade Center in New York and the Pentagon in Washington, DC, is similar in many respects to the Brotherhood of Assassins of the Middle Ages. Like the Assassins, modern fedayeen find strength in the promise of a reward in paradise. Unlike the earlier sect, however, these modern zealots believe they will receive their reward in a spiritual paradise, not in the courtyard of the caliph. Religion is the narcotic that serves to motivate their terrorist actions, and to deaden their consciences to the horror of the slaughter that they inflict on innocent persons.

TABLE 2.1   Radical Religious Groups

Group	Description	Activities
al-Qaeda	Islamic extremist group, maintaining a network of supporters with cells in perhaps 40 countries, but based in Afghanistan	Attacks on World Trade Center and Pentagon in United States Bombing of U.S. embassies in Kenya and Tanzania
Armed Islamic Group (a.k.a.) GIA	Islamic extremist group, operating in Algeria against sectarian state	Civilian massacres, often of entire villages
Sikh groups Include, among others: *Dashmesh* (active in India, Germany, and Canada); *Dal Khalsa* (active in India, Pakistan, and Germany); *Babbar Khalsa* (active in India, Germany, and Canada)	Several domestic and international groups that seek to establish an independent Sikh state called Khalistan	Regular and bloody attacks against Hindus Blamed for bombing of Air India airline (329 people killed) Desecration of Hindu holy places, bombings, and assassinations
Aryan Nations Active in United States	Advocates race war against non-Christian, non-Aryans to protect Christian values	Linked to wide range of attacks on individuals in state and national governments

Thus, the mixture of religion and politics in the commitment of terrorism today is not new, but continues to be quite deadly. History enables us to place current mixtures such as these in context, which makes understanding easier. It has not yet made it possible for governments or organizations to prevent the explosion of these potentially lethal elements.

TYRANNICIDE: "TO GO TOO FAST"

Assassination, in fact, has become both an ideological statement and a powerful political weapon, using the vehicle of the doctrine of **tyrannicide,** *the assassination of a (tyrant) political leader*. Throughout Italy during the Renaissance, tyrannicide was fairly widely practiced, while in Spain and France during the Age of Absolutism it was at least widely advocated. The leading advocate of the doctrine of tyrannicide as an acceptable solution to political repression was a Spanish Jesuit scholar, Juan de Mariana, whose principal work, *De Regis Institutions,* was banned in France.[4]

In the words of Mariana we find much of the same political justification as that used by leaders of national liberation movements today. Mariana asserted that people necessarily possessed not only the right of rebellion but also the remedy of assassination, stating that "if in no other way it is possible to save the fatherland, the prince should be killed by the sword as a public enemy."[5]

Only 10 years after Mariana's words were uttered, the king of France, Henry III, was assassinated by the monk, François Favaillac. Many leaders since that time have been struck down by persons who claimed to have acted as instruments of justice against a tyrant. Even President Lincoln's assassin, John Wilkes Booth, saw his act in such a light, as evidenced by his triumphant shout, *"Sic semper tyrannis!"* (Thus always to tyrants!).[6]

Political assassins, like those committing murder in the name of religion, have frequently claimed to be acting as "divine instruments" of justice. At the very least, such assassins have viewed themselves as the chosen instruments of a popular legitimacy, rightly and even righteously employed in the destruction of illegitimate regimes and tyrannical rulers. The robes of martyrdom have been donned as readily by political as by religious zealots. Like the religious fanatics, political assassins have had no hesitation in acting as judge, jury, and executioner, assuring themselves and others that their appointment to these offices was made, not by them, but by a "higher" will or authority.

The concept of **jihad** or *holy war* continues to permeate the mixture of religion and politics in the Middle East today. Indeed, the words of al-Qaeda spokesman Suliman Abu Geith, in a videotaped statement on Al Jazeera in October 2001, echoed this ancient concept of terror-violence by divine instruments, when he stated that

> Allah says fight, and for the sake of Allah, uphold the name of Allah . . . . I thank Allah for allowing us to start this *jihad* and ask Allah to give us victory in the face or our enemy.[7]

The impact of this concept of holy war on the forms of terrorism in the Middle East will be explored in a later chapter; the focus here is on the linkage of politics and religion in efforts to topple nations and rulers.

During the latter part of the eighteenth century and early nineteenth century, the **divine right of kings** theory, *that kings rule by divine appointment,* began to lose its political grip on Europe. As the theory of the existence of a social contract between a people and their government began to gain acceptance, those who carried out political offenses such as tyrannicide gradually found a more benign atmosphere in which to act.

As one acting to right the wrongs committed by government, the political assassin was no longer regarded with universal disfavor. Vidal, a leading French legal scholar, noted:

> Whereas formerly the political offender was treated as a public enemy, he is today considered as a friend of the public good, as a man of progress, desirous of bettering the political institutions of his country, having the laudable intentions, hastening the onward march of humanity, his only fault being that he wishes to go too fast, and that he employs in attempting to realize the progress which he desires, means irregular, illegal, and violent.[8]

Not until the middle of the twentieth century was the murder of a head of state, or any member of his family, formally designated as terrorism. Even today, those who commit the political crime of murder of a head of state can often enjoy a type of special protection, in the form of **political asylum,** a type of *sanctuary or refuge for a person who has committed such a crime granted by one government against requests by another government for extradition of that person to be prosecuted for this political crime.*

STATE TERRORISM

The use of "irregular, illegal, and violent means" was not, of course, limited to lone political assassins. The execution of Marie Antoinette on October 16, 1793, was one of the first incidents actually called terrorism. In this instance, the terrorists were not trying to *overthrow* the government—they *were* the government! The Committee of Public Safety, led by Robespierre, chief spokesman of the Jacobin party, governed France during the tumultuous period known as the Reign of Terror (September 1793–July 1794). It is from this period, during which an estimated 20,000 persons were killed, that the word *terrorism* has evolved.

It is interesting, is it not, that modern terrorism derives its name from a gross example of **state terrorism,** *acts of terrorism that a state commits against defenseless victims,* rather than from terror-violence by a lone assassin or small, fanatic, nonstate group? Although most state-crafted definitions of terrorism do not include terrorism initiated by a state (focusing instead on substate groups), states have been, and continue to be, involved in a wide variety of violent acts against their own citizens and those of other nations.

Consider the case of piracy. From the sixteenth century forward, pirates and piracy have been considered by lawmakers to be the "common enemies of humanity." Blackstone's *Commentaries* referred to piracy as "an offense against the universal law of society."[9] Yet both England (for whom Blackstone wrote) and America (whose law frequently cites his precepts) licensed **privateers,** *private ships outfitted as warships and given letters of marque and reprisal, allowing them to make war on vessels flying foreign flags.*

Under the reign of Queen Elizabeth I of England, the Elizabethan Sea Dogs, privateer ships sailing under the protection of the English flag, carried out violent acts of piracy against the Spanish fleet. American privateers, too, played a fairly significant role in both the American Revolution and the War of 1812. Both nations, then, have commissioned pirates to carry out acts of terror-violence for them on the high seas, acts that both nations publicly deplore as "offenses against humanity" in their courts today. Modern terrorism continues to occasionally take the form of piracy, but today the piracy is often of aircraft rather than sea vessels. This interesting change will be discussed later, with particular attention to its impact on legal remedies for terrorism.

GUERRILLA WARFARE: SELECTIVE VIOLENCE

Since the French Revolution, terrorism and guerrilla warfare have become increasingly difficult to separate clearly. **Guerrilla warfare** is, essentially, *an insurrectionary armed protest, implemented by means of selective violence.* To the extent that the violence remains "selective" and the choice of targets military rather than civilian, it is possible to distinguish between guerrilla warfare and terrorism.

The term *guerrilla,* meaning "little war" evolved from Spanish resistance to the invasions of Napoleon in 1808. This war on the Iberian peninsula, in which Spanish guerrillas were aided in making increasingly successful attacks on French encampments by the British military, has become in some measure a prototype for the twentieth-century wars of national liberation. In such contemporary struggles, indigenous vigilante groups are often supported openly (as were the Spanish) or covertly by the military of other nations.

Ideology and nationalism combined with terror-violence in the Internal Macedonian Revolutionary Organization (IMRO), a group that made its first appearance in 1893. For several years the IMRO waged guerrilla warfare, sometimes employing terrorist tactics, against the Turkish rulers of their region. As in the Iberian conflict, other nations both assisted and interfered in the struggle. Bombings and kidnapping, as well as the murder of civilians and officials, were frequent in this "little war." Violence escalated into the Saint Elliah's Rebellion in August of 1903, which was dealt with ruthlessly by Turkish authorities. This struggle left thousands dead on both sides, at least 70,000 homeless, and 200 Macedonian villages in ashes.

Turkey's suppression of similar nationalist struggles on the part of its Armenian population in the early part of the twentieth century helped to create Armenian groups willing to engage in terrorist activities today. These activities, which include bombings and murder reminiscent of the IMRO, have been directed less by nationalism than by a desire to have revenge for the ruthless suppression of that earlier nationalism. In this case, savagely suppressed nationalism has spawned vengeful terrorism by individuals and groups whose demands are perhaps even harder to satisfy than were those of the nationalists of earlier decades.

Events of the 1990s in the former Yugoslavia give credence to the concept that repressed nationalism can, in a resurgent form, exact a bloody toll on innocent civilian populations. In the turbulent years before the outbreak of World War I, the Balkan states were engaged in a wide variety of revolutionary violence. Brigands, calling themselves *comitatus* (committee men), covertly sponsored by Greece, Serbia, and Bulgaria (which was also involved in the IMRO struggles), roamed the countryside. In the worst, not the best, tradition of revolutionaries, these brigands terrorized their own fellow citizens, burning, murdering, and robbing all who stood in their way. The incredible destruction and genocidal murders that took place in the Balkans in the 1990s parallel, and even exceed, this pattern.

World War I was, in fact, triggered by a transnational assassination that had its roots in revolutionary terrorism. A secret Serbian terrorist organization, popularly known as the Black Hand, was both an organization employed by the Serbian government as an unofficial instrument of national foreign policy and a lethal weapon of political protest against the Austro-Hungarian Empire. On June 28, 1914, a 19-year-old Serbian, Gavrilo Princip, trained by the Black Hand, murdered the heir to the imperial throne of that empire, Archduke Franz Ferdinand, in Sarajevo. This assassination was the catalyst for a series of events that, within a month's time, grew into a global conflagration.

Revolutionary terror-violence triggered international devastation on a scale unprecedented at that time. Conflict in and around Sarajevo in the 1990s is partially explained, too, by this early pattern of revolutionary terror-violence. At least twice within the twentieth century, revolutionary terror-violence was unleashed by groups, governments, and militias against a civilian population. This type of violence makes reconciliation extremely difficult, if not impossible, to achieve. Memories of violence against women and children within families are hard to relinquish, and repetition of such violence within less than a century makes the creation of a sense of common identity (nationalism) and reconciliation between populations within that region perhaps an impossible goal.

Revolutions are not by definition terrorist events. Indeed, some have been successfully carried out without resort to terrorist tactics. It is increasingly difficult, however, for an untrained and sparsely equipped indigenous army to wage a successful guerrilla war against a national standing army. With mounting frustration in the face of apparently insurmountable odds, it is increasingly easy to resort to terror-violence to achieve by psychological force what it is not possible to achieve by force of arms.

Perhaps nowhere else in this century has the role of liberationist combined more thoroughly, until recently, with that of terrorist than in the actions of the militant group usually known as the Irish Republican Army (IRA). This group's guerrilla campaign of murder and terror, growing out of the Sinn Fein movement in 1916, provoked the British to respond in kind, with a counterterror campaign. Although this revolutionary terrorism may be said to have stimulated the creation of an independent Irish Republic, the violence did not end with this "success." In the mid-1950s the Provisional IRA began a second wave of anti-British terror, which continued until 1994.

This struggle offers insights in several historical respects. In addition to being, in part, a blend of nationalism and terrorism, it is also a contemporary example of the potent mixture of religion and politics. Catholic Ireland has long resented Protestant Britain's domination of its politics. Northern Ireland, which remains under British rule, is predominantly Protestant, with a Catholic minority.

Thus, the lines of battle are drawn along both nationalistic and religious lines. Catholics in Northern Ireland have tended to support a unification of those northern provinces with the Irish Republic, while Protestants in Northern Ireland have demanded continued British rule. The legacy of hatred and mistrust bred by generations of violence is so bitter that an end to the violence seemed, until the end of the twentieth century, unlikely. The cyclical nature of violence can indeed create a deadly spiral.

CYCLICAL NATURE OF TERROR

Violence, particularly terrorist violence, has too often created a **cycle of violence,** *with those against whom the terror-violence is first carried out becoming so angered that they resort to terrorism in response, directed against the people or institutions regarded as responsible for the initial terrorist acts.* Each violent act frequently causes equally violent reactions. When the violence is unselective, when innocent people are victimized, the reactive violence is also likely to break all the rules in the selection of targets, and thus be terrorist.

Most revolutionary groups assert that it is terrorism by the *state* that provokes, and by its presence justifies, acts of terror-violence by nonstate groups seeking to change the government or its policies. The relationship between terror-violence by the state and that of nonstate groups and individuals is evident in the history of many modern nation-states. But the nature of that relationship is still the subject of much debate.

Since the French Revolution, terrorism and guerrilla movements have become inextricably intertwined. Perhaps the most prominent proponents of individual and collective violence as a means of destroying governments and social institutions were the Russian anarchists, revolutionaries within Russia who sought an end to the Czarist state of the latter nineteenth century. "Force only yields to force," and terror would provide the mechanism of change, according to Russian radical theorist Alexander Serno-Solovevich.[10] In the writings of two of the most prominent spokesmen for revolutionary anarchism, Mikhail Bakunin and Sergei Nechaev, one finds philosophies often echoed by modern terrorists. Bakunin, for example, advocated in his *National Catechism* (1866) the use of "selective, discriminate terror." Nechaev, in his work, *Revolutionary Catechism* (1870), went further in advocating both the theory and practice of pervasive terror-violence. He asserted of the revolutionary:

> [D]ay and night he must have one single thought, one single purpose: merciless destruction. With this aim in view, tirelessly and in cold blood, he must always be prepared to kill with his own hands anyone who stands in the way of achieving his goals.[11]

This is surely a very large step in the evolution of a terrorist from the lone political assassin of earlier centuries. Even the religious fanatics of the Assassins' genre and the privateers of Elizabethan times were arguably less willing to kill anyone to achieve a political objective. But this difference may well have existed more on paper than it did in practice. In spite of this written willingness to kill anyone who stood in the way, even the Socialist Revolutionary Party resorted primarily to selective terror-violence and took special pains to avoid endangering innocent bystanders. For instance, the poet Ivan Kalialev, who assassinated the Grand Duke Sergius on the night of February 2, 1905, had passed up an opportunity earlier that evening to throw the bomb because the Grand Duchess as well as some of her nieces and nephews were also in the Grand Duke's carriage.[12]

Although an attempt was made to kill Alexander II as early as 1866, the first generation of Russian terrorists generally resorted to violence only to punish traitors and police spies, or to retaliate against brutal treatment of political prisoners. (Odd, isn't it, that these same reasons are frequently quoted today as justifications for similar use of "extralegal violence"?)

With the creation of the *Narodnaya Volya* (The Will of the People) in 1879, political assassination of a wide range of targets began to become a normal form of political protest, becoming part of an intense cycle of terror and counterterror. This revolutionary group believed terrorism should be used to compromise the best of governmental power, to give constant proof that it is possible to fight the government, and to strengthen thereby the revolutionary spirit of the people and its faith in the success of the cause.[13]

It is quite easy to note the blending of revolutionary and state terror-violence during this time. The assassinations of Czar Alexander II in 1881 and of First Minister Peter Stolypin in 1911 were incidents that produced periods of counterterrorism (in the form of state repression). This repression probably accelerated the revolutionary movement responsible for those assassinations. Thus, the terrorist acts of assassination, inspired by brutal repression in the Czarist state, provoked further state terrorism, which in turn inspired revolutionary movement to further acts of violence.

The formation of the Union of Russian Men to combat the growing revolutionary movement "by all means" was not only sanctioned by the Czar, but also granted special protection by him. This reactionary group engaged in a variety of terrorist activities, including but not limited to political murders, torture, and bombing. The Okrana (the Czarist secret police) also wreaked fierce counterterror against the militant revolutionaries in an unabated attack, until World War I.

George Kennan, commenting on the rising tide of terrorism in Russia during the last half of the nineteenth century, explained the relationship of state and revolutionary terrorism in this way:

> Wrong a man . . . deny him all redress, exile him if he complains, gag him if he cries out, strike him in the face if he struggles, and at the last he will stab and throw bombs.[14]

Still, while some of the seeds of a more widespread and random terror-violence were sown in the revolutionary and anarchistic movements of the late nineteenth century, by the beginning of the twentieth century, terror-violence was still principally directed toward political assassination. Between 1881 and 1912, at least 10 national leaders had lost their lives to assassins, as Table 2.2 indicates.

TABLE 2.2   Assassinated Leaders, 1881–1912

Individual	*Nation*	*Year of Death*
President James Garfield	United States	1881
Czar Alexander II	Russia	1881
Lord Frederick Cavendish Chief Secretary	Ireland	1882
President Sadi Carnot	France	1894
Premier Antonio Canavos del Castillo	Spain	1897
Empress Elizabeth	Austria-Hungary	1898
King Umberto I	Italy	1900
President William McKinley	United States	1901
Premier Peter Stolypin	Russia	1911
Premier Jose Canalejas y Mendez	Spain	1912

The cyclical nature of terror is also evident in the events surrounding the creation of the state of Israel. The terrorism spawned in Nazi Germany helped to create a cycle of violence that still grips the Middle East today. After the military collapse of the Central Powers and the Armistice Agreement of November 1918, a large number of largely right-wing paramilitary organizations grew within Germany. In ideology, terrorist method, and political role, these groups were in many respects the historical heirs of the Brotherhood of Assassins. They were also the nuclei for the German *Reichswehr*.

Under the leadership of such men, Germany perpetrated upon innocent persons the greatest atrocities the world has ever recorded. Organized state terrorism reached its zenith in Nazi Germany, and its victims numbered in the millions. Of those victims, the majority were Jewish. Many who sought to flee the terror tried to emigrate to Palestine, which at that time was under British mandate. But the British Mandate Government, by 1940, was engaged in closing the gates to Jewish immigration into this land, which was, in fact, already occupied by Arabs. As the population balance began to swing away from the indigenous Arab population toward the immigrant Jews, the British government sought to stem the tide of refugees.

The *Haganah,* a Zionist underground army, and the *Irgun Zvai Leumi,* a Zionist militant force willing to use terrorist tactics, waged terrorist warfare on the British forces in Palestine. Bombing, murder, and assassination became the order of the day, as British counterviolence met with escalating Irgun and Haganah intransigence. With the Irgun bombing of the King David Hotel in 1946, in which many innocent people died or were seriously injured, British determination to quell the rebellion diminished. In 1947, Britain turned Palestine over to the fledgling United Nations.

But during the struggle to gain a homeland free of Nazi terror, the Irgun had practiced terror against the indigenous population. When Israel declared itself to be an independent state in 1948, some of the dispossessed people within its borders and those who fled to surrounding states began a war of revolution and of terror against Israel.

Israel's revolutionary terror-violence against the Palestinian people has spurred a conflict that continues to rend the fragile fabric of peace in the Middle East. Born in bloodshed, violence, and desperation, Israel continues to struggle against the terrorist violence that its very creation evoked.

CONCLUSIONS

Is contemporary terrorism different? In what ways? One reason for briefly reviewing the historical pattern and roots of terrorism is to be able to discover whether that pattern remains accurate in the contemporary world. If terrorism today is just like terrorism of previous centuries, then we can use historical patterns to predict behavior and to construct responses based on successful attempts to combat this phenomenon in the past.

If terrorism today is different, however, then historical patterns will be less useful in designing responses, though still of use in understanding the dynamics of the phenomenon. Terrorism has clearly existed before this century. What we need to know as we prepare for yet another century is whether twentieth-century terrorism was significantly different from its historical counterparts.

We have established that prior to the twentieth century, terrorism existed in many forms: political assassinations, lethal groups of religious and/or drug-crazed murderers and zealots, state-sponsored as well as nonstate pirates, and dedicated revolutionaries whose resort to violence is often tied to state repression. All of these forms of terrorism still exist in the modern world.

But there are important differences. Examination of these differences may help us to understand our contemporary terrorism.

Political Assassinations

Terrorist acts are no longer directed solely or even primarily at heads of state. Security precautions to guard such persons against attack have made it very difficult for a lone assassin to successfully murder such a person. The assassination of Yitzhak Rabin, prime minister of Israel in 1995, demonstrated that it is not, of course, impossible for such an attack to occur with success. However, in the latter part of the twentieth century, attacks have been made with greater frequency on individuals of less significance but easier access. This broadens the range of acceptable victims well beyond those justified under the doctrine of tyrannicide.

Drugs, Religion, and Political Murders

This lethal combination still exists in the contemporary world, but the relationship among these elements has changed considerably. During the Middle Ages, the caliph rewarded his assassins with drugs for successfully completed murders of religious opponents. Today, drugs are used to finance the lethal expeditions of religious zealots whose targets are not only those of another religion within their community, but also whole nations or groups of nations whose citizens are regarded by the zealots as legitimate targets for murder. Again, this is a drastic broadening of the category of acceptable potential victims. Osama bin Laden's call for Muslims to attack any Americans in the waging of a holy war dramatically illustrated this broadening of targets, particularly in the September 11 attacks.

Piracy

Although piracy of the sea has waned somewhat in recent years (even though the incident involving the *Achille Lauro* reminded us that such piracy still occurs), air piracy has more than taken its place. During the 1970s and 1980s, airline hijacking became a fairly commonplace occurrence. Where pirates of old, however, sought primarily material gains (with political gain a pleasant by-product for certain governments), modern air pirates tend to seek political gain first. So although the treatment of victims of piracy has remained essentially the same (pirates throughout the ages have tended to treat their victims as completely expendable), the purpose or goal of the act has changed radically.

State-Sponsored Terrorism

Modern governments have expanded the concept of "licensed" pirates. Terrorism became an institutionalized form of foreign policy for many nations in the twentieth century. Governments privately and sometimes publicly sponsor groups involved in terrorist activities. Moreover, in the latter half of the twentieth century, governments increasingly became involved in revolutionary movements, providing assistance for either the revolutionaries or the regime against which the revolution was fighting. This has blurred the lines between those involved in the fighting of a war and those who are merely innocent bystanders.

Modern Travel and Communication

Technology has widened the field of possibilities for contemporary terrorism. Modern methods of travel, for example, make it possible to carry out an assassination in the morning of Country Q, and be halfway around the world from that nation within a matter of hours. Modern communication, too, has made this a smaller world in that events in, for instance, Yemen are of immediate notice and interest in New York. Such communications also have served to expand the theater to which the terrorist plays. Thus, to catch the attention of the United States, the terrorist need not travel to New York City with a bomb—he needs only to plant a bomb in a boat in Yemen's harbor.

Terrorism today seems to be evolving into a violent form of **netwar,** as well. The term *netwar* refers to

> an emerging mode of conflict and crime at societal levels, involving measures short of traditional war, in which the protagonists use network forms of organization and related doctrines, strategies, and technologies attuned to the information age.[15]

Groups like al-Qaeda and HAMAS appear to consist of loosely organized, semi-independent cells that lack any central command hierarchy. These decentralized, flexible structures make counterterrorism efforts such as the recent U.S. war on terrorism very difficult to wage successfully, since it is difficult to determine when the "enemy" is defeated or captured.

Weapons

The dramatic increase in the arsenal of weapons available to modern terrorists is also worth noting. No longer need the would-be assassin rely on a small handgun to eliminate his or her victim. A letter bomb will do the job without endangering the perpetrator, as the Unibomber in the United States has demonstrated. Revolutionaries are no longer confined to simple rifles; SAMs (surface-to-air missiles) are all too accessible.

The potential for destruction through chemical and biological weapons has not yet been fully tapped, although the events in Japan in 1995 and the United States in 2001 gave ample evidence of the potential for such weapons when used in the very vulnerable mass transit system or the mail system of modern nation-states. Perhaps, until recently, the consequences of using such weapons were too dramatic for most groups to contemplate. But modern technology has certainly put at the terrorist's disposal a vast array of lethal and largely indiscriminate weapons, of which the sarin toxin used in Japan and the anthrax sent through the mail in the United States, represent only very simple examples. With the arsenal, the selection of victims has become devastatingly indiscriminate. One can be a victim simply by riding a subway train to work or opening the mail—basic and essential acts for millions of innocent people.

As historical precedents for terrorism grow, it becomes very hard to distinguish between legitimate and illegitimate violence. As the nation born in illegitimate violence, such as occurred in Northern Ireland and Israel, becomes the state, it is increasingly difficult to condemn as terrorist (and thus illegitimate) the methods employed in the struggles for independence and survival of persons within those states. The longer the history of terrorism grows, the harder it is to make a label of terrorism stick to the actions of any group, individual, or nation.

EVALUATION

Modern Piracy and Government Responses

In October 1985, the news flared across the world: A group of American and European tourists had been taken hostage aboard a pleasure ship, the *Achille Lauro,* by a handful of Palestinian terrorists. The ship wandered north along the coast of Lebanon as the hijackers sought a safe haven. Bit by bit, news of the horror aboard leaked out: 69-year-old Leon Klinghoffer of New York City was murdered in his wheelchair.

The Egyptian government called in a negotiator, Abu Abbas, leader of the Palestinian splinter group to which the hijackers claimed to belong. He ordered them to release the ship and come into port, where they were promised safe passage out of the country.

At the same time, U.S. intelligence sources, monitoring the exchanges between President Mubarak of Egypt and Yasser Arafat, leader of the Palestinian Liberation Organization, gained enough information to enable the United States to spring a trap. The EgyptAir plane aboard which the hijackers were being smuggled out of Egypt was ambushed by U.S. warplanes, and forced to land in Italy, where the hijackers were taken into custody by the Italian government.

This modern incident of terrorism and counterforce raises some important questions for discussion:

1. Were the hijackers pirates, "common enemies of mankind," or revolutionaries using the means at their disposal to wage war on oppressive governments?
2. Was Egypt wrong to allow the hijackers into port and assist them in leaving the country, since in doing so they secured the release of the rest of the hostages?
3. Was the United States justified in its actions against the hijackers, or was it guilty of terrorism as well?
4. Do, in fact, "rights" (to commit acts of terror-violence) derive from "wrongs"?

SUGGESTED READINGS

Laqueur, Walter. "PostModern Terrorism." *Foreign Affairs* (September/October 1996).

Miller, Judith, Stephen Engelberg, and William Broad. *Germs: Biological Weapons and America's Secret War.* New York: Simon & Schuster, 2001.

Nyatepe-Coo, Akorlie A., and Dorothy Zeisler-Vralsted, ed. *Understanding Terrorism: Threats in an Uncertain World.* Upper Saddle River, NJ: Prentice Hall, 2004.

Schultz, George. "Low-Intensity Warfare: The Challenge of Ambiguity." Address to Low-Intensity Warfare Conference, Washington, DC, January 15, 1986.

Simonsen, Clifford E., and Jeremy R. Spindlove. *Terrorism Today: The Past, the Players, the Future.* Upper Saddle River, NJ: Prentice Hall, 2004.

Slann, Martin. "The State as Terrorist." In *Multidimensional Terrorism,* ed. Martin Slann and Bernard Schechterman. New York: Rienner, 1987.

NOTES

1. Robert Friedlander, *Terrorism: Documents of International and Local Control* (Dobbs Ferry, NY: Oceana, 1979), 7.

2. Funk and Wagnall's *Standard Dictionary: Comprehensive International Edition,* vol. 1, 86, col. 3.

3. See M. Hodgson, *The Order of the Assassins* (San Rafael, CA: Presidio Press, 1960); B. Lewis, *The Assassins: A Radical Sect in Islam* (San Rafael, CA: Presidio Press, 1968).

4. See O. Zasra and J. Lewis, *Against the Tyrant: The Tradition and Theory of Tyrannicide* (Boston: Little Brown, 1957).

5. Quoted by B. Hurwood, *Society and the Assassin: A Background Book on Political Murder* (London: International Institute for Strategic Studies, 1970), 29.

6. Carl Sandburg, *Abraham Lincoln: The War Years* (Cambridge, MA: MIT Press, 1939), vol. 4, 482.

7. "Allah Says Fight." Transcript of Statement by al-Qaeda Spokesman. ABC News.com, October 9, 2001.

8. Vidal, *Cours de Droit Criminal et de Science Pententiare,* 5th ed. (Paris: Institute de Paris Press, 1916), 110–12.

9. William Blackstone, *Commentaries on the Laws of England* (1749), vol. 4, 71.

10. Quoted by F. Venturi, *Roots of Revolution: A History of the Populist and Socialist Movements in Nineteenth Century Russia,* trans. F. Haskell, (New York: Norton, 1966), 281.

11. Venturi, *Roots of Revolution,* 366.

12. Irving Howe, "The Ultimate Price of Random Terror," *Skeptic: The Forum for Contemporary History* 11 (January–February 1976): 10–19.

13. Sandra Stencel, "Terrorism: An Idea Whose Time Has Come," *Skeptic: The Forum for Contemporary History* 11 (January–February 1976): 4–5.

14. Quoted by Friedlander, *Terrorism: Documents,* 26.

15. John Arquilla, David Ronfeldt, and Michele Zanini, "Networks, Netwar, and Information-Age Terrorism," in *Terrorism and Counterterrorism: Understanding the New Security Environment,* ed. Russell D. Howard and Reid L. Sawyer (McGraw-Hill: Guilford, CT, 1999), 101.

CHAPTER 3

Ideology and Terrorism: Rights from Wrongs?

Key Concepts

anarchism
jus ex injuria non oritur
right of self-determination
image of the enemy
images of themselves
nature of the conflict
image of the victims
theme of millenarianism

religious fanaticism
neo-Nazism/neofascism
separatism
nationalism
issue orientation
ideological mercenaries
pathological terrorists
counterterror terrorists

"I have always dreamed," he mouthed, fiercely, "of a band of men absolute in their resolve to discard all scruples in the choice of means, strong enough to give themselves frankly the name of destroyers, and free from the taint of resigned pessimism which rots the world. No pity for anything on earth, including themselves, and death enlisted for good and all in the service of humanity . . ."

Joseph Conrad

Can rights ever derive from wrongs? Can one injustice truly justify the commission of another injustice? There are, of course, no easy answers to such loaded questions. In the same manner, there may be no clear or absolute answer to the question of whether there could be a justifiable terrorist act.

Most individuals or groups who claim that an act is justified, mean that it has a purpose that is "just," one that can be given a "reasonable explanation." So to determine whether or not terrorism is justified, we must study the reasons or justifications given for the terrorist acts. Because we have already reviewed the transformation of terrorism over the centuries, from the lone assassin executing an unjust ruler to the revolutionaries of modern Russia, we will confine our study to the reasons for terrorism to the terrorism that has existed in the twentieth century.

This will not limit the usefulness of our observations, since the basic reasons for terrorism have not, in fact, changed as rapidly as have the tactics of terror. The forces of oppression that have caused men to rebel have not changed over the centuries; what has changed is the willingness of the oppressed to use previously unthinkable means to achieve their objectives.

The reasons for this willingness to use extraordinary means are important; they are, in many ways, the "justification" for modern terrorism. It has always been possible to murder innocent persons. Why is it no longer an unthinkable option for revolutionary groups?

This is the crucial question. It is unarguable that states throughout history have used terrorism on their citizens, on the citizens of other nations, and as an instrument of war. Biblical and historical accounts abound of conquering armies who slaughtered innocent men, women, and children; and who took slaves and captives, perpetrating all manner of atrocities on their innocent heads.

But those rebelling against such tyrannous brutality have heretofore eschewed a comparable brutality. Indeed, the lodestar of revolutionary theory has been its vehement condemnation of the brutality of the existing regime.

Why, then, during this century have revolutionary groups become more and more willing to perpetrate equally brutal acts against similarly innocent persons? Oppression is not new, nor is the presence of a few desperate persons willing to risk all to oppose a system they abhor. What is new is the willingness of these "desperate people" to use tactics that, until very recently, were the sole provenance of the despised state.

This, it seems, is the phenomenon of modern terrorism: that revolutionaries, those rebelling against state oppression, are now willing to use weapons of terror against an innocent citizenry. In the past, revolutionaries and the theorists who espoused their causes have defended their actions in terms of ridding the world of oppressive states whose leaders committed unthinkable, barbarous acts upon the citizenry. By committing similar unthinkable, barbarous acts upon the citizenry, revolutionaries have fundamentally altered their philosophy. It is important to understand the substance of this changed philosophy, and the reasons for the change, in order to understand modern terrorism.

THE RATIONALIZATION OF VIOLENCE

The terrorist revolution is the only just form of revolution
Nikolai Morozov (1880)

Revolutionaries such as Morozov came to view terrorism as the only chance for successful revolution in czarist Russia. **Anarchism,** *which advocated "propaganda of the deed,"* became increasingly committed to nonselective violence, as the possibility of forcing change within the structure of the existing state became less feasible.

Indeed, anarchism, as a theory, is less strict in its adherence to the injury of only "guilty" persons than were most revolutionaries of nineteenth-century Russia. Louis August Blanqui asserted that the transformation of society could only come about from a small, well-organized group of "terrorists" acting as the vanguard of the revolutionary process.[1] With the imperial abdication in France in 1870 and the establishment of the Paris Commune in March 1871 (composed as it was of a Blanquist majority), "a red terror once again came into being, accentuated by class division and violence."[2]

The anarcho-syndicalist credo expressed by American revolutionary propagandist Emma Goldman offers another insight into the transition of revolutionary theory. Goldman advocated "direct action against the authority of the law, direct action against the invasive meddlesome authority of our moral code."[3] This rejection of a moral code as "invasive" and "meddlesome" and belonging to those in authority is certainly a shift in philosophy. Revolutionaries of previous centuries had claimed that such a code "justified" their actions against a clearly immoral state. This change in perception of the existing moral code will be explored shortly, in the context of discussion of the self-justification of modern terrorists.

Franz Fanon, the theoretical architect of the Algerian independence movement, also offered some changes to traditional revolutionary theory. He argued for the use of "the technique of terrorism" that, he asserted, consisted of individual and collective attempts by means of bombs or by the derailing of trains to disrupt the existing system.

Both of these theorists express a philosophy radically different from that espoused by the early Russian revolutionaries or earlier advocates of tyrannicide. The legitimate victim of violence need no longer be exclusively either the soldier or the government official. Rather, with increasing frequency, he or she is an innocent civilian third party, whose injury or death is intended to hurt or frighten the entire body politic.

In the United States, anarchist philosophy also began to engender radical demands for indiscriminate violence. Anarchist publications in the 1880s were candid in their enthusiasm for the widespread use of explosives. One letter that appeared in one extremist paper, *Alarm,* enthused:

> Dynamite! Of all the good stuff, this is the stuff . . . . Place this in the immediate vicinity of a lot of rich loafers who live by the sweat of other people's brows, and light the fuse. A most cheerful and gratifying result will follow.[4]

Anarchist violence did indeed claim innocent lives, often through the use of dynamite, during the following decades. Although strains of both nonviolent socialism and violent anarchism mixed in the labor movement, unfairly tainting much of labor's legitimate attempts to organize, acts of random violence were unabashedly carried out by anarchist extremists within the movement.

On October 1, 1910, the *Los Angeles Times* building was destroyed by dynamite. Two young ironworkers eventually confessed to this crime, in which 20 innocent persons died and another 17 were injured. On September 16, 1920, an explosion on New York's Wall Street claimed an even larger number of innocent lives. Forty people were killed in this blast, and another 300 were injured. A hitherto unknown group, calling itself the American Anarchist Fighters, claimed credit for this devastating attack whose victims were ordinary working people. In spite of the fact that anarchists were, in theory, committed to conflict with the "rich ruling elites," victims of its violence were in many cases *not* wealthy or powerful persons, but innocent bystanders.

CASE STUDY   Tupamaros (Uruguay Faction)

Violence among groups seeking to correct societal injustices has not been limited to anarchistic rationalization. In Uruguay, terrorism was justified by the Tupamaros on nationalistic and socialistic grounds. Uruguay, until the late 1950s a model of democracy and prosperity in a largely authoritarian sea of South American nations, began to falter economically in 1958. Young middle-class professionals and intellectuals, hit especially hard by the economic difficulties and moved by the wretched living and working conditions of many groups in the country, began to seek radical solutions to the nation's woes.

The Tupamaros, named for Tupac Amaru, a Peruvian rebel Indian leader of that name who was burned at the stake in the eighteenth century, began a nationalist movement in 1962. It was led in the beginning by Raúl Sendic, born in 1925 in the Flores province of Uruguay in an upper middle-class family. Sendic became unhappy with his law studies and dropped out of school, heading to the northern part of Uruguay to work among poor sugar beet laborers. In 1962, Raúl went to Cuba for a few months, returning to organize the sugar plantation laborers in their first march on the capital, Montevideo. As support grew for Sendic and the sugar beet laborers, the Tupamaros movement was launched.

The Tupamaros protested against what they considered to be a democratic, quasi-welfare state, viewing it as an attempt to destroy the political soul of the masses with economic incentives. Over the next few years, their activities ranged from the hijacking of trucks carrying food (which they subsequently distributed to needy people), to bank robbery and kidnapping for ransom. Seeing themselves as the "Robin Hood" of their country, they robbed banks and corporations, then distributed the money to the poor. Kidnapping was another profitable method of financing their activities, and their victims included a Brazilian consul, a U.S. advisor to the Uruguayan police (whom they later killed), and the British ambassador to Uruguay. They also assassinated leading figures, including the chief of the civil defense forces.

These activities alone would not constitute terrorism, perhaps. However, the targets for the kidnapping were frequently foreign diplomats or employees of foreign companies, whose only "crime" was their presence in Uruguay. Assassinations of police officers were so common that some police officers refused, in fear, to wear their uniforms to work.

Convinced that the Tupamaros constituted a threat to democracy in Uruguay, President Gestido banned the Socialist Party in 1967, and the government declared an internal war against the Tupamaros. By 1972, more than 4,000 Tupamaros sympathizers had been arrested, and the government passed the Law of State Security, suspending the normal time period allowed for the holding of suspects. It also permitted military trials of suspected Tupamaros supporters. Free press and free speech were also suspended by the government in order to curb the media coverage of the Tupamaros.

The desire to drive out foreign influence and to forcibly redistribute wealth served, in the case of the Tupamaros, as the justification for its acts of terror-violence. In response, the government declared a state of war to exist, making it difficult to justify the killing of those innocent persons by the group, since the consequences for much of the population were actions of state terrorism. The cycle of violence generated by terrorist acts by a group spiraled out of control, and hence the justification for the terrorism by the revolutionaries diminished in credibility.   ❏

REBELLION AND THE RIGHT
OF SELF-DETERMINATION

The evolution of revolutionary violence into terrorism is significant. It has long been a stumbling block in the creation of effective international law concerning terrorism. Revolutions have occurred throughout history without recourse to terror-violence; an effort made to understand why such revolutions do not continue to occur without the use of terrorist tactics. Do they not occur, or can they not occur successfully without the use of terrorism?

Although rebellion cannot be separated from violence, certain types of violence, as noted earlier, have not been acceptable. Violence directed deliberately against innocent parties is destructive not only of law and of legal systems, but also of civilized society, according to one expert on international law.[5]

As the United Nations (UN) Secretariat, in its study of the nature and causes of terrorism, concluded: "The legitimacy of a cause does not in itself legitimize the use of certain forms of violence, especially against the innocent." Paragraph 10 of the Secretariat's study notes that this limit on the legitimate use of violence "has long been recognized, even in the customary laws of war."[6] Both the General Assembly and the Security Council of the United Nations have passed resolutions stating that "criminal acts intended or calculated to provoke a state of terror in the general public, a group of persons or particular persons for political purposes are in any circumstances unjustifiable, whatever the considerations of a political, philosophical, ideological, racial, ethnic, religious or other nature that may be invoked to justify them."[7]

Two points here are worth noting. One is that the community of nations regards the limits on the legitimate use of violence as being of long standing, not the product of twentieth-century governments seeking to prevent rebellions. Although many nations have come into being during this century through both rebellion and peaceful decolonization, the customary laws restraining the use of force were not created to harness this explosion of nationalism.

The second point is that the community of nations, not just in the Secretariat's report but in many documents and discussions, has agreed that there are in fact limits to the legitimate use of violence, regardless of the justice of the cause. Moreover, these limits are acknowledged to exist even in times of war. Indeed, it is *from* the laws of war that we obtain our clearest understanding of precisely what these limits on the use of violence are.

Therefore, a condemnation of terrorism is not a denunciation of revolutionaries or guerrillas. It is only a reiteration of the limits on violence that a civilized society is willing to permit. It does not in any sense preclude the right to revolution, which is a recognized and protected right under international law.

As one scholar pointed out, those who attack "political and military leaders . . . will not be called terrorists at all" in international law.[8] Another knowledgeable expert remarked that "today's revolutionaries want to be guerrillas, not terrorists," as there is no stigma attached to the status of rebels.[9] Most resolutions passed by the UN General Assembly on terrorism contain, at the beginning, a reaffirmation of "the inalienable right of self-determination and independence of all peoples."[10]

No pejorative status is attached to rebels and revolutionaries, but even armies engaged in warfare must by law recognize certain limits on the use of violence. The right to revolution and self-determination cannot be predicated upon the wrongful deaths of innocent persons, nor is it prevented in any meaningful way from other nonprohibited activity by the condemnation of terrorist tactics.

To cite a venerable legal maxim, *jus ex injuria non oritur,* meaning *"rights do not arise from wrongs."* Revolutions have occurred throughout history without depending on the use of terrorism for success. There seems no legitimate reason why they cannot continue to occur successfully in spite of a ban on terrorist tactics. The position of governments committed to this concept was stated in part by former U.S. Secretary of State William Rogers when he spoke at the 1972 opening of the UN General Assembly:

> [T]errorist acts are totally unacceptable attacks against the very fabric of international order. They must be universally condemned, whether we consider the cause a terrorist invoked noble or ignoble, legitimate or illegitimate.[11]

Not all nations, governments, or individuals agree with this assessment. Even the nations who subscribe to this assessment are not unfailingly willing to adhere to it. For instance, during World War II, Nazism was regarded as "an ultimate threat to everything decent . . . an ideology and a practice of domination so murderous, so degrading even to those who might survive it, that the consequences of its final victory were literally beyond calculation, immeasurably awful."[12]

But nonstrategic, random terror bombing by those same nations who have authored and defended the current laws against terrorism resulted in the deaths of thousands of German civilians. These persons were apparently sacrificed for "psychological" purposes (i.e., to create fear and chaos in an audience). Such "sacrifices" and indiscriminate destruction of civilians today would be roundly condemned by those same nations if they were performed by a revolutionary or guerrilla force or by a rogue state carrying out terror-violence against its own citizens.

So the distinction between acceptable and unacceptable use of force is not always clear and is influenced, of course, by the nations responsible for making the rules. But as noted earlier, the *mores* prohibiting certain forms of violence are not of recent vintage: they have been evolving over many centuries.

One of the ingredients in the formulation of the rules that govern civilized society today that *is* new is the **right of self-determination.** The UN Charter, written in 1945, states that *people have a right to determine for themselves the form of state under which they choose to live.*[13] Since that time, nations and legal scholars have been trying to work out just which people have this right and how extensive a justification this right confers on individuals engaged in wars of self-determination.

The answers to these and related questions are not readily attainable. As one scholar noted:

> [A]ccording to United Nations practice, a "people" is any group that August organization wishes to liberate from "colonial and racist regimes." Thus, the Puerto Ricans are a people but the Kurds are not; the Namibians are a people and possess their own state but the population of East Timor (or what remains of it) is without identity and without hope.[14]

East Timor is now a state (making the observation by Friedlander in the 1980s no longer completely accurate), but the lack of clarity as to who are a "people" by law remains, since this right is not clearly defined by the concepts essential to it. Nor is it clear just how fundamental or extensive this right to self-determination is. Is it more fundamental than the right to life? If not, then the pursuit of self-determination cannot intentionally jeopardize any person's right to life. Does the right to self-determination supercede the right of a state to protect itself and to provide for its citizens a safe and stable system of government?

No people seeking to exercise their right to self-determination do so today in a vacuum. Their actions in the course of their struggle necessarily have an effect, often a negative one, on other persons within their community. As in any other armed struggle, there must remain limits within which their right to pursue self-determination must operate, to limit the adverse effects of such a course of action on the rights of others.

The problem that this newly articulated right to self-determination has created in terms of the limitation of armed warfare is important. This right is readily conferred upon, or claimed by, many groups who do not enjoy, and probably can never gain, majority support among the indigenous population of their state. This means that many groups of disaffected persons may claim this right who have no hope of ever waging even a successful guerrilla war against an established state. The argument has been made, of course, that these groups therefore cannot reasonably be held to conventional rules of warfare, for to hold them to those rules is to condemn them to inevitable failure.

CASE STUDY   The Palestinians

Faced with the overwhelming odds in favor of the well-established and well-armed state, many of the peoples seeking to exercise their right to self-determination have been increasingly willing to use less conventional methods and means of waging war. Lacking large popular support from the indigenous population, facing a state whose trained army and weaponry make conventional resistance a mockery, such groups are increasingly willing to use the illegal tactic of terrorism to achieve their right.

The difficulties facing such groups seeking self-determination are very real, but the problems that they create are also formidable. What happens, for example, if two "peoples" claim that their right to self-determination gives them the right to occupy and control the same piece of land? Who decides which group's right should prevail?

Should it be decided based upon which group can establish control or on which has the better legal claim to the land? Again, who or what is to make such a determination?

This is not a hypothetical situation. There exist such dilemmas in the world at this very moment. The rival claims of the Palestinians and the Israelis to the same land have provoked decades of bloodshed and bitter fighting. Each people in this struggle claim an historic right to the land.

For more than five decades, Israel managed to secure its right to determine its own form of government and to exercise control over its own people. But it has had to do so through force and to maintain, through the end of the twentieth century, its existence through occupation of additional land. Peace is seldom achieved, in the long term, through occupation, and Israel has struggled with the difficult issue of the need to pull out of those occupied lands. But as Israeli settlements in the occupied territories continue to expand, there are Jewish settlers who have now lived in those lands for years, whose identity and security as a people are threatened by the withdrawal and whose right to self-determination they fear will be lost in the peace process. As long as there exists within or near the borders of this troubled land a people whose right to self-determination remains unsatisfied, terrorist acts may well continue to be a threat to peace in the region.

The assassination in late 1995 of Yitzhak Rabin, prime minister of Israel, by a Jewish student seeking to derail this withdrawal of Israel from the occupied territories, makes this threat very clear. Certainly, the satisfaction of the Palestinians' right to self-determination will be difficult to achieve in any way that is acceptable to all of the people of Israel. One Israeli military officer noted that even children born and raised in Palestinian refugee camps, will state that they are from Jaffa and other coastal cities (of what used to be Palestine). Since this land is now an integral part of Israel, there seems little likelihood that the aspirations of those Palestinian adults who have fostered this sense of belonging to old homelands can ever be satisfied.

Violent actions taken during the peace process that began in 1993 have made it clear that some factions of Palestinians do not want independence in the West Bank or the Gaza Strip. They want to return to, and to claim, their "homeland" of Palestine, including the land that is today Israel. It would appear impossible to satisfy their right to self-determination without infringing upon Israel's right to exist. Just as the Jewish people rejected other offers of homelands around the turn of the century, insisting on their right to return to the homeland of their theological ancestors, Palestinians have found it difficult to accept alternatives that fall short of a return of *their* homeland.

On whose side does "right" rest in this conflict? The right of self-determination that the Palestinians seek to exercise is the same one for which the Haganah fought against the British occupying forces in the 1930s to 1940s. Just as the Jewish Irgun and its radical off shoot, the Stern Gang, used terror tactics to force out an occupying power, the Palestinians have resorted to terrorist acts to rid themselves of what they perceive to be an occupying power.

This right to self-determination is, by its very lack of clarity, a dangerous justification for unlawful violence. Because neither the peoples nor the extent of the right itself appear to have any specific legal limitations, the exercise of such rights can lead to vicious spirals of violence, as rival peoples seek to claim their rights within an international system whose state of flux lends credence to first one and then the other's rights. ❏

TERRORIST BELIEFS AND IMAGES

Terrorism, then, has been justified by relatively sophisticated theories, such as anarchism, and by less well-defined concepts, such as that of the right of self-determination. But how do modern terrorists justify themselves, on a personal level, for their actions? Do they indeed think in terms of broad theoretical justifications, or is their belief system less complex?

The content of terrorist belief systems has not, in fact, been the subject for much systematic study. The reasons for this neglect are in some respects understandable. For one thing, the study of terrorism is a relatively new field, with very little emphasis placed thus far on the world's view of terrorists.[15]

Another more serious problem in analyzing terrorist belief systems lies in the difficulties in acquiring and interpreting data. Few if any extensive memoirs, minutes of meetings, or interviews with terrorist decision makers are available to facilitate a reconstruction of events. Much of the existing data is classified by governments in ways that make it virtually inaccessible to researchers.

This does not mean that no studies exist of terrorist belief systems. Gerald A. Hopple and Miriam Steiner, in 1984, employed content analysis to evaluate 12 factors as potential sources of action, applying the techniques to 46 documents from the German Red Army Faction, the Italian Red Brigades, and the Basque ETA. Their findings indicated that emphasis within belief systems changes over time and that different groups stress different motivations.[16]

From the studies made, some significant components of terrorist belief systems have emerged. A brief review of these, although not sufficient to explain why *all* terrorists do what they do or believe what they do, will offer insights into the framework of logic by which a terrorist justifies his or her actions.

One of the significant components of a belief system is the **image of the enemy.** Dehumanization of the enemy is a dominant theme. *The enemy is viewed in depersonalized and monolithic terms,* as capitalist, communist, the bourgeoisie, or imperialist. It is not human beings whom the terrorist fights; rather, it is this dehumanized monolith.

As one group of researchers noted, for many terrorists, "the enemy is nonhuman; not good enough. He is the enemy because he is not the hero and is not friendly to the hero."[17] This rationalization is particularly prominent among right-wing terrorists, whether neofascist or religious extremist. Like other right-wing theorists, such groups tend toward prejudicial stereotyping, based on class, ethnic, or religious attributes. The enemy thus might be all journalists, lawyers, students, intellectuals, or professors, who are regarded by such terrorists as leftist or communist.

Making war, even illegal, "unthinkable" war, on an inhuman enemy is all too easy. As long as that enemy does not have a face, a wife or child, a home, grieving parents or friends, the destruction of that enemy is a simple matter, requiring little or no justification beyond the enemy status.

Viewing the enemy in these terms also makes the depiction of the struggle in which the terrorists see themselves as engaged in relatively simple. It is a struggle in which good and evil, black and white, are very obvious. The enemy is often seen as much more powerful in its monolithic strength, with many alternative courses of action from which to choose. The terrorists, on the other hand, have no choice except to resort to terrorism in confronting this "monster," which becomes, in their view, a response to oppression, not a free choice on their part but a duty. Osama bin Laden, in his call for a jihad against America, stated, "The ruling to kill the Americans and their allies—civilians and military—is an individual duty for every Muslim who can do it in any country which it is possible to do it."[18]

Also of interest in this belief system is the terrorists' **images of themselves.** Terrorists of both the left and right tend to think of themselves as belonging to an *elite*. Most left-wing revolutionary terrorists view themselves as the *victims*, rather than the aggressors, in the struggle. The struggle in which they are engaged is an obligation, a duty, not a voluntary choice, because they are the enlightened in a mass of unenlightened.[19] For the religious zealot, the image tends to be of being *chosen* by a supreme being to lead the struggle and to be a martyr in confronting the monster that threatens the world of the *faithful.*

Like terrorists of the right, revolutionary terrorists seem to view themselves as above the prevailing morality, as morally superior. Normal standards of behavior do not apply to them. They do not deem themselves in any sense bound by conventional laws or conventional morality, which they often regard as the corrupt and self-serving tool of the enemy. It would clearly be useless to condemn as immoral an action by a terrorist, because it is quite likely that the those embracing terrorist tactics have already reached the belief that the morality condemning their action is inferior to their own morality.

This view of morality is integral to the terrorists' view of the **nature of the conflict** in which they are engaged. *Not only is this a moral struggle, in which good and evil are simplistically defined, but terrorists tend to define the struggle also in terms of elaborately idealistic terms.* Terrorists seldom perceive what they do as the murder or killing of innocent persons. Instead, they are wont to describe such actions as executions committed after trials of traitors.

Menachem Begin offered insights into this legalistic rationalization. He noted that, in terrorist struggles, "what matters most necessary is the inner consciousness that makes what is 'legal' illegal and the 'illegal' legal and justified."[20]

Also of importance in understanding the belief system of terrorists is the **image of the victims** of the violence. *If the victims are fairly easily identifiable with the enemy, then as representatives of the hostile forces, they are despised and their destruction is easily justified, even if such victims have committed no clear offense against the terrorist or his group.* As Michael Collins, founder of the Irish Republican

Army, noted with reference to the killing of 14 men *suspected* of being British intelligence agents, such persons were "undesirables . . . by whose destruction the very air is made sweeter." This remained true, according to Collins, even though not all of the 14 were guilty of the "sins" of which they were accused.[21]

Innocent victims, persons whose only "crime" was in being in the wrong place at the wrong time, are generally dismissed as unimportant by-products of the struggle. "Fate," rather than human acts, is often blamed for the deaths of such persons. Thus, the persons in the airplanes flown into the World Trade Center towers and the Pentagon were only victims because they were on the wrong flight; those killed in the towers and at the Pentagon were part of the American "monster" against which bin Laden had called for a jihad.

This brings up one last important point about terrorist belief systems: the predominant **theme of millenarianism.** *Personal redemption through violent means* is a millenarian theme found in many terrorist belief systems. Violence is often viewed as being essential to the coming of the millennium, whose coming may be hastened by the actions of believers willing to violate the rules of the old order in an effort to bring in the new order (often conceived of in terms of total liberation).

Such beliefs have led to a deliberate abandonment of restraints. Coupled with the tendency to divide the world into clear camps of good and evil, as noted earlier, this abandonment of restraints usually entails a strong conviction that no mercy can be shown to the evil that the enemy embodies. Terrorists are wrapped in an impenetrable cloak of belief in the absolute righteousness of their cause and the ultimate success that will inevitably come. If all violence brings the millennium closer, then no violence, regardless of its consequences, can be regarded as a failure. The terrorist always "wins" in this struggle.

Other elements are common to some terrorist belief systems. Some, for instance, place a premium on martyrdom, suggesting this as a desirable goal. A statement from the "Ladenese Epistle" illustrates the strength of this commitment to martyrdom:

> Those youths know that their rewards in fighting you, the USA, is double than their rewards in fighting some one else not from the people of the book. They have no intention except to enter paradise by killing you.[22]

Understanding at least these few fundamental elements of terrorist beliefs may facilitate an ability to deal with terrorism in its many forms and to anticipate its future growth patterns. Certainly the modern terrorist appears to hold belief systems very different from that of either soldiers or criminals.

CAUSES OF THE LEFT AND RIGHT

In addition to having belief systems that help the individual to justify terrorist actions, there are a wide variety of causes for which men and women have committed terrorism. Let us briefly consider a few of the motives for modern terrorism.

Religious Fanaticism

Bin Laden's al-Qaeda network has given the world a dramatic example of the destructive power of *individuals committed to waging holy war on religious principles,* disciples of **religious fanaticism.** The holy war called for by bin Laden from Islamic fundamentalists caused the death of thousands of innocent people in the attack on the World Trade Center in 2001 and continues to feed the flames of conflict within Afghanistan, Iraq, and the rest of the world.

In their religious fervor, religious fanatics of all faiths have been unrepentantly responsible for the loss of thousands of lives. Planes are sabotaged, temples stormed, and unrelenting guerrilla warfare waged, all in the name of "religion." Such a war pits Shi'a Muslims against Sunni Muslims, Catholics against Protestants, Hindus against Muslims across all forms of political and physical boundaries.

Modern "crusaders," often taking the form of suicide bombers in the Middle East today, offer some of the most chilling evidence of the impact of religion on terrorism. Martyrdom is a compelling lure and self-sacrifice is valued above many other virtues, including mercy or pity. In the name of a supreme being, rivers of blood have flowed, and will no doubt continue to flow, for fanatics of any sort are seldom ever satisfied by any gain.

Anarchism

Few groups still operate today that hold strictly to this cause. Over the last three decades of the twentieth century, we witnessed the growth and demise of the Weather Underground and the Symbionese Liberation Army in the United States. The Japanese Red Army, in its rhetoric, has espoused anarchistic beliefs, as did the Red Army Faction in Germany. Such groups have tended to be small and short-lived, perhaps because their goals are somewhat nebulous, and thus they find it difficult to draw others into their ranks. Anarchism's more extreme form, nihilism, in which the destruction of *all* structure and form of society is sought, still exists as an ideology among certain Western European terrorist groups.

Neo-Nazism/Neofascism

In recent years, a number of groups have sprung up throughout Western Europe and the United States, embracing **neo-nazism/neofascism.** In the United States, for example, the Aryan Nations, and several related groups including the Christian Identity Movement and the Christian Patriots, have been involved in armed conflict with the authorities and have been responsible for several bombings in which innocent people were killed. Indeed, many of these groups have been involved in the arming and training of paramilitary troops in almost every state in the United States. The devastating bomb blast in Oklahoma City in 1995, after which a shocked nation watched the bodies of small children carried lifeless or dying from the rubble, was carried out by a person who had been a member of a paramilitary group in Michigan and whose mother, not surprisingly, had involved him at an early age in the Christian Identity Movement.

Separatism

Perhaps the best-known group embracing **separatism** is the ETA, the Basque separatists who seek independence or at least autonomy from Spain, and have used bombs and machine guns to try to force the Spanish government to accede to their demands for independence. The violent group of French-Canadian separatists, the FLQ, was essentially inactive by the 1990s, but was responsible for several acts of terrorism during the 1960s and 1970s. The Abu Sayyaf Group in the Philippines has carried out numerous kidnappings for ransom in an effort to gain separation for the Muslim portion of the country from the government in Manila.

Nationalism

It is difficult to separate **nationalism** from separatism as a motivator of terrorism. The distinction is somewhat unclear in many cases. Groups whose motivation is nationalism are those who seek for their portion of society, which is sometimes but not always a minority, to gain control of the system of government and the allocation of resources within that nation-state. Such groups do not seek independence or separation from the nation. With this in mind, the IRA, whose terrorist acts in Northern Ireland are the source of infamous legend, could conceivably have been classed in this category prior to the peace process of the 1990s. The Tupamaros in Uruguay and the Sendero Luminoso in Peru could also be placed within this category.

Issue Orientation

During the latter part of the twentieth century, various forms of **issue orientation** aroused such violent sentiments that adherents to one side or another have resorted to terrorist violence to enforce their beliefs. Abortion is one such issue: its opponents have actually bombed abortion clinics. Oddly enough, environmental and animal protection activists, during the last decade of the twentieth century, became increasingly militant in their insistence that protection of the environment and/or of animals is critically important and worth fighting for. Placing spikes in trees and in paths through the woods and burning down animal testing centers have become common actions by such groups. Doctors have been killed to save the fetuses that those doctors may have been willing to abort. The Earth Liberation Front, one militant environmental group in the United States, rationalized that, if it was necessary to kill people to save the trees, then they would be justified in killing people!

The issue of nuclear power and nuclear weapons, too, has provoked violence. Several modern novelists and screenwriters have created all-too-realistic scenarios concerning the possibility of antinuclear activists detonating a nuclear weapon to illustrate their contention that such weapons must be banned. Thus far, such an incident exists only in fiction, but the growing intensity of the debate on this issue makes such an incident uncomfortably close to reality.

As Figure 3.1 indicates, the causes for which terrorism is committed today encompass a wide spectrum. Many of these reasons for terror do not fit comfortably into the lineup, but may be associated with a cause, depending upon the type of group

Japanese Red Army	Irish Republican Army	ETA	Aryan Nations	al-Qaeda
Anarchist	Nationalist	Separatist	neo-Nazi/neofascist	Religious Fanatic
		Ideological mercenaries Pathological terrorists Counterterrorist terrorism		

FIGURE 3.1   Spectrum of Causes, from Left to Right, with Groups.

or state perpetrating it. Visualizing this line of causes is useful, but it is also useful to remember that the causes of the extreme left and the extreme right too often meet on the fringe of a circle rather than being separated to the ends of a straight line, because groups at both ends of this spectrum may desire the same thing: an absolute end to the authority structure that currently exists.

Ideological Mercenaries

The legendary Illich Ramirez Sanchez, known to the world as Carlos the Jackal, and more recently Sabri al-Banna (Abu Nidal), have given rise to a fear of the proliferation of *"terrorists-for-hire,"* or **ideological mercenaries.** Although it is beyond debate that such persons do exist and cause considerable violence, little evidence suggests the development of a mercenary army of terrorists. Indeed, the arrest of Carlos from his abode in the Sudan and his removal for trial in France, indicates that the twenty-first century may have less tolerance politically for such individuals, in a world in which nations no longer can count on a cold war to protect them from direct intervention by a stronger nation, if they harbor such a mercenary. Instead, the rise of individuals like Osama bin Laden suggests that terrorists who can themselves hire or fund terrorist activities constitute a greater threat.

Pathological Terrorists

Some persons kill and terrorize for the sheer joy of terrorizing, not for any "cause" or belief. Charles Manson was perhaps one such; those who commit so-called serial murders are of the same cast. **Pathological terrorists** *have no cause; they are sick and twisted individuals,* whom Frederick Hacker has called "crazies."[23] Perhaps the youths responsible for the massacres in schools during the 1990s were enjoying terrorizing and were thus pathological but not necessarily terrorists, because they lacked definable political motive.

Counterterror Terrorists

Perhaps the most frightening development toward the end of the twentieth century is the proliferation of so-called **counterterror terrorists,** the *death squads that*

mete out summary justice to those judged by their leaders to be terrorists. Several authoritarian states, threatened by political change, have resorted to these semiofficial
troops, thereby inspiring that spiral of terror-violence discussed earlier. Several
countries in Central and South America have fallen prey to the lure of counterterror
tactics to control terrorism. Even Israel, itself prey to countless terrorist suicide
bombings, has resorted to the use of helicopter gunship attacks on civilian communities in their attempts to kill suspected leaders of the militant groups.

CONCLUSIONS

Terrorism *is* different today, with many different forms and many different causes.
The argument continues to be made that the justice of the cause, the nobility of the
motive, in some way makes the terrorist act less heinous. To understand the cause for
which one fights and the belief system in which one operates, it is said, makes it less
likely that one will whole-heartedly condemn the actions taken.

But does the woman whose legs are blown off in an explosion in the supermarket understand that the bomb was placed by persons who bore her no personal grudge
but were merely seeking independence or separatism for a disenfranchised minority?
Will the family of a child killed in an airline explosion accept the explanation that the
group responsible for the explosion had not enough weapons to fight a legitimate battle with an authoritarian government? Can those who lost family members and other
loved ones in the World Trade Center attacks accept their losses more easily by understanding the desperation of those who saw their faith threatened by the presence
of the United States in the Middle East?

No cause, however just or noble, can make such actions acceptable. Understanding cannot diminish the horror of the atrocity committed against the innocent.
The right of self-determination, if it must be secured by the wrong of the murder and
maiming of innocents, is not worth the price in the eyes of the rest of the world.

EVALUATION

If a group is exercising its right to self-determination, does this give it the right to
commit a wrong on other persons? To what extent is one justified in committing a
wrong in order to secure a right? Is there ever a time in which, as some have argued,
the needs of the many—to secure the right of self-determination or freedom—can be
said to outweigh the needs of the few—victims of the violence?

Consider and discuss the following incidents, keeping in mind several questions: Were these acts of terrorism? For what cause were they committed? Were they
in any sense justified?

1. *Assassination of Franz Ferdinand.* Shot to death by a man who felt, with some justice,
   that the rights of the minority of which he was a part were being cruelly ignored in the
   carving up of Europe. Ferdinand's death precipitated the events leading up to World War
   I. His death was, in some ways, the catalyst to that calamity.

2. *Assassination of Anwar Sadat.* Shot by men who felt Sadat had betrayed the Arabs by his willingness to establish a peaceful relationship with Israel, Sadat's death considerably slowed down the peace process in the Middle East. His successor, Hosni Mubarak, was understandably reluctant to take similar unpopular steps.

3. *Bombing of the U.S. Marine barracks in Lebanon.* Carried out by militants who regarded the U.S. military presence in Lebanon as an invasive influence in their civil war, this attack resulted in over 200 deaths and the diminishing of the U.S. presence in that war-torn country. Syrian and Israeli influence and presence remains strong in that country's territory.

4. *Bombing of Hiroshima.* Carried out by U.S. bombers carrying atomic weapons, this attack was designed to bring a quick halt to the devastating war in the Pacific. It did indeed achieve this, at the cost of countless thousands of Japanese civilian dead or maimed and many more who bore disease and deformity for generations.

SUGGESTED READINGS

Bergen, Peter L. *Holy War, Inc.: Inside the Secret World of Osama bin Laden.* New York: The Free Press, 2001.

Brown, Michael. "Right Wing Extremism as an Extension of American Frontier Tradition of Violence." Unpublished manuscript, Missouri State University, Academy of Criminal Justice Scientists, 1987.

Crenshaw, Martha. "Ideological and Psychological Factors in International Terrorism," paper presented to the Defense Intelligence College Symposium on International Terrorism. Washington, DC: December 2–3, 1985.

Gunaratna, Rohan. *Inside Al-Qaeda: Global Network of Terror.* New York: Columbia University Press, 2002.

Hacker, Frederick J. *Crusaders, Criminals, and Crazies: Terror and Terrorism in Our Time.* New York: Bantam Books, 1978.

Jenkins, Brian. *The Terrorist Mindset and Terrorist Decisionmaking: Two Areas of Ignorance.* Santa Monica, CA: Rand Corporation, 1979.

Peters, Rudolph. *Jihad in Classical and Modern Islam.* Princeton, NJ: Princeton University Press, 1996.

Ranstorp, Magnus. "Terrorism in the Name of Religion." In *Terrorism and Counterterrorism: Understanding the New Security Environment,* ed. Russell D. Howard and Reid Sawyer. Guilford, CT: McGraw-Hill, 1999.

"Turner Diaries: Blueprint for Right-Wing Revolution." *Law Enforcement News.* June 30, 1987.

NOTES

1. R. Blackey and C. Payton, *Revolution and the Revolutionary Ideal* (New York: Pergamon Press, 1976), 91–93. See also B. Croce, *History of Europe in the Nineteenth Century,* trans. H. Furst (New York: Rienner, 1953).

2. Sandra Stencel, "Terrorism: An Idea Whose Time Has Come," *Skeptic: The Forum for Contemporary History* 11 (January–February 1976): 51.

3. Emma Goldman, *Anarchism and Other Essays* (New York: Dover, 1969), 66. This is a republication of the original 1917 edition. Of particular note to the student of terrorism are Goldman's essays on the meaning of anarchism and the "psychology of political violence."

4. Quoted by Jonathan Harris in *The New Terrorism: Politics of Violence* (New York: Messner, 1983), 141.

5. Robert Friedlander, "On the Prevention of Violence," *The Catholic Lawyer* 25, no. 2 (Spring 1980): 95–105.

6. UN Secretariat Study, "Measures to Prevent International Terrorism" (November 2, 1973), UN Doc. A/C.6/418. Prepared as requested by the Sixth Legal Committee of the General Assembly.

7. United Nations General Assembly Resolution 51/210, "Measures to Eliminate International Terrorism" (January 16, 1997).

8. C. Leiser, "Terrorism, Guerrilla Warfare, and International Morality." *Sanford Journal of International Studies* 12 (1974): 39–43.

9. J. Bowyer Bell, "Trends of Terror: Analysis of Political Violence." *World Politics* 29 (1977): 476–77.

10. United Nations General Assembly Resolution 44/29, "Measures to prevent international terrorism which endangers or takes innocent human lives or jeopardizes fundamental freedoms and study of the underlying causes of those forms of terrorism and acts of violence which lie in misery, frustration, grievance, and despair and which cause some people to sacrifice human lives, including their own, in an attempt to effect radical changes" (December 4, 1989).

11. For the full text of his remarks, see State Department Bulletin no. 67 (1972), 425–429.

12. Quoted by Robert Friedlander. "On the Prevention of Violence," 67.

13. The United Nations Charter entered into force on October 24, 1945.

14. Robert Friedlander, "The PLO and the Rule of Law: A Reply to Dr. Annis Kassim," *Denver Journal of International Law and Policy* 10, no. 2 (Winter 1981): 231.

15. Brian M. Jenkins, *The Terrorist Mindset and Terrorist Decisionmaking: Two Areas of Ignorance* (Santa Monica, CA: Rand, 1979), 6340.

16. Gerald W. Hopple and Miriam Steiner, *The Causal Beliefs of Terrorists: Empirical Results* (McLean, VA: Defense Systems, 1984).

17. Franco Ferracuti and Francesco Bruno. "Italy: A Systems Perspective," in *Aggression in Global Perspective* ed. A. Goldstein and M. H. Segall (New York: Pergamon, 1983), 274.

18. Osama bin Laden, "World Islamic Front Statement: Jihad Against Jews and Crusaders," *The Washington Post,* February 23, 1998.

19. Martha Crenshaw, "Ideological and Psychological Factors in International Terrorism," paper prepared for the Defense Intelligence College Symposium on International Terrorism, Washington, DC: December 2–3, 1985.

20. Quoted by Martha Crenshaw, "Ideological and Psychological Factors in International Terrorism," 8.

21. Rex Taylor, *Michael Collins* (London: Hutchinson, 1958), 17.

22. Osama bin Laden. "Ledanese Epistle: Declaration of War (Part III): A Martyr Will Not Feel the Pain of Death," *Washington Post,* September 21, 2001.

23. Frederick J. Hacker, *Crusaders, Criminals, Crazies: Terror and Terrorism in Our Time* (New York: Bantam Books, 1978).

CHAPTER 4

Criminals or Crusaders?

Key Concepts

crazies
criminals
crusaders
characteristics of a "successful"
  terrorist
fedayeen
HAMAS
Irish Republican Army

soldiers of the revolution
al-Qaeda
motivation
group dynamics
religion as a factor
trends in recruitment and membership
socialization toward violence
Sicariis

Nothing is easier than to denounce the evil doer; nothing is more difficult than to understand him.

Fedor Dostoevsky

What kind of person becomes a terrorist? Perhaps an understanding of the dynamics of becoming a terrorist will increase our understanding of this phenomenon. As noted in the previous chapter, terrorist acts are committed for a wide variety of causes. It is also true that there are a wide variety of individuals and groups who commit terrorist acts. Although studying all such persons in detail is not feasible, a brief analysis of some of the important characteristics of modern terrorists might be informative.

The political world changed a great deal in the last two decades of the twentieth century. These political changes influenced the type of persons more likely to be recruited into terrorist groups. A study of the type of individuals known to be drawn to terrorism in the twentieth century will, perhaps, help us to predict the most probable type of twenty-first century terrorist. This could be an extremely useful tool for governments and institutions confronted with the need to plan to cope with terrorism.

PROFILE OF A TERRORIST

Why do people become terrorists? Are they crazy? Are they thrill seekers? Are they religious fanatics? Are they ideologues? Is there any way to tell who is likely to become a terrorist?

This final question provides a clue as to why political scientists and government officials are particularly interested in the psychological factors relating to terrorism. If one could identify the traits most closely related to a willingness to use terrorist tactics, then one would be in a better position to predict, and prevent, the emergence of terrorist groups.

Unfortunately, identifying such traits is not easy. Just as not all violence is terrorism, and not all revolutionaries are terrorists, not all persons who commit acts of terrorism are alike. Frederick Hacker suggests three categories of persons who commit terrorism: *crazies, criminals,* and *crusaders.* He notes that an individual carrying out a terrorist act is seldom "purely" one type or the other, but Hacker suggests that each type offers some insights into why an individual will resort to terrorism.[1]

Understanding the individual who commits terrorism is vital, not only for humanitarian reasons, but also to decide how best to deal with those individuals *while they are engaged in planning or carrying out terrorist acts.* From a law enforcement perspective, for example, it is important to appreciate the difference between a criminal and a crusading terrorist involved in a hostage-taking situation. Successful resolution of such a situation often hinges on understanding the mind of the individuals perpetrating the crime.

Let us consider the three categories of terrorists suggested by Hacker: crazies, criminals, and crusaders. For the purposes of this study, we need to establish loose descriptions of these three types. Hacker offers some useful ideas on what is subsumed under each label. **Crazies,** he suggests, are *emotionally disturbed individuals who are driven to commit terrorism "by reasons of their own that often do not make sense to anybody else."*

Criminals, on the other hand, *perform terrorist acts for more easily understood reasons: personal gain.* Such individuals transgress the laws of society knowingly and, one assumes, in full possession of their faculties. Both their motives and their goals are usually clear, if still deplorable, to most of mankind.

This is not the case with the **crusaders.** These individuals commit terrorism for reasons that are often unclear both to themselves and to those witnessing the acts. Their ultimate goals are frequently even less understandable. While such individuals are usually idealistically inspired, their idealism tends to be a rather mixed bag of half-understood philosophies. Crusaders, according to Hacker, *seek not personal gain, but prestige and power for a collective cause.* They commit terrorist acts in the belief "that they are serving a higher cause," in Hacker's assessment.

What difference does it make what kind of terrorist is behind the machine gun or bomb? To the law enforcement personnel charged with resolving the hostage situation, it can be crucial to know what type of person is controlling the situation. Criminals, for instance, can be offered sufficient personal gains or security provisions to induce them to release the hostages. Crusaders are far less likely to be talked out of carrying out their threats by inducements of personal gains, since to do so they would have to betray, in some sense, that higher cause for which they are committing the action.

For the same reason, it is useful for security agents to know what type of individual is likely to commit a terrorist act within their province. A criminal, for example, would be more likely to try to smuggle a gun aboard an airline than a bomb, since the criminal usually anticipates living to enjoy the reward of his or her illegal activities. Crusaders, however, are more willing to blow themselves up with their victims, since their service to that higher cause often carries with it a promise of a reward in the life to come.

The distinction between criminals and crusaders with respect to terrorism needs some clarification. Clearly, when anyone breaks the law, as in the commission of a terrorist act, he or she becomes a criminal, regardless of the reason for the transgression. The distinction between criminal and crusader, though, is useful in understanding the differences in the motives and goals moving the person to commit the act.

The majority of the individuals and groups carrying out terrorist acts in the world in the last decade of the twentieth and the beginning years of the twenty-first century have been crusaders. This does not mean there are not occasional instances in which individuals who, reacting to some real or perceived injury, decide to take a machine gun to the target of their anger and kidnap or destroy anyone in sight. Nor does it mean there are not individual criminals and criminal organizations that engage in terrorist activities.

Nonetheless, it is true that the majority of individuals who commit modern terrorism are, or perceive themselves to be, crusaders. According to Hacker, the typical crusading terrorist appears to be normal, no matter how crazy the cause or how criminal the means used for this cause may seem. He or she is neither an idiot nor a fool, neither a coward nor a weakling. Instead, the crusading terrorist is frequently a professional, well trained, well prepared, and well disciplined in the habit of blind obedience to a cause.

Table 4.1 indicates a few dramatic differences between the types of terrorist Hacker profiles. One is that crusaders are the least likely to negotiate a resolution to a crisis, both because such action can be viewed as a betrayal of a sublime cause and because there is little that the negotiator can offer, since neither personal gain nor safe

TABLE 4.1   Hacker's Typology of Terrorists

Type of Terrorist	*Motive/Goal*	*Willing to Negotiate?*	*Expectation of Survival*
Criminal	Personal gain/ profit	Usually, in return for profit and/or safe passage	Strong
Crusader	"Higher cause" (usually a blend of religious and political)	Seldom, since to do so could be seen as a betrayal of the cause	Minimal, since death offers reward in "afterlife"
Crazy	Clear only to perpetrator	Possible, but only if negotiator can understand motive and offer hope/alternatives	Strong, but not based on reality

passage out of the situation are particularly desired by true crusaders. Belief in the cause makes death not a penalty, but a path to reward and glory; therefore the threat of death and destruction can have little punitive value. What can a police or military negotiator offer to a crusader to induce the release of hostages or the defusing of a bomb?

Similar problems exist with crazies, depending upon how much in touch with reality such an individual is at the time of the incident. Negotiation is difficult, but not impossible, if the negotiator can ascertain the goal or motive of the perpetrator and offer some hope (even if it is not real) of success in achieving that goal by other, less destructive means. One of the critical elements is that crazies, according to Hacker's evaluation, have a limited grip on the reality that they themselves may die in the course of this action. Thus, the threat of death by a superior force carries diminished weight if the perpetrator cannot grasp the fact that he or she may die in this encounter. Just as very young children find the reality of death a difficult concept to grasp, Hacker suggests that crazies offer serious difficulties for negotiators because they often cannot grasp this reality.

Criminals, then, are the preferred perpetrators, since they will negotiate; their demands are generally logical (although often outrageous) and are based in terms that can be met or satisfied with rational alternatives. Criminals know they can be killed and have a strong desire to live to enjoy the rewards of the actions they are taking. Thus, negotiators have specific demands to be bartered, and their "clients" can be expected to recognize superior force and to respond accordingly in altering demands and resolving the incident.

These differences are critically important in at least two contexts: (1) resolving situations in which hostages are held by terrorists and (2) establishing security measures and training for vulnerable targets. The type of terrorist engaged in the incident significantly impacts the successful resolution of the situation. Hostage negotiators need to know whether they are dealing with a crusader or a criminal, know whether there is any potential for negotiation. If the individual(s) perpetrating the crime are crusaders, then an immediate hostage rescue attempt may be more appropriate than the initiation of a negotiation process.

In terms of security devices and training, the profiles become even more vital. The events of September 11, 2001, illustrate dramatically the consequences of training and equipping for the wrong type of perpetrators. Airline pilots in the United States had been trained to respond to attempts to take over flights as hostage situations. Thus the pilots of the doomed September 11 flights were engaged in trying to keep the situation calm and to "talk down" the plane, to initiate a hostage release without violence. But the individuals engaged in the takeover were crusaders, not criminals or crazies, who did not plan to live through the incidents. Only the passengers on the flight that crashed in Pennsylvania were able to offer substantial resistance— perhaps in part because they had not been trained to assume a peaceful solution could be negotiated with hostage takers.

This does not suggest that the pilots and crew were not vigilant and did not make every effort to save the lives of the passengers. But because the profile they had been trained to respond to did not match that with which they were confronted, they were unable to respond successfully to the demands of the situation. Thus, inaccurate profiling in pilot training was a serious contributing factor to the sequence of events on that day.

To political scientists, as well as to military, police, and other security and intelligence units assigned the task of coping with terrorism, an understanding of the type of person likely to commit acts of terrorism is invaluable. As our understanding of a phenomenon increases, our ability to predict its behavior with some accuracy also increases. Thus, as we try to understand who terrorists are and what they are like, we should increase our ability to anticipate their behavior patterns, thereby increasing our ability to respond effectively and to prevent more often the launching of successful terrorist attacks.

CAN WE GENERALIZE ABOUT A "TYPICAL" TERRORIST?

What, then, do we know about the type of individual who becomes a terrorist? Until fairly recently, with the in-depth coverage given to Osama bin Laden, we usually had very little personal data about successful perpetrators of terrorist attacks, because successful terrorists depend upon secrecy for protection. Through the capture of those less efficient in the art of terrorist operation, we have learned some useful information; our security and intelligence organizations continue to add substantially to that data pool.

Nevertheless, it remains true that to generalize about the "typical" terrorist can be very difficult with any degree of accuracy. The search for a "terrorist personality" is a legitimate exercise, but it is unlikely to produce any common denominator capable of uniting a wide variety of countries, periods of time, cultures and political alliances. In other words, the community of nations is unable, at this point, to agree on such a profile.

Some scholars, of course, have attempted to create a profile of a typical terrorist. Their successes are mixed, at best, but do offer some ideas that help us not only to understand what a typical terrorist may be like (if such a creature can be said to exist), but also to evaluate how terrorists as well as terrorism have changed in recent years.

Edgar O'Ballance offers one such critique of what he calls a "successful" terrorist (by which he appears to mean one who is neither captured nor dead). In his book, *The Language of Violence,* O'Ballance suggests several essential **characteristics of the "successful" terrorist:**

1. *Dedication.* To be successful, a terrorist cannot be a casual or part-time mercenary, willing to operate only when it suits his convenience or his pocket. He must become a **fedayeen,** a "man of sacrifice." Dedication also implies absolute obedience to the leader of the political movement.
2. *Personal Bravery.* As the terrorist must face the possibility of death, injury, imprisonment, or even torture if captured, O'Ballance regards this trait as important, to varying degrees, depending upon one's position within the terrorist group's hierarchy.

3. *Without the Human Emotions of Pity or Remorse.* Since most victims will include innocent men, women, and children, whom he or she must be prepared to kill in cold blood, the terrorist must have the killer instinct, able to kill without hesitation on receipt of a code or signal. As this expert notes, many can kill in the heat of anger or in battle, but few, fortunately, can do so in cold blood.

4. *Fairly High Standard of Intelligence.* As the would-be terrorist has to collect, collate, and assess information, devise and put into effect complex plans, and evade police, security forces, and other hostile forces, intelligence would appear to be a requisite.

5. *Fairly High Degree of Sophistication.* This is essential, according to O'Ballance, for the terrorist to blend into the first-class section on airliners, stay at first-class hotels, and mix inconspicuously with the international executive set.

6. *Be Reasonably Well Educated and Possess a Fair Share of General Knowledge.* By this, O'Ballance means that the terrorist should be able to speak English as well as one other major language. He asserts that a university degree is almost mandatory.

O'Ballance notes that "all terrorists do not measure up to these high standards, but the leaders, planners, couriers, liaison officers, and activists must."[2] This assertion is difficult to challenge effectively, because if the terrorist is successful, then the implication is that he or she has succeeded in evading law enforcement, security, and intelligence officers, and hence the information about the individual is necessarily either scant or unconfirmed.

We could conclude, with some justice, that most of O'Ballance's assertions, like most generalizations, are at least half-true, half-false, and largely untestable. But these generalizations, with their grains of truth, are still useful in analyzing terrorism and terrorist behavior. Let us instead examine each of his suggested attributes of a terrorist to discover whether they can be substantiated by insights into contemporary behavior.

Dedication certainly appears, on the surface, to be characteristic of modern terrorists. Palestinians involved in various groups, for example, have indicated a willingness to wait for as long as it takes them to realize their dream of a return to a nation of Palestine. They have been willing to wait as long as the Irgun waited, or longer, and many are reluctant to accept the current peace settlements, because that represents at this point less than full national independence for a nation of Palestine. Like the Irgun, they have unbounded faith in the justice of their cause and seem willing to die to achieve it.

The progress toward a comprehensive peace settlement in the Middle East in the last years of the twentieth century indicated that this tenacity may be a liability to the government established by Yasser Arafat in Gaza and parts of the West Bank, because this represents only a portion of the land that was Palestine and does not constitute full sovereignty from Israel for the Palestinians, particularly with the construction by the government of Israel of a formidable wall slicing through the West Bank and decimating parts of Palestinian territory. Anger by the Palestinian group **HAMAS,** *a radical Islamic movement supported throughout the Middle East by Iran,* indicates that a significant portion of the Palestinians remain committed to full restoration of Palestine to the Palestinian people. The suicide bombings in this area since 1994, which have claimed the lives of innocent men, women, and children, provoking harsh response by Israel in attacks that have claimed far more Palestinian lives, have given credence to this absolute resolve.

Nor is such dedication limited to Palestinians and Israelis. Observers in Northern Ireland have suggested that religious fanaticism is handed down from generation to generation in this region as well, carrying with it a willingness to fight and die for a cause. Schoolchildren in Northern Ireland have exhibited an intolerance and a bitterness that is too often translated into violence, and parents have even attacked groups of children walking to school. When children, parents, preachers, and priests join to commit murder in a "holy" cause, "dedication has produced countless bloody massacres and seemingly endless terrorism."

However, unlike the continuing violence in the Middle East, progress is being made toward a political settlement of the problem of Northern Ireland. Like the situation of Palestine, though, the solution will probably not satisfy all of the truly dedicated terrorists. The willingness of the **Irish Republican Army,** *radical Irish Catholics committed to the removal of British forces from Northern Ireland and to the unification of Ireland,* to negotiate a peace has angered radical elements in the Catholic community, and the movement of the British to negotiate with the IRA openly has raised equal anger in militant Protestant groups. If a resolution of the dispute of the British with the IRA *is* reached and a merging of Northern Ireland with the Republic of Ireland planned, there is reason to fear that a similarly dedicated group of terrorists will emerge, determined to force the United Kingdom into retaining sovereignty (thus keeping Protestant control).

Such dedication is not always directed at so specific a nationalist cause. The Japanese Red Army (JRA), for instance, founded in 1969, described themselves as **soldiers of the revolution,** *pledged to participate in all revolutions anywhere in the world through exemplary acts.* This group was responsible for the massacre of 26 tourists at Lod Airport in Tel Aviv, Israel. These dedicated revolutionaries undertook numerous terrorist attacks, many of which, like the Lod Airport massacre, were essentially suicide missions, because escape was scarcely possible.

The dedication of Osama bin Laden and his **al-Qaeda** network—*created by bin Laden in the late 1980s to bring together Arabs in Afghanistan against the Soviet Union and now engaged in attempting to establish an Islamic Caliphate throughout the world*—has also become apparent, as evidence has emerged that most of the attacks generated by this network involved years of preparation. Some of the individuals who carried out the September 11 attack came to the United States years in advance, slowly and carefully planning each stage of the operation. The dedication involved for those willing to leave home and live for years in the country to be attacked—learning about its airport security systems, taking lessons in the flight of its airliners, even traveling on the airlines to time and plan each step with accuracy—is difficult to assimilate but is clear from the evidence of their activities.

Personal bravery is also a characteristic often attributed to modern terrorists. There are, however, two views of the bravery that terrorists may possess. One might argue, with a great deal of justice, that it can scarcely be termed "brave" to use weapons mercilessly against unarmed and defenseless civilians. The men, women, and children at Lod Airport were wholly unable to defend themselves against the vicious attack of the JRA. Was it "brave" of the JRA to slaughter these innocent and unarmed people?

The opposing view, which does in fact attribute bravery to those perpetrating acts of terror, is that to be willing to carry out missions in which one's own death or imprisonment are inevitable argues no small degree of personal courage. A willingness to give one's life for a cause has commanded, throughout history, at least a reluctant admiration, even from one's enemies.

Bravery is, at best, a very subjective term. One may feel oneself to be very cowardly but be perceived by others to be quite fearless. The audience for one's deeds is often able to judge one's bravery only by the commission of the deed and is unaware of the inner doubts or demons that may have driven one to the act. Nor is the individual necessarily the best judge of his or her own personal bravery, since a person's capacity for self-deception makes it so that we often do not consciously admit (or refuse to be aware of) our true motives and fears.

The question as to whether or not terrorists who murder innocent persons, with the knowledge that their own survival is problematic, are brave may never be answered to anyone's satisfaction. Much depends on the way in which one describes the situation.

According to O'Ballance, a successful terrorist should be without the human emotions of pity or remorse. Given the necessity of being able to kill, in cold blood, unarmed and innocent persons, this would appear a reasonable assumption regarding the terrorist personality. Unlike criminals who may kill to prevent being captured or to secure some coveted prize, terrorists must, by the very nature of the act that they are often called upon to commit, kill persons against whom they have no specific grudge, whose life or death is not really material to their well-being or security. Hacker states:

> Often, the terrorists do not know whom they will hurt, and they could not care less. Nothing seems important to them except they themselves and their cause. In planning and executing their deeds, the terrorists are totally oblivious to the fate of their victims. Only utter dehumanization permits the ruthless use of human beings as bargaining chips, bargaining instruments, or objects for indiscriminate aggression.[3]

This description creates a vivid portrait of a ruthless and, one would think, thoroughly unlikable killer. Yet those guilty of such acts have not always presented to the world such a vision of themselves.

Consider the following case: On July 22, 1946, an Irgun team, dressed as waiters, rolled seven milk churns full of dynamite and TNT into the empty Regency Grill of the King David Hotel in Jerusalem. At 12:37, the TNT in the milk cans exploded, creating pressure so great that it burst the hearts, lungs, and livers of the clerks working on the floors above.

Thurston Clarke gives a gruesome description of the fate of the people in the King David Hotel at that time:

> In that split second after 12:37, thirteen of those who had been alive at 12:36 disappeared without a trace. The clothes, bracelets, cufflinks, and wallets which might have identified them exploded into dust and smoke. Others were turned to charcoal, melted into chairs and desks or exploded into countless fragments. The face of a Jewish typist was ripped from her skull, blown out of a window, and smeared onto the pavement below. Miraculously it was recognizable, a two-foot-long distorted death mask topped with tufts of hair.
>
> Blocks of stones, tables and desks crushed heads and snapped necks. Coat racks became deadly arrows that flew across rooms, piercing chests. Filing cabinets pinned people to walls, suffocating them. Chandeliers and ceiling fans crashed to the floor, empaling and decapitating those underneath.[4]

Ninety-one people died in that bomb blast. Of these, 28 were British, 41 were Arabs, and 17 were Jews. Another 46 were injured.

Listen to the words of the person who commanded this attack:

> There is no longer any armistice between the Jewish people and the British administration of Eretz Israel which hands our brothers over to Hitler. Our people are at war with this regime—war to the end.[5]

Was this bombing the deed of a fanatic, a person who could murder in cold blood many innocent people in this "war to the end"? Certainly it would seem the case.

And yet the perpetrator of this atrocity, the man responsible for the terrible destruction of 91 lives, was Menachem Begin, who in the 1970s served as prime minister of Israel. The Irgun terrorist who plotted to destroy the hotel was the same man who, working with President Carter of the United States and President Anwar Sadat of Egypt, made significant efforts to move Israel on the road to peace with its Arab neighbors, signing the famous Camp David Accords, bringing a measure of peace between Israel and Egypt.

Are terrorists cold-blooded killers only at the time of the commission of their crime, or is that a trait endemic to their character? Do they, in fact, commit such acts because of a fatal flaw in their character that makes them unable to feel pity or remorse, or are they driven by circumstances and forces to commit acts that are personally abhorrent to them?

Just as there is no safe generalization with regard to the personal bravery of terrorists, so there seem pitfalls in making too broad a characterization of a terrorist as incapable of pity or remorse. Perhaps of all that O'Ballance had to say about this particular aspect of a terrorist's characteristics, it is accurate only to say that terrorists appear to have an image of the enemy that allows them to be willing to use lethal force.

Some may indeed kill without pity or remorse and may in fact be incapable of such emotions. But to say that terrorists as a whole are so constructed is a generalization for which there is insufficient data and conflicting indicators in known cases.

The characteristics that O'Ballance suggests of sophistication and education are less true of post-1970s terrorists than they were of terrorists prior to that time. Many nineteenth-century revolutionary terrorists were indeed intelligent, sophisticated, university educated, and even multilingual. Those responsible for the murder of Czar Alexander II of Russia in March 1881 were men and women who possessed a much higher level of education and sophistication than most other young people of their nation. They were led by Sophia Perovskaya, daughter of the wealthy governor-general of St. Petersburg, the empire's capital.

Similarly, the Tupamaros of Uruguay were primarily composed of the young, well-educated liberal intellectuals who sought, but never fully gained, the support of the less educated masses. The Baader-Meinhoff gang in West Germany, which terrorized that nation throughout the 1970s, was also composed of middle- and upper-class intellectuals. This gang's master strategist was Horst Mahler, a radical young lawyer, and it drew its membership and support system heavily from the student body of German universities.

The founder of one of Italy's first left-wing terrorist bands, the Proletarian Action Group (GAP), was Giangiacomo Feltrinelli, the heir to an immense Milanese fortune and head of one of Europe's most distinguished publishing houses. Like the Red Brigades, which would succeed this group as Italy's leading left-wing terrorist group, the GAP drew much of its initial membership from young, often wealthy, intellectuals.

Terrorists, in fact, tended to be recruited from college campuses until the 1980s. Many came from well-to-do families, so that sophistication and an ability to mix with the international set were well within their grasp. Intelligence, sophistication, education, and university training: not only the leaders but also many of the practitioners of both nineteenth-century anarchism and contemporary terrorism possessed these attributes.

But standards and modes of behavior among terrorists as we move forward in the twenty-first century are changing. The French anarchists would not have abducted children and threatened to kill them unless ransom was paid. The Narodnaya Volya would not have sent parts of their victims' bodies with little notes to their relatives as the right-wing Guatemalan National Revolutionary Unity did. Neither French nor Russian anarchists would have tormented, mutilated, raped, and castrated their victims, as too many terrorist groups have done in the latter part of the twentieth century. The Baader-Meinhoff would not have flown passenger airlines into the World Trade Center, killing thousands.

As Walter Lacquer pointed out:

> Not all terrorist movements have made a fetish of brutality; some have behaved more humanely than others. But what was once a rare exception has become a frequent occurrence in our time.[6]

According to Lacquer, the character of terrorism has undergone a profound change. Intellectuals, he contends, have made "the cult of violence respectable." In spite of the violence characterizing their movement, he asserts that no such cult existed among the Russian terrorists, a difficult claim to either prove or disprove.

Nevertheless, Lacquer is correct in his assertion that the terror of recent decades is different. That much has already been established in preceding chapters. It is also true that modern terrorists are significantly different and that the difference in the type of person becoming a terrorist today has a great deal to do with the difference in terrorism.

TERRORISM IS DIFFERENT TODAY

Motivation

Part of the difference lies in the **motivation** that drives individuals to embrace terrorism. Walter Lacquer summed up the situation very well in the 1980s:

> Whatever their motives may be, the "ardent love of other" which Emma Goldman observed is not among them. The driving force is hate not love, ethical considerations are a matter of indifference to them and their dreams of freedom, of national and social liberation are suspect. Nineteenth-century nationalist terrorists were fighting for freedom from foreign domination. More recently, appetites have grown, the Basques have designs on Galicia, the Palestinians not only want the West Bank but also intend to destroy the Jewish state, and the IRA would like to bomb the Protestants into a united Ireland. The aims of terrorism, in brief, have changed, and so have the terrorists.[7]

In the twenty-first century, a less-than-clear political purpose seems involved in much of the terrorism perpetrated. Moreover, the motives of individuals involved in a struggle against a cruel oppressor are surely significantly different from those of persons rebelling against a democratically elected government. Although idealism, a social conscience, or hatred of foreign oppression can serve to drive one to commit acts of terrorism, so can boredom, mental confusion, and what psychologists term "free-floating aggression."

Certainly religious fanaticism is today as strong a motivator for the commission of terrorism as it has been in previous centuries. The holy war waged by some Muslims on Christians and fellow Muslims is no less violent than that waged during the Middle Ages. The mixture of political and religious fanaticism has always been a volatile and often violent combination.

What difference does it make whether terrorism is committed by social idealists or persons suffering from free-floating aggression? We could speculate that a social conscience would be more likely to inhibit the perpetrator from the use of indiscriminate violence against the unprotected masses. Perhaps mental confusion contributes to an inability to recognize limits on the use of terror-violence.

Unfortunately, terrorists of the twenty-first century appear more willing to use weapons of mass destruction than have those of preceding decades, perhaps because more states have used these weapons in internal wars in recent years. Iraq's use of cyanide gas on the Kurds in Halabja in March 1988 dramatically illustrated the willingness of states to use such weapons. Thus, the news that al-Qaeda tested an air dispersal mechanism for cyanide, although a chilling thought, should hardly be surprising. If states, which set the norms that limit the use of such weapons, are using these weapons openly against their own citizens, then individuals engaged in terrorist acts can scarcely be expected to continue to refrain from the use of such weapons.

Group Dynamics

These are, at best, only suppositions as to why modern terrorists, although they may still be idealistic, are more brutal than their predecessors. Before considering demographic information that might help to substantiate and explain this difference, let us first consider the impact of the terrorist *group* upon the terrorist. If **group dynamics** *helps to shape terrorist thought and action,* then its impact must certainly be understood in order to comprehend the contemporary terrorist.

Modern terrorists are, for the most part, fanatics, whose sense of reality is distorted. They operate under the assumption that they, and they alone, know the truth and are therefore the sole arbiters of what is right and what is wrong. They believe themselves to be moralists, to whom ordinary law does not apply, because the law in existence is created by immoral persons for immoral purposes.

They are not, of course, consistent in their logic. For example, they demand that governments who capture terrorists treat them as prisoners of war, as they are involved in a war against either a specific government or society in general. But they vehemently deny the state's right to treat them as war criminals for their indiscriminate killing of civilians. In other words, they invoke the laws of war only in so far as it serves their purposes, but reject any aspect of such laws that limit their ability to kill at will.

Two other points should be made with respect to understanding the contemporary terrorist. The first point is relatively simple and involves what seems like a truism. *The less clear the political purpose that motivates terrorism, the greater its appeal is likely to be to unbalanced persons.* A rational individual will be more likely to require a clear purpose for the commission of an extraordinary act. Thus an act whose motivation is unclear is more likely to appeal to an irrational mind.

As already noted, contemporary terrorism has significantly less clear political purpose than that of earlier centuries. Thus, it seems fair to say that a larger proportion of contemporary terrorists may well be unbalanced persons, the crazies that Hacker described.

The second point relates to what psychologists term *group dynamics. If it is true that a terrorist's sense of reality is distorted, as discussed earlier in the context of terrorist images, then the greater the association the terrorist enjoys with his or her group of fellow terrorists, the greater that distortion will be.* The more, in other words, an individual perceives his or her identity in terms of the group of fellow terrorists, the less will be his or her ability to see the world as it really is. For the terrorist who is a member of a close-knit organization, reality is defined by the group. Remember, too, that this group rejects the reality of laws as they currently exist and morality as defined by anyone except the group itself.

Thus, conventional moral and legal constraints have little meaning to an individual deeply involved in a terrorist group. The group determines for itself what is moral and what is legal. An individual who has just joined the group may be able to perceive the difference between what the group declares to be morally or legally justified. The longer he or she remains with the group or the stronger the individual identifies with the norms of the group, the less able the individual becomes to see the difference between reality and "reality" as it is defined by the group.

The strength of the individual's acceptance of the group's definition of reality is particularly evident in situations in which terrorism has been a significant part of the culture for several generations. In Northern Ireland, for instance, young people have been "brought up to think of democracy as part of everyday humdrum existence, but of recourse to violence as something existing on a superior plane, not merely glorious but even sacred."[8]

Religion as a Factor in Group Dynamics

Consider the case of the individual who commits terrorism as a member of a fanatic religious group. Religions, as a rule, offer their own versions of reality, as well as a promise of reward for conformity to the norms of that reality. The reward is usually promised for a future time, when the present reality has passed away.

Thus, religious zealots committing an act of terrorism are assured by their religion and its leaders that their acts are acceptable to a higher morality than may currently exist. They are reinforced in their belief that what they are doing is right by the approval of their fellow zealots. Further, religious fanatics are assured of immortality and a suitable reward therein if they should die in the commission of the act of terrorism.

It would be difficult if not impossible to persuade such persons out of their beliefs by reasonable arguments. Little could be offered to such persons as an inducement for discontinuing the act of terrorism. What reward can compete with the promise of immortality, approval by one's peers, and religious sanctification?

Obviously, the dynamics of some groups are much more powerful than those of others whose reward system and expensive spiritual support system is less organized or persuasive. Certain types of terrorists are thus, much more difficult to deal with on a rational basis, due to this ability of a group to distort reality.

TRENDS IN TERRORIST RECRUITMENT AND MEMBERSHIP

So groups have an impact on modern terrorist behavior; some groups have more than others. Motivation has some effect on the type of individual involved in contemporary terrorism. Yet we have not established what a modern terrorist is really like, beyond a few generalizations. Is it, in fact, possible to be more specific about a typical terrorist personality?

It is unlikely that this search for a terrorist personality could be successful in creating a set of common denominators that could span several continents, time periods, cultures, and political configurations. All that most experts seem to agree on regarding terrorists today is that they are primarily young people. There are, it seems, very few old terrorists.

However, some demographic **trends in recruitment and membership** in modern terrorist affiliations offer clues as to who is currently becoming a terrorist. While this falls short of providing a profile of a modern terrorist, it does yield insights into not only who modern terrorists are, but also the impact of such a demographic configuration on contemporary terrorism.

Age

Terrorism is not only a pursuit of the young, it also became in the late 1970s and 1980s a pursuit of the *very* young. Although terrorists during the time of the Russian anarchists tended to be at least in their mid-20s, during these two decades in the late twentieth century, the average age steadily decreased. During the turbulent 1960s, many terrorists were recruited from college campuses throughout the Western world. This brought the average age down to around 20, give or take a year, because the leaders were several years older, often in their early thirties.

Research in 1977 indicated that the usual urban terrorist was between 22 and 25 years of age. Among the Tupamaros, the average age of arrested terrorists was around 24.1, while in Brazil and Argentina, the average was 23 and 24, respectively. These figures remained true for the ETA, the IRA, and groups in Iran and Turkey during that time.

As early as the spring of 1976, however, evidence of a change in the age level of terrorists began to emerge. Arrests of Spanish Euzkadita Azkutasuna (ETA) members revealed a number of youths in their teens. In Northern Ireland, some of the terrorists apprehended were as young as 12 to 14.[9]

Today, although the majority of active terrorists are in their twenties, there has been a tendency, particularly among the Arab and Iranian groups, to recruit children of 14 or 15 years of age. These children are used for dangerous, frequently suicidal, missions, partly because their youth makes them less likely to question their orders and partly because their extreme youth makes them less likely to attract the attention of the authorities.

One explanation of this phenomenon is that the anarchistic-revolutionary philosophy that had begun to infiltrate the province of the university students has begun to infiltrate the secondary school level, but this is a less persuasive explanation. Instead, researchers note the increasing level of media violence, access to weapons, development of satanic cults, and other sociological phenomenon are more likely to be found in young people today than in earlier decades.

Although these social patterns may explain part of this demographic trend, another explanation may lie in the number of children growing up in cultures in which violence is a way of life. In the Middle East and in Northern Ireland, for instance, children growing up in violent community struggles could easily become a part of terrorist activities spanning successive generations within the same family. Children were thus recruited, not by philosophy learned at university or secondary school, but by the dogma and lifestyles of their parents, facilitating a potentially more comprehensive assimilation into the terrorist group.

However, by the 1990s, this trend became less clear, as peace within at least one of these regions came closer to reality. Religious fanaticism is still a highly motivating factor compelling young teenagers into roles as suicide bombers; yet, studies of groups like HAMAS and Ansar al-Islam indicate most members are closer in age to the early 1970s terrorist profile. The individuals responsible for the bombing of the Pan Am flight over Lockerbie and those involved in either the 1993 bombing or the dramatically more successful 2001 attacks on the World Trade Center in New York City were certainly not 12 or 13 years of age!

Sex

During the earlier part of the twentieth century, the leaders of terrorist cadres included some women among their numbers, but the rank and file were usually predominantly male. In many such groups, women were assigned the less life-threatening roles of intelligence collection, courier, nurse or medical personnel, and maintenance of "safe houses" for terrorists on the run.

Terrorism of the late twentieth century, however, was an equal opportunity employer. The commander of the JRA for years, Fusako Shigenobu was a woman, and of the 14 most wanted West German terrorists in 1981, 10 were women. Moreover, studies have shown that female members of terrorist groups have proved to be tougher, more fanatical, more loyal, and possessors of a greater capacity for suffering. Women have also, in some terrorist groups, tended to remain members longer than men, on the average.

One example serves to demonstrate the difference in the roles played by women in terrorism today. It was a pregnant woman who was given the task of carrying a suitcase loaded with explosives aboard an airplane in the 1980s. Only a few decades ago, she would have been, at best, allowed to provide a safe haven for the man entrusted with that task. This is *not* to suggest that this is in any way "progress," but it does indicate a difference in the role women now play in terrorism.

Education

Until the mid-1970s, most of the individuals involved in terrorism were quite well educated. Almost two-thirds of the people identified as terrorists were persons with some university training, university graduates, or postgraduate students. Among the Tupamaros, for example, about 75 percent of their membership were very well educated, and of the Baader-Meinhof organization in West Germany, the figure reached almost 80 percent.

In the Palestinian groups, most members were university students or graduates, frequently those who, by virtue of their middle-class wealth, had been able to study at foreign universities. By 1969, several thousand Palestinians were studying abroad at universities, particularly in Europe, where they were exposed to anarchistic-Marxist ideas. This group became an important recruiting pool for the Popular Front for the

Liberation of Palestine (PFLP). Indeed, the chief of the PFLP for decades, George Habash, was a medical doctor who obtained his degree abroad.

But the level of education of the average terrorist is declining today, partly because of the trend in recruitment age of the last two decades of the twentieth century already noted. If young people are being recruited out of secondary school rather than out of college, then the number of individuals in terrorist groups with college educations will necessarily decline as well.

This trend brings with it another important decline: a diminishing of the understanding by the rank and file among terrorists of the political philosophies that have supposedly motivated the groups to adopt terrorist activities. As a rule, elementary school children are clearly unable to grasp the impetus of Marxist philosophy toward social revolution. Unlike the college students of the 1960s who studied and at least half-understood radical political philosophies, today's new terrorist recruits are fed watered-down versions of Marx and Lenin or religious philosophy by leaders whose own understanding of these philosophers is certainly suspect.

This downward trend in education and understanding of political philosophy is exhibited by terrorist leadership figures as well as by the cadres' rank-and-file memberships. The notorious terrorist, Abu Nidal, leader of the group bearing his name, only attended college in Cairo for two years. Contrary to his claim in subsequent years, he never obtained an engineering degree, or indeed any other degree.

Economic Status

During the 1960s, many young people joined terrorist organizations as a way of rejecting the comfortable, middle-class values of their parents. They were often children of parents who could afford to send them to private colleges, and they were rejecting the comparative wealth of their surroundings to fight for justice for those less fortunate.

Today's terrorists tend to be drawn more from the less fortunate than from the comfortable middle-class homes. Although some come from families who have had wealth but lost it through revolution or confiscation, most are from absolute destitution, individuals for whom terrorism represents the only way to lash out at society's injustices. In the terrorist group, these individuals find a collective wealth and ability to improve one's financial situation that is enormously appealing to the impoverished.

Again, Abu Nidal provides insight into the change in the economic circumstances of the type of person who becomes a terrorist today in many parts of the world. Nidal, born Sabri al-Banna, was the son of wealthy Palestinian parents who lost everything. From the lap of luxury, his family moved into the extreme poverty of refugee camps. The bitterness and frustration of this life of endless poverty and statelessness may well have produced the catalyst for the terrorist he was to become.

Osama bin Laden, however, clearly does not fit this trend in economic status. The son of a multimillionaire, inheriting substantial wealth, bin Laden was, in this respect, more like the terrorists of the 1970s, rejecting the life of wealth and perceiving himself as fighting on behalf of those victimized by the very economic system from which his family benefited. This is remarkably similar to the attitude of the founders of the Tupamaros in Uruguay.

Disturbing Patterns

Although the trends in recruitment of individuals into terrorist acts offer insights into the demographics of groups engaged in terrorism today, there are several more disturbing patterns also emerging. Many individuals who engage in terrorist acts share either a lack or a rejection of the desire for a peaceful society. Among many groups, too, is an emerging, and violent, antipathy toward Western cultures. When these two factors combine with religious fanaticism, the potential for escalating terrorism against Western targets by individuals and groups who share a common enemy and even a common religious motivation easily becomes a holy war of immense proportions.

Socialization toward Violence

As noted earlier, intellectuals have, during the past few decades, helped to make the cult of violence respectable. But for today's terrorists there has been a **socialization toward violence** in ways never experienced before in civilized society. Intellectual terrorists of the 1960s were, for the most part, first-generation terrorists. Today we see an increasing number of third- and even fourth-generation terrorists. Young people recruited in such circumstances have been *socialized to accept violence as a normal pattern of life*. Peace, as much of the rest of the world knows it, has no meaning for them, and the related values of a civilized society have equally little relevance in their lives.

In Northern Ireland and parts of the Middle East, until the peace efforts of the 1990s, this pattern of successive generations of terrorism has produced terrorists who have no understanding of the kind of limits on the use of violence regarded by much of the world as fundamental. Violence is not only a normal pattern of life, but also a means of survival. Its successful use offers a means of security and enhancement of one's own and one's family's, life.

This role of violence is made vividly clear by remarks made by the Reverend Benjamin Weir, a former U.S. hostage held by terrorists in Lebanon in the 1980s. He suggested that, for many Lebanese youths, the only employment open to them that offered both an income and some form of security for their families was with one of the warring militia factions. College was for decades either unavailable or unaffordable, and alternative employment in a nation whose economy was in shambles was unlikely. Life as a terrorist was, in some respects, the *only* alternative for many young people in that war-torn country.

Alienation toward Western Systems

Globalization has left at least 20 percent of the world's population completely stranded, alienated, and desperate, without hope of catching a ride on the

accelerating economic train led by the West. Terrorism and violent religious fundamentalism, however complex their causes, grow well in the soil of poverty and
hunger. For people who struggle to feed their families and feel left behind by
economic globalization, the call to radicalism is powerful. More than 800 million
people globally are chronically undernourished, a condition with devastating consequences for their health and for the welfare of their communities. The poverty
and hunger in the developing nations threaten social and political stability, while
providing fertile ground for those who want to blame the Western governments for
these conditions.

Clearly, many who responded to bin Laden's call for holy war against the
United States were among those stranded and alienated by the Western-led pattern of
globalization. Not only did the poverty and hunger breed resentment of those who
appear to enjoy so much of the world's wealth, but the presence of the West, particularly the United States, in the Middle Eastern region provided a focus for the anger.
When the U.S. presence could be described as desecrating the holy sites of Islam,
then the fires of religious zeal could be added to the desperation of poverty and
hunger, creating a lethal combination. Globalization was linked in the minds of many
with the destitute living to which many were reduced and to threats to the culture by
the presence of heretics within the region.

Religious Fanaticism

Like some of the earliest forms of terrorism, drawn from Muslim and Jewish
histories, terrorists in the twenty-first century are increasingly motivated by religious
zealotry, seeking not only to change a political system but also to purify a religious community. Seeing themselves as called upon to engage in a holy war against infidels who
threaten their faith, these modern zealots have begun to have an impact not enjoyed by
their predecessors of earlier times. The **Sicariis,** *dagger-wielding Jewish zealots of ancient Rome who sought to provoke an apocalyptic confrontation between Rome and
the Jewish nation,* and the Assassins, noted in an earlier chapter, who tried to purify the
Muslim community by assassination in order to hasten the arrival of the Imam, the heir
of the Prophet, who would establish a new and just society, had either a negative or at
best a relatively insignificant impact on the growth of their faith community.

Modern religious zealots emerging today have been able to seriously impact
both political systems and the strength of faith communities in their movement
toward holy wars. Extremists carrying out terrorism—by the state, by groups, or by
individual suicide bombers—are making the emergence of a political state of Palestine and the survival of the state of Israel problematic. Religious leaders in several
countries in the Middle East advocate instructing the very young to commit themselves to religious fanaticism, which makes peace in that region unlikely. Religiously
inspired terrorists carried out the attacks of September 11 and impede the rebuilding
of both Afghanistan and Iraq by calls for a holy war to purify and protect a faith community. Clearly, religious motivation for terrorism today has not only increased, but
is also becoming more successful.

CASE STUDY   **Osama bin Laden**

Mastermind of the attacks on the World Trade Center and the Pentagon, as well as the alleged architect of the bombings of the U.S. embassies in Kenya and Tanzania and the attack on the USS *Cole* in Yemen, Osama bin Laden is perhaps the world's best known terrorist. A brief review of his life to date offers interesting insights into the profile of this modern crusader terrorist.

Osama, which means "young lion," in Arabic, was born on March 10, 1957, in Riyadh, Saudi Arabia. His family moved to Medina when he was six months old, later dividing their time between Jeddah and the holy cities of Mecca and Medina. He was the seventeenth son of Mohammed, who had more than 50 sons and daughters by several wives. The construction company that Mohammed founded in 1931 helped to rebuild the al-Aqsa mosque in Jerusalem—the site to which the Prophet was transported in his Night Journey from Mecca—and to renovate the holy places in Mecca and Medina. Mohammed died in a plane crash in 1967, when Osama was 10 years old.

At 17, Osama married a Syrian relative (the first of his four wives) and began his studies at King Abdul-Aziz University in Jeddah soon after this, receiving his degrees in economics and public administration in 1981. At the university, bin Laden became acquainted with both the Muslim Brotherhood, an Islamic group, and the leading teachers in Islamic studies, Abdullah Assam and Muhammad Qutb. Both of these men would influence Osama's life significantly. Azzam would eventually create the first contemporary international jihadist network, and Qutb was the brother of Sayyid Qutb, author of *Signposts,* the key text of the jihadist movement.

Bin Laden absorbed Sayyid's writings with intensity; indeed, they shaped the way he saw the world and his role in it. Sayyid Qutb suggested that the way to establish the Islamic order desired by true Muslims is through an offensive jihad against the enemies of Islam, whether they be non-Islamic societies or Muslim societies that are not following the precepts of the Koran. As one scholar notes, "This is the ideological underpinning of bin Laden's followers, who target not only the West but also such rich Muslim regimes as Saudi Arabia, which they regard as apostates."[10]

In the middle of his studies of these writings, the Muslim world was undergoing a period of substantial change. In 1979, the shah of Iran was overthrown and a Muslim state under the leadership of Ayatollah Khomeini came to Tehran. Egypt and Israel signed a peace agreement in March of that year; in November, hundreds of armed Islamic militants seized the Grand Mosque in Mecca; and the Soviets invaded Afghanistan in late December.

Muslims from around the world were drawn to fight the Soviets in Afghanistan during the 1980s. Rob Schultheis, one of the few journalists who covered this largely ignored war, called it "the holiest of wars," as the Afghans rose up under the banner of Islam to drive the infidels out and to stop the carnage, which ultimately cost more than a million Afghan lives and displaced at least another five million.[11]

Bin Laden, then 22, headed to Pakistan to meet with the Afghan leaders who were calling for support from the Muslim world. He then returned home to Saudi

Arabia to lobby his family and friends for support of the mujahideen. During the next few years, he made several trips to Afghanistan, taking hundreds of tons of construction machinery from his family construction business, which he made available to the mujahideen to build roads, dig tunnels into the mountains for shelter, and build simple hospitals for the wounded.

Having lost his deeply religious father at a very early age, bin Laden was influenced throughout his life by older religious men, often radicals, but always men of strong faith. Each contributed to Osama's vision of the call for a holy war and of the focus of this struggle against the enemies of Islam. He told a Pakistani journalist that his father "was very keen that one of his sons should fight against the enemies of Islam," and he clearly saw himself as fulfilling his father's wishes.[12]

Bin Laden's contribution to the Afghan war was primarily in terms of the fundraising that he did for it and the intensity with which he advocated support for the mujahideen. Like most Afghans who fought in the war, the significance of their interaction lay in the lessons they learned from it, the network that emerged from contact with militants from dozens of countries, and the indoctrination in the most extreme ideas of jihad. All received at least some military training, a little battlefield experience, and went home to continue this jihad on another front.

The war in Afghanistan profoundly affected bin Laden, in what he viewed as a spiritual rather than a political or military context. In an interview with CNN, he stated:

> I have benefited so greatly from the jihad in Afghanistan that it would be impossible for me to gain such a benefit from any other chance . . . . What we benefited from most was [that] the glory and myth of the superpower was destroyed not only in my mind, but also in [the minds] of all Muslims.[13]

Bin Laden's subsequent willingness to call for a jihad against the remaining superpower, the United States, clearly grew from his experiences in the Afghan war. This, from his perspective, was his destiny. The events of September 11, 2001, although not necessarily planned by him, were certainly a fulfillment of his desire for such an attack on what he viewed as enemies of Islam.   ❏

CONCLUSIONS

These trends present an alarming portrait of modern terrorists. Some are younger, much younger than in previous centuries. As any parent (or older sibling) knows, younger children are harder to reach by logical argument. Their values are less clearly formed or understood. They are, as a whole, less rational, more emotional than their elders. They are also less likely to question the orders of their leaders, more likely to follow blindly where their trust is given.

Younger or older, they are less educated, so they are less likely to be following the dictates of their social conscience, or their political philosophy, and more likely to be simply following orders. It is very difficult to reason with someone who is "just following orders." Some of the world's greatest atrocities have been committed by those who were just following orders—who did not even have the excuse of being children.

Individuals committing terrorist acts today are less likely to have a comfortable home to fall back on or to cushion their failure. Instead, their families are increasingly likely to be extremely poor. For these new recruits, membership—and success—in a terrorist group is the only way out of abject poverty. For them, there can be no turning back.

They are used to violence; it is for them a daily occurrence. They neither understand nor recognize the need for limits on that violence. They have seen homes destroyed, families killed, in endless wars of attrition. The idea that civilization wishes to impose limits on the types or victims of violence is beyond their understanding, because they have seen almost every type of violence used against almost every conceivable victim.

Too often, their faith and the teachings of their religious leaders not only justify their actions but call upon them to do more. The agents of socialization—family, community, religion—are now offering increasing support for young people to carry out extreme acts of violence against enemies of their faith community.

These are the new terrorists, and they are a formidable force. Their youth and their patterns of socialization make them unique, even in the long history of terrorism. Whether it is possible for modern civilization to successfully counter this radicalization of the very young toward the violence of terrorism is questionable. What is beyond question is that unless we *can* reverse these trends, civilization will have to cope with an increasing spiral of terror-violence.

EVALUATION

The modern terrorist *is* different. The requisites suggested by O'Ballance are met less frequently, even by terrorist leaders, and the trends in terrorist recruitment suggest an increasing deviation from those norms suggested by that expert.

Taking Osama bin Laden as an example of a modern terrorist leader, try to resolve the following questions:

1. To what extent does bin Laden meet, or fail to meet, the criteria suggested by O'Ballance?
2. To what extent does bin Laden exemplify the trends discussed (toward youthful recruitment, education, etc.)?
3. If bin Laden is a "typical" modern terrorist, what does that suggest about terrorist acts today (more cruel, more indiscriminate)?
4. Are there other leaders who are more typical of modern terrorists?
5. Judging by the trends, from what areas or groups are terrorist recruits more likely to come?
6. Do the individuals who committed the September 11 attacks on the World Trade Center or the Oklahoma City bombing fit the typical pattern offered here?
7. What does this suggest for those who seek to diminish the incidence of terrorism in today's world?

SUGGESTED READINGS

Bergen, Peter L. *Holy War, Inc.: Inside the Secret World of Osama bin Laden.* New York: The Free Press, 2001.

Clarke, Thurston. *By Blood and Fire: The Attack on the King David Hotel.* New York: Putnam, 1981.

Hacker, Frederick J. *Crusaders, Criminals, Crazies: Terror and Terrorism in Our Time.* New York: Norton, 1976.

Hoffman, Bruce. "Defining Terrorism." In *Inside Terrorism.* New York: Columbia University Press, 1998.

Juergensmeyer, Mark. *Terror in the Mind of God: The Global Rise of Religious Violence.* Berkeley, CA: California University Press, 2000.

O'Ballance, Edgar O. *The Language of Violence: The Blood Politics of Terrorism.* San Rafael, CA: Presidio Press, 1979.

Pillar, Paul R., ed. "Dimensions of Terrorism and Counterterrorism." In *Terrorism and U.S. Foreign Policy.* Washington, DC: Brookings Institute Press, 2001.

NOTES

1. Frederick J. Hacker, *Crusaders, Criminals, Crazies: Terror and Terrorism in Our Time* (New York: Norton, 1976), 8–9.

2. Edgar O'Ballance, *The Language of Violence: The Blood Politics of Terrorism* (San Rafael, CA: Presidio Press, 1979), 300–301.

3. Hacker, *Crusaders,* 105.

4. Thurston Clarke, *By Blood and Fire: The Attack on the King David Hotel* (New York: Putnam, 1981), 45.

5. Quoted by Milton Meltzer, *The Terrorists* (New York: Harper & Row, 1983), 111.

6. Walter Lacquer, *The Age of Terrorism* (Boston: Little, Brown, 1987), 92.

7. Ibid., 93.

8. Connon Cruise O'Brien, "Reflecting on Terrorism," *New York Review of Books* (September 16, 1976): 44–48.

9. Charles Russell and Bowman Miller, "Profile of a Terrorist," *Terrorism: An International Journal* 1, no. 1 (1977): 20.

10. Peter L. Bergen, *Holy War, Inc.: Inside the Secret World of Osama bin Laden* (New York: The Free Press, 2001), 48.

11. Rob Schultheis, *Night Letters: Inside Wartime Afghanistan* (New York: Crown, 1992), 155.

12. Bergen, *Holy War,* 52.

13. Bin Laden interview with Peter Bergen and Peter Arnett, May 1997, CNN.

CHAPTER 5

Terrorism by the State

Key Concepts

internal terrorism

external terrorism

intimidation

coerced conversion

genocide

desaparecidos

"dirty wars"

Universal Declaration of Human Rights

state-directed terrorism

state-supported terrorism

"fishing in troubled waters"

arms bazaar

terrorist-supported states

intifada

Terror is an outstanding mode of conflict in localized primitive wars; and unilateral violence has been used to subdue satellite countries, occupied countries or dissident groups within a dictatorship.

Thomas Schelling

Individuals and groups are not the only perpetrators of terrorism. Political leaders have used terrorism as an instrument of both domestic and foreign policy for centuries. From the time when centralized governments were first organized, rulers resorted to the use of terror tactics to subdue their subjects and to spread confusion and chaos among their enemies.

Terrorism remains a formidable weapon in the hands of a ruthless state. It is still used primarily for those two purposes: to subdue a nation's own people or to spread confusion and chaos among its enemies.

Internal terrorism, *practiced by a state against its own people,* has produced some of the most flagrant violations of human rights that the world has ever known. **External terrorism,** *practiced by one state against citizens of another,* is less often cited as a form of state terrorism. Its perpetrators tend, as a rule, to try to conceal their roles as the instigators or supporters of the terrorists.

INTERNAL TERRORISM: THE BEAST
THAT LURKS WITHIN

No matter how chilling the atrocities committed by individuals or groups, these crimes pale into insignificance beside the terror inflicted by a state on its own people. Because governments have a much greater array of power, they are capable of inflicting a much greater degree of terror on their citizenry.

A look at casualty figures gives some perspective on the magnitude of the harm states can inflict on their people, compared to the damage caused by nonstate terrorists. In the decade between 1968 and 1978, about 10,000 people were killed worldwide by terrorist groups. In just *one* of those years, 1976–1977, the military dictatorship in Argentina was responsible for almost that same number of deaths.

Throughout history states have used terrorist acts of violence to subdue groups or individuals. States have from time to time used such violence to create a climate of fear in which citizens will do whatever the government wants.

The history of state terrorism stretches back at least into the legacy of ancient Rome. The Roman emperor Nero ruled by fear. He ordered the deaths of anyone who either opposed him or, in his mind, constituted a threat to his rule, including members of his own family. He was responsible for the slaughter of many of the nobility and for the burning of Rome in A.D. 64. To him, everyone was an enemy, and with his power he made them all victims of his terrorism.[1]

What a state does to its own people was, until very recently, strictly its own business. Neither the rulers nor concerned citizens in other countries usually interfered with what a sovereign government chose to do with its citizens. Even today such interference is largely limited to diplomatic or economic pressures and to the problematic effects of an informed world opinion.

At least three levels of internal state terrorism have been identified as useful gradations in understanding the scope of terrorism practiced by the state. The first is **intimidation,** *in which the government tries to anticipate and discourage opposition and dissent,* frequently through control of the media and prolific use of police force. This form of state terrorism has existed in almost every nation-state at some point in its history, most often during times of war. Chile, Argentina, South Africa, and Uganda offered, at several points in the twentieth century, excellent examples of this type of internal state terrorism. **Coerced conversion,** *involving government efforts to create a complete change in a national lifestyle,* is not unusual in the aftermath of a revolution, as the Soviet Union experienced in the early twentieth century, and Iran in the 1980s.

Nations in the twentieth century have also practiced the third level of internal state terrorism, **genocide,** *the deliberate effort to exterminate an entire class, ethnic group, or religious group of people,* for ideological reasons, while the rest of the civilized world watched in horror, disbelief, or studied indifference.[2] Nor was this destruction of innocent persons confined to Nazi Germany or Stalin's Soviet Union. Certain tribes in African nations were all but obliterated by rival tribal leaders who grasped the reins of government. Rwanda, in the mid-1990s, experienced at least one wave of this form of terror. In the early 1990s, Bosnia was the scene of mass slaughter

Intimidation	*Coerced Conversion*		*Genocide*
State-tolerated	**Covert state-supported**	**Overt state-supported**	**Genocide**
◄————————			————————►
Ku Klux Klan	*"hit squads"*	*"dirty war"*	*Holocaust*

FIGURE 5.1

of people of one ethnic group by leaders of another. In Argentina, thousands of persons "disappeared" during an oppressive regime.

State internal terrorism can be placed on a spectrum to facilitate understanding, because state internal terror takes a variety of forms to varying degrees of state participation. Using the gradations of terrorism—intimidation, coerced conversion, and genocide—it becomes clear that state terror can range from forms of intimidation that the state simply allows to occur to that for which the state is fully responsible. Placing state-tolerated terrorism at one end of the spectrum, moving on to covert state terror, then to overt state terror, culminating in genocide organized by the state, offers a useful tool in visualizing the range of internal state terrorism. (See Figure 5.1.)

Let us look at some of these examples of state terrorism a little more in depth to better gauge a comparison between their destructiveness and the destructiveness of terrorist groups. State terrorism during the twentieth century was not confined to one nation or to one continent. Although history is sprinkled with examples of gross state terrorism, such as that practiced by Nero or by the Jacobins in the French Revolution, many modern nations must share the "honors" as terrorist states today.

One of the nations that comes readily to most people's minds when one refers to a modern terrorist state is Nazi Germany (1933–1945). Hitler moved swiftly after he rose to power to create an authoritarian regime. He suspended all civil rights, eliminated the non-Nazi press, and banned all demonstrations. The Gestapo, his secret police, was given the power to arrest and even to execute any "suspicious person."

In the beginning thousands of people were imprisoned, beaten, or tortured to death. But this did not end Hitler's terrorism of the remaining population. Instead, borrowing the idea of concentration camps from Russia, he created such camps in Germany and in occupied nations, and he gave the Gestapo the power to send anyone it wanted to the camps, without trial or hope of appeal.

These camps became the instruments for Hitler's "final solution" for ridding himself of all his "enemies." It is estimated that during his 12-year rule of terror, between 10 and 12 million people died. Some were gassed, others hung; some faced firing squads; countless others died by other equally violent and vicious means. In 12 years, one state murdered between 10 and 12 *million* innocent people and was responsible, through the war it initiated, for the deaths of countless more. It is a record of terror almost unparalleled in modern history, even by the most vicious terrorist.

But it is only *almost* unparalleled: the Soviet Union under Stalin was responsible for millions of deaths as well. Only estimates have been given for the number of people who fell victim to Stalin's totalitarian society. By the time of Stalin's death in

1953, scholars have estimated that between 40 and 50 million people were sent to Soviet jails or slave labor camps. Of these, between 15 and 25 million died there—by execution, hunger, or disease.

In some ways it is difficult for the world to grasp the magnitude of the terror inflicted by such regimes because the numbers are so large and the masses of individuals relatively faceless. We are able to identify with Alexander Solzhenitsyn in his description of the terrors of the psychiatric-ward prison in his book *The Gulag Archipelago,* but we find it difficult to identify with the 25 million who died, unheralded, in the labor camps.

Dictators, as a whole, have found it easier to commit terrorism without world censure than have individuals, because state terrorism is committed, generally, in secret. The shadowy world of state terrorism is thus less susceptible to the pressures of world opinion than the activities of terrorist groups, who actively seek this spotlight of global attention.

Cambodia, under the rule of the Khmer Rouge, illustrates this point. During its rule of less than four years, the state's systematic terrorism was responsible for over 1 million deaths. When one notes that there were only about 7 million people in that land, the magnitude of the terror becomes evident. This regime committed genocide against its own people.

Africa has had its share of state terrorism. Colonial powers used terrorism, often in the form of summary imprisonment and execution, to suppress national liberation movements. But this was not the only form that terrorism has taken in Africa. Uganda, under Idi Amin, was clearly a terrorist state. Between 1971 and 1979, over 100,000 Ugandans lost their lives to his terrorist state.

Latin America, too, continues to have regimes that practice terror on their people. At least five nations on this continent—Argentina, Bolivia, Chile, Paraguay, and Uruguay—have suffered under cruel and repressive regimes. In Uruguay, the terrorism instigated by the leftist Tupac Amaru was repaid 100-fold by the repressive military regime that came to power in the wake of the collapse of what was, at the time, South America's only democracy.

Argentina suffered under the yoke of a brutally repressive military regime, which finally ended in 1983. Leftist terrorism in that nation provoked a right-wing military-backed response so savage that it staggered the imagination. For a time the press reported the appearance of bodies in ditches and mutilated corpses on garbage heaps and in burned-out vehicles. People "disappeared" by the thousands, abducted by armed men claiming to be members of "security forces." Although the "disappearances" became less frequent as the nation moved toward democracy, the legacy of brutality continues to burden the government in its quest for legitimacy and acceptance.

CASE STUDY   Argentina's Military Dictatorship

Argentina offers an excellent, chilling example of the potential for state terrorism in all three gradations to be carried out, unchecked, for more than a decade. It clearly meets the criteria for internal terrorism by a state and indicates the desire of a state to "clean up" its own problems and to punish, if necessary within rather than submit to international adjudication.

Although Argentina's 1853 constitution placed strong emphasis on protecting individuals from abuse by authority, repressive military rule made this a difficult tradition to maintain. In 1930, the military deposed President Hipolito Yrigoyen, beginning a trend of regimes. After five military coups and 30 out of 46 years spent under military rule, the 1976 military coup that overthrew President Isabel Perón was hardly remarkable in itself, but the "dirty war" carried out during the next seven years remains a dark period of state terrorism tarnishing Argentina's history.

General Juan Domingo Perón became president of Argentina twice, in 1946–1955 and again briefly from 1973 to 1974. Perón's advocacy of social justice and a "third way" between capitalism and socialism generated animosity among both the military and the Catholic bishops, leading to his ouster and flight into exile in 1955. In exile, he remained a powerful political figure and "Perónism" continued to make the country difficult to govern for a succession of anti-Peronist military regimes. The Perónist movement splintered into several factions, several of which were violent and carried out terrorist activities.

To combat the activities of the opposition groups, the Argentine government resorted to the use of death squads as a form of counterterrorism. The Argentine Anti-Communist Alliance (AAA or Triple A) was the most notorious of the death squads during this time. The Triple A was established under the government of Isabel Perón, who became president upon the death of her husband, Juan, in 1974. Her social security minister, Jose Lopez Rega, created the Triple A, and his close relationship with Isabel Perón gave him the freedom to carry out operations under the Social Welfare Ministry. About 200 of the security forces were recruited to carry out special tasks, including terrorism against opposition political groups and any individuals thought to have leftist ideas or contacts. These individuals included journalists, actors, singers, socialists, academicians, and many university professors. During what came to be called Black September in 1975, these individuals were given 72 hours to leave the country, following a warning by Triple A.

In 1976, a new military junta, comprised of three commanders of the military (army, navy, and air force), took control of the government. General Jorge Rafael Videla was the leader of the coup and president of Argentina from 1976 to 1981. Under his direction, the government issued a Process of National Reorganization (PRN), which sought to eliminate all opposition. Together with General Robert Viola, who succeeded him as president in 1981, Videla developed a myth of necessary counterterrorism and security, which later became known throughout the world as a "dirty war." Exaggerating the violence of the Perónist left, Videla called for increases in counterterrorism in the form of secret police, death squads, and censorship of the media and the universities. Although the Montoneros, a group whose members were drawn from the Perónist left, had engaged in acts of violence and terrorism, they were all but extinct by the time Videla came to office. Yet this group became the focus of the Videla government's counterterrorism and the basis for his claim that a civil war was occurring that required strong government action in the subsequent "dirty war."

Although it is impossible to be certain of the exact number of deaths generated in this state terrorism, which included extrajudicial killings, abductions, and torture executed by the military regime from 1976 to 1983, at least 30,000 people were killed and another 9,000 "disappeared" during that time. The ***desaparecidos,*** or "*disappeared ones*" include those who, after being kidnapped by secret police or military units, were never traced. Secret police and military units maintained secret lists of names of those targeted for abduction, torture, and murder. Clandestine places of detention were known as "holes," and many of those taken to these secret camps were tortured for information. Most were eventually killed, and their bodies disposed of secretly.

Victims of this period of state terrorism included trade unionists, artists, teachers, human rights activists, politicians, Jews, and all of their respective relatives. Virtually no one was safe, and the intense mood of fear generated by this state terrorism lingered long after the war ended. One well-documented example of this state terrorism was known as the Night of the Pencils. High school students decided to protest for lower bus fares, specifically a half-rate fare, already in existence for younger children. The government labeled these protests "subversion in the schools" and ordered the death of those who participated. More than 20 students were kidnapped from two schools.

Only 3 of the 15 children seized in La Plata survived. One of them was 16-year-old Pablo Dias, who described how their captives blindfolded them, put them in front of a mock firing squad, and asked questions. His captors stripped him, tied him down, and began to burn his lips. They subjected him to electric torture in his mouth and on his genitals. They pulled out one of his toenails with tweezers, an action that became almost a signature of the army torture. He was beaten with clubs and fists, and kicked repeatedly. He related that his friend Claudia, who was also kidnapped, had been raped at the detention camp. The ordeal lasted from September to December of 1976.

Scholar Martin Andersen in his book, *Dossier Secreto: Argentina's Desaparecidos and the Myth of the "Dirty War,"* noted that in the **dirty wars,** *the Argentine military practiced a forged disappearance of people that was modeled on the tactics of Hitler's might-and-fog decrees, a systematic, massive, and clandestine operation.* The government built 340 secret camps in which the victims were housed and prepared mass graves for their burial. Prisoners in these camps, like those in Nazi concentration camps, were lined up or made to kneel in front of large, previously dug graves, blindfolded, and gagged. Although some were put in the grave alive, they were then doused with oil and burned with tires to cover the smell. Indeed, disposal of bodies became an exercise in creativity, and many were dumped in rivers or even in the South Atlantic from airplanes or ships. According to Andersen, detainees were usually tortured to the maximum extent before being killed. Torture methods used by the military were intended to produce pain, a breakdown of resistance, fear and humiliation, a strong sense of imminent death, and weakness. Anyone who escaped or survived these camps were changed forever by the terrorism endured.[3]

Nine of the top officials responsible for these acts of violence and mass terror were brought eventually to trial under the rule of President Alfonsin. Two of them,

Videla and Viola, were sentenced to life imprisonment, with the others also receiving substantial prison terms. In 1990, however, President Carlos Menem issued pardons to every official involved in the dirty war, intending to help Argentina "move forward." None were ever indicted in an international forum for crimes against humanity. ❑

THE CONTINUING REALITY OF STATE TERROR

In 1972, a young woman named Ayse Semra Eker was abducted off the street by Turkish military police. For the next 10 days she was tortured. She was tied spread-eagle to pegs on the floor and beaten repeatedly, on her naked thighs, on her palms, and on the soles of her feet. She was beaten so hard and so often her feet turned black, and she was unable to walk. Electric wires were attached to her fingertips and toes, and she was shocked, again and again. Then the wires were moved to her ear lobes, and the current was turned up until her teeth broke and her mouth spewed blood. Electric probes were inserted in her anus and vagina, and she passed out from the pain. She awakened to find her fingernails had been burned with hot cigarettes.[4]

Dozens of nations today use terrorism as (unofficial) government policy to secure and ensure control over their citizens. Amnesty International reports that foreign "experts" in torture have been sent from country to country. Schools of torture teach and demonstrate methods to government officials, particularly electroshock techniques, because that is the easiest and most commonly used form of scientific torture.

Modern torture equipment is exported regularly. Some of the shock machines used by governments to torture their citizens are made in the United States.[5]

Torture falls within the form of state terrorism called "covert state terror," because few states openly admit to practicing this lethal abuse of citizens. In using the power of the state, its laws and courts, to stifle dissent and compel the people through fear into compliance, the ability of a state to intimidate or to force a change in its people is almost unchecked. Unfortunately, the use of murder, slavery, and terror to subjugate and intimidate people taints the history of almost every modern nation.

Even the United States has experienced such abuses of power by persons in authority. The U.S. history of violence in the labor movement provides several examples of government abuse of power. The events in Ludlow, Colorado, offer a poignant vignette of state terrorism. On Easter night in 1914, members of the Colorado National Guard, aided by the company police of Colorado Fuel and Iron Company (owned by John D. Rockefeller, Sr.), poured oil on the tent city of miners, and set them ablaze. The miners, who had been on strike and evicted from their homes in the company town, had dug a cave under the largest tent and placed the children there for safety. Even so, 11 children and one pregnant mother burned to death, while five men and one boy were shot to death as they tried to run to safety.

Similar blots on U.S. history also exist in the treatment of Blacks. Slavery was enforced by government law and police power for decades. Even with its official end, through the Thirteenth Amendment to the Constitution, unofficial persecution of Blacks continued unchecked. The Ku Klux Klan and similar groups murdered, lynched, beat, and raped, in a concerted effort to terrorize the freedmen after the Civil War and Reconstruction. Although such groups were not in any sense arms of the state, they were allowed until the 1960s to carry out their terror campaigns relatively unhampered by a sympathetic or uncaring government.

The state uses many weapons to conduct terrorism, including arrest (usually in the dead of night to maximize the psychological impact), summary deportation of dissidents or subversives, incarceration without trial for indefinite lengths of time, and of course, torture. It is torture that is the ultimate weapon of state terrorism.

Amnesty International's *Report on Terrorism* provides horrifying details of state torture and terror, including the following description of torture in Chile:

> Many people were tortured to death by means of endless whipping as well as beating with fists, feet and rifle butts. Prisoners were beaten on all parts of the body, including the head and sexual organs. . . . There were many cases of burning (with acid or cigarettes), of electricity, of psychological threats including simulated executions and threats the families of the prisoners would be tortured. At times the brutalities reached animalistic levels.[6]

The report goes on to tell of rape, sexual depravities, abortions forced by rifle butts, force feeding of excrement, immersion in ice-cold water or tanks of petrol, and countless other atrocities too horrible to recount. They sicken the reader—but they are true, and they are happening now. Such bestiality did not stop with the death of Hitler or Stalin. There still exist many governments today with so little regard for human life and dignity that they are willing to perpetrate such acts of terror on their citizens.

If, as Hannah Arendt suggests, "lawlessness is the essence of tyranny, then terror is the essence of totalitarian domination." In her essay "On Violence," this same expert notes that "terror is not the same as violence; it is, rather, the form of government that comes into being when violence, having destroyed all power, does not abdicate but, on the contrary, remains in full control." State terrorism, thus described, is the quintessential form of terrorism.[7]

INTERNATIONAL EFFORTS TO RESTRICT INTERNAL STATE TERRORISM

In the wake of discovering just how ruthless some rulers could be in dealing with their subjects, leaders of victorious nations after World War II tried to create international laws that would restrict the ability of governments to use terrorism against their citizens. Attempts to create such laws by consensus were only marginally successful.

On December 10, 1948, the General Assembly of the United Nations adopted the **Universal Declaration of Human Rights** without dissent, calling on all member countries to publicize the text of the declaration, and to "cause it to be disseminated, displayed, read and expounded principally in schools and other educational institutions, without distinction based on the political status of countries or territories."[8]

This document states that *"everyone has the right to life, liberty, and security of person," and that these rights may not be taken away by any institution, state, or individual.* According to this declaration, it is not acceptable for states to administer collective punishment or to punish any person for a crime that he or she did not personally commit. The declaration, too, emphasizes the necessity of fair trials and equal justice before the law. Since terrorism by a state often involves the summary punishment of individuals not for any specific crime but because their deaths or incarceration will result in a climate of fear among other citizens, this declaration would appear significant in the effort to curb state terrorism. However, it has no binding effect in international law. It is, in some respects, only a statement of concern among some states about the presence of state terrorism.

If this declaration is only a statement of principles lacking mechanisms for enforcement, the subsequent Covenant on Civil and Political Rights has tried to remedy that flaw.[9] Although this covenant has more explicit provisions for enforcing compliance, it has a much worse record for ratification. Less than one-third of the nations in existence today are a party to this treaty, which is designed in part to protect individuals from state terrorism. The United States, for instance, refused to ratify this covenant, just as it also refused for over 40 years to become a party to the convention outlawing genocide.

The problem, both in terms of ratification and enforcement, is largely a political one. States do not openly interfere in the domestic affairs of other states, because such interference would leave them open to similar intrusions. Conventions such as those protecting human rights are often viewed as dangerous, even by states with relatively clean records in terms of state terrorism, in that these conventions open avenues for hostile governments to interfere with the internal affairs of the nation.

Kren and Rappoport argue that

> within certain limits set by political and military power considerations, the modern state may do anything it wishes to those under its control. There is no moral ethical limit which the state cannot transcend if it wished to do so, because there is no moral-ethical power higher than the state. Moreover, it seems apparent that no modern state will ever seriously interfere with the internal activities of another solely for moral-ethical reasons.[10]

Most interference in the internal affairs of a sovereign state is based on national security rather than on ethical or moral grounds. Although the Nuremberg trials offered some evidence that the principle of nonintervention was being challenged by nations motivated by moral-ethical concerns, since that time few nations have indicated that crimes against humanity undertaken within a nation's own borders are a basis for international intervention. Even evidence of "ethnic cleansing" in Bosnia during the early 1990s, although generating the formation of an international criminal tribunal, did not produce on the part of nations a willingness to send indicted criminals to succumb to the justice process at The Hague. Justice remains largely within the purview defined by the rulers of the individual nation-states.

At least one action taken by a state in 2001, however, encourages hope that states will begin to effectively bring pressure on each other to comply with punishments for crimes against humanity. The carefully orchestrated arrest and extradition of Slobodan Milosevic, former leader of Yugoslavia, by his successor as president of that state, to the War Crimes Tribunal meeting in The Hague suggests that economic promises and pressures by the international community led the emerging leadership to submit former leaders to trial by the international community for crimes that they allegedly committed while in office. This abrogation of the concept of immunity from prosecution in international courts of state leaders for actions, however outrageous and illegal, committed while in office suggests that the international norms for human rights are beginning to take a stronger legal hold in the international community than mere treaty ratification might imply.

International cooperation on efforts to contain state terrorism remains sketchy at best, though. Efforts to create an international criminal court, the focus of conference in Italy in the summer of 1998, highlight the problem. Although agreement has slowly evolved on the need for such a court, its structure and mandate remain sources of contention. Moreover, the conference stated early in its meetings that the issue of terrorism, by individuals or states, would not be codified for such a court, because this issue was too political, presenting too many points of controversy for successful resolution.

The linkage between revolution and violence has already been discussed. A similar relationship exists with respect to the right of a state to protect itself from revolutionary violence. Most modern states experienced a period of revolutionary violence. During and after such periods, however, the right of a state to protect itself remains restricted by even more rules than those that apply to its revolutionary enemies. In addition to abiding by the laws of warfare, states are entrusted with the responsibility for preserving and protecting human rights and freedoms.

Thus, a state has an abiding obligation to restrain its use of violence against its citizens. Both at war and at peace, a state is supposed to recognize a legal commitment toward the preservation of the rights of the individual. If it is true that insurgent terrorists frequently try to provoke government repression in the hope of generating greater sympathy and support for the terrorists' cause, then it is obviously extremely important that governments *not* respond in kind.

This does not mean that governments are, or should be held to be, impotent in the face of flagrant attacks on law and order. Certainly a state is responsible for protecting its citizens from violence. But the means used to ensure law and order must be carefully balanced against the responsibility of the government to ensure the maximum protection of civil rights and liberties. Too great a willingness to sacrifice the latter in order to preserve stability within a state would not only be giving the terrorists the impetus for their cause, but would also be placing the state in the invidious position of breaking international law in order to stop someone else from breaking it.

A state that violates international law by committing acts of genocide, by violently suppressing fundamental freedoms, or by breaking the laws of war or the Geneva Convention on the treatment of prisoners of war and civilians, can be considered guilty of state terrorism.[11] If terrorism is defined to include acts of political violence perpetrated without regard to the safety of innocent persons in an effort to evoke a mood of fear and confusion in a target audience, then surely states have been as least as guilty of such acts as have individuals and groups.

Indeed, it is useful to remember that the word *terror* derives from the actions of a government—the Jacobin government of revolutionary France. In fact, terrorist regimes have been far more deadly than group or individual actors in this century, even after the end of World War II.[12] The word *totalitarian* has become part of the political lexicon of this century as a result of state terrorism in Nazi Germany and Stalinist Russia. Both systems relied upon organized, systematized discriminate terror to create bondage of the mind as well as of the body.[13]

State terrorism is frequently a nasty combination of personality and ideology. "Nazism and Stalinism were personifications of the evil genius of their leaders, but they could not have succeeded without a disoriented, terrorized citizenry," according to one expert.[14]

Totalitarianism and state terrorism aim not only at the transmutation of society, but also at the fundamental change in human nature itself. The basic goal of terrorist states is mass disorientation and inescapable anxiety. Modern governments whose actions have earned for themselves the soubriquet "terrorist," such as Indonesia in the 1960s or Chile in the 1970s, have employed terror-violence as an integral part of the governing process.[15]

Governments, then, have been, and continue to be as likely to commit terrorist acts as individuals and groups. Moreover, it is probably true that "as violence breeds violence, so terrorism begets counter-terrorism, which in turn leads to more terrorism in an ever-increasing spiral."[16] So state domestic terrorism not only transgresses international law, but it often creates the political, economic, and social milieu that precipitates acts of individual and group terrorism. It is thus a causal factor in the perpetration of further terrorism.

TERRORISM AS AN INSTRUMENT OF FOREIGN POLICY: WAGING WAR BY PROXY

Coercive measures within the state are only one form of state terrorism. At least two other forms of state terrorism have become prevalent in recent years. Terrorism has been used by national leaders as an instrument of foreign policy, particularly in the waging of irregular warfare. This has usually taken the form of covert terrorism, because the acts are generally expected to be committed without the state being openly involved.

This state form of terrorist behavior usually falls into one of two categories: state-directed terrorism and state-supported terrorism. In **state-directed terrorism,** *there is more involvement by the state, sometimes as direct as decision making and control of the group's activities.* In **state-supported terrorism,** *the state usually aids or abets existing terrorist groups that have varying degrees of independence.*[17] In both types of state terror, the state uses groups engaged in terrorist acts to enhance state goals in other countries. Unlike the internal coercive diplomacy (which may be obvious to all observers, whether or not they are willing to label it as such), clandestine operations are, by their very nature, conducted in secrecy. Consequently they are often difficult to document. Thus, there is often little verifiable data that can be used to study this phenomenon. This makes the use of terrorism an attractive, but potentially dangerous, weapon for states seeking to carry out hostile acts without initiating a war.

Because it is often almost impossible to distinguish, in the absence of clear lines of connection, whether a state is engaging in state-directed or state-supported terrorism, the use of external terrorism by states continues to be an attractive foreign policy option. State-directed and state-supported terrorism are primarily used to produce fear and chaos within potentially unfriendly or hostile states. It is used, for example, to weaken the resistance or diminish the intransigence of states, as the cost of such antagonism is made plain. Such activities are also designed to demonstrate the weaknesses and vulnerabilities of opponents, in an effort to make such adversaries more willing to bargain.

Such activities have been described as attempts to "destabilize" unfriendly regimes. Central Intelligence Agency (CIA) efforts in Chile in the early 1970s took this form. This organization was not only involved in clandestine efforts—including the assassination of Rene Schneider, the commander-in-chief of the Chilean Army who refused to approve plans to remove Salvador Allende from office—but it was also involved in numerous other efforts to remove Allende. Records indicate that at least $7 million were authorized by the United States for CIA use in destabilizing Chilean society, including the financing of opposition groups and right-wing terrorist paramilitary groups.

Similar clandestine efforts in Nicaragua provoked a great deal of undesirable attention (from the U.S. government's point of view). Efforts to destabilize the Sandinista regime supposedly came to an official halt in 1982, when the U.S. House of Representatives voted to halt covert activities abroad by the CIA for the purpose of overthrowing the government of Nicaragua.[18] But, as the Iran-*contra* affair indicated, efforts to conduct clandestine terrorist operations did not cease with the passage of that law. Instead, such activities became one step *more* covert.

Claire Sterling conducted serious research into the networks of support and sponsorship that terrorist organizations enjoy. According to Sterling, nations such as the former Soviet Union were heavily involved in sponsoring terrorism:

> Direct control of the terrorist groups was never the Soviet intention. All were indigenous to their countries. All began as offshoots of relatively non-violent movements that expressed particular political, economic, religious or ethnic grievances.[19]

States have chosen to support terrorism abroad directly, or more often, indirectly. Let us consider at least one compelling reason for indirectly supporting terrorism. It may be that such support offers a low-risk avenue for redressing an international grievance. Some Arab states chose to sponsor Palestinian groups engaged in terrorist acts as a less risky method of redressing the Palestinian problem—less risky than provoking another open and costly war with Israel.

Certainly Iran, under the direction of religious leaders, engaged in this practice throughout the Middle East. Some nations within the former communist bloc also offered support to terrorist groups in the form of equipment and training camps, purportedly as a way of exporting the communist revolution or perhaps as a means for weakening an adversary state (a reason often cited to explain support for terrorist activities against Israel). Libya has used terrorism as an instrument to help the state track down and eradicate exiled dissidents (or intimidate them into silence), offering sanctuary and assistance to the Abu Nidal Organization and a variety of other Palestinian resistance groups.

Again we can turn to Sterling's assessment of the former Soviet Union's reasons for becoming involved in state-supported terrorism. She suggests that [t]he heart of the Russian's strategy is to provide the network with the goods and services necessary to undermine the industrialized democracies of the West.[20]

Even in the light of information unearthed by Sterling and other journalists who sought to uncover the support network by which terrorist organizations operate, a significant lack of verifiable data exists to link states thought to have logical policy reasons for supporting such groups with actual instances of substantive support. Although few would dispute the evidence of relatively low-level sponsorship (providing safe houses, travel documents, and similar assistance), there is a lack of hard evidence as to any "control" exercised by the Soviets or other states or participation by those states in any hostile events.

Most researchers recognize that the Soviets had an interest in actions that would spread fear and chaos in the Western world, but many are unprepared to go further than that assessment. What is often referred to as **"fishing in troubled waters"**—that is, *assistance to those already engaged in opposition to states that are one's enemies*—is not an unusual policy, nor is it necessarily illicit. Does such "fishing" make the state giving the assistance culpable for the offenses committed by those receiving the assistance?

Sterling suggests that "the Soviet Union had simply laid a loaded gun on the table, leaving others to get on with it."[21] By inference, the issue of whether a state directs or merely benefits from terrorist actions carried out with that "loaded gun," is less significant, while the linkage to the state and its state policy is fairly clear. Activities carried out by groups provided with those "loaded guns" are nonetheless incidents of state-supported terrorism.

In fact, governments may engage in terrorism for a variety of reasons, which become blurred even in their own minds and are often indistinguishable in the eyes of horrified observers. One cause may be the principal motivator for a particular act, but it may have numerous desirable side effects, which become in time prime motivators, too. A state may decide, for example, to assist an organization carrying out terrorist acts or field an organization of its own, to try to redress a particular international grievance. In the course of events, the state may discover that the terrorism has helped to weaken an adversary state against which it would not ordinarily have had the strength to wage a regular war. After a time, it becomes difficult for the state to decide which is the most important reason for its decision to engage in terrorism by proxy.

In the legions of states offering support to terrorist groups or nations, there are no villains in black hats. Usually the state is at pains to conceal the linkage or to rationalize its necessity. Even more often, the links are hidden through many channels and transfers of equipment and assistance.

RELUCTANT BEDFELLOWS: THE ARMS BAZAAR

Let us briefly examine the booming sale of arms to individuals, groups, and nations engaging in terrorist acts who make no secret (until after the September 11 attack) of their propagation of terrorism. Even among the Western allies, who on paper oppose these regimes and groups, there remained, until the close of 2001, strong support channels. Through these channels, with the knowledge and support of the state, many companies circumvent national law in selling arms to hostile or warring nations or groups.

France sold to Libya dozens of Exocet antiship missiles, which were subsequently used by Muammar al Qadhafi on the U.S. Sixth Fleet. Germans traveled to Iran to work out details on a contract for the sale of four diesel submarines, which would presumably be added to the armada with which Iran has threatened the shipping lanes in the Persian Gulf. Austria officially condemned Iraq's use of gas in the Iran-Iraq war and offered the use of its hospitals for the treatment of Iraqi victims of gas attacks. Yet Austria exported the chemicals used to make the poisonous gas—to Iraq! From the former West Germany, via Greek shipping offices, Iran obtained optics and range-finding equipment, as well as the G-3 assault rifle, its standard infantry weapon.

Nor is it only Iran and Iraq who have benefited from industrial nations' desires to cash in on the arms market. Libya, which made little secret during the last three decades of the twentieth century of its support for and commitment to groups and individuals engaging in terrorism against the West, has been the recipient of considerable European assistance, only a part of which took the form of arms sales. The former West Germany, for instance, opposed sanctions against states supporting terrorism each time such sanctions were proposed. It may be fair to assume that part of that opposition stemmed from the fact that West Germany bought 191,000 barrels of oil from Libya in 1985.

Italy, too, has had a strong trade relationship with Libya, averaging approximately $5 billion per year during the 1980s, when Libya owned 15 percent of Fiat Corporation. In May 1986, the former chief of the Italian intelligence service admitted that his service had helped Qadhafi get arms and assisted him on intelligence matters. Italy also sold a wide variety of arms to Libya, including Augusta antitank helicopters, Assad-class missile corvettes, self-propelled howitzers, Otomat missiles, and acoustic mines and torpedoes. Many of these weapons have subsequently found their way into the hands of terrorists.

Athens, Greece, known as the cradle of democracy, has for years been the middleman through which transactions from the West are channeled to various protagonists in the Middle East and North Africa. Members of the Islamic Jihad, the Abu Nidal Organization, and Abbu Abbas have operated freely through Greek borders.

Cooperation between governments in the sales of arms has certainly resulted in some strange bedfellows. None is perhaps stranger that the relationship between Israel and Iran in the 1980s. Israel was one of Iran's biggest suppliers of armaments. In 1984, for example, Israel sold 20 F-4 jet engines to Iran, routing the transaction through Greece to Tehran. In January 1985, Israel offered to sell (via telexes to brokers, including those in Iran) 150 U.S. Sidewinder air-to-air missiles.

Some defenders of such sales argue that the nations or groups would purchase such arms anyway, so why should Western nations not make the profit to be made in these "inevitable" transactions? Such an argument is, of course, merely a rationalization of an economic reality that contravenes political policy.

The economic ties forged by such transactions make it difficult for nations to take firm stands against terrorism or terrorist groups sponsored by the recipient nations. The stronger the economic linkage, the weaker is a government's response to restrict terrorism. The uneasy relationship between these buyers and sellers of arms clouds the issue of each nation's policy on terrorism. The seller nations, the purveyors of arms, find themselves in the dubious position of appearing to sponsor terrorism, indirectly, which is an allegation they cannot completely dismiss.

WEAPONS OF MASS DESTRUCTION ON THE ARMS BAZAAR

As the **arms bazaar** expands today to include weapons of mass destruction, the stakes for the peace and security of the international community escalates dramatically. A quick look at several suppliers of weapons of mass destruction (WMDs) makes clear the potential dangers:

> *Russia.* Because Russia's defense, biotechnology, chemical, aerospace, and nuclear industries are eager to raise much-needed funds, there is a large potential for the export and transfer of weapons, as well as training in the use of these weapons. During the first half of 2002, Russian entities were a key source of dual-use biotechnology, chemicals, production technology, and equipment for other states seeking to develop WMD capabilities, such as Iran.
>
> *North Korea.* Through the first half of 2002, North Korea continued exporting significant ballistic missile related equipment and technical expertise. It is a critical source of hard currency for this cash-strapped system.
>
> *China.* China has, since the mid-1990s, provided material support for Iran's chemical weapons program. Since Iran continues to arm many groups engaged in terrorism and is not a party to the Chemical-Biological Warfare agreement, the probability of Chinese chemical weapons supplies reaching the hands of terrorists is high.[22]

SILENT PARTNERS: WAGING SUBTLE WAR

Syria

Syrian president Hafez al-Assad long sought to become the dominant power broker in the Middle East, and until the fall of 1986, he came close to achieving that objective. Until that time Assad contrived to mask his support for terrorists beneath a cloak of state secrecy. By distancing himself from the terrorists, he managed to preserve deniability; and when it seemed strategically expedient, he renewed his credit with the West by intervening on behalf of Western hostages.

Assad's secure power base at home and close ties with Moscow made diplomats hesitant to openly criticize him. In the absence of evidence to the contrary, some observers have even assumed that he was a "helpful partner" in Mideast negotiations concerning Lebanon.

Evidence of his duplicity eventually came to light, after the demise of the Soviet Union. As *U.S. News & World Report* noted, "even in the diplomatic world of studied indirection and strategic dissembling, the evidence has become impossible to ignore, and it points straight at Syrian strong man Hafez Assad."[23] Former secretary of state George Schultz noted that the case of Nezar Hindawi's unsuccessful attempt to blow up an El Al jetliner in London provided "clear evidence" of Syrian involvement in terrorism. Ariel Merari, director of Tel Aviv University Project on Terrorism, suggested that "there is no doubt that the general policy of sponsoring terrorist activity in Western Europe is done with Assad's approval and probably his initiative."[24] The same report contained one expert's comments that

> For years, Libya's Muammar Qadhafi has been the international outlaw, condemned for his wide-ranging support of terrorism. But now it is clear that Qadhafi is an erratic bumbler compared with Assad, a hard-eyed strategist who uses terror as an essential tool of statecraft.[25]

Assad's preferred tool of persuasion was terror, according to some Middle East experts. During the early 1980s, he began exporting his deadly product, by increasingly indirect means. The CIA made public evidence that the Syrian intelligence services gave logistical support to the individuals who bombed the U.S. Marine barracks in Lebanon. After the attack, the National Security Agency also intercepted messages showing payments were sent through Damascus to the Iranian-sponsored terrorist group responsible for the bombing.

Nor was this the only evidence of Assad's involvement in terrorism. *U.S. News & World Report* published what it termed a "bill of particulars" concerning Syria's links to terrorist events in the early 1980s. Since these events were also noted in the U.S. State Department's annual report on global terrorism, there is little reason to doubt the link to terrorism that the "bill" implies belongs to Syria. The following are a few of the incidents detailed during that period:

> *September 8–16, 1986, Paris.* Bombings kill 10 persons, and injure more than 160. An obscure Mideast group, thought to be a cover for the Syria-linked Lebanese Armed

Revolutionary Faction, claimed responsibility. The series of bombings were carried out by brothers of jailed terrorist Georges Ibrahim Abdallah, held in a French prison.

September 6, 1986, Istanbul. Arab terrorists fired on Jewish worshipers at a synagogue, killing 22 and wounding 3. Experts claim the Syrian-backed Abu Nidal group was responsible. (Abu Nidal himself, architect of the Rome and Vienna airport massacres, lived at the time in a heavily guarded apartment building on the outskirts of Damascus.)

September 5, 1986, Karachi. Twenty-one were killed and more than 100 wounded in a massacre aboard a hijacked jet. Four gunmen, later linked to Syria, were seized after commandos stormed the plane.

November 23, 1985, Malta. An Egyptian jetliner was hijacked; 60 people were killed, 2 by the terrorists and 58 by Egyptian commandos who stormed the plane. The Syrian-backed Abu Nidal group claimed responsibility.

April 12, 1985, Madrid. A restaurant bombing killed 18 and wounded 82. Islamic Jihad, backed by Syria, was among the groups claiming responsibility.

September 20, 1984, Beirut. Fourteen are killed and 70 are injured when a car bomb explodes at the U.S. Embassy. Islamic Jihad claimed responsibility.

April 18, 1983, Beirut. In the suicide bomb attack on the U.S. Embassy, 57 persons are killed and 120 are injured. Responsibility is claimed by Islamic Jihad.

This is by no means an exhaustive summary of Syria's dealings in terrorism. There were, for instance, five bases near Damascus and at least 20 other Syrian-controlled camps where instruction in the techniques of terrorism was provided. Yarmouk, in Damascus, was the camp most often used for advanced terrorist training. Skills acquired at these camps were tested in Lebanon's Bekaa Valley, which Syria controlled.

General Mohammed Khouli, at one time head of the Syrian Air Force (which was Assad's personal intelligence service and base of power), directed most of these training operations. One of his deputies, Colonel Haitham Sayeed, was also the intelligence coordinator for Abu Nidal. Khouli and Sayeed, according to Western intelligence agents, directed the Hindawi case.

Yet Assad managed to maintain relatively cordial relations with Western nations. Part of his ability to continue to be acceptable (or at least be difficult to condemn) lay in the care with which he distanced himself from actual terrorist attacks. He also won approval by helping in hostage crises. Indeed, he became a master at the strategy of helping groups to take hostages with one hand and gaining favor with the West by aiding in their release with the other hand. Until the Hindawi case, no one could prove that what to the West seemed to be the "helping" hand knew what the "terrorist" hand was doing.

Unlike Libya's Qadhafi, Assad seemed to prefer secrecy to the spotlight of international attention in the drama of terrorist involvement. Assad relied on sporadic, preferably untraceable attacks, which allowed him to avoid retribution. Qadhafi, in the 1980s, treated terrorism like a banner to be waved before the troops; for Assad, it was instead as quick and silent as an assassin's bullet.

Assad had no wish to make himself an obvious target for retribution in a terrorist incident, as Qadhafi has done. He did not underestimate the desire for revenge of a nation whose citizens have been attacked, and he clearly did not wish to make himself or his country a tempting target. He preferred to wage a hit-and-run war, in which it was hard to find the guys wearing the black hats. He was, at heart, a pragmatic politician, a survivor.

One expert at the Foreign Policy Research Institute summed up sponsors of terrorism during the 1970s and early 1980s in this manner:

> Of the four major sponsors of terrorism—the Palestinian Liberation Organization (PLO), Libya, Iran, and Syria—the first two get all the attention. But it's the other two we should be watching, and particularly Syria. It is quiet and deadly in its effectiveness, and until this slipup with Hindawi, it has always managed to stay in the shadows.[26]

The end of the cold war at the beginning of the 1990s changed Syria's position significantly. Losing the Soviet Union as an ally, capable of support and willing to protect, appears to have strengthened Assad's determination not to be directly involved in planning or executing terrorist attacks. As the 1997 U.S. State Department's *Global Terrorism* report notes, there has been no evidence that Syrian officials have been directly involved in planning or exeuting terrorist attacks since 1986.[27]

Assad's death near the end of the 1990s did not substantively change Syria's role as a quiet supporter of terrorism. Syria continued to provide safe haven and support for several groups that engage in terrorist attacks. Ahmad Jibril's Popular Front for the Liberation of Palestine–General Command (PFLP–GC) and the Palestinian Islamic Jihad (PIJ), Abu Musa Fatah-the-Intifada, and George Habash's PFLP have maintained their headquarters in Damascus. The Syrian government allowed HAMAS to open a new main office in Damascus in March 2000, while HAMAS continued to seek permission to reestablish its headquarters in Jordan. Syria also granted to several groups practicing terrorism (including HAMAS, the PFLP–GC, and the PIJ) basing privileges or refuge in areas of Lebanon's Bekaa Valley under Syrian control, privileges that remained in place through the end of the twentieth century.

In the wake of the Gulf War, Syria began to distance itself from its role as sponsor of terrorism. Seeking to improve its relations with the Western nations, Syria moved away from obvious links with various Middle Eastern groups engaging in terrorism. Whether this move was permanent or only a feint designed to deflect Western criticism remains unclear. The situation in Lebanon has not yet stabilized and the groups have not yet been forced to leave that country to seek sanctuary and assistance elsewhere. The Middle East peace process tests Syria's willingness to cooperate in the control of violence against Israel by refusing to provide shelter and assistance to such groups.

Iran

According to the U.S. State Department, Iran was clearly the most active state sponsor of terrorism through the year 2003. Following their success in the 2004 elections, conservative clerics and the more radical anti-Western fundamentalists continue to be actively involved in the planning and execution of terrorist acts and to support a variety of groups that use terrorism to support their goals. Iran has been a strong sponsor of extremist Islamic and Palestinian groups, providing safe haven, funds, weapons, and training. The Lebanese Hezbollah, one of Iran's most important "clients," was responsible for some of the most lethal acts of the 1980s and early 1990s, including the 1983 suicide truck bombing of the U.S. embassy and U.S. Marine barracks in Beirut, the hijacking of TWA Flight 847 in 1985, the 1992 car bombing of the Israeli embassy in Argentina, and rocket attacks on civilians in northern Israel.

Iran has openly supported many other radical organizations that have resorted to terrorism, including the PIJ, the PFLP–GC, and HAMAS. The latter group was particularly active during the 1994–1996 portion of the peace process, with numerous car and suicide bombings carried out in Israel, the West Bank, and the Gaza Strip. The intifada, which emerged when the peace process faltered during the late 1990s, was often marked by suicide bombers encouraged by HAMAS and the Islamic Jihad and supported by Iran.

Iran's support of terrorism has been somewhat open, unlike Syria's more covert assistance. This has made it easier to link the state to the terrorist acts, but difficult to prevent such support, because the government appeared unconcerned with international disapproval or condemnation until the international community came together to condemn terrorism after the attack on September 11, 2001. Iran, in some respects, has been a crusader in state terrorism, willing to accept death for a cause in the confident expectation of eternal reward. Moreover, Iran's strong position as an oil-producing nation made many nations unwilling to support direct action against Iran in retaliation for such support.

Tehran conducted at least 13 assassinations in 1997, according to the U.S. *Global Report on Terrorism,* the majority of which were carried out in northern Iraq. The targets of Iran's attacks were usually members of the state's main opposition groups, such as the Kurdish Democratic Party of Iran (KDPI) and the Mujahedine Khalq (MEK), an Iranian terrorist group that opposes the current Iranian regime and is based in Iraq.

Perhaps the most compelling evidence of Iran's involvement in terrorism was reviewed in the trial in Germany of an Iranian and four Lebanese for the 1992 killing of Iranian Kurdish dissidents in Berlin's Mykonos restaurant. Finding the four guilty of murder, the court stated that the government of Iran had followed a deliberate policy of assassination of enemies of the regime living outside of Iran. The judge noted further that the Mykonos murders were approved at the most senior levels of the Iranian government, by an extralegal committee that included the president, the foreign minister, the supreme leader, and the minister of intelligence and security.

Iran continues to provide support (training, money, and/or weapons) to several groups engaged in terrorism, including those mentioned earlier. The government has encouraged the violent rejection of the Middle East peace process. Indeed, in the fall of 1997, Tehran hosted a conference of "Liberation Movements," whose participants included HAMAS, Lebanese Hezbollah, the PIJ, and Egypt's al-Gama'a al-Islamiyya. At this conference, there was open discussion of the jihad and of establishing greater coordination between certain groups.

As noted earlier, the elections in May of 1997 were indicative of a move in a more moderate direction. Iran's new foreign minister publicly condemned the attack by Egypt's al-Gama'a al-Islamiyya on tourists in Luxor, Egypt, in November of that year. In a CNN interview on January 7, 1998, President Khatami agreed that terrorist attacks against noncombatants, including Israeli women and children, should be condemned. These are encouraging signs of change in what the State Department's Report continues to characterize as the most active state sponsor of terrorism.

Libya

Libya, while also an oil state, has been less obvious in its support for terrorism since 1985, when linkage to a terrorist act in West Germany evoked a bombing attack on Tripoli by the United States. Indeed, Libya's support for acts of terrorism continued to cause economic and political penalties during the 1990s, following the bombing of Pan Am Flight 103 in 1988 over Scotland. The UN Security Council passed Resolution 731, which demanded that Libya take steps to end its state-sponsored terrorism, including extraditing two Libyan intelligence agents indicted by the United States and the United Kingdom for their role in that bombing. The resolution also required that Libya accept responsibility for the bombing, disclose all evidence related to it, pay appropriate compensation, satisfy French demands regarding Libya's alleged role in bombing UTA Flight 772 in 1989, and cease all forms of terrorism.

In 1992, the UN Security Council adopted Resolution 748, imposing an arms and civil aviation embargo on Libya. This resolution demanded that Libyan Arab Airlines offices be closed and required that all states reduce Libya's diplomatic presence abroad. When these measures failed to elicit full compliance from Libya, the Security Council adopted Resolution 883 in 1993, imposing a limited assets freeze and oil technology embargo on Libya and strengthening existing sanctions against that nation.

In 1999, Libya surrendered the two suspects accused of the 1988 bombing of Pan Am Flight 103 over Lockerbie, Scotland, to a court in The Hague, presided by international jurists. On January 31, 2001, the court found Abdel Basset al-Megrahi guilty of murder, concluding that he caused an explosive device to detonate on board the airplane, resulting in the murder of the flight's 259 passengers and crew as well as 11 residents of Lockerbie, Scotland. The judges found that he acted "in furtherance of the purposes of . . . Libyan Intelligence Services."[28] The other defendant, Al-Amin Kalifa Fahima, was acquitted based on a lack of sufficient evidence of "proof beyond a reasonable doubt."

In 1999, Libya paid compensation for the death of a British policewoman, a move that preceded the reopening of the British Embassy in Tripoli. The policewoman was killed and 11 demonstrators were wounded when gunmen in the Libyan People's Bureau in London fired on a peaceful anti-Qadhafi demonstration outside their building. Libya also paid damages to the families of victims in the bombing of UTA Flight 771. Six Libyans had been convicted in absentia in that case.

In the wake of UN intervention in the Lockerbie case, in fact, the regime in Libya largely avoided open association with acts of terrorism and terrorist groups. Although Qadhafi offered public support for radical Palestinian groups opposed to the PLO's Gaza-Jericho accord with Israel in 1993, and openly threatened to support extremist Islamic groups in neighboring Algeria and Tunisia, the level of practical open support by Libya for terrorism decreased substantially.

Instead, Libya played a high-profile role in negotiating the release of a group of foreign hostages seized in the Philippines by the Abu Sayyaf Group, reportedly in exchange for a ransom payment. The hostages included citizens of France, Germany, Malaysia, South Africa, Finland, the Philippines, and Lebanon. Libya also expelled the Abu Nidal organization and distanced itself from Palestinian groups engaged in terrorism against Israel, although it maintained contact with groups such as the PIJ and the PFLP–GC.

In the wake of the September 11 attacks on the United States, Libya was vehement about its noninvolvement and in its condemnation of the actions. Clearly, Libya is seeking to redefine itself with regard to the soubriquet of "state sponsor of terrorism." In 2004, Libya joined the international community in condemning terrorism, and sanctions were lifted against its economy as it began to rebuild relations damaged by its long-term role as state supporter for terrorism.

TERRORIST-SUPPORTED STATES

A situation has begun to emerge in recent years adding a new twist to the linkage of states and terrorism. Globalization, corruption, poverty, and a variety of factors are generating "failed states," whose governments are too weak and often too impoverished to provide for themselves or for their citizens. Some of these failed states have become the anomaly of **terrorist-supported states,** who *receive support from unexpected sources: affluent terrorist groups*. The groups then use these states as training grounds, recruitment centers, and procurers of useful technologies, making the state a partner in the terrorism being planned or perpetrated. A brief look at two such states offers interesting insights into this modern problem.

Few if any states today can afford, politically or economically, to openly support terrorism. Instead, the phenomena of the twenty-first century may well be the emergence of states supported by terrorist groups, rather than vice versa. There are groups today with sufficient resources, economic and personnel, that can actually receive safe haven and access to land for training facilities from political systems too weak to survive as effectively without their support. A brief look at two case studies—Afghanistan under the Taliban, and the emerging state of Palestine, under the PLA and Arafat—may help to make this new development clearer.

CASE STUDY   Afghanistan under the Taliban Leadership

Afghanistan, under the leadership of the Taliban, was a primary hub for terrorists and a home or transit point for the loosely organized network of "Afghan alumni," a web of informally linked individuals and groups that were trained for and fought in the Afghan war. These alumni have been involved in several major terrorist plots and attacks against enemies, including but not limited to the United States and other

Western nations. The leaders of some of the most dangerous groups engaged in terrorism emerging during the last two decades of the twentieth century have had headquarters or major offices in Afghanistan.

From this network have come attacks throughout the world, from the Philippines to the Balkans, Central Asia to the Persian Gulf, Western China to Somalia, and South Asia to Western Europe. But the most visible group in recent years has been al-Qaeda, bin Laden's group, blamed for the attacks on September 11, 2001. International concern for this state sponsorship was articulated in 2000 by UN Security Council Resolution 1333, which levied sanctions on the Taliban for harboring Osama bin Laden and failing to close down terrorist training camps established and funded by bin Laden in Afghanistan.

The problem was that bin Laden's organization provided financial and material support for the Taliban, as well as espousing the more fundamentalist view of Islam popular with both bin Laden and the Taliban leadership. Thus, it was not a situation in which a state government offered support and protection to a group practicing terrorism; rather, it was a group that offered support and assistance to a shaky leadership that controlled only a part of a state and lacked international diplomatic recognition as a state government.

Lacking this recognition, it was clearly impossible to bring diplomatic pressure on the Taliban to evict bin Laden and the al-Qaeda network from Aghanistan. Moreover, it is unclear whether the Taliban, even if they had wished to do so, could have mustered the force necessary to capture or evict bin Laden and his followers. In this case, it was the group that sponsored the state in many respects, making a demand to end state sponsorship of the group illogical, in many respects.   ❏

CASE STUDY   Palestine Liberation Authority

In this case, as well, the leadership responsible for supporting terrorism is not a recognized state entity in the international community. The Palestine Liberation Authority (PLA) has a limited role in the governing of the territories relinquished by Israel according to the 1994 Oslo accords. Yet in this limited territory, more acts of individual and group terrorist violence have occurred than in virtually any other contest during the 1990s. With the encouragement and support of groups like HAMAS, suicide bombers have killed people in shopping centers, on buses, in a wide range of public venues during the **intifada,** which in this case refers to *the violent civil disobedience of Palestinians in the occupied territories to Israeli rule,* that arose after the Oslo accords began to fall behind schedule.

Israel continued to blame Yasser Arafat, elected as the first president of the PLA, for failure to control the violence, accusing him of sponsoring terrorism within the territories by failing to arrest and punish those responsible for attacks. Arafat argued that he did not support the attacks, but was unable to control the violence, within the extremely limited context that Israel allowed for his police to exercise power.

Again, in this case as in Afghanistan, the ability of a not-quite state to exercise effective control over groups and individuals engaged in terrorism within its territories is debatable. Given the high political and economic costs engendered by the attacks by HAMAS on the future of Palestine, it was unlikely that Arafat actually supported the attacks. But his government's ability to control such individuals and groups was problematic, and he had to depend on some of these people for support in maintaining his leadership role in ongoing negotiations for the future of the state of Palestine. So it is perhaps less a state "sponsoring" terrorism than a group or individuals using terrorism to "sponsor" the emergence of the state.　❏

Conclusions

State terrorism, then, whether it is internal or external, offers a real threat to international peace and security. Internal terrorism breeds resistance movements, which often resort to terrorist tactics. This cycle of terror-violence can result in a whirlwind that will destroy all within its reach, innocent and guilty.

External terror, as practiced by some states, has resulted in the proliferation of terror worldwide. States whose policy specifically rejects the use of terror have been guilty of giving aid, often clandestinely, to states or groups that promote terrorism. With the exception of a few states such as Iran and Libya, most states have sought to keep their dealings with terrorists a secret.

State sponsorship of terrorism decreased during the last decade of the twentieth century. This became increasingly evident in the fall of 2001, as the international community became a part of the "war" declared by the United States on terrorism, in the wake of the September 11 attacks. Open support for terrorism, or for groups actively engaged in terrorist activities, became too politically costly, and because of the increasingly globalized economy, too economically costly as well. As the case studies of Afghanistan and Palestine graphically illustrate, although groups carrying out terrorist acts continue to find safe haven of a more discreet sort in some countries today, most are tolerated rather than openly supported by states whose ability to govern is frequently questionable and thus whose ability to control the use of its territory by such groups is often marginal.

Evaluation

Will terrorism become the accepted method of warfare in the future for disenfranchised and alienated peoples? As more and more states emerge that cannot govern their territories effectively enough to control the access of their territory to terrorist groups, can the international community cope with this emerging challenge? This may be a critical question, particularly since terrorism offers so many appealing attributes as an instrument of war:

1. *Low cost, financially.* It offers a relatively inexpensive method of operation for insurgent groups who lack the money, the manpower, and the armament to take on a powerful army. It also offers states a fairly inexpensive way to wage war, openly or clandestinely, on a hostile state whose resources make a full-scale war undesirable.

2. *Low cost, politically.* For states, particularly those who engage in clandestine support for terrorist groups, the political cost can be quite low while the profit in, for example, arms sales can be temptingly high. As long as the support is not obvious, as it was in Libya's case, the leaders of other nations have shown a tendency to look the other way.

3. *High yield, financially.* States engaged in arms sales to terrorists can profit quite handsomely, while suffering little if any political or economic reprisals. Assad's involvement in the Hindawi affair, for instance, resulted in the recall of a couple of ambassadors, but not the complete rupture of any diplomatic or trade relations.

4. *High yield, politically.* For freedom fighters who engage in terrorism, the yields can indeed be significant. Government reaction or overreaction can lead to a weakening or even the fall of a regime. Major concessions or changes can also be bought at the price of a successful terrorist incident.

5. *Low risk, politically and financially.* Because the cost of financing these operations is considerably less than that required for a fully equipped and trained army, the loss of the individuals carrying it out is minor. If it succeeds, the rewards can be enormous. If it fails, the loss is usually minimal, *unless* the failure is openly linked to a state. Since the end of the cold war, such linkage has become increasingly costly, both in financial and political terms.

What, then, is to deter individuals and nations from engaging in this high-profit, low-risk form of warfare? If nuclear warfare is unthinkable and unconventional warfare is, as both Vietnam and Afghanistan have illustrated, expensive and counterproductive today, will individuals and nations turn more often to this unpleasant alternative?

SUGGESTED READINGS

Andersen, Martin Edwin. *Dossier Secreto: Argentina's Desaparecidos and the Myth of the "Dirty War."* Boulder, CO: Westview Press, 1993.

Guest, Ian. *Behind the Disappearances: Argentina's Dirty War Against Human Rights and the United Nations.* Philadelphia: University of Pennsylvania Press, 1990.

Gunson, Phil, Andrew Thompson, and Greg Chamberlain. *The Dictionary of Contemporary Politics in South America.* New York: Macmillan, 1989.

Simonsen, Clifford E., and Jeremy R. Spindlove. *Terrorism Today: The Past, The Players, The Future,* 2nd edition. Upper Saddle River, NJ: Pearson Prentice Hall, 2004.

U.S. Department of State, *2003 Global Terrorism Report.* Washington, DC: Government Printing Office, 2004.

Wolosky, Lee S. Statement before the First Public Hearing of the National Commission on Terrorist Attacks Upon the United States. April 1, 2003.

NOTES

1. Milton Metzer, *The Terrorists* (New York: Harper & Row, 1983), 193.
2. Martin Slann, "The State as Terrorist," in *Annual Editions: Violence and Terrorism 91/92*, ed. Martin Slann and Bernard Schecterman (Guilford, CT: Dushkin, 1991), 69.
3. Martin Anderson, *Dossier Secreto: Argentina's Desaparecidos and the Myth of the "Dirty War"* (Boulder, CO: Westview Press, 1993), 57.

4. Robert A. Liston, *Terrorism* (New York: Elsevier/Nelson Books, 1977), 67.

5. Amnesty International, *Report on Terrorism* (New York: Farrar, Straus, and Giroux, 1975), 27.

6. Liston, *Terrorism,* 79.

7. Hannah Arendt, *The Origins of Totalitarianism* (New York: Harcourt, Brace, & World, 1973), 464.

8. This declaration was adopted with 48 states voting in favor, none against, and 8 abstentions (including Saudi Arabia, the Union of South Africa, the Union of Soviet Socialist Republics, and Yugoslavia). For a full copy of the text of this declaration, see Louis Henkin, Richard Pugh, Oscar Schachter, and Hans Smit, *International Law: Cases and Materials* (St. Paul, MN: West, 1980), 320.

9. International Covenant on Civil and Political Rights, 21 U.N. GAOR, Supp. (no. 16), 52, U.N. Doc. A/6316 (1966). Entered into force March 23, 1976.

10. George Kren and Leon Rappoport, *The Holocaust and the Crisis of Human Behavior* (New York: Holmes and Meier, 1980), 130.

11. See Nicholas Kittrie, "Response: Looking at the World Realistically," *Case Western Journal of International Law* 13, no. 2 (Spring 1981): 311–313.

12. See, for further documentation of this trend, the Annual Reports by Amnesty International, as well as that organization's *Report on Torture* (1975).

13. Carl J. Friedrich, "Opposition and Government Violence," *Government and Opposition,* 7 (1972): 3–19.

14. See Erich Fromm, *The Anatomy of Human Destructiveness* (New York: Holt, Rinehart, and Winston, 1973), 285–288.

15. Ted Gurr, *Why Men Rebel* (Princeton, NJ: Princeton University Press, 1970), 213.

16. United Nations Secretariat Study, "Measures to Prevent International Terrorism," U.N. Doc. A/C.6/418 (November 2, 1973). Prepared as requested by the Sixth Legal Committee of the General Assembly.

17. Bernard Schechterman and Martin Slann, eds. *Violence and Terrorism 98/99* (New York: Dushkin/McGraw-Hill, 1998), 42.

18. Robert Slater and Michael Stohl, eds. *Current Perspectives on International Terrorism* (New York: MacMillan/St. Martin's Press, 1988), 169.

19. Claire Sterling, "Terrorism: Tracing the International Network," *New York Times Magazine,* March 1, 1981, 19.

20. Sterling, "Terrorism: Tracing the International Network," 54.

21. Claire Sterling, *The Terror Network* (New York: Holt, Rinehart, and Winston, 1981), 293.

22. www.fas.org/irp/threat/bian_apr_2003.htm.

23. "The Unmasking of Assad," *U.S. News & World Report,* 101, no. 19 (November 10, 1986): 27.

24. Ibid., 26.

25. Ibid., 28.

26. Ibid., 29.

27. U.S. Department of State, "State-Sponsored Terrorism," in *1997 Global Terrorism Report* (Washington, DC: Government Printing Office, 1998), 6.

28. U.S. Department of State, "Overview of State-Sponsored Terrorism," in *Patterns of Global Terrorism* (Washington, DC: Government Printing Office, April 2000), 3.

6

Terrorism, Inc.

Key Concepts

networking	Shura
international terrorism congress	netwar
strategic planning	chain networks
revolutionary taxes	hub or star networks
hawala	all-channel network
bonuses	narcoterrorism
Libyan connection	unholy triangle
fedayeen	
fighting fund	

Terrorism can be viewed as a warped mirror image of the new economy.

Don van Natta, Jr.

NETWORKING

The three Japanese who disembarked from Air France Flight 132 at Lod International Airport in Tel Aviv, Israel, in May 1972 appeared no different from the other tourists bound for the Holy Land. Chatting pleasantly to the other passengers, they made their way swiftly to the luggage conveyor belt, where they retrieved their bags.

Opening one suitcase, they extracted a lightweight Czech-made submachine gun and a few hand grenades. They then opened fire on the crowd of disembarking passengers and visitors, using their weapons to strafe the airport lounge from side to side. From time to time they lobbed the grenades into the groups of terrified people.

In this attack, 26 people died. At least six of them were decapitated. One child of about seven was cut in half twice by the barrage of bullets. More than half of the dead were Puerto Ricans on a tour of the Holy Land. An additional 78 persons were wounded, many of them dismembered. The entire episode was over in seconds.

As an example of the **networking** of international terrorists, *in the creation of an interconnected system linking groups with common goals,* this incident excels. Here Japanese members of the JRA killed Puerto Ricans on behalf of Palestinian Arabs who sought to punish Israelis.

Cooperation between terrorist groups with, if not a common cause, at least a shared hatred, has occurred with alarming frequency for two decades. Anti-NATO sentiment, for example, drew several European groups into cooperative action. A communiqué on January 15, 1986, declared that the Red Army Faction (RAF) of West Germany and Action Direct (AD) of France would together attack the multinational structures of NATO. Shortly thereafter, assassins killed the general in charge of French arms sales and a West German defense industrialist. On August 8, 1985, two Americans were killed in a bomb blast at a U.S. air base in Frankfurt, West Germany. The RAF and AD claimed joint responsibility for this attack.

These French and German terrorists used explosives stolen from a Belgian quarry, suggesting a connection with Belgium's Fighting Communist Cells. This latter group bombed NATO pipelines and defense-related companies. Portuguese and Greek terrorists have also attacked NATO targets in their homelands, although evidence of collaboration in these countries is less clear.

Linkage between terrorist groups *does* exist, however. It appears in the form of shared members, training camps, weaponry, and tactics. It is obvious in the propaganda being disseminated by the groups. Perhaps the most obvious linkage—funding—became evident after the September 11 attacks. Each of these aspects of linkage will be explored to assess the extent to which "terrorism, inc." exists.

Study of contemporary terrorist groups suggests that terrorists in the latter part of the twentieth century shared intelligence information, weapons, supplies, training facilities and instructors, sponsors, and even membership. Such frequent *ad hoc* sharing does not necessarily constitute an organized "network of terror," as some have suggested. But the dimensions of cooperation between groups with unrelated or even opposing ideological bases offer useful insights to police, military, intelligence, and academic personnel who understand the web that does from time to time link terrorists.

That web is tenuous for the most part, constructed in a pragmatic fashion to meet common needs for relatively scarce resources. This does not, of course, diminish the potential for serious damage posed by such linkages. It simply makes the danger more difficult to assess, as the linkages are not only usually covert, but also appear to be in an almost constant state of flux.

Let us examine, then, some of those linkages as they have been shown to exist (usually after the fact in a terrorist event or confrontation). It is not necessary to study *all* of the available data on such linkages to establish that such connections exist. A brief survey of some of the evidence of cooperation or collusion will suffice to illustrate both the reality and the hazards of this insidious merging of terrorist interests and assets.

SHARED STRATEGIC PLANNING

In 1975 French police learned that the international terrorist known as "Carlos the Jackal" was running a clearinghouse for terrorist movements. His clients included the Tupamaros, the Quebec Liberation Front, the IRA, the Baader-Meinhof gang from West Germany, Yugoslavia's Croatian separatists, the Turkish People's Liberation Army, and the Palestinians.[1]

An **international terrorism congress,** *a meeting of terrorists from all over the world to work out agendas and to organize cooperative efforts,* took place in Frankfurt, Germany in 1986, reportedly attended by no less than 500 people. Meeting under the slogan "The armed struggle as a strategic and tactical necessity in the fight for revolution," it proclaimed the U.S. armed forces in Europe to be the main enemy.[2]

At this congress, it was decided that the correct strategy was to kill individual soldiers in order to demoralize their colleagues and lower their collective capacity to kill.

Among those represented at this congress, or present as guests, were German, French, Belgian, Spanish, and Portuguese terrorists, as well as members of the PLO, the PFLP, the ANC, the IRA, the Tupamaros, the Italian Red Brigades, and the ETA (Basque separatists). Most of the manifestos issued by this congress were basically Marxist-Leninist in style. The congress was financed largely by Libya.

Reports that surfaced in May of 1987 tell of Khomeini making the following offer to Nicaragua: Tehran would raise its $100 million in annual economic and military aid by 50% if Nicaragua would help recruit Latin American immigrants in the United States to join Iranian expatriates in forming joint terror squads. The mission of these squads: to strike back if the Americans made any attack on Iran.[3]

Some evidence indicates that attempts at coordinating activities have been made by various terrorist groups, but concrete proof of shared strategies demonstrating a "terrorist conspiracy" perhaps manipulated by a common hand—such as bin Laden— is insufficient. One prominent expert, James Adams, has suggested instead that terrorist groups act more like a "multi-national corporation with different divisions dotted around the world, all of which act in an essentially independent manner."[4]

In his book, *The Financing of International Terrorism,* Adams illustrates his analogy by suggesting that these "independent divisions" offer to the head of another operation, when he or she comes to town, the use of the company apartment, advances against expenses, and perhaps access to local equipment. In a similar manner, terrorist groups carrying out an operation in a foreign country may be granted such assistance by the "host" country's terrorist groups.

This analogy between different divisions in a multinational corporation and terrorist groups is more credible than that of a conspiracy, based on the fragmentary and often subjective nature of the evidence brought forth as proof of a true conspiracy among terrorist groups. The cooperation in terms of **strategic planning** that has been authenticated to date between terrorist groups has been (1) ad hoc, *focused on the planning of just one particular operation between groups whose other contacts remain fragmentary;* and/or (2) bombastic, *consisting primarily in the issuing of declarations by "congresses" or transient alliances between groups briefly united against a perceived common target.*

But contact between various terrorist groups does exist and has been documented. Adam Cohen, writing for *Time* in the aftermath of September 11, suggested that Osama bin Laden led a "global terrorist network," where bin Laden "creates the service and brand, but the cells largely fund their activities."[5] Moreover, Western intelligence believes that between 1970 and 1984, 28 meetings involving different terrorist groups were held around the world. While these meetings were generally called to discuss cooperation rather than coordination or revolutionary activities, it is difficult to establish precisely what plans and agreements have emerged from these contacts.

TERRORISM IS BIG BUSINESS

If the PLO were an American corporation, it would have been on the list of Fortune 500 companies. What was the PLO worth in the mid-1980s? James Adams calculated the organization's financial empire at $5 billion. Return on investments was the group's largest source of income at that time, bringing in about $1 billion per year.

Let us take a look at the financial headquarters of this group, as James Adams describes it:

> Just off Shah Bander Square in downtown Damascus is a five-story building of light brown cement. It looks more like the office of a low-level government department, unpainted since the colonials departed, than the headquarters of one of the wealthiest multinational corporations in the world.[6]

On the top floor of this building were banks of Honeywell computers, which were tended by young Palestinians. Most of these computer experts were trained in the United States, some at MIT and some at Harvard. From this world of high-tech and superefficiency, the Palestinian National Fund managed investments that generated a total annual income greater than the total budget of some Third World countries, an income that made the PLO the richest and most powerful terrorist group in the world during the 1980s.

Almost all of the PLO's assets were held indirectly through private individuals and in numbered bank accounts in Switzerland, West Germany, Mexico, and the Cayman Islands. Its primary banking institution was the Palestinian-owned Arab Bank, Ltd., headquartered in Amman, Jordan. The chairman of the Palestine National Fund at that time, Jawaeed al-Ghussein, administered the PLO finances.

PLO financiers invested money in the European market, as well as a few blue-chip stocks on Wall Street. The PLO also held large amounts of lucrative money certificates in the United States. These and other investments were said to provide as much as 20 percent of all of the group's revenues.

The PLO, like many multinational corporations, was also involved in a wide variety of business ventures, not all of which generated a monetary profit. Some were primarily political, made to win friends for the PLO. PLO money flowed covertly, through dummy corporations established in such places as Liechtenstein and Luxembourg, into investments in Third World countries. Much of this investment money passed through the Arab Bank for Economic Development in Africa and the Arab African Bank.

The PLO owned dairy and poultry farms and cattle ranches in the Sudan, Somalia, Uganda, and Guinea. It reportedly purchased a duty-free shop in Tanzania's Dares Salaam International Airport, and then negotiated for similar shops in Mozambique and Zimbabwe.

The point is, the PLO not only had cash assets of staggering proportions, it succeeded in investing them for capital, political, and strategic gains. Its stock and bond investments were exemplary and brought in considerable revenue; its investment in Third World ventures brought it considerable support and goodwill from many nations; and its ventures into such operations as duty-free airport concessions provided it with security-proof access through which to transfer materials from country to country. The PLO not only had money—it learned how to use much of it wisely.[7]

Not all groups carrying out terrorist acts are so well endowed. Most have to depend on the largess of patrons or on their own success in staging robberies and ransom situations. The ETA, which had close ties with the IRA and the PLO, adopted one of the PLO's less-publicized methods of raising money. Funds for this group, which received training and support from Libya and the PLO, were generated through **revolutionary taxes,** which were *levied on Basque businessmen. The PLO levied such a tax against the wages of Palestinians working abroad throughout the Arab world.*

Of the financial patrons of contemporary terrorist groups, two nations and one individual created networks that deserve special attention. These networks alone have been responsible for the training and arming of countless terrorist teams during the latter part of the twentieth century. Under their aegis, international terrorism took on a truly international flavor.

CASE STUDY   Bin Laden's al-Qaeda Network

Osama bin Laden, son of a billionaire Saudi construction magnate with an estimated worth of hundreds of millions of dollars, runs a portfolio of businesses across North Africa and the Middle East. Companies in sectors ranging from shipping to agriculture to investment banking throw off profits while also providing al-Qaeda's movement of soldiers and procurement of weapons and chemicals. Saudis, Pakistanis, Yemenis, Egyptians, Algerians, Lebanese, Mauritanians, Palestinians, and more have carried out terror operations linked to al-Qaeda. Many of these men were originally affiliated with a specific national organization like Egypt's Islamic Jihad or Algeria's Armed Islamic Group, but their allegiance shifted to bin Laden, and they fight for his causes.

Some of bin Laden's money is in mainstream institutions, as investigations after the September 11 attack indicated when the United States requested banks worldwide to cooperate in freezing al-Qaeda's assets. But al-Qaeda also clearly makes use of **hawala,** *an informal Islamic banking network that links brokers around the world who advance funds to depositors on a handshake and, sometimes, a password.* Hawala, Hindi for "in trust," has operated for generations in Asia and the Middle East. In remote areas, a broker may have little more than a rug and a phone, and the transfers leave little or no trail for investigators to follow, because they involve no wire transfers, balance sheets, or financial statements.

Hawala is used to transfer small amounts of money—usually less than $1,000—around the world. The transaction is almost immediate, based entirely on trust and requires no certification that might leave a paper trail. This system is an excellent example of the Islamic world's unique approach to finance. Services and training are provided interest-free for rich and poor, personal relationships and trust replace collateral, and accounting is a luxury often not included. Donating money for the advancement of Islam—building a mosque or funding an Islamic exhibit—is a religious obligation.

Financial services like hawala are a quick and inexpensive way for Muslims in the West to send funds to poorer relatives back home. For example, Al-Barakaat, a Somali-based organization, has outlets in cities across Europe and North America through which Somali abroad send vital cash to families at home.

Extremists have begun exploiting the religious rather than the financial motives of hawala, and its lack of detailed bookkeeping makes it difficult to track the source of money used by groups engaged in terrorist acts. Islamic charities also take in billions each year, most of which is used for good causes, but not all. Some of these millions make it into the hands of Islamic fighters and terrorists. Al-Qaeda's financial structure was built, as a recent report noted,

> from the foundation of charities, nongovernmental organizations, mosques, web sites, fundraisers, intermediaries, facilitators, banks and other financial institutions that helped finance the mujahideen throughout the 1980s. This network extended to all corners of the Muslim world.[8]

In Sudan, where bin Laden established himself in 1991, he launched several companies. One of these, the Al Shamal Islamic Bank, had a complete Web site with a list of correspondent banking relationships, including institutions in New York, Geneva, Paris, and London. Bin Laden also set up agricultural and construction companies.

One former al-Qaeda member, Jamal Ahmed al-Fadl, a Sudanese man, suggested in testimony at the trials of those accused of the bombing of the U.S. embassies in Kenya and Tanzania that bin Laden's organization has been beset by the usual office politics, ruthless cost cutting, and even corruption by some of its members. Al-Fadl complained bitterly about his $500 monthly salary, which was lower than other members' salaries, particularly certain Egyptians who seemed to enjoy preferential treatment. Bin Laden's response, according to al-Fadl, was that the Egyptians were paid more because they had more skills than the Sudanese, like the ability to obtain forged documents.

In this sense, terrorism in the al-Qaeda network resembles a warped mirror image of an international corporation, in its financial structure with corporate chieftains who manage lean, trimmed-down firms and bring in consultants and freelancers to perform specific jobs. As one author notes, "The specialists work as a team to complete an assignment, then move on to other jobs, often for other companies."[9] In this image, too, bin Laden is much like a terror "mogul," a man with the power to approve projects suggested to him, who has final veto over the content or timing, but often little to do with the project's actual creation. His most important contribution is the money.

The formalized merging of al-Qaeda with the Egyptian Islamic Jihad in 1998 greatly enhanced bin Laden's global reach and organizational ability. In early 1998, when the two groups announced they had formed the World Islamic Front for Jihad Against Jews and Crusaders, the focus of Islamic Jihad shifted from overthrowing the current Egyptian government to attacking U.S. interests, bin Laden's focus. The scope of the Jihad network is illustrated by the countries where 107 defendants in the 1999 trial were arrested—Albania, Bulgaria, Azerbaijan, the United Arab Emirates, and Egypt.

The leaders of this expanded network used the Muslim pilgrimages to Islamic holy sites in Saudi Arabia as a cover for recruiting new members or passing cash from one member to another. They shifted money around the world to bail members out of jail in Algeria or Canada and to finance applications for political asylum to enable the planting of terrorist cells in Western Europe.

One example of such a cell is emerging from a trial in Spain of an individual accused of assistance in the September 11 attacks. The cell began to take shape in 1994, when a group of radicals sought to take over a mosque in central Madrid to impose more fundamentalist teachings. The attempt failed when the insurgents argued among themselves, splitting into rival factions, one of which coalesced under the leadership of Anwar Adnan Mohamed Saleh, a Palestinian. This group, known as the Soldiers of Allah, distributed literature at the mosque about the activities of Muslim militants in Algeria, the Palestinian territories, Egypt, and Afghanistan, including communiqués issued by Osama bin Laden. According to a report submitted in the trial, Saleh and his associate, Imad Eddin Barakat Yarkas, a Syrian, began to indoctrinate young Muslims who expressed an interest in the literature, recruiting several to fight in Bosnia, where Muslims were at war with the Serbs.

Saleh left Spain abruptly in 1995, moving to Peshwar, Pakistan, where he began to work with the fledgling organization that would become al-Qaeda, moving Muslim militants across the border into Afghanistan for training in terrorist camps established there by bin Laden. In Spain, Yarkas took over the cell created under Saleh's leadership. Eventually, Spanish authorities charged eight men with complicity in the September 11 attacks. The officials marveled that these men had posed patiently for years as middle-class householders, occasionally moving into the shadows to recruit young Muslim fighters for bin Laden's camps or to commit crimes to raise money for guns and explosives. The bombing attacks on the Madrid subway system in March 2004 offered evidence of the expertise clearly developed by such cells; it also suggested the linkage of such al-Qaeda units with local groups like the ETA, who local authorities initially blamed for the attacks.

Evidence of al-Qaeda cells emerged in more than 40 countries after the September 11 attacks, as the United States urged other states to "follow the money" to determine the extent of the network of terrorism and its financial support structure. Bin Laden's degree in economics and his experience as part of a multibillion dollar, multinational construction company has made this task quite challenging.

Al-Qaeda resources have been invested in industries as diverse as trade in honey and in diamonds. American officials noted evidence that bin Laden used a network of shops that sell honey—a staple of Middle Eastern life since biblical times—to generate income, as well as to secretly move weapons, drugs, and agents throughout his terrorist network. Honey is deeply rooted in Middle Eastern culture, religion, and trade. In Saudi Arabia, which produces relatively little honey, families consume on average more than two pounds a month, according to a 1998 report by the U.S. Department of Agriculture.

The honey business is less significant for the income it generates, however, than for the operational assistance it provides. The shops allow al-Qaeda to ship such contraband as money, weapons, and drugs. "The smell and consistency of honey makes it easy to hide weapons and drugs in shipments. Inspectors don't want to inspect that product. It's too messy."[10]

Al-Qaeda, like other groups, have exploited the corruption and chaos endemic to the Democratic Republic of the Congo (DRC) to tap into the diamond trade and funnel millions of dollars into their organizations. U.S. officials investigating the financing of al-Qaeda indicated that they had greatly underestimated the amount of money this group and other organizations controlled, not only in the diamond trade, but also in the trade of gold, uranium, and tanzanite in this troubled region. The diamonds, and other precious and semiprecious materials, are bought at a small fraction of their market value, then smuggled out of the country and sold, frequently in Europe, for sizable profits.

Viewed in this context, al-Qaeda is clearly a financial structure willing to break moral laws to further its cause. Preying on the failed or collapsed states like the DRC, Liberia, and Sierra Leone, this organization profits from the chaos, violence, and intimidation of this region to secure funds for its operatives to carry out terror in other states. ❏

Although state-sponsored terrorism is increasingly less common, as organizations such as al-Qaeda develop international networks to finance their operations, it is useful to remember that state sponsorship played a significant role in the development of some of the terrorist networks that exist today. One of the principle players in this development has been the state of Libya, under the leadership of Muammar Qadhafi. A brief look at this state-sponsored network is enlightening.

CASE STUDY   Libyan Protector

Under Qadhafi, Libyan agents dispersed huge amounts of aid during the 1970s and 1980s to various terrorist groups. That this dispersal appeared to depend greatly on whim, and consequently caused a great deal of frustration among terrorists dependent upon his support, does not detract from the substantial contributions he made to the financing of terrorism worldwide.

Qadhafi supported Palestinian groups, including the PFLP, the DFLP, and the PFLP–GC, with donations of as much as $100 million a year. He also assisted the IRA, the ETA, the Baader-Meinhof gang, the JRA, the Red Brigade, the Tupamaros, and the Moros (in the Philippines).

His assistance was not confined to the financing of the terrorist operation itself. Israeli intelligence suggested that Qadhafi paid a $5 billion bonus to the Black September terrorists who were responsible for the Munich massacre in 1972. Western intelligence also believed Qadhafi paid Carlos the Jackal a large bonus, around $2 billion, for his role in the seizure of the Organization of Petroleum Exporting Countries (OPEC) oil ministers in Vienna in December 1975.

Bonuses were *payments given for success,* such as that paid to Carlos, and *for "injury or death on the job."* By the 1990s, these significantly decreased in amount. Qadhafi reportedly paid only between $10,000 and $30,000 to the families of terrorists killed in action in the late 1980s, down considerably from the $100,000 reportedly paid to a terrorist injured in the OPEC incident in 1972.

So Qadhafi has given money to support terrorist groups, and he has furnished monetary incentives for participating in terrorist events. Other leaders throughout history have supported dissident groups and provided for the survivors of their military or quasi-military activities. But Qadhafi has taken his support of terrorists to greater lengths. When the United States carried out air raids on Libya on April 15, 1986, Qadhafi was, of course, furious. He offered to *buy* an American hostage in Lebanon, so that he could have him killed. On April 17, Peter Kilburn, a 62-year-old librarian at American University who had been kidnapped on December 3, 1984, was executed after Qadhafi paid $1 million to the group holding him. He paid $1 million to be able to kill an elderly librarian, in order to punish the United States.

Declining oil revenues, particularly due to UN sanctions, diminished Libya's role in financing terrorism. In six years, this income fell from $22 billion to about $5.5 billion, seriously reducing Qadhafi's ability to bankroll terrorism. Although he remained after this loss involved in the training of terrorists, his role as the "godfather" of terrorism decreased dramatically during the last decade of the twentieth century, making it difficult to predict his role for the twenty-first century.

Libya's role decreased at this point, but did not end. This became obvious when, after having been expelled from both Iraq and Syria, Abu Nidal, the Palestinian master terrorist who planned the *Achille Lauro* hijacking, was given refuge in Tripoli. Western sources feared that, under Libya's protection, Nidal could repay Qadhafi by striking at more American targets.

Moreover, Libya developed a strong "connection" in Central and South America through its ties to Nicaragua. The Sandinista government of Nicaragua was, until the early 1990s, the **Libyan connection** in this region, *supplying arms, training, and logistical support to revolutionary groups in that region.*

In 1986, Daniel Ortega wrote to Libya's leader,

> My brother, given the brutal terrorist action launched by the U.S. government against the people of the Libyan Arab Jamahiriyah, I wish to send sentiments and solidarity from the FLSN National Directorate and the Nicaraguan people and government.[11]

This was not the first time these leaders had pledged friendship and support. Long before they came to power in 1979, Sandinista leaders had been training in

PLO camps in Libya and Lebanon. When the Sandinistas finally seized power, Qadhafi promised political and financial aid, promises that he indeed kept over the years.

In the early years, the Sandinistas received a $100 million "loan" from Libya. In 1983, Brazilian authorities inspecting four Libyan planes bound for Nicaragua discovered that crates marked "medical supplies" actually contained some 84 tons of military equipment, including missiles, bombs, cannons, and two unassembled fighter planes.

In Managua, leaders from Germany's Baader-Meinhof gang, Spain's ETA, Colombia's M19, Peru's Sendero Luminoso, and El Salvador's FMLN met with Libya and the PLO. Through Nicaragua, Libya was able to funnel arms to many of these groups.

M19's attack on Colombia's supreme court, in which more than 100 were killed, was carried out with arms supplied, through Nicaragua, by Libya. Many of the guns captured in that raid were linked to Libya, some of which reached M19 through conduits in Vietnam, Cuba, and of course, Nicaragua.

Nicaragua's Libyan connection highlights the continuing spiral of terror funded by Qadhafi. Libya supported a revolutionary group with money and arms, and when it had managed to seize control of Nicaragua, Libya used that government as a conduit to funnel arms and support to other groups engaged in terrorism in similar struggles throughout Central and South America.

The peaceful end of the Sandinista regime, through democratic elections, brought this "Libyan connection" to a halt. Since Libya's profile in supporting terrorist groups similarly declined in the latter part of the 1990s, this transition has left several groups without a sponsor or support system. Some have begun to link with the illicit drug cartels in Colombia, providing "security" for drug lords and the shipment of their goods. This has diminished, to some degree, the revolutionary focus of such groups, but has helped to fill the gap left by the loss of Libyan patronage. ❑

CASE STUDY   Iran's Support Network

Libya was certainly not the only Middle Eastern nation to support terrorism, openly during the 1970s and 1980s, more discretely in the 1990s. As James Adams noted, when one prime supporter falls away, another tends to rise to take its place. Iran was able, to a large degree, to take Libya's place as the leading patron of terrorism in the Middle East, Europe, and the Americas.

In order to understand Iran's commitment to terrorism, one can look back 900 years to the time of al-Hassan ibn-Sabbah. Sabbah, a leader of the dissident Muslim Ismaili group (which in turn is one of the two divisions of the Shi'a sect), was the founder of the previously mentioned "Assassins," the hashish-smoking terrorists who terrorized the Persian Gulf region in the twelfth century. Sabbah called his followers **fedayeen**—meaning either *adventurers or men of sacrifice,* an acronym adopted by many terrorists today. Palestinian suicide bombers in Israel and those engaged in bin Laden's holy war against the West have both been called fedayeen.

Iran is the home of the Shi'a branch of Islam, which has been in conflict with the majority Sunni branch for centuries. When Ayatollah Khomeini came to power after the fall of the shah, he began to rally Shi'a globally to this ancient conflict. In March 1982, clergy and leaders of Shi'ite revolutionary movements from all over the world came to Tehran. At this meeting, in addition to agreeing to establish a number of training camps for terrorists in Iran (which was after all the home of the Assassins), it was agreed that $100 million would be immediately allocated as a **fighting fund,** *established by Iran to support worldwide terrorism.* Moreover, an additional $50 million was designated to be spent each year for an indefinite period of time to bankroll specific acts of terrorism.[12]

From this capital outlay have come a variety of terrorist activities. Several powerful groups operating in Lebanon were financed by Iran during the last two decades of the twentieth century. Bomb attacks on moderate Arab states, including Kuwait, Saudi Arabia, and Egypt, caused serious personal and monetary damage. Islamic fundamentalism rose rapidly in southern Asia, supported by substantial cash infusions. Hit squads were dispatched throughout Europe to eliminate "enemies" of Shi'a Islam. And a global network of clergy-dominated religious groups was formed, whose purpose was to mastermind further terrorism and recruit new assassins to serve in Iran's holy war. (The concept of a holy war against the West did not originate—nor will it end—with bin Laden!)

In the mid-1990s, France was a target of attacks by Algerians angry about French support for the military regime, which prevented the strong Islamic fundamentalist parties from winning the election in Algeria. Attacks in this case included a hijacking and numerous bomb attacks, including attacks on the subways and monuments in Paris.

Faced with the threat of continuing Iranian-sponsored terrorist bombings and hijackings, some wealthy Kuwaiti citizens began taking extended vacations during the late 1980s in other Arab states and Western Europe. The Kuwaiti government naturally was concerned that too large an exodus of such persons could set off panic among Egyptians, Palestinians, Pakistanis, and other guest workers, who made up 70 percent of the Kuwaiti workforce. Accordingly, Kuwait moderated its antagonism toward Iran, fearing that Iran's terrorist retaliation might cripple beyond repair the Kuwait economy. In light of Iraq's subsequent invasion of Kuwait, this move to placate Iran by not appearing to favor Iraq too much in the previous conflict appears quite ironic.

Saudi Arabia, which was also a victim of Iranian-directed terrorism, was also very cautious in taking public stands in the Iran–Iraq conflict. Although many Saudi officials, including Prince Bandar ibn Sultan, the Saudi ambassador to the United States in the 1980s, urged a tough stance toward Tehran, King Fahd maintained an extremely cautious approach. Remembering the violence of the Iranian-provoked riot in Mecca in July 1987, which left more than 400 dead, the Saudis were careful not to deliberately antagonize the state of Iran. The bombing in late 1995 of the building used as U.S. military training headquarters for years in Riyadh indicated that such caution might not have been sufficient.

Months before a bloody street battle on July 31, 1987, between Iranian pilgrims and Saudi security forces, Saudi intelligence knew that a specialist unit of Iran's

Revolutionary Guards had been training for a major sabotage action during the pilgrimage season in Mecca. Unable, as custodians of Islam's holiest shrines, to ban Iranian pilgrims, they could only respond to the deadly violence instigated by the pilgrims.

Despite Saudi political wariness, however, terrorism continued to pour from Iran in an unpredictable flow, encompassing friend and foe alike in the Arab world. Originating from Bangkok, Kuwait Airways 422 was hijacked on April 5, 1988, in a plot hatched four months earlier in Tehran by Shi'a radicals from Bahrain, Lebanon, and Iran. The mastermind of the plot was apparently Immad Mughniye, a Shi'a religious fanatic responsible for planning bombings of the U.S. embassy and the U.S. Marine headquarters in Lebanon five years earlier.

The world, with the possible exception of Iran, watched in horror as the bodies of innocent persons on Flight 422 were thrown from the plane by the terrorists, whose demands for the release of other terrorists held in Kuwaiti prisons the Kuwaiti government steadfastly refused to meet. Those imprisoned terrorists were responsible for Iranian-directed bombings of the U.S. and French embassies in Kuwait.

Intelligence sources have indicated that a dozen terrorists drawn from Hezbollah—the Iranian-backed Party of God group engaged in terrorism against Israel—and the Bahrain Front, also led from Tehran, were sent for training in the Bekaa Valley of Lebanon in March 1988. At the same time, Iranian agents checked Bangkok airport for security weaknesses that could be exploited in the hijack. So blatant was Iran's involvement in this terrorist episode that when the plane reached Mashad Airport in Iran, while the hijacking was in progress, the Iranians allowed the hijackers a "crew change." It is also thought that the Iranians allowed the hijackers to take aboard sophisticated two-way radios at this point, giving them a link to the persons directing the hijack during the subsequent negotiations in Cyprus and Algeria. ❏

Support networks for terrorists do not only occur in the Middle East. The United States, recently a victim of the worst terrorist attack in recent history, has nevertheless allowed a network of support for a group involved in terrorism to exist in its domain for several decades.

CASE STUDY   NORAID—A U.S. Terror Connection

According to James Adams:

> From the onset of modern terrorism in Northern Ireland in 1969, the United States has played a key role in its support. The enormous Irish-American population has always felt a strong sentimental attachment to "the old country," and this has been translated into a steady stream of cash and guns to the IRA, which has, in part, enabled them to survive.[13]

Michael Flannery, a former IRA member living in New York, in 1969, established Irish Northern Aid—generally known as NORAID. Its purpose was to facilitate the giving of assistance to the IRA. Headquarters were established at 273 East 194th Street, in the Bronx, New York City.

Conflicting reports are offered about the importance of NORAID for the IRA (now known as the Provisional IRA or PIRA, after the 1969 split in the IRA leadership) during the last three decades of the twentieth century. Certainly in the early 1970s, NORAID could be termed crucial to the PIRA's survival, since it supplied over 50 percent of the cash needed by the PIRA. By the end of the twentieth century, however, the PIRA could expect to receive less than $200,000 of its estimated $7,000,000 budget from NORAID.

During the late 1980s, NORAID no longer supplied only cash to the PIRA. Instead, cash raised at traditional annual dinners was frequently used to purchase arms, which were then smuggled to Ireland. Because each dinner was expected to generate between $20,000 and $30,000, and such dinners were held in cities throughout the United States during the 1980s, the supply of arms that could be purchased and smuggled was substantial.

Following the murder of 79-year-old Lord Mountbatten and other members of his family, including his 14-year-old grandson by the IRA in 1979, U.S. intelligence agencies, including the FBI, began to cooperate with the British in attempting to stem the flow of arms from NORAID to the IRA. Although initial successes in this effort were few, by 1984 the cooperation yielded significant results. In early September of that year, for instance, an 80-foot trawler, registered in Ipswich, Massachusetts, left Boston bound for Ireland. In its cargo were rockets, grenades made in Korea, 100 German automatic rifles, 51 pistols and revolvers, shotguns, and a 0.50 caliber heavy machine-gun. A CIA surveillance satellite tracked the trawler to its rendezvous with an Irish trawler. A report on this cargo and its transfer was made to the Irish government, which subsequently seized the ship and confiscated its $500,000 cargo of illegal arms.

NORAID was crippled in the last two decades of the twentieth century by more than the stepped-up scrutiny and cooperation between intelligence services of the United States and Britain. In the chapter that discusses methods of combating terrorism, more details will be given. At this point the court challenges to NORAID members in the United States, based on claims for injuries incurred by victims of the weapons purchased by NORAID money, have substantially drained NORAID coffers, making the donation of cash and the purchase of arms difficult, if not completely impossible. Moreover, the peace process, begun in the mid-1990s, has helped to make the transfer of this type of aid to the IRA much less politically acceptable in the United States. ❑

THE INTERNATIONALIZATION OF TERRORISM

Although terrorism has clearly been "internationalized" in the Middle East, frequently around a religious war against a commonly hated heretic state, Europe has also had to cope with the networking of terrorist groups into a web whose strength is difficult to measure. Study of one of Europe's most networked group, the RAF, offers insight into this phenomenon.

The RAF was the oldest and the most ruthlessly violent left-wing terrorist movement in Germany in the late twentieth century. Emerging from a small residue of left-wing extremists from the student protests of the late 1960s, it was responsible for half a dozen bombing attacks in 1972. Although it suffered large defeats in 1977 and again in 1982 (due to the arrest of many of the original leaders), it continued to successfully regroup and reemerge as a violent political force until Germany was reunited in the early 1990s.

Early generations of the RAF were to some degree international in the struggle that they waged against imperialism. In 1977, the RAF carried out a PFLP plan to hijack a Lufthansa aircraft to Mogadishu. The PFLP plan was designed to captilize on the Schleyer kidnapping. Two members of the RAF, Hans-Joachim Klein and Gabriele Krocher-Tiedemann, were recruited by Carlos the Jackal to assist in the raid on the Vienna OPEC conference in 1975. Another two members of the RAF, Wilfred B'o'se and Brigitte Kuhlmann, participated in the 1976 hijack to Entebbe.

But in July 1984, West German police found documents indicating that the RAF planned to further internationalize their struggle by uniting with other terrorist groups in attacks on the representatives of repression, specifically NATO allies. This anti-imperialism brotherhood of bombers and assassins began to wage war throughout Europe in the 1980s.

German, French, and Belgian radicals assassinated prominent members of Europe's defense establishment and set off explosives at such targets as a U.S. air base, military pipelines, and a variety of other NATO installations. Nor did the targets remain specifically military. A Berlin nightclub filled with off-duty soldiers and German civilians was bombed in 1984, allegedly by this terrorist alliance.

One source close to the German underground noted,

> From the Red Army Faction point of view, the only opportunity to fight NATO suppression around the world is to organize a kind of illegal guerrilla war and get in contact with more and more people.[14]

This transformation apparently took concrete form first in 1981. Italian counterterrorist forces revealed that in that year, exiles from the RAF, the Italian Red Brigades, and other groups met in Paris. From this meeting, the order went out to kidnap James L. Dozier, a U.S. Army brigadier general stationed in Rome. From being indigenous terrorist groups, operating primarily on their own soil for essentially nationalistic purposes, these groups began to focus their attention and activities against an international enemy: NATO.

Working together, these European terrorists created an informal network helping them to strike at a variety of NATO targets throughout that region. With relatively open borders between nations in the European Union (EU), these terrorists managed to operate in a manner that made it difficult for law enforcement officials to predict and prevent their attacks or to capture them after the events. Evidence suggests that they shared personnel, resources (explosives and weapons), and safe houses, as well as the low-level support system involved in such activities as the production of travel documents.

CASE STUDY   September 11, 2001 and Beyond

In the year of intense effort on the part of the United States and its allies in the international community to "search out and destroy" al-Qaeda, it became obvious that the organization had developed new bases and a looser structure; it was still quite capable of attacking Western targets. An examination of some of the individuals, the cells scattered worldwide, and the pattern of activities still taking place offers insights into the new "netwar" being waged by this particular brand of "terrorism, inc." today.

The "Lieutenants"

Osama bin Laden could not have carried out the attacks of September 11, 2001, without widespread help from a network of talented and committed "lieutenants." These men were sought intensely by the United States following the attacks in 2001, because their participation was believed to be crucial to the attack's success:

> *Ayman Zawahiri:* Widely believed to be bin Laden's deputy, Zawahiri was the leader of the Egyptian Islamic Jihad, the group blamed for the assassination of President Anwar el-Sadat in 1981, and a member of the **Shura**—*a body of al-Qaeda that contains members of other terrorist groups.* Zawahiri, a surgeon, was sought by the U.S. military in Iraq in 2004, where it was believed that he continued to coordinate attacks against U.S. military in that country. "Al-Zawahiri's experience is much broader than even bin Laden's," according to Dia'a Rashwan, one of Egypt's top experts on militants. "His name has come up in nearly every case involving Muslim extremists since the 1970s."[15]

> *Muhammad Atef:* Thought responsible for carrying out the detailed mechanics of the plan to hijack four aircraft simultaneously on September 11, Atef is also believed responsible for planning the 1998 bombings of U.S. embassies in Kenya and Tanzania. Responsibility for these attacks was claimed by the Islamic Army for the Liberation of Holy Sites, led by Sobhi al-Sitta, also a bin Laden lieutenant. Atef operated his own military training camps in Afghanistan, where he apparently trained members of the Islamic Army group.

> *Mustafa Ahmad:* Ahmad, as Osama's "money man," financed the hijackers while they were in the United States. In fact, he was in the United Arab Emirates before the September 11 attacks, waiting for the hijackers to return their unused U.S. dollars to him there.

> *Abu Zoubeida:* This Palestinian was responsible for overseeing al-Qaeda's training camps. He is thought to have masterminded the "millennium bombings," including a plot to blow up the Los Angeles airport on New Year's Eve in 1999.

> *Saif al-Adel:* This man, described by the FBI as one of the most dangerous al-Qaeda leaders, was responsible for training elite terrorist recruits in handling explosives. Several of the September 11 hijackers were reportedly schooled by al-Adel in Afghanistan.   ❑

THE NETWORK AND NETWAR

After the destruction of the Afghan training camps in 2001, many al-Qaeda operatives returned to their homelands or to third countries, where they made common cause with other Islamic groups to wage a jihad against the United States and its allies. These separate cells or factions, inspired by the events of September 11, do not appear to have needed contact with one another or a central authority to carry out successful terrorist attacks on al-Qaeda's behalf. As one news agency reported, "al-Qaeda supporters in 60 countries range from small cells to allied terrorist groups to guerrilla gangs."[16]

First, a quick look at the "al-Qaeda affiliates" in this netwar helps to make the dimensions of the conflict visible:

In Europe, small cells plot new attacks, recruiting second-generation European Muslims. Members of some cells report directly to al-Qaeda, while others belong to allied North African groups.

In Sub-Saharan Africa, al-Qaeda maintains support for a variety of Muslim rebel groups from Eritrea to South Africa, including the Eritrean Islamic Jihad Movement and al-Ittihad al-Islamiya.

In Pakistan, al-Qaeda members co-opt local groups, such as Jaish-e-Muhammad and Lashkar-i-Jhangvi, to launch attacks on foreigners.

In Yemen, bin Laden's ancestral home, al-Qaeda maintains a very active base, because the government here remains able to exert very little control over much of the country.

In North Africa, al-Qaeda allies, operating from Morocco to Egypt, include the Salafi Group for Call and Combat, Takfir Wal Hijra, and Egyptian Islamic Jihad.

In Southeast Asia, al-Qaeda cells have been active in Indonesia, Malaysia, Singapore, and the Philippines, with a list of allies that include the regional Jemaah Islamiah and local groups like the Philippines Moro Islamic Liberation Front.

In Central Asia, trouble continues to foment from the Islamic Movement of Uzbekistan and the Eastern Turkestan Islamic Party, whose members trained in Afghanistan under al-Qaeda.

Terrorism is clearly taking on a new dimension, described as **netwar,** an *asymmetric mode of conflict and crime at societal levels, involving measures short of conventional war carried out by protagonists using network forms of organization and related strategies and information-age technologies to carry out attacks.* The individuals involved in a netwar usually connect in small groups, which communicate and coordinate their activities, but which generally lack an organized central command authority.

Networks of terror groups, similar to the structures emerging in the world of business, generally organize in one of three types: chains, hubs, or all-channel. **Chain networks** are organized much like an organization of smugglers, where *goods, information, and even people are passed along a line of separate contacts, from one end of the chain to the other*. In contrast, **hub or star networks** are similar to the structure of a drug cartel, *with actors and cells tied to a central cell or actor that controls communication and coordinates action*. In the **all-channel network,** however, *each small group or cell is connected to every other group in a collaborative effort, but without a central command cell.*[17]

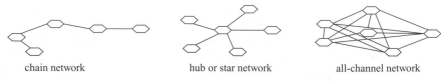

chain network   hub or star network   all-channel network

FIGURE 6.1

Source: John Arquilla, David Ronfeldt, and Michele Zanini, "Networks, Netwar, and Information-Age Terrorism," in *Terrorism and Counterterrorism: Understanding the New Security Environment,* ed. Russell D. Howard and Reid L. Sawyer (Guilford, CT: McGraw-Hill, 2003), 101.

Figure 6.1, created by the authors of an excellent article on networks and netwars in the context of terrorism, offers a useful visualization of these forms of terror structure. As they note, "each node in the diagram . . . may be an individual, a group, an institution, part of a group or institution, or even a state."[18]

A brief overview of the wave of attacks carried out by the disparate cells of al-Qaeda in 2002 offers a disturbing view of this new form of warfare:

> *Wall Street Journal* reporter Daniel Pearl was kidnapped and murdered in Karachi by members of a Pakistani organization with ties to al-Qaeda.
>
> A church in Islamabad frequented by Westerners is bombed, killing five people. A group linked to al-Qaeda is suspected.
>
> In Tunisia, an al-Qaeda cell attacks North Africa's oldest synagogue with a natural gas truck rigged with explosives, killing 19 people, most of whom were tourists.
>
> An explosion in a karaoke bar in Zamboanga on Mindanao Island in the Philippines kills three people, including an American. The local Abu Sayyaf group claims responsibility.
>
> The French oil tanker *Limburg* is rammed by an explosives-laden boat off the coast of Al Mukalla, Yemen.
>
> A bomb blast outside a Bali, Indonesia, nightclub kills more than 180, mostly foreign tourists. Jemaah Islamiah is suspected.
>
> Two bombs explode in department stores in Zamboanga, killing seven. Authorities suspect a faction of Abu Sayyaf.[19]

Clearly, al-Qaeda *is* decentralized, but its capacity to commit acts of terror has in some respects actually increased as its territory and targets have expanded. Terrorism, in this netwar form, offers a challenge to international security unlike that faced by most modern law enforcement or military.

NARCOTERRORISM

Terrorists of the future may be even less dependent than those of the present on the sponsorship of patron states or individuals to create a network to support their violent activities. A new source of revenue has come into the hands of terrorist groups in the last decades of the twentieth century, prompting some experts to decry the existence of what they call **narcoterrorism,** *a networking of the trade in drugs and terrorism.* *U.S. News & World Report* called this "the unholiest of alliances, a malevolent marriage between two of the most feared and destructive forces plaguing modern society— terror and drugs."[20]

The use of drugs to underwrite the costs of terrorism adds a new dimension to law enforcement efforts to combat both drugs and terrorism. The drug trade offers vast profits, too, for nations who, while wanting to continue to sponsor terrorist groups, find their coffers seriously depleted in recent years. Syria, for example, and more recently Afghanistan, have engaged in international drug smuggling to help finance their support for terrorist groups.

The nether world of narcoterrorism has three main players: the terrorist groups such as al-Qaeda, the ETA, or Sendero Luminoso; the government officials and intelligence services of nations such as Iran and Cuba, whose foreign policy includes the exporting of revolution; and the narcotic-dealing gangsters, such as Juan Mata Ballesteros, who also deal in political violence and terror. Through a complex network of contacts, these narcoterrorists deal in weapons, launder money, share intelligence information, trade false passports, share safe havens, and offer other forms of assistance.

It is a loose global alliance of two elements of the criminal world. Those who deal in drugs have long become inured to dealing in death and find little incongruent in their relationship with terrorists. In spite of the apparent callousness in such groups as the PLO toward the taking of human life, these groups are very sensitive to charges that they deal in drugs.

Indeed, PLO treasurer Jaweed al-Ghussein vehemently repudiated such charges. "We are fighting for our homeland. We are not drug smugglers. That is against our values."[21]

Regardless of such denials, it is true that in war-torn Lebanon, the annual 1500-ton hashish trade (recently supplemented by opium and heroin) has supported terrorists of many ideologies for years. "Lebanese hashish helps to pay for everything from hijacking and bombing spectaculars in Europe and the Middle East to a simmering revolt by Moslem insurgents in the Philippines."[22]

It is certain that Syria would be unable to conduct its assistance to insurgent groups without the infusion of millions of dollars in drug profits. Without such profits, the Syrian economy would be even more threadbare than it has become in the years since the collapse of the Soviet Union. Intelligence agencies suggest that Syrian government involvement in the drugs-for-terrorism trade involves persons at high levels of the Syrian government.

Nor is the Middle East alone in experiencing the impact of narcoterrorism. In Peru, as one researcher noted, the coca growers and drug traffickers are in a working alliance with the Sendero Luminoso, or Shining Path. Although the ultimate ends sought by each group are different, their alliance does benefit each significantly, and the stability and legitimacy of the Peruvian government is constantly sabotaged. Because this destabilization is a shared goal (as well as the shared desire to make a profit) and because all members of this network want "liberation" from interference by the police and the military, there is a strong network of cooperation in Peru in narcoterrorism.

The Sendero Luminoso is one of the best armed militia in the region. Peru's police and military were, until recently, viewed as underequipped in comparison. The successful resolution of the takeover of the Japanese Embassy in Lima in 1997 changed international perception of the capabilities of Peruvian counterterror forces. But the situation with the drug traffickers and Shining Path remains unresolved. Few economic enterprises can command the market power and earning potential that the contemporary narcotics trade commands today. As one expert on the situation in Peru noted:

> Narcoterrorism is a growing movement. The police and the military have not been able to solve the problems of the Peruvian people; the Senderos provide a solution, however risky it might be. The Senderos have literally taken over hundreds of towns, usually welcomed in because they provide order and freedom to produce coca.[23]

What are the implications of this new source of financial independence for terrorist groups and states? Is this alliance of drugs and terror a result of temporary coincidence of needs, or does it have longer-term, broader, more strategic aims? It has been said that drugs could destroy the Western world; is the **unholy triangle** *of drug traffickers, terrorists, and state officials committed to the destruction of that world* just a mischance, or is it of deliberate design? How will this affect the way nations deal with drug traffic? Will there be any attempts to effect cooperation between agencies charged with combating drugs and those pledged to combating terrorism, similar to that attempted between Mexico and the United States in the mid-1990s?

CONCLUSIONS

Terrorism today is big businesss. No one country is wholly responsible for terrorism's scope, nor is any single individual so essential to the existence of terrorism that his loss would seriously diminish terrorism's spread. The continuation of terrorist attacks, in Europe, the Middle East, and now in the United States, after the collapse of the Soviet Union, has made it clear that no one state's support is essential to the survival of international terrorism. States like the former Soviet Union made it *easier* for terrorists to network, but such support, while no longer available, is clearly not critical to the survival or the networking of many groups.

Similarly, even in the wake of U.S. attacks on Afghanistan that destroyed the physical terrain of bin Laden's camps and headquarters, terrorism by his supporters has not ended. In spite of intense U.S. efforts to capture or kill bin Laden, his death or capture would not end al-Qaeda's capability as a terrorist network.

Moreover, evidence indicates that terrorist groups are becoming increasingly self-sufficient. As noted earlier, the PLO blossomed from a group that hijacked planes in the 1960s into a sophisticated multinational corporation that used both terrorism and sound investments to achieve its goals. Unlike its earlier years, when its ability to operate depended upon substantial contributions from sympathetic Arab states, the PLO by the final decade of the twentieth century obtained about five-sixths of its annual expenditures of $600 million from its own operations, not from terrorism.

Organizations such as the PLO and the IRA have become increasingly entrenched, both in the communities in which their followers live and in the governments that do business with them. The PLO, for instance, invested in farms, factories, the import-export business, and real estate. These investments provided revenues and jobs; they helped to integrate the PLO into the local economy, and they provided members of the organization with valuable experience as managers of both personnel and money, all of which should benefit the Palestinians as they establish self-government in the West Bank and the Gaza Strip.

Furthermore, governments in Europe now have bureaus created to deal with these groups. The PLO now has a mission to the United Nations in New York, and it has begun to operate as a government, in the form of the Palestine Liberation Authority, over a population and territory. Even before the peace accords in the 1990s, the PLO was able, due to its structure and resources, to act more as a government in exile than a terrorist operation. This does not suggest that it automatically abandoned its terrorist operations when it secured funds and investments—just that it, like the government of Syria, began trying to distance itself from the use of terrorist tactics.

However, many terrorist organizations still exist that are capable of lethal operations and networking on their own. Bin Laden's al-Qaeda is clearly such an entity.

Three final points need to be made with regard to this concept of a terror network. The first has to do with the transition of terrorist organizations into "corporations." As such groups become institutionalized, in terms of formalized government contacts and offices, entrenched in the local economics of many nations, and independent of a need for sponsor financing, *they become increasingly difficult to destroy.* Their adherents begin to include government bureaucrats whose offices regularly deal with them, businesses who share joint economic interests, and communities whose livelihood depend upon its employment.

The second point is that, with the increasing contact and sharing of support between terrorists, *there is a potential for greater sophistication in the carrying out of terrorist acts.* Terrorists operating in a foreign country, if they are able to avail themselves of the local expertise of indigenous groups, can carry out more efficient operations.

Thus far, evidence of this increase in expertise is limited. Indeed, evidence exists that terrorists operating on foreign soil are still receiving inadequate or incorrect intelligence information about their targets and intended victims. On September 3, 1985, for instance, the Palestine Popular Struggle Front, a small PLO faction, carried out what it supposed was an attack on a hotel swimming pool in Athens, Greece, frequented by American military personnel. Instead, the two grenades this group tossed over the wall killed two and wounded 13 handicapped British tourists! Bungling such as this increases, rather than decreases, the work of security forces charged with combating terrorism, of course, since the selection of victims is not just arbitrary, it is illogical.

Ironically, cooperative assistance may increase the ability of a group to select an appropriate target. But such cooperation also increases the likelihood that the group can in fact penetrate that target, as local expertise is added to fanatical commitment. Sharing information, arms, and training, terrorists of the next century can brandish a stronger, if still not coordinated, array of daggers at the throat of the civilized world.

The final point is that, after the September 11 attacks on the United States, *a concerted effort has begun worldwide to infiltrate the network of terrorism,* particularly but not exclusively that of al-Qaeda. The United States began to use a Foreign Terrorist Asset Tracking Center (FTAT), designed to dismantle terrorists' financial bases. The FTAT has begun to examine terrorist organizations worldwide, not just pinpointing financial data relating to a single crime. The information gathered would be used to identify and disrupt terrorists' funding, according to U.S. officials.

In this effort to cut off sources for terrorist funding, some Islamic charities will be impacted. Nada Management, founded in 1987 under the name Al Taqwa, is one of the world's largest financial institutions dedicated to Muslim clients and Islamic business activities. Organizations like Nada Management have offices in scores of countries, some of which may see no justification for the legal crackdown on these funds.

But Italy has deployed a new 600-strong multidisciplinary force to investigate the finances of al-Qaeda and other terrorist groups. In September 2001, the United States released a list of 88 groups and individuals it suspects of aiding al-Qaeda. In at least nine countries, law enforcement officials made concerted efforts to freeze millions of dollars in assets and shut off affiliates of two groups the United States accused of bankrolling al-Qaeda's terrorist activities.

Police in Italy raided the homes of Youssef M. Nada and Ali Ghaleb Himmat, top executives of Nada Management, whose offices in nearby Lugarno, Switzerland were searched. Both men were detained for questioning and released; both are members of the Muslim Brotherhood, a fundamentalist group whose long struggle to establish an Islamic state in Egypt could make it a natural ally for the Egyptian Islamic Jihad, with which al-Qaeda has networked.

While these efforts to "break up" terrorist support networks is certainly an encouraging development, the ability do so effectively remains unproven. On the other hand, terrorists have clearly demonstrated in recent years that they can survive the loss of support states, and can even internationalize and establish diverse funding structures quite effectively. Terrorism remains, essentially, a thriving international business.

EVALUATION

Consider these examples of contemporary terrorisms network and funding:

1. On December 22, 2001, Robert Reid, a British citizen, was restrained by passengers on a Paris-to-Miami American Airlines flight after flight attendants noticed a burning smell and found him using matches to try to light his sneakers. Preliminary FBI tests on the shoes detected the presence of two compounds—PETN (pentaerythritol tetranitrate), one

of the most powerful bases of plastic explosives, and TATP (triacetone triperoxide), another explosive compound. According to reports, Reid was the son of Jamaican and British parents, and had converted to Islam recently networking with individuals in Europe to aid in his efforts to follow the dictates of holy war as a suicide bomber.

2. Israeli naval commandos in rubber boats commandeered a cargo ship in the Red Sea and found 50 tons of Iranian-made weapons meant for the Palestinian Authority, according to the Israeli army chief in a report on January 5, 2002. The cargo included rockets with a range of 12 miles—enough to reach most areas of Israel from Palestinian-controlled territory. The Palestinian Authority vehemently denied involvement in weapons smuggling, and Arafat promised an investigation.

3. An ex-CIA officer discovered that bin Laden's al-Qaeda network had produced a bomb-making guide, written as part of an encyclopedia of the Afghan jihad. Volume one of this encyclopedia is entitled "Explosives," and is, in this officer's words, a "portable university for the militant common man, nothing less than a terrorist's how-to guide." It starts with relatively simple stuff: how to rig letter bombs, exploding books, chairs, sofas, beds, any of a variety of household items. It gradually moves to bigger items: bombs for trucks, cars, houses, buildings, laying out details on fuses, timing switches, even brewing instructions for the terrorist who can't get his hands on Libyan stockpiled plastic Semtex explosives. Copies of this encyclopedia are held by individuals from many countries who have been trained in the jihad spreading from Afghanistan.

The networking of terrorism, including the funding, the training, and the willingness of people from very diverse backgrounds to cooperate to carry out terrorist attacks, raises many concerns for the nations seeking to secure themselves from terrorist attacks. As the events of September 11 graphically demonstrated, terrorist activities are global in reach, in nationality of perpetrators, and in sophistication. The ability to cope depends on the degree to which one is able to understand and predict. As the scope of individuals and nations involved in carrying out attacks broadens, can states adequately predict and thereby protect themselves against future attacks by terrorists trained, armed, and carrying how-to manuals?

SUGGESTED READINGS

Adams, James. *The Financing of Terrorism*. New York: Simon & Schuster, 1986.

Gunaratna, Rohan. *Inside Al-Qaeda: Global Network of Terror*. New York: Columbia Univeristy Press, 2002.

Laqueur, Walter. *The New Terrorism: Fanaticism and the Arms of Mass Destruction*. Oxford: Oxford University Press, 1999.

McCormick, Gordon H. *The Shining Path and the Future of Peru*. Santa Monica, CA: The Rand Corporation, 1990.

———. *From the Sierra to the Cities*. Santa Monica, CA: The Rand Corporation, 1992.

Rosewitz, Barbara, and Gerald F. Seib. "Big Business: Aside From Being a Movement, the PLO is a Financial Giant." *The Wall Street Journal,* July 21, 1986, A28.

Scott, Marvin. "What is the PLO Worth?" *Parade Magazine,* September 21, 1986, 17–28.

Segaller, Stephen. *Invisible Armies: Terrorism in the 1990s*. New York: Harcourt Brace Janovich, 1987.

NOTES

1. When French police moved in to capture Carlos at his headquarters, he escaped in a spectacular shoot-out, during which he killed two French police officers. For further information and commentary, see *Terrorism,* by Thomas P. Raynor (New York: Franklin Watts, 1982).
2. Walter Laqueur, *The Age of Terrorism* (Boston: Little, Brown, 1987), 290. Laqueur describes both the participants and the agenda of this congress in some detail.
3. "Iran's Offer," *U.S. News & World Report,* May 25, 1987, 17.
4. James Adams, *The Financing of Terrorism* (New York: Simon & Schuster, 1986), 16.
5. Adam Cohen, "How Bin Laden Funds His Network," *Time,* October 1, 2001, 63.
6. Adams, *The Financing of Terrorism,* 107.
7. Marvin Scott, "What Is the PLO Worth?" *Parade Magazine,* September 21, 1986, 17.
8. Statement of Lee S. Wolosky to the National Commission on Terrorist Attacks Upon the United States, April 1, 2003.
9. Don van Natta, Jr., "Running Terrorism as a Business," *The New York Times,* November 11, 2001, A1.
10. Judith Miller and Jeff Gerth, "Trade in Honey Is Said to Provide Money and Cover for bin Laden," *The New York Times,* October 11, 2001, A3.
11. *U.S. News & World Report,* May 4, 1987, 16.
12. Adams, *The Financing of Terrorism,* 73.
13. Ibid., 134.
14. Charles J. Hanley, "Reborn Terrorist 'Armies' Target NATO," *The Winston-Salem Journal,* April 9, 1986, 1.
15. Douglas Jehl, "Egyptian Doctor Believed to Be Bin Laden's No. 2," *The New York Times,* September 24, 2001, 1.
16. "Terror's New Wave," *Time,* October 28, 2002, 28.
17. John Arquilla, David Ronfeldt, and Michele Zanini, "Networks, Netwar, and Information-Age Terrorism," in *Terrorism and Counterterrorism: Understanding the New Security Environment,* eds. Russell D. Howard and Reid L. Sawyer (Guilford, CT: McGraw-Hill, 2003), 101.
18. *Ibid.,* 103.
19. *U.S. News & World Report,* May 4, 1987, 17.
20. "Terror's New Wave," *Time,* October 28, 2002, 28–36.
21. Scott, "What Is the PLO Worth?" 8.
22. "Narcotics: Terror's New Ally," *U.S. News & World Report,* May 4, 1987, 37.
23. Rebecca Knickerbocker, "Narcoterrorism," in *Sendero Luminoso and the Threat of Narcoterrorism,* Center for Strategic and International Studies, Washington, DC (The Washington Papers), 1990.

7

Terrorist Training

Key Concepts

safe haven	counterintelligence
explosive bombs	weapons
incendiary bombs	shaped-charge principle
plastic explosives	precision-guided munitions
disguise techniques	organophosphates
clandestine travel	botulinal toxins
sleepers	backpack nukes
recruitment	dirty bombs
communication	threat/hoax
intelligence collection	phases

So in the Libyan fable it is told
That once an eagle, stricken with a dart,
Said, when he saw the fashioning of the shaft,
"With our own feathers, not by others' hands,
Are we now smitten."

Aeschylus

THE "HOW" QUESTIONS

Thus far we have noted who is likely to become a terrorist, who trains a person to become a terrorist, and the purposes for which a person might resort to terrorism. We have, in part, attempted to answer the *who* question (who becomes a terrorist and who supports him or her) and some of the *why* question. Part of the *where* questions—relating to where terrorists operate and where they are trained—have also been discussed.

There remains a need to discuss the important question of *how* terrorists operate. How are they trained—at what sites and on what topics? How are they equipped, in terms of weapons available to them? How do they tend to operate—that is, what tactics do they choose and why do they choose to use or not use certain weapons?

Some of these *how* questions can be answered simply by listing the important points. Others, such as those relating to the type of weaponry available to contemporary terrorists, require considerable explanation. None of these questions needs be answered in depth here, for two reasons. One is that this is, at best, a cursory look at terrorism, a brief sketch of only a minimum of the points relating to this complicated subject. The other is that, just as terrorism is itself in considerable flux today, so the lists of training sites and topics of today's terrorists may well be inadequate for understanding and predicting the actions of tomorrow's terrorist. The topics and tactics are unlikely to become obsolete, but the list may well be expanded as the twenty-first century unfolds.

TRAINING SITES

Until the final decade in the twentieth century, more than a dozen nations were offering training camps for terrorists globally. Some of these camps were specifically for terrorists, whereas others were camps used by the host country for military or intelligence training as well as by terrorists.

Figure 7.1 contains a list that, although not comprehensive, details most of the major training facilities for terrorists (known to intelligence services) until the collapse of the Soviet Union in 1990. These former sites are listed by country, rather than by size or affiliation with particular terrorists organizations, to demonstrate the geographic distribution of these camps.

A number of countries from the 1960s through the 1990s operated training facilities within the structure of their own military services. Names for these terrorist

Nation	Location of Training Camp(s)
Bulgaria	Varna
Cuba	Camp Matanzos
Czechoslovakia	Ostrova and Karlovy Vary[*,†]
East Germany	Pankow[*,†,‡,§]
Hungary	Lake Belaton
Lebanon	Boalbok
Libya	Res Hilal[*,†,§]
	Misurata
	Sirte
	Tameona
	Focra
North Korea	Three major centers (names not available at this time)
South Yemen	Khayat[*,†]
Syria	Bekaa Valley (area under Syrian control in Lebanon)[*,†,§]

FIGURE 7.1

Note: Four symbols have been used in this list to indicate additional assistance given at and through these camps to terrorists.
[*] Terrorists were also provided with arms at these camps.
[†] Money was channeled to terrorists from the host country, usually through these training facilities.
[‡] Host country shared its personnel with the terrorist in the training camp.
[§] Host country provided intelligence information to terrorists at the camp.

training facilities are still not readily available for release to the general public. But a list of training sites would be inadequate without including at least the names of such countries.

> *Algeria* offered arms, training, funding (occasionally totaling between $5 and $7 million per year), a safe haven for terrorists, diplomatic assistance, and even assistance in acquiring passports.
>
> *Iran,* in addition to providing training to terrorists, also gave funding (already discussed in a previous chapter), a safe haven for terrorists on the run, and passport and diplomatic assistance.
>
> *Iraq,* in spite of the drain on its resources made by its war with Iran, still provided some training for terrorists, as well as arms, funding, a safe haven, and diplomatic and passport assistance. This did not end with Iraq's defeat in the war with Kuwait.
>
> *The People's Republic of China* began to offer both training and arms to terrorists during the 1980s and continued through the beginning of the twenty-first century.

This is not, of course, a comprehensive list of all locations at which terrorists received training during the latter part of the twentieth century. Some nations were more discrete than others in the training opportunities they provided. Moreover, information concerning such camps necessarily came from some national intelligence services, meaning that the information was certainly biased according to how that nation defined terrorism. It is unlikely, for instance, that such an intelligence assessment would list "friendly" nations as hosts for terrorist camps, instead citing such camps as training sources for legitimate insurgent or revolutionary groups.

In addition, the dramatic changes that occurred in the world in the early 1990s seriously impacted the ability of the listed states to offer training, arms, or specific support to terrorist groups. Of the states on this list, only a few still offered significant levels of training and support in the 1990s. Iran remained a major supporter, providing weapons, funds, and training primarily to Hezbollah, but also to the PIJ, Ahmad Jibril's PFLP–GC, the Kurdistan Workers' Party, and of course, HAMAS. Iraq, too, continued to defy international concern, as articulated through UN resolutions, and offered training facilities and safe haven to several groups, such as the Palestine Liberation Front (Abu Abbas's organization), the Abu Nidal Organization (ANO), and the Arab Liberation Front.

Cuba, however, could no longer financially or politically afford to flout Western censure by openly offering training to terrorist groups. While it continued in the 1990s to offer safe haven to members of the ETA (Basque separatists) and to members of the Manuel Rodriguez Patriotic Front (Chilean insurgent group), as well as to the Revolutionary Armed Forces of Colombia (FARC) and the National Liberation Army (from Colombia), Cuba could no longer provide weapons or training on the scale that had been available before the fall of its sponsor, the Soviet Union.

Nations such as Syria and North Korea became similarly unable or unwilling to openly offer terrorist training and support after 1987. Although Syria continued to offer **safe haven,** or *sanctuary,* to the PFLP–GC, HAMAS, the PIJ, the JRA, and other groups, the training assistance and access to weapons was no longer made freely available. The political costs, lacking the shelter of a superpower, were simply too high.

Perhaps one of the most dramatic highlights of the diminishing role of states involved in providing sanctuary to terrorists came in August 1994, when the Sudanese government handed over notorious terrorist Illich Ramirez Sanchez (a.k.a. "Carlos"). Carlos had been given sanctuary in the Sudan in 1993, but was peacefully handed over to French authorities one year later. Open sanctuary to internationally known terrorists is obviously less attractive a policy option today.

Training camps offered to terrorists today are less likely to be state funded, but are located in states where no government controls all of the territory effectively or in states where the governments will permit the establishment of such camps but do not staff or support them. Instead, as noted in the previous chapter, individuals and groups with funding and leadership are establishing camps in these countries, with often no more than the tacit consent of the state.

After the September 11 attacks, information surfaced about terrorist training camps in Afghanistan established by al-Qaeda under bin Laden's leadership and funding. Islamic militants from more than 40 countries have received training in these camps, which the Taliban permitted to operate for years. U.S. bombing attacks in the fall of 2001 devastated many of these facilities. Although such attacks were aggressive acts of war in the territory of another state, the United States stated, and the international community in UN debates agreed, that the willingness of a state to allow the training of terrorists in its territory made that government's leadership responsible for the actions of the camps' trainees. Since the Taliban refused to help to close the camps and turn over the al-Qaeda leadership, including bin Laden, to U.S.-led forces, the destruction of the camps was argued to be a legal means to end a form of state support for terrorism.

Unfortunately, terrorist camps of the sort built in the mountains of Afghanistan were not buildings, but were caves that had existed for centuries and were merely reinforced and used to harbor the training facilities. Thus, the bombs certainly made the use of those particular caves as terrorist camps impossible but did not necessarily cost the terrorist leadership much in terms of lost facilities. The pounding with bombs of those camps was satisfying to governments angry about the existence of such training facilities, but it did not necessarily end the camps. It merely rearranged the rocks and made access more difficult. Indications initially were that most personnel had fled in relative safety to neighboring states, possibly to regroup and rebuild in another passive host state.

TRAINING TOPICS: WHAT DO THEY LEARN AT CAMP?

In 2001, four people were convicted by a New York court for their roles in the August 1998 bombing of the American embassies in Kenya and Tanzania, a double atrocity that cost 224 lives and apparently took five years to plan. From this case, and a separate hearing in New York on the conspiracy by a group of Algerians to set off a suitcase bomb at Los Angeles airport at the turn of the millennium, evidence emerged about what is taught at training camps today.

One witness, who gave evidence for the prosecution, disclosed that he had received six months of training at a camp in Afghanistan in 1998. He, along with volunteers from many other places including Algeria, Jordan, Yemen, Saudi Arabia, France, and Chechnya, were trained in how to blow up the infrastructure of a country, including "airports, railroads, and large corporations."[1] They were also taught how to wage urban warfare by blocking roads, storming buildings, and assassinating individuals.

Terrorists do not go to training camps just to acquire arms, intelligence information, or funding. They undergo, at most such camps a rigorous program of activities gaining proficiency in a variety of skills. A brief review of some of the topics taught at these training camps provides useful insights into the type of tactics that terrorists employ in their ventures.

Such a review of topics also yields a better understanding of the depth and breadth of the training available to terrorists today. In fact, many terrorists are more highly trained in a wider array of tactics than the police forces of the nations whose task it often is to combat terrorism.

Again, the following sketch of training topics is not intended to be exhaustive. It is merely meant to offer a rudimentary understanding of the scope of training available today, with the intent of making one more aware of the potential array of tactics from which contemporary terrorists may choose.

Arson and Bombs

Since about 50 percent of all terrorist incidents involve bombings, this ranks as one of the most prevalent and most popular training topics. Terrorists are, as a rule, taught how to make and use two types of bombs: explosive and incendiary. **Explosive bombs** are *generally of either fragmentation or blast type.* The most commonly utilized fragmentation bomb at these camps is the pipe bomb, usually employing gunpowder as the explosive agent. Terrorists are taught how to use commercial- or military-type dynamite with a blasting cap for detonation in the creation and use of blast-type bombs.

Information about camps in Afghanistan yielded useful insights into the training in bombs. The encyclopedia of Jihad mentioned earlier, for example, gave directions in Arabic paired with diagrams for a host of explosive devices, including instructions on how to turn a wide range of common objects, such as hairbrushes, radios, and whistles, into lethal devices. According to experts who reviewed portions of the information on explosives, the writers had obviously gotten their hands on, among other things, U.S. special forces manuals, training guides the CIA produced in the late 1950s and early 1960s, and other explosives literature available from Paladin Press, the militia's favorite guide to weaponry and guerrilla tactics.[2]

Terrorists are also taught how to create and use incendiary bombs, as such bombs are quickly and easily constructed. **Incendiary bombs** are simply *fire bombs, generating extensive fire damage.* These are also inexpensive yet capable of inflicting extensive damage. Terrorists are often taught, for instance, how to make a simple fire bomb, consisting of a glass bottle filled with an inflammable mixture, to which a fuse is attached. Fire bombs can vary in sophistication from time-delay fused and barometric bombs to fertilizer mixed with fuel oil. The bomb blast in Oklahoma City in 1995 was clearly the latter type of incendiary bomb, simple in construction but incredibly destructive.

Not every training camp offers instruction on all such bombs, nor is every trainee instructed in the construction and use of all bomb types. But the array of weapons of destruction from just instruction in arson and bomb usage is of great use to every terrorist recruit.

Plastic explosives, *made of plastique,* are the newest editions to the weapons for which terrorists may receive training in camps. Access to such material is supposedly restricted, but Libya's stockpile of the plastique Semtex made it possible for terrorists to use this more sophisticated explosive, which is virtually undetectable by most modern airport security devices. Moreover, as the capture of Robert Reid mentioned earlier indicates, chemical equivalents of Semtex are also in use, though not always with sufficient training, as was clearly the case with Reid.

Assassination and Ambush Techniques

Terrorists are usually taught how to penetrate personal security systems in order to kill at close hand. They are instructed in the proficient use of handguns and silencers. Methods of clandestine approach, disguise, and escape are generally incorporated into this part of every terrorist's training. Increasingly, modern terrorists in some parts of the world, notably Central America, are being instructed in the commission of flamboyant, execution-style assassinations, instead of the unobtrusive-gunman-in-a-crowd techniques favored by the anarchists of earlier years.

Extortion, Bank and Armored Car Robberies

Contemporary training courses for terrorists often now include information on how to raise money for indigent terrorist groups. Among the instruction offered in this part of the curriculum is information on how to extort money from wealthy sources, usually the families or employers of kidnap victims.

In the 1970s, this was a source of considerable wealth, particularly for groups operating in Central or South America. U.S. firms in these areas were at first willing to pay large sums for the safe return of their kidnapped executives. However, during the 1980s, businesses began making it a formal part of their policy *not* to submit to ransom demands. As a result, kidnapping for ransom money became for a time a less profitable enterprise.

In the 1980s, terrorists were trained in the use of kidnap victims for the extortion of *political* rewards or concessions as well as money. Although many governments have a states policy of not conceding to terrorist extortion demands, most have from time to time found it expedient to yield rather than allow a kidnap situation to drag on indefinitely or to end disastrously.

Events in the Philippines, however, particularly the actions of the Abu Sayyaf Group during the late 1990s, give credence to the credible and profitable use by terrorist groups of this tactic, at least in the kidnap of tourists for ransom. Libya's payment of a ransom in 2000 for an international group of tourists held by this organization made this clearly a low-risk, high-profit operation.

Disguise Techniques, Clandestine Travel, Recruitment, and Communications

Terrorists today are trained in many of the same techniques the counterintelligence services utilize. They are taught methods of **disguise techniques** and **clandestine travel,** including *how to travel inconspicuously* (contrary to popular belief, an Arab engaged in a terrorist attack does *not* routinely wear a burnoose, nor does he or she travel by camel). Instruction is also given in *the procuring of false passport and identification papers,* and *the skill of altering one's appearance to permit one to slip through surveillance nets.*

The trainees are taught how to blend in with the country in which they will operate. As one official speaking of a cell uncovered by the French put it, "They all carefully applied the technique taught in Afghan camps: act, look, talk and dress like the impious and corrupt people around, in order to better plan the blow against them."[3] With training like this, the people who carry out terrorist attacks are most often those you would never suspect, the handful of **"sleepers,"** *agents recruited, trained, sent to blend in unnoticed, but not put into operation for a period of time.* Hiding among millions of potential suspects and victims, such sleepers, if well trained in blending in may evade security systems for years, as some of those who carried out the September 11 attacks clearly did.

Most terrorists are also trained in the techniques of **recruitment,** as all terrorist groups must seek to *draw in new members* but must constantly beware of the dangers of counterintelligence penetration. The screening and selection of potential recruits is thus a vital talent for every successful terrorist group.

Terrorists are also trained in sophisticated methods of **communication.** Recognizing the importance of *reliable and secure means of communicating during a terrorist incident,* leaders of terrorist organizations are having larger numbers of their recruits trained in the advanced technology of communication. Not for the modern terrorists are the simple two-way radios still favored by many police forces.

Intelligence Collection and Counterintelligence Methods

Not surprisingly, many modern terrorists are more skilled at the collection of intelligence information than are many members of the intelligence organizations of some nations. Terrorists can now receive comprehensive training not only in the techniques of intelligence gathering, but also in the equally important methods of counterintelligence operations.

Intelligence collection instruction involves teaching terrorists *how to infiltrate target areas, gather relevant data, and return that information to headquarters.* The use of codes and the translation of intelligence data bits into comprehensible information is basic to the education of today's terrorist.

Terrorists are also being taught methods of **counterintelligence,** including *how to disseminate misinformation designed to confuse their enemies.* Such instruction generally includes as well information on how to *protect the organization from infiltration by police, military, and governmental intelligence operatives.*

This does not mean, of course, that all terrorists are trained in all of these methods. Most organizations can usually afford to train only a carefully selected number in the more sophisticated techniques. But the ability of most terrorist organizations to have at least a few such skilled recruits is becoming a matter of survival. Lack of information or misinformation can seriously cripple an organization's ability to carry out a successful operation. So the extent to which a terrorist group can field operatives skilled in intelligence matters is crucial to that group's success today.

Weapons

This last item is by no means the least important in the repertoire acquired by terrorists in training facilities. The number and variety of **weapons** available to terrorists through the different training camps over time certainly has varied considerably, making generalizations difficult. Without detailing all of the weapons available to modern terrorists (which is covered in the following section), it is well to note the types of weapons for which terrorists are being trained.

In addition to being trained in the use of small firearms, including pistols, rifles, and sawed-off shotguns, terrorists are currently being trained in the use of automatic and semiautomatic weapons. Training is regularly given in the use of machine guns and machine pistols, particularly those manufactured in the former Soviet Union and several other countries in the former Eastern Europe, including Poland and the Czech Republic, and those produced in Israel, the United Kingdom, and the United States.

Training is also available in light-tank antirocket launchers, principally the Soviet-made RPG-7 and the U.S. LAW. Use of the French Strim F-1 has also been taught at some camps. Such weapons are portable and easy to conceal. Surface-to-air missiles (SAMs), known to be in the hands of terrorists, are also a part of some training programs, including those led by the United States.

There is now evidence of training being given to terrorists in the use of some of the more exotic weapons, such as chemical or biological agents. While use of such weapons remains relatively infrequent today, the use of sarin gas by the AUM Shinrikyo group in Japan on the subway in the middle of the 1990s opened the specter of vast destruction presented by such weapons in the hands of individuals willing to use them. Moreover, it should be noted that *states* in the twentieth century have been distressingly willing to use such weapons in wars (biological and chemical weapons were used in the world wars) and internally against dissident populations (as the Iraqis did to the Kurds).

The anthrax attacks in the United States following the September 11 events should not, therefore, have been a complete surprise to government experts, but it was. Agencies in the United States charged with responding to such a crisis have admitted to being unprepared to deal with it appropriately, giving those responsible for the attack a fairly low-cost victory in terms of the disruption of the system. Part of the problem, as these agencies assessed their responses, seems to have been that they were preparing to respond to a massive attack by an enemy at war, who would seek destruction by the use of such a weapon. Terrorists, however, would seek only disruption, inflicting pain but not destruction—goals which the U.S. response allowed them to achieve.

The training process for terrorists appears quite comprehensive, even formidable in its potential for turning out proficient terrorists. The camps created by bin Laden in post-Soviet Afghanistan became a kind of "university of terrorism, offering courses in murder and mayhem to which radical Islamic movements all over the world were invited."[4]

CASE STUDY September 11, 2001, Attacks on the United States

In the bloodiest day on American soil since the Civil War, the United States experienced a terrorist attack in two cities, New York City and Washington, DC, which resulted in thousands of casualties and billions of dollars in damage. Although the investigation continues concerning the individuals responsible for the attack, the events chronicled offer insight into the most devastating terrorist attack to date, one that triggered a war on terrorism to be fought, under UN auspices, by a coalition of states from across the world who share the United States's desire to end the potential for future such acts.

Sequence of Events

The cycle of events on September 11, 2001, began with the departure of two planes from Boston's Logan Airport. One was a Boeing 767, American Airlines Flight 11, bound for Los Angeles with 81 passengers, which took off at 7:59 a.m. and headed west over the Adirondacks before taking a sudden turn south and diving toward the heart of New York City. The second flight involved in the incident was a United Airlines Flight 175, leaving Boston at 7:58 a.m. Meanwhile, American Flight 77 had left Dulles Airport in Washington, DC, and United Flight 93 left Newark at 8:01 a.m., bound for San Francisco. Because all of these flights were transcontinental, they were heavily loaded with fuel.

At 8:45 a.m., American Airlines Flight 11 hit the World Trade Center's (WTC) north tower, ripping through the building's skin and setting its upper floors ablaze. Bits of plane, a tire, office furniture, glass, a hand, a leg, whole bodies began falling all around, stunning the people in the streets who had at first assumed it was perhaps a sonic boom, or a construction accident, or at worst a dreadful airline accident. Inside the building, people began to run down the flights of stairs from the offices below the crash point. The lights stayed on, but the lower stairs were filled with water from broken pipes and sprinklers. The smell of jet fuel filled the building as hallways collapsed and flames erupted. Others leaped to their deaths from the 110-story tower as the fires trapped them in the upper floors. Pedestrians watched in horror as a man tried to shimmy down the outside of the tower, making it about three floors before flipping backward to the ground. Many escaping the tower were burned over much of their bodies, with hair burned off and compound fractures from falls in the plunge down to escape.

At 7:58 a.m., United Airlines Flight 175, also a Boeing 767 filled with fuel for the transcontinental flight from Boston to Los Angeles with 65 passengers aboard, left the airport about 20 minutes behind flight schedule. After passing the Massachusetts-Connecticut border, it made a 30-degree turn, then an even sharper turn, and flew down through Manhattan, between the buildings, slamming into the south tower of the WTC at 9:06 a.m. The short delay at the Boston airport caused this flight to hit the Trade Center more than 20 minutes after the first crash, a delay that may have saved thousands of lives, because it allowed that much time for escape from the blazing north tower.

After the initial impact in the north tower, employees ran to the windows and saw debris falling, and sheets of white building material, and bodies. As one employee, Gilbert Richard Ramirez, employed by BlueCross/BlueShield on the 20th floor, noted, "someone pulled an emergency alarm switch, but nothing happened. Someone else broke into the emergency phone, but it was dead. People began to say their prayers."

Stumbling out of the office doors, down the smoky stairs, those fleeing saw suffering on every side: people who had been badly burned, their skin appearing to be dripping or peeling from their bodies. Apparently some were thrust out of windows by the force of the blast, and bodies rained down on those below as others jumped to escape the inferno engulfing the building.

Each of the towers, more than 200 feet wide on each side, contained a central steel core surrounded by open office space. Eighteen-inch steel tubes ran vertically along the outside, providing much of the support for the buildings. One of the planes damaged the central core, redistributing the weight to the outer steel tubes, which were slowly deformed by the added weight and the heat of the fires. Steel starts to bend at 1,000 degrees Fahrenheit. The floors above where the second plane hit in 1 World Trade Center—each floor weighing millions of pounds—were resting on steel that was softening from the heat of the burning jet fuel, softening until the girders could no longer bear the load. As one retired ATF (Bureau of Alcohol, Tobacco, and Firearms) investigator described it, "all that steel turns to spaghetti, and then all of a sudden that structure is untenable, and the weight starts bearing down on floors that were not designed to hold that weight, and you start having collapse."[5] Because each floor dropped down onto the one below, the building did not topple—it came straight down, flattening all of the floors below, with all of the people trapped on those floors.

At 10:00 a.m., the sudden collapse of the south tower trapped hundreds of rescue workers below, in addition to thousands of workers in the building. The debris from this collapse gutted the 4 World Trade Center building below it. Twenty-nine minutes later, weakened by its imploded twin, the north tower collapsed, pouring more debris and crushing buildings and rescuers below. The third building to collapse was 7 World Trade Center, which fell at 5:25 p.m.

The first crash was shocking, but the second changed everything. The event was not a dreadful accident or an isolated incident. Facing the catastrophe and the threat clearly demonstrated, the system responded with emergency plans. Traffic stopped—the bridges and tunnels in the city were shut down at 9:35 a.m. as warnings were issued. The Empire State Building, the Metropolitan Museum of Art, and the even the United Nations buildings were evacuated. First the airports in New York, then Washington, and then all airports nationwide were closed for the first time in the nation's history.

As the second plane was crashing into the south tower, President Bush was in an elementary school in Sarasota, Florida, meeting second graders. Informed of the first crash just after he arrived, news of the second plane striking the north tower came as he was watching the students' reading drills. The president continued to listen to the students, but at a news conference after his time with the students, he ordered a massive manhunt to find the people responsible for the attacks. The bomb dogs checked Air Force One again and an extra fighter escort was added.

The attacks continued in a different city: Washington, DC. At 9:40 a.m., American Airlines Flight 77 hit the Pentagon. The jet came in, its wings wobbling and appeared to be aimed straight for the Pentagon. The plane was about 50 feet off the deck when it came in, sounding to spectators on the ground as though the pilot had the throttle wide open. The plane rolled left, back to the right, then the edge of the wing touched down at the helicopter pad in front of the Pentagon's side, and the plane cartwheeled into the building.

Within minutes, a "credible threat" prompted the evacuation of the White House and eventually all of the federal office buildings, including both the State and Justice departments. Although Washington had contingency plans for emergencies such as this, the chaos on the streets by 10:45 a.m. gave evidence that the plans needed improvement. Traffic in and around the Capitol and the government buildings was gridlocked by 11 a.m., with people trying to leave. Although most plans to evacuate government leaders, including the vice president and the Senate's president pro tempore (fourth in line to the presidency), worked fairly efficiently, most government workers were unable to escape the city. Security units had closed both the 14th Street Bridge and the Arlington Memorial Bridge leading into Virginia and past the Pentagon, as well as the airports and Union Station.

The aircraft carrying Federal Reserve Chairman Alan Greenspan en route from Switzerland was ordered to turn back. Greenspan, however, reached his vice chairman Roger Ferguson by phone and Ferguson coordinated contacts with Reserve banks and governors around the country to ensure that U.S. banks would continue to function. Vice President Dick Cheney told the president, who was returning from Florida, that law enforcement and security agencies believed the White House and possibly Air Force One were targets, suggesting that Bush head to a safe military base. Air Force One made a brief touchdown at Barksdale Air Force Base outside of Shreveport, Louisiana, at 11:45 a.m., with fighter jets hovering beside each wing during the descent.

By this time a third attack had occurred as well. United Flight 93, which had taken off from Newark, New Jersey, headed for San Francisco, took a sudden, violent left turn as it passed south of Cleveland, Ohio, and headed back into Pennsylvania. Although air-traffic controllers tried frantically to raise the crew via radio as the plane and its 38 passengers passed Pittsburgh, there was no response from the plane. At 9:58 a.m., the Westmoreland County emergency-operations center, 35 miles southeast of Pittsburgh, received a frantic cell phone call from a man who said he was locked in the restroom aboard United Flight 93, who repeated frantically, "We are being hijacked!"

Many citizens later reported having cell phone messages from loved ones on the plane, who described the planned efforts of the passengers to thwart the hijackers' intent, if possible. The plane flew over woodland, pastures, and cornfields, crashing into a reclaimed section of an old coal strip mine at 10:06 a.m., barely two miles short of the Shanksville-Stonycreek School with its 501 students.

Insights into Those Responsible

At Dulles International Airport in Virginia, two polite young men of Arab origin handed over their prepaid $2400 each first-class tickets to the American Airlines agent. Both men appeared to be around 20 years of age, had valid identification, and gave the right answers to standard security questions. The two brothers, Nawaq Alhamzi and Salem Alhamzi, boarded American Airlines Flight 77 for Los Angeles. They were 2 of the 19 men who hijacked the four planes on September 11.

The real names of those 19 involved are not positively known at present, since intelligence officials believe many used false identities. On the American Airlines Flight 11, which crashed into the north tower of the WTC, Mohamed Atta, Satam Al Suqami, Waleed M. Alshehri, Wail Alshehri, and Abdulaziz Alomari were the names of those identified as those in the cell who carried out the hijacking. Hani Hanjour, Khalid Al-Midhar, Majed Moqed, Nawaq Alhamzi, and Salem Alhamzi carried out the hijacking on American Airlines Flight 77, which crashed into the Pentagon. Aboard United Airlines Flight 175, Marwan Al-Shehhi, Hamza Alghamdi, Ahmed Alghamdi, Fayez Ahmed, and Mohald Alshehri hijacked the plane and crashed it into the south tower of the WTC. Only 4 have been identified as being aboard the flight that crashed in Pennsylvania, United Airlines Flight 93: Ziad Jarrahi, Ahmed Alnami, Ahmed Alhaznawi, and Saeed Alghamdi.

As investigators and intelligence services worldwide rushed to trace the movements of these 19 men, it became increasingly clear that they were part of a much larger network and that years of planning had been a part of this operation. Hani Hanjour, for example, may have lived in Arizona since 1990. He took flight lessons nearby in 1996 and 1997. Nawaq Alhamzi joined him later at this location. Nawaq and Khalid Al-Midhar lived together in San Diego, California, from 1999 to 2000 and took a few flying lessons from a school close to their home. From July 2000 until September 2001, Mohamed Atta and Marwan Al-Shehhi traveled around South Florida, taking flying lessons and meeting accomplices. All 5 Flight 175 hijackers and some of those on Flight 93 appear to have lived in Delray Beach, Florida, and in nearby Deerfield Beach during the summer of 2001.

U.S. authorities believe Mohamed Atta was the ringleader of the 19 hijackers, but that he was working under the direction of someone from the network of Osama bin Laden and his al-Qaeda organization. The 19 blended in well with their American neighbors, living in inexpensive apartments, eating pizzas, wearing khakis and polos, and working out at local gyms. Experts think that it cost at least several thousand dollars to carry out the attack and that the money for both the attack and the support network for the agents in place came from bin Laden's resources.

This whole operation demonstrated to the world that terrorists were indeed capable of carefully planned, brilliantly executed relatively low-cost attacks. Reconnaissance, timing, and planning were clearly techniques with which terrorists were becoming increasingly familiar. In time, an increasingly sophisticated arsenal of weapons would make such an attack many times more lethal. ❑

POTENTIAL FOR DESTRUCTION: A TERRORIST'S ARSENAL

Before examining the tactics chosen by trained terrorists, it is appropriate to look briefly at the arsenal of weapons available to the terrorist today. From contact in training camps, certain weapons are favored by some terrorist groups. Other weapons have gained popularity due to their proven effectiveness or their relative availability.

Explosives

Terrorists worldwide continue to use explosives, frequently in the form of homemade devices. These are most often blast rather than fragmentation bombs. Explosives, as Kupperman and Trent have pointed out, "offer many advantages to a terrorist: they are available everywhere and crude bombs can be fabricated locally; they are concealable and can be readily disguised so that X-ray and magnometer inspections are ineffective defenses."[6] As the capture of Robert Reid mentioned earlier demonstrated, more sophisticated types of explosives are already in use, fortunately not always effectively. Also note that the planes flown in the September 11 attacks were fully fueled "bombs" flown into their targets with devastating results—and without having to smuggle bombs aboard the planes.

The destructive quality of bombs does not depend necessarily on the sophistication of their construction. Trucks packed with forms of TNT have created substantial damage and caused innumerable deaths. One truck laden with fertilizer and gasoline in Oklahoma City in 1995 destroyed a federal building and left hundreds of casualties, dead or injured.

But the ability of a small amount of explosive to create a large amount of damage has been enhanced by terrorists, using the **shaped-charge principle,** *focusing the force of the explosion in a desired direction.* Terrorists have shown themselves to be proficient in the use of both conical or "beehive" bombs (which increase the charge's penetration), and linear bombs, which have a "cutting" effect.

Small Arms

In recent years, terrorists have continued to use pistols, rifles, and such crude weapons as the sawed-off shotgun. The supply of such weapons is vast, the cost relatively small, and the training for their use fairly simple to accomplish, making these popular weapons for small or underfinanced terrorist groups.

Handguns continue to be the weapon of the political assassin, but more importantly in terms of modern terrorism, they are often the preferred weapons of those taking hostages. Moreover, unlike the automatic weapon, laws limiting the sale and possession of handguns are either very lax or nonexistent in many countries.

Automatic Weapons

The automatic weapon is essentially an antipersonnel weapon, but it has also been used by terrorists to assault cars and even airplanes. It is a favorite weapon of terrorist groups for several reasons: its availability, ease of concealment, high rate of fire, and perhaps most importantly, its psychological impact on unarmed civilians or lightly armed security forces.

There are two basic types of automatic weapon: the assault rifle and the submachine gun.[7] Both are easily obtained through arms dealers or the military of various nations, particularly since the demise of the Soviet Union. The Soviet AK-7 is one of the most popular weapons of terrorists today, due to its accessibility as well as to its performance record. Assault rifles can be obtained in either their military form, such as the AK-7 assault rifle, or in their semiautomatic commercial version.

In recent years, the "little brother" of the submachine gun, the machine pistol, has become popular among terrorist groups and police forces. This is particularly true of European terrorists, where such weapons can easily be procured.

Portable Rockets

In recent years, training of terrorists in the use of **precision-guided munitions** (PGMs)—*devices that can launch missiles whose trajectories can be corrected in flight*—has increased dramatically. Most, but not all, PGMs are portable, meaning they are fairly lightweight and can be both carried and operated by one or perhaps two persons.

Such weapons are designed to destroy aircraft and, on the battlefield, tanks. There are documented incidents, to date, in which terrorists have attempted to use weapons such as the Soviet-made SA-7 (code-named *Strela*) against aircraft. In 1973, for instance, a Palestinian group planned to use two SA-7's to shoot down an El Al airliner near Rome, but the attempt was foiled. A similar plot in Kenya in 1975 also failed, but by 1978 the SA-7 was apparently used successfully against a commercial airliner.[8]

Of the surface-to-air rocket systems currently available, the most popular appear to be those of the United States, Russia, and the United Kingdom. The US-made Stinger (the successor of the Redeye), the aforementioned Russian-made SA-7, and the British Blowpipe have achieved a considerable degree of popularity among contemporary terrorists.

Most such rockets employ infrared devices, heat-seeking sensors that, as a rule, serve to guide the missile to a heat source, presumably the aircraft engine. They generally weigh between 30 and 40 pounds, with an effective range of at least several kilometers.

Worst of all, from a security standpoint, such weapons are becoming all-too-readily available to terrorist organizations. It is interesting to note the observations made by Rand Corporation's terrorist expert, Brian Jenkins, two decades ago, with regard to the proliferation of these weapons:

> First-generation PGMs such as the Strela and the Redeye will be available to 30 or 40 countries in the Third World. It is not realistic to expect that all of these countries will maintain strict security measures; some may find it in their interest to make these weapons available to nongovernmental groups. If we postulate a conservative loss rate worldwide by theft or diversion of one-tenth of one percent over the next five years, then man-portable PGMs will be "loose" in the hundreds by the beginning of the 1980's.[9]

Such weapons *were* loose in at least the hundreds if not the thousands in the 1980s. Not only did Third World nations allow and even assist in their dissemination, but Western nations whose laws forbade the "sharing" of such weaponry were guilty of allowing these missile systems to come into the hands of terrorists.

Less sophisticated but about as lethal are the light antitank rocket launchers, such as the U.S. Viper and the Russian RPG-7, which have been used with increasing frequency by terrorists. Such systems are compact, self-contained, lightweight, and easily transported (once dismantled) in a suitcase. Terrorists could use such weapons with devastating effect against limousines, aircraft, transformer banks, vehicles transporting radioactive wastes, and oil or natural gas pipelines.

"Science Fiction" Weapons

Robert Kupperman, in a report prepared for the Department of Justice in October 1977, made a useful analysis of the devastation that could be wrought by chemical, biological, and radiological weapons and nuclear explosives:

> In terms of fatalities, conventional weapons such as machine guns and small bombs constitute the least threat. They can produce tens or hundreds of casualties in a single incident. Chemical weapons such as nerve agents constitute a substantially greater threat, being capable of producing hundreds to thousands of fatalities. A small nuclear bomb could produce a hundred thousand casualties, but biological agents—both toxins and living organisms—can rival thermonuclear weapons, providing the possibility of producing hundreds of thousands to several millions of casualties in a single incident.[10]

Let us first consider the possibilities (for as yet they remain primarily possibilities, with only a few attempts at use, fortunately) of a terrorist group using chemical or biological agents of mass destruction. That most groups have not yet done so is less a factor of the difficulties and dangers involved in producing such weapons than in the problems in effectively disseminating the toxic material.

There are tens of thousands of highly toxic chemicals, some of which are available to the general public in the form of, for instance, rodenticides. **Organophosphates,** *the so-called nerve agents,* could be synthesized by a moderately competent chemist with limited laboratory facilities. Indeed, for terrorist groups lacking even such a chemist and laboratory, some forms of these agents, such as TEPP (tetrathylpyrophosphate), are available commercially as insecticides.

The use of an organophosphate by a group in Japan in 1995 demonstrated both the effectiveness of the agent and the vulnerability of major urban centers to such attacks. The injury to thousands, generated by a relatively small amount of substance, makes clear that Kupperman's assessment was distressingly accurate. The relatively small number of casualties from the incident is attributable to the inability of the AUM Shinrikyo to place the agent in the appropriate place for maximum dissemination, according to experts.

The dissemination of such agents of destruction is not simple. Aerosol dispersal would be difficult and risky in some areas, although subways, trains, planes, and buses make inviting targets. Contamination of a large water supply is normally inhibited by such factors as hydrolysis, chlorination, and the required minimum quantity of toxic material per gallon of water for effectiveness.

Similar problems inhibit the dissemination, if not the production, of even more lethal **botulinal toxins,** *highly toxic nerve agents created by anerobic bacterium,* often found in spoiled or ill-prepared food. Although compared to the most toxic nerve agent, botulinal toxin is at least a thousand times more dangerous, there are problems in the dissemination of botulinal toxins. Dissemination through the food supply is an obvious route, and one that concerns the food industries.

Unfortunately, botulinal toxins are easily produced. There is a vast array of literature on their growth, serological typing for virulence, the techniques for continuous culturing, separation, and purification of the toxin. The toxin that causes botulism is produced by the organism *Clostridium botulinium,* which is found almost everywhere.

Kupperman produced an interesting data set for the comparison of the lethality of such weapons with more conventional (and better-understood) weapons. According to his data, although it would take *320 million* grams of fuel air explosives (such as the crude truck load of fertilizer and gasoline used in Oklahoma City) to produce heavy casualties within a square-mile area, it would take only *8 grams* of anthrax spores to produce the same approximate casualty count if properly disseminated.

There are several important limits on the usefulness of this anthrax data. First, agencies in the United States assessing the response to the anthrax attack in the fall of 2001 noted that most U.S. assessment of the toxicity of anthrax was probably inaccurate, grossly overestimated in fact. Much of the research on this agent was based on the casualties reported by a few incidents, including one in the former Soviet Union, which apparently did not include the number infected who recovered with treatment. When all that is reported is the number who died, the fatality rate appears effectively 100 percent, making the agent appear incredibly lethal. In the wake of the 2001 attacks, it became apparent that most of the research on this agent is not accurate and needs reexamination.

Moreover, Kupperman's data set postulates *ideal* conditions (including requirements for dissemination), making his projections somewhat suspect since such conditions rarely exist. Nevertheless, such studies highlight how powerful these small but toxic agents potentially are, as well as suggest that certain chemical and biological weapons are potentially even more lethal than nuclear devices.[11]

Many chemical and biological agents are fairly readily produced or obtained, often through legitimate sources. They are also incredibly deadly, capable of killing thousands, even hundreds of thousands, of people. Thus far, the difficult step of dissemination may be one of the only remaining reasons why contemporary terrorists have not yet used these agents of mass destruction. The success of the use of such an agent in Japan in 1995 may well encourage other groups to begin to use these "science fiction" weapons.

Brian Jenkins, in 1975, suggested another reason might exist that inhibits terrorists' use of such weapons. According to his understanding of terrorism at that time:

> Incidents in which terrorists have deliberately tried to kill large numbers of people or cause widespread damage are relatively rare. Terrorists want a lot of people watching, not a lot of people dead—which may explain why, apart from the technical difficulties involved, they have not already used chemical or bacteriological weapons, or conventional explosives in ways that would produce mass casualties.[12]

However, it is no longer true that all modern terrorists eschew mass violence. Bombs have been placed aboard airliners, like the Pan Am flight over Lockerbie, Scotland, killing hundreds. Explosives have been used in vast quantities, as in Oklahoma City, resulting in hundreds of casualties both injured and dead. Hundreds have been injured on subways with toxic materials. The thousands of deaths resulting from the September 11 attacks made clear that terrorists involved in a holy war may not feel any more restraint from the use of nonconventional weapons than have the states that developed and sold them such devices of destruction.

It seems, then, that Jenkins' premise regarding terrorists' reluctance to use weapons of mass destruction proved less accurate in the twenty-first century. It may well be that the reason few groups have yet used such weapons rests upon the difficulty in disseminating the toxic substance in sufficient quantities. That is, surely, a frail defense for those nations who may find themselves the target of such attacks.

Nuclear Weapons

For years modern nations have tried both to secure the materials necessary for the production of nuclear weapons and to remain secure in their belief that, even if some small portions of such materials should fall into terrorist hands, the terrorists would lack the technical skill to manufacture such weapons. The former is a manifestly false premise, particularly since the breakup of the former Soviet Union, and the latter is, at the very least, an arguable premise.

Experts have estimated that, in order to produce a crude nuclear weapon, terrorists would perhaps need to have a half dozen technologically trained individuals (trained in subjects such as nuclear chemistry, physics, metallurgy, electronics, and the handling of high explosives) and considerable time, space, and money. Let us consider each of these requisites to determine whether such a weapon does in fact lie within the realm of possibility for some terrorists today.

The financial resources of terrorists have already been discussed in some detail. Oil revenues (which had enabled patron states to be generous in their support) and more recently, drugs have served to swell the coffers of many terrorist groups. An organization such as the RAF could well afford the necessary funds to procure the materials, trained technicians, and facilities necessary to build such a weapon.

For small, poorly financed groups, a lack of time as well as money could inhibit the production of a nuclear weapon. Such groups are compelled to produce results at once if they are to obtain the funding and support from the patron states that they require to survive. They cannot afford to wait while technicians are either trained or recruited and suitable facilities are constructed.

Well-financed groups can afford, however, to wait while personnel are put into place in an adequately constructed facility. With their contacts among friendly governments, they might even be able to secure a safe testing ground for the weapon prior to its use although such a step would not be essential. Military experts are concerned with such matters as high reliability and predictability yield. All terrorists need be concerned with is that the bomb produces a sufficiently audible "bang" and visible mushroom cloud.

The requirement of space is one that well-established and funded groups can manage. Because considerable hazards are attendant upon working with radioactive materials, a laboratory of fairly substantial size, equipped, with specialized equipment, would be necessary. Like the fissionable materials, it has become increasingly probable that the acquisition of such facilities are within the grasp of some groups today. If such groups can gain access to military training facilities as described earlier, then the possibility exists that terrorists can also gain access to the use of suitable research and development facilities.

Trained personnel are also obtainable for groups and states that can afford market prices for such personnel, after the demise of the Soviet Union. According to one study, about one-third of individuals identified as terrorists were persons with some university training, university graduates, or postgraduate students. In some groups, such as the Tupamaros (Uruguay), the Argentine Revolutionary People's Army, and the Monteneros, the figure was nearly 75 percent in the 1970s. Even in Turkey and Iran, university-trained terrorists were the rule rather than the exception, according to this study. In Turkey and Iran, too, the fields of study tended to be the more exact sciences such as engineering.[13]

Thus, even though it might not be feasible to train a recruit with only grade school or even high school education in the technology necessary for the construction of nuclear weapons, terrorists have a large pool of university graduates from which to select, as well as a large number of trained scientists seeking employment following the crash of the Soviet system.

However, those terrorists who may possess or be able to obtain the necessary resources to construct a crude nuclear weapon are those who are least likely to benefit from the commission of such a barbarous act. Well-established terrorist organizations have tended to try to distance themselves from acts of barbarity, as did the group leadership in Japan following the use of gas on the subways. The reason for such distancing is obvious: these organizations have attachable assets and fixed locations and personnel upon which retribution could be meted.

Yasser Arafat for instance, when he led the PLO, would have been extremely reluctant to use the resources of his organization for the construction and subsequent detonation of a nuclear device. To do so, even before the peace process began in the 1990s, would have irreparably damaged his credibility with the United Nations and would have played into the hands of his enemies, giving them good reason for condemning him as a murderer of unparalleled proportions.

Access by terrorist groups to **backpack nukes** (*small, portable nuclear devices developed by the military of both sides of the cold war*), or the creation of so-called **dirty bombs,** in which *explosives are attached to nuclear waste products to disperse radioactive materials,* is increasingly possible. In the wake of the September 11 attacks, the United States articulated the growing fear among Western states of this latter form of weapon and began to study more intensely the need for security at nuclear power plants from attacks similar to those on the World Trade Center.

Two forms of nuclear terrorism remain feasible, however. One is the **threat/hoax** *by which leaders are frightened or blackmailed into acceding to terrorist demands, based on the threat of detonating a hidden nuclear device in a crowded area, such as a city.* Although it sounds more like the stuff of which science fiction books and movies are made, such threats have in fact already been made. Leaders in several nations, including the United States, have already had to deal with such threats.

To date that is all they have been: threats and hoaxes. But the time may well be at hand when leaders may no longer be so confident that terrorists do not truly possess a nuclear device that they are prepared to detonate. The increasing willingness of some terrorists to commit carnage on a large scale must surely give pause to those who would claim that the devastation wrought by a nuclear device would be on too large a scale for contemporary terrorists. As terrorism continues to become more violent, nuclear terrorism becomes a greater possibility.

The greatest potential for a nuclear disaster, and one that has concerned governments more, is the possibility of an attack or sabotage of an existing nuclear facility. With the growing number both of nuclear power plants inside countries that have for some years produced nuclear power and weapons and of nuclear facilities in previously nonnuclear states, the possibility of these types of situations has dramatically increased.

In either case, great damage could be done without the expenditure of either a great deal of time, money, or personnel recruitment and training. In other words, such an action is well within the reach of most contemporary terrorists. Security protections at such facilities, although gradually increasing, are at present inadequate to prevent a determined and well-planned assault. Such an assault could be carried out by indigenous or foreign groups, as long as sufficient intelligence gathering and reconnaissance measures had been taken.

The "science fiction" terrorism of earlier years, then, is rapidly becoming part of the potential pattern of terrorism today and tomorrow. Chemical, biological, and nuclear terrorism is technically within the grasp of some terrorists today. That they have, for the most part, not chosen to pursue such tactics—yet—is a subject for conjecture. It would be unwise to rely, however, on the terrorists' need for popular approval or goodwill as an indefinite defense against an attack with weapons of this kind.

The recent record in the use of nontraditional weapons will be explored in more depth in two succeeding chapters: the chapter on domestic terrorism in the United States and the final chapter, which examines trends in modern terrorism. At this point, it is simply important to be aware of the very real and rapidly increasing possibilities for the use of chemical, biological, and nuclear agents.

TERRORIST TACTICS

It may be useful at this point to briefly review what we know about the tactics used by contemporary terrorists. We have already discussed how they are trained and what kind of weapons they use. The tactics chosen, given these variables of training and weapons, should prove illuminating in discerning patterns of contemporary terrorist tactics and perhaps enable us to more accurately predict patterns of terrorist acts in the twenty-first century.

Described here are various types of terrorist tactics reported worldwide, together with a few brief remarks about their use. Although not an exhaustive list, it features most of the major tactics employed by terrorists to date.

Bombing

Bombs are the most common tool of contemporary terrorists. About 50 percent of all terrorist incidents are bombings. Most recent trends in the use of this tactic include efforts to maximize the casualties, the use of secondary explosives, and the use of highly sophisticated devices. The letter bomb of earlier years has in large measure been replaced (except in the case of the U.S. Unibomber) by vehicle bombs, which can carry a larger charge.

CASE EXAMPLES

Review of a few examples of the use of bombs by terrorist groups indicates that the use of such weapons is becoming common throughout the world and that such attacks are extremely lethal. These examples were selected to give a sense of the geographical scope and variety of groups involved and types of bombs used, as well as this lethality.

December 1988, Lockerbie. Pan Am Flight 103 airliner exploded from bomb, killing over 200 people. Responsibility for planning and support for the bombing was traced to Libya, Iran, and Syria.

March 1991, Sri Lanka. State Minister for Defense Wijeratne killed in a car bombing in Colombo along with 50 other victims. The LTTE was responsible.

June 1991, Honduras. The Morazanist Patriotic Front launched an RPG-7 rocket at the UN Observer Group headquarters in Tegucigalpa.

February 1993, New York. Explosion of a massive van bomb in an underground parking garage below the WTC killed six and wounded over 1,000. Islamic extremists were convicted.

June 1993, Egypt. A bomb exploded beneath an overpass as a tour bus traveled to the Giza pyramids killing two Egyptians and injuring six British tourists, as well as nine Egyptians and Syrians.

August 1995, Oklahoma City. Truck bomb at a federal building injured or killed hundreds, including children in a day care center. A member of a militia group was charged with the crime.

January 1996, Israel. Suicide bombers caused civilian deaths in Jerusalem and the West Bank. HAMAS extremists, in efforts to stop the peace process, took responsibility.

September 11, 2001, United States. Two airplanes loaded with passengers and fully fueled for transcontinental flight were flown into the WTC in New York City. Another similarly loaded passenger plane was flown into the Pentagon in Washington, DC. More than 4,000 people were killed in these two attacks.

April 2004, Madrid, Spain. Bombs exploded in train stations, killing hundreds of commuters and wounding many more. Muslim extremists were arrested and charged.

This does not, of course, detail all of the bombings occurring in the past two decades. It is intended only to demonstrate the wide range of bombs used, the variety of targets chosen, and the global nature of the utilization of this type of tactic.

Arson

Arson accounts for approximately 14 percent of all terrorist incidents. The use of this tactic often involves the employment of an incendiary explosive device.

Again, a brief look at some of the terrorist events in which this method has been employed may offer insights into its usefulness. It is, for example, used more frequently to destroy property and to create a climate of fear than to destroy lives.

March 1982. A U.S. International Communications Office in Pusan, South Korea was burned by a band of youths killing one visitor.

October 1993. Terrorists threw a firebomb into the Turkish-owned Bosporus Bank in central Paris. No serious damage resulted.

November 1993. The PKK staged a round of coordinated attacks against Turkish diplomatic and commercial facilities in six West European countries. The assaults consisted mainly of firebombings and vandalism, but one person was killed and about 20 other injured.

Hostage Taking and Kidnapping

This tactic allows terrorists to maximize the publicity surrounding the event. By employing such a tactic, terrorists are able to control both the length of the event, and media coverage of the event, at least in terms of interviews with the hostages. Since audience is important to terrorist events, this makes this tactic particularly enticing to terrorists. The feelings of power, of being in control, of playing before a worldwide audience are indeed heady sensations for terrorists.

The headlines have been full, in recent years, of spectacular and not-so-spectacular hostage takings. Indeed, as shock has succeeded shock, the taking of yet another individual by extremists is no longer even considered newsworthy in some parts of the world. A brief glimpse at the endless list of hostage takings gives an indication as to why this should be so. Note also that virtually all such reports refer to the incident as "kidnapping."

October 1986, Lebanon. Edward Austin Tracy, an American and long-time resident of Moslem-controlled West Beirut, was kidnapped. A group calling itself the Revolutionary Justice Organization claimed responsibility.

August 1991, Turkey. The PKK kidnapped 10 German tourists near Lake Van. The tourists were later released. That same month, PKK kidnapped three Americans, one Briton, and one Australian near Bingol. They were released after a month.

February 1993, Colombia. Eight Ejército de Liberación Nacional (ELN) terrorists kidnapped U.S. citizen Lewis Manning, an employee of the Colombian gold-mining company, Oresom, in the Choco area.

March 1993, Costa Rica. Four terrorists kidnapped 25 persons in the Nicaraguan Embassy in San Jose, including the Nicaraguan ambassador. The hostages were held for several days while negotiations were conducted.

October 1993, Algeria. Terrorists kidnapped from the company cafeteria a Peruvian, a Filipino, and a Colombian—technicians employed by an Italian construction firm in Tiaret. Two days later, the three were found dead with their throats cut. The extremist Armed Islamic Group claimed responsibility for this and other attacks against foreigners.

January 8, 1996. In Indonesia, 200 Free Papua Movement guerrillas abducted 26 individuals in the Lorenta nature preserve. Indonesian Special Forces rescued nine of the hostages on May 15.

March 1, 1999. 150 armed Hutu rebels attacked three tourist camps in Uganda, killed four Ugandans and kidnapped 16 tourists. Eight of the hostages were subsequently killed by their abductors.

May 1, 2000. Revolutionary United Front militants in Sierra Leone kidnapped at least 20 members of the UN Assistance Mission to Sierra Leone (USAMSIL) and surrounded and opened fire on a UNAMSIL facility.

Unlike hostage taking, kidnapping is a covert act. Since secrecy is required, kidnapping is usually preceded by considerable planning and rehearsal. Terrorists tend to kill the victims, even if their demands are met. This may be because a dead body is infinitely more dramatic than a quietly released hostage. To be effective, terrorism requires an element of drama.

In the news items cited previously, the events could in some cases be termed "kidnapping," planned and executed in secrecy. The victims, however, were in a very real sense hostages to political and/or monetary demands made by their kidnappers. Some were killed, but others remained in captivity as hostages to demands that could not be met.

Assassinations and Ambushes

Targets for such attacks have been selected both for their publicity and their symbolic value. In Lebanon, Bosnia, and other places where UN forces are involved, victims have included officers involved in peacekeeping efforts. In other areas, the victims were as likely to be priests as college personnel. This tactic, since it requires an element of surprise, usually involves careful planning and execution.

Assassins and their victims come in all shapes and sizes. Although government officials make attractive targets, a variety of others have come under the assassin's gun. Note in the brief list below the diversity of targets.

1984: Malcolm Kerr, President of American University of Beirut, was shot and killed as he stepped off the elevator to his office on the West Beirut campus. Islamic Jihad claimed responsibility.

Leamon R. Hunt, the American director of the Multinational Force and Observers peacekeeping force in the Sinai peninsula, was shot and killed as he drove to his home in southwestern Rome. A radical offshoot of the Red Brigades claimed responsibility.

1985: Terrorists shot and killed 13 people as they sat at a sidewalk cafe in San Salvador. Two days later the urban guerrilla, Mardoqueo Cruz, associated with the Farabundo Martí National Liberation (FLMN), took responsibility.

A coalition of Palestinian and Japanese Red Army terrorists attacked airports at Rome and Vienna with grenades and machine guns, killing 18 and wounding 116. Abu Nidal's Revolutionary Fatah group was responsible.

1991: The Red Army Faction claimed responsibility for firing approximately 250 rounds of small-arms fire at the U.S. Embassy in Bonn. This was the first RAF attack against a U.S. target since 1985.

An Iranian dissident leader was stabbed and killed in the lobby of his apartment building in Paris.

Senderao Luminosa killed the Canadian director of the humanitarian organization World Mission in a Lima suburb.

Former Prime Minister Rajiv Gandhi was assassinated by a suspected Liberation Tigers of Tamil Eemal (LTTE) suicide bomber while campaigning in southern India.

1992: An Italian businessman was shot and wounded by a terrorist as he left his residence in a suburb of Algeria.

A police officer was killed and six others wounded when a group of terrorists opened fire on two movie houses that were showing foreign films. Al-Gama's al-Islamiyya claimed responsibility, stating that the attack retaliated for the screening of "immoral" films.

1995: Yitzhak Rabin, Prime Minister of Israel, was assassinated by a Jewish student, claiming that Rabin had given away too much of Israel in the peace process.

1996: A bomb exploded at the home of the French archbishop of Oran, killing him and his chauffeur. The attack occurred after the archbishop's meeting with the French foreign minister. The Algerian Armed Islamic Group was suspected.

June 8, 2000: In Athens, Greece, two unidentified gunmen killed British Defense Attaché Stephen Saunders in an ambush. The Revolutionary Organization 17 November claimed responsibility.

Aerial Hijacking

Skyjacking, as such events have been called, has been used by terrorists to maximize spectacular situations. This type of event allows the terrorist to maximize shock value and to grab world attention. Moreover, it provides the terrorist with an escape vehicle, until international law closed this loophole.

These spectaculars have provided extensive media coverage, at fairly minimal cost to the hijackers. Although the psychological costs for the victim are high, the loss of lives has also tended to be less than in other types of terrorist events—except when things go wrong.

1985: Shi'a gunmen hijacked TWA Flight 847 from Athens, Greece. The hijackers shot and killed U.S. Navy diver Robert Stetham in Beirut and dispersed the remaining hostages throughout the city.

Four Palestinian gunmen hijacked the Italian cruise ship *Achille Lauro* off Alexandria, Egypt, with 80 passengers and 320 crew aboard, sailed to Syria and Cyprus (where it was refused port entry) and back to Egypt. While off the Syrian port of Tartus, the terrorists killed wheelchair-bound American Leon Klinghoffer.

Arab gunmen hijacked an Egypt Air flight and landed at Malta after an in-flight gun battle with Egyptian security guards. Five passengers were shot at close range and dumped on the runway.

1986: Pan Am Flight 73 was hijacked in Pakistan. At 5:55 p.m. (Eastern Standard Time), four Arab-speaking gunmen seized a Pan Am 747 at Karachi International Airport as the plane was loading passengers for a flight to Frankfurt, Germany. The hijackers held 374 passengers and 15 crew members hostage for 16 hours while sporadic negotiations were attempted. Suddenly, at 9:45 p.m. the following night when the ground power units ran out of gas and the lights dimmed on the plane, the gunmen panicked and began firing indiscriminately at the huddled passengers. Before Pakistani commandos could storm the plane, 21 hostages were dead and more than 60 were seriously wounded.

1991: Four Pakistanis claiming to be members of the Pakistani People's Party hijacked a Singapore Airlines flight en route from Kualu Lumpur to Singapore and demanded the release of several people reportedly imprisoned in Pakistan.

1999: Five militants hijacked a flight bound from Katmandu to New Delhi carrying 189 people. The plane and its passengers were released unharmed on December 31.

Sabotage

Highly industrialized Western nations are particularly vulnerable to this type of terrorist tactic. It is possible, for example, to disrupt utility services or shut down industrial complexes. Japan in 1987 suffered a disruption of its commuter rail services by terrorists armed with nothing more than a few sharp blades. Such an incident can clearly have tremendous symbolic value, providing to the watching governments the power that even a relatively obscure group may wield. Such actions serve the terrorist goals of disrupting and perhaps destabilizing governments, but they are not necessarily terrorist acts, because no innocent victims are injured or killed in the action (disturbed, imposed upon, perhaps, but not casualties).

Threat/Hoax

This is another low-cost tactic, with varying potential for disruption, without making innocent victims of anyone. It forces governments to assess the vulnerability of the targets and the history of the group claiming responsibility. The cost of reacting to such a hoax may well be crippling to the authority involved, whereas the consequences of not responding could be equally dreadful.

Chemical-Biological Attacks

Agents for this type of tactic are, as noted earlier, available commercially or can be developed without undue difficulty by some groups. The possibility of a successful poisoning of a city's water supply has concerned some governments in recent years. Individuals in the United States have already demonstrated that it is possible to poison medicines on drugstore shelves and poison food supplies. The toxic agent attack on Tokyo subways in 1995 proved the effectiveness of this tactic and demonstrated that groups can no longer be assumed to be unwilling or unable to use them. Use of toxic agents against the Kurds by the government of Iraq during its conflict with Iran had already made it clear that states were increasingly willing to use this weapon against women and children. As noted earlier, the use of this type of tactic will be discussed in later chapters.

Nuclear Threat

As noted earlier, nuclear technology and materials are available to terrorists today. While the devices may be difficult to manufacture, it is not impossible to do so, and they could be stolen, purchased, or supplied by a supporting state. Sabotage or bombing of a nuclear facility is also feasible and far less expensive.

Information regarding these last four forms of terrorism is less readily available. Sabotage, as note earlier, is not a terrorist act in the strict definition of the term. Threat holders, according to most terror-specific statutes, are not legally punishable crimes of terrorism, either. Thus, the reporting for such crimes is less complete. The use of chemical and biological weapons by terrorists has thus far remained quite limited—no longer a "science fiction" tactic, but not yet widely used. The increased use of such weapons by nation-states at war, however, makes the likelihood of terrorist acquisition and use of such methods much more probable.

In the Iran-Iraq war, as noted earlier, Iraq spread poison gas against its enemies. For a time such measures were reserved for desperate military situations, when confronted with overwhelming Iranian forces. But there was gruesome evidence of an increase in the use of this lethal weapon against villages and cities. The city of Halabja, near the Iran-Iraq border, was covered with a poison cloud, which one survivor described as "a dense choking pancake that settled over many square blocks."[14] Very few of those left in the center of town survived. Medical evidence suggests that Iraq dropped mustard gas, a relatively common poison; hydrogen cyanide, a chemical combination used for executions in U.S. prisons; and possibly sarin, a nerve gas that is one of the deadliest chemical weapons ever developed by mankind.

When nation-states themselves use such weapons, even on civilian populations, how can the civilized world prevent or even proscribe the use of such weapons by terrorists? Certainly the use of such weapons by nations engaged in conflict lessens both the strength of the laws designed to control or prohibit their use and makes more difficult the means by which the production of such weapons are controlled. If production of such chemical weapons cannot be effectively limited, then the dissemination of such weapons becomes even more difficult to control.

Today, intelligence sources say that some 37 countries are full or potential members of the "chemical weapons club."[15] Although all but six of these—North and South Korea, Laos, Angola, Albania, and Nicaragua—have signed the 1925 Geneva Convention banning chemical warfare, several signatory nations are flagrant violators of the pact. Iran is one whose violations are well documented. Evidence exists that others, including Ethiopia, Mozambique, Libya, Vietnam, and even the former Soviet Union, violated the agreement.

CASE STUDY   Al-Qaeda's Quest for a Biological Toxin

Material and testimony recovered from the training camps in Afghanistan has indicated this organization at one time was interested in acquiring chemical and/or biological weapons. It is becoming clear, however, that this organization is still involved in attempts to manufacture and utilize such weapons. The efforts of recently discovered cells of this group appear to have focused on the production of ricin, a biological toxin found in castor beans.

In France in 2001, one al-Qaeda trainee, Menad Benchellali, set up a laboratory in his family's spare bedroom in Lyon and began to manufacture ricin. Blending the ingredients in a coffee decanter and scooping the dough-like mixture onto newspapers to dry, he was able to produce a powdered substance, which he stored in small jars. Benchellali and others like him have discovered it is inexpensive and reasonably simple to produce a WMD for their group to use.

Unfortunately, this is hardly a surprising choice of weapon, since ricin is very accessible, relatively easy to make, safe to handle, and extraordinarily lethal. In fact, a single particle of ricin the size of a pinhead could kill an adult if injected into the bloodstream. Although a biological weapon, ricin also has the advantage of being noncontagious and therefore not likely to set off epidemics that could kill the very persons for whom the politically motivated action is being taken. It cannot be absorbed through the skin, like the very lethal nerve agent VX, however, meaning that inhalation or injection must occur for dissemination to be successful—neither of which are simple methods of deployment.

To date, no ricin attacks by al-Qaeda have been carried out, perhaps because the problem of creating a weaponized form capable of effective dissemination are not yet resolved. But it is clear that they and many other groups (domestic as well as international) are trying to create this new weapon. As one expert notes, "biological and chemical weapons are more important than ever to al-Qaeda."[16] While ricin is not, in many respects, a feasible weapon of mass destruction (given its limitations in contagion and dissemination), it appears that groups like al-Qaeda will continue to seek to acquire such substances and to learn how best to use them.   ❏

PHASES OF A TERRORIST INCIDENT

Having assessed the training topics and chosen tactics of terrorists, it is also useful to note the patterns that have emerged in modern terrorist incidents. Much of what was taught in the training camps is clearly used in the structuring of the incident itself, at least by well-trained operatives.

Since it is clear that some organizations, like al-Qaeda, have very intelligent and organized lieutenants orchestrating the training of operatives, it should not be surprising to find that modern, well-planned terrorist incidents often have five discernible **phases,** which for the purpose of this study will be called *preincident, initiation, negotiation, termination, postincident.* Each of these stages deserves attention, for each offers both insights into the sophistication of the group carrying out the operation and indicators that might be useful to law enforcement personnel seeking to prevent or resolve such incidents.

Figure 7.2 illustrates the projected flow of a terrorist event, broken down into these five phases.

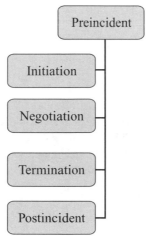

FIGURE 7.2

In the preincident phase, the individuals or groups planning the incident will generally carry out two important functions: intelligence gathering and rehearsal of the event. At this point, nothing illegal has yet occurred. Members of the group are gathering information about the target, making plans for the attack, and often rehearsing the event before it is initiated. At this stage, training in clandestine travel and intelligence gathering becomes useful, as does training in evaluation of security systems and access routes.

This phase differs from the others in one critical respect: no law has yet been openly violated and therefore surveillance and intervention by law enforcement is difficult to justify. Unless the intelligence gathering and rehearsal offer sufficient evidence for an investigation—that is, there is information about the group or plot *before* the incident, or the individuals are careless and/or ill-trained in their intelligence-gathering efforts—intervention by law enforcement at this point is difficult. This issue will be pursued in more depth in the discussion later about U.S. efforts to expand law enforcement capabilities in this area, particularly with the so-called PATRIOT Act.

Phase Two, the initiation phase, entails exactly what it suggests: the beginning of the implementation of the incident. This involves moving the individuals involved to the location(s) necessary for the event, as well as any equipment needed. During this phase a diversion is also planned, by the more well-organized groups, to draw the attention of law enforcement and the media away from the intended target. Thus, those seeking to protect the public from the planned attack may have to be able to discern which is the real target and which is the diversion during this initiation stage.

The third phase, negotiation, does not occur in every terrorist incident. If there is only the placing of a bomb or the driving of a truck filled with explosives to a desired target, there may well be no negotiation phase, because there is nothing to discuss about the act. This phase occurs when an individual or group has a demand (or a list of demands) to communicate and is willing to talk to someone in authority about meeting those demands. Generally, this involves either the taking and negotiated release of hostages and/or the threatened detonation of a bomb or other weapon capable of mass destruction. During this phase, the training that members of the group have received in the making of explosives and in the framing of demands for ransom or release of prisoners can significantly impact the flow of events.

What often appears to be the final stage, called here the termination phase, is not actually the end of the event in most cases today. This phase simply involves either the escape, surrender, capture, or death of the individuals involved in the incident. Here, planning for a "back door" escape, a diversion to draw some of the attention away to allow this escape, or a demand that includes safe passage out for the perpetrators often depends on the quality of training and experience the terrorists have.

For law enforcement, the primary focus is usually on the safety of the hostages, not the capture or killing of the criminals. If the event is handled by a military authority, however, the focus is most often on the capture or death of the individuals responsible. Thus, the success of this phase may depend on the nature of the enforcement officials seeking to end the incident.

The final phase is in many respects the most important, and unfortunately the least understood. In the postincident phase, the remaining members of the group that planned the attack will regroup to *learn* from the mistakes as well as the successes of the incident. By studying what went right and what went wrong in the event, groups learn how law enforcement met the challenges and can then plan how to exploit the weakness of those protecting the public. The group members, in fact, do what military forces do in their debriefing after an incident.

The important point here is that *terrorists planning these events are not stupid.* They learn from mistakes and from successes, and they use those lessons in the next plans. Although there may be copycat perpetrators who will repeat the group's initial mistakes, the perpetrators, if they are well organized and trained, will not repeat their errors. Thus, if security forces only copy the attacks made by groups in planning security, they will miss a critical point, because no future attack by that group will be just like the one that occurred. Instead, the next incident will reflect the learning curve of the group from its postincident evaluation.

EVALUATION

Terrorists today have a variety of tactics from which to choose, and sufficient training and support systems to make the most of the tactics within their grasp, should they choose to use them. While most terrorist groups continue to rely on the tactics proven successful in earlier years, such as bombing and hostage taking, recent developments make it possible that different choices may be made in the near future.

Potentially conflicting forces seem to be influencing the terrorists' choice of tactics. Consider these factors carefully and decide what you think will be the trends in future terrorist attacks.

1. Some terrorist groups have become financially stable, with established ties to governments, individuals, and/or banks. Although governments have been willing to supply training, arms, personnel, intelligence, and travel assistance, they are somewhat more vulnerable than the group itself to retaliation in the event of a terrorist attack. The U.S. war on terrorism, on Afghan soil in 2001–2002 gives credibility to this point. Moreover, the demise of the Soviet Union made the political risks for supporting such groups much higher and the risks of military retaliation much less calculable.

2. The technology for developing more sophisticated weapons is now more readily accessible to terrorists. At the same time, restraints against the use of widespread violence in terrorist attacks appear to be diminishing. In other words, it is now possible to construct instruments of vast destructive power at a time when inhibitions against the committing of such atrocities seems to be vanishing. If terrorists groups (or states) are willing to be responsible for hundreds of deaths in an airline bombing, will they continue to be reluctant to use weapons capable of even greater destruction, such as toxins, if they can obtain them?

3. Terrorists today can inflict more harm with more sophisticated weapons and with larger quantities of weapons than ever before in part because of the eagerness of the rest of the world to *sell* arms to anyone who has the money. How much responsibility rests with the arms merchants of the so-called civilized world for making weapons so easy to obtain?

4. Dr. David Hubbard, a psychiatrist who has interviewed scores of imprisoned hijackers, contends that TV news broadcasts of ongoing terrorist events is "social pornography" because it "caters to the sick, unmet needs of the public" (*Skyjacker: His Flights of Fancy*). He is convinced that world terrorism would decrease if television brought its coverage under control.[17] How accurate do you think this assessment is? What kind of controls can a democratic society afford to impose on its media? What are the dangers of such controls? How effective do you think either voluntary or involuntary controls on media coverage of terrorism would be in reducing either the number or the violence of terrorist events?

SUGGESTED READINGS

Crenshaw, Martha, ed. *Terrorism in Context*. University Park: Pennsylvania State University Press, 1995.
Hickey, Neil. "Gaining the Media's Attention." In *The Struggle against Terrorism.* New York: Wilson, 1977.
Hoffman, Bruce. *Inside Terrorism*. New York: Columbia University Press, 1998.
Jenkins, Brian. "Will Terrorists Go Nuclear?" P-5541. Santa Monica, CA: Rand, November 1985.
Laqueur, Walter. *The New Terrorism: Fanaticism and the Arms of Mass Destruction*. Oxford: Oxford University Press, 1999.
Stern, Jessica. *The Ultimate Terrorists*. Cambridge, MA: Harvard University Press, 1999.

NOTES

1. "The Spider in the Web," *The Economist,* September 22, 2001, 5.
2. Reuel Marc Gerecht, "Blueprint for Terror," *Talk,* October 2000, 91.
3. Bruce Crumley, "Breaking a Web," *Time,* Saturday, October 6, 2001, 2.
4. "How Bin Laden Set Up Shop in Southeast Asia," *Time,* October 10, 2001, 2.
5. Peter Grier, "A Changing World," *The Christian Science Monitor,* September 17, 2001, 3.
6. Robert H. Kupperman and Darrell M. Trent, *Terrorism: Threat, Reality and Response* (Stanford, CA: Hoover Institution Press, 1979), 80.
7. Ibid., *Terrorism,* 54.
8. In that year, evidence indicates that a Rhodesian airliner was shot down with an SA-7.
9. Brian Jenkins, *Terrorism: Trends and Potentialities* (Santa Monica, CA: Rand, 1977), 80.
10. Kupperman and Trent, *Terrorism,* 83.
11. Kupperman and Trent, *Terrorism,* 57. This agent comparison was derived by Conrad V. Chester of the Oak Ridge National Laboratory, transmitted in a June 20, 1975, letter entitled "Perspectives on the CB Terrorist Threat."
12. Brian Jenkins, "Will Terrorists Go Nuclear?" P-5541 (Santa Monica, CA: Rand, November 1975).
13. Charles A. Russell and Bowman H. Miller, "Profile of a Terrorist," *Terrorism: An International Journal* 1, no. 1 (1977): 27–28.
14. "New Horrors in a Long-Running Horror Show," *U.S. News & World Report,* April 4, 1988, 11.
15. "A Plague of 'Hellish Poison,'" *U.S. News & World Report,* October 26, 1987, 32.
16. Joby Warrick, "Al-Qaeda's Quest for a Toxin," *The Washington Post National Weekly Edition,* May 17–23, 2004, 15.
17. David Hubbard, *Skyjacker: His Flights of Fancy* (New York: Wilson, 1997), 133.

CHAPTER 8

The Media: A Weapon for Both Sides?

Key Concepts

amplification effect	interactive relationship	denial of platform
right of access	built-in escalation	information and
prior restraint	imperative	cooperation
censorship	publicity	copycat operation
prisoners of war	tactical and strategic gains	disinformation
complicity	favorable understanding	getting a scoop
arousal hypothesis	legitimacy and identity	dramatic presentation
disinhibition hypothesis	destabilizing the enemy	protection of rights
social learning theory	criminality of act	personal security

If terrorism is seen as political theater performed for audiences . . . clearly the mass media plays a crucial role. Without massive news coverage the terrorist act would resemble the proverbial tree falling in the forest.

Brigette L. Nacos

PROPAGANDA BY THE DEED

Terrorism has been called "propaganda by the deed." This particularly violent form of propaganda has captured the attention of millions of people today. To what extent has the media become a weapon of the terrorists about whom it reports? Who is exploiting whom in this vicious scramble for worldwide audience?

Many of today's terrorists have learned an important lesson about this technological age: television news organizations can be forced into becoming the link between terrorists and their audience. What is needed to forge this link is a crime sufficiently newsworthy—which has come to mean outrageous, dramatic, even barbaric enough. According to Brian Jenkins, a Rand Corporation expert on terrorism, "terrorists want a lot of people watching and a lot of people listening, not a lot of people dead. . . . I see terrorism as violence for effect. Terrorists choreograph dramatic incidents to achieve maximum publicity, and in that sense, terrorism is theater."[1]

Terrorists benefit from what has been called an **amplification effect,** *when their activities are broadcast through the media to a much larger audience than* *would be available on the spot where the action occurs.* For instance, insurgents carried on rural guerrilla warfare in several countries, including Angola and Mozambique, for more than a decade without receiving much attention from the rest of the world. But when a similar number of Palestinians carried their warfare into the urban centers of Europe and the Middle East, their actions and their causes became dinner table conversation for TV audiences around the world, because in the urban centers of Europe and the Middle East, the terrorists were within reach of TV newsmen and their cameras.

This confluence of interest between the media—who thrive on sensational news—and terrorists—who are only too happy to provide the sensational events—has raised questions about the possible complicity of the media in today's terrorism. Students of terrorism have suggested that the media today are in fact a contributing factor—a weapon—in the hands of modern terrorists. A quick survey of the opinions of a few of these experts is illuminating:

> *Frederick Hacker,* a California psychiatrist who has served as negotiator in terrorist incidents, notes that "if the mass media did not exist, terrorists would have to invent them. In turn, the mass media hanker after terrorist acts because they fit into their programming needs: namely, sudden acts of great excitement that are susceptible, presumably, of quick solution. So there's a mutual dependency."
>
> *Walter Laquer,* chairman of the International Research Council of the Center for the Strategic and International Studies, stated, "The media are a terrorist's best friend. . . . [T]errorists are the super-entertainers of our time."
>
> *Raymond Tanter,* political scientist at the University of Michigan, makes the relationship dilemma a bit clearer in his statement: "Since the terror is aimed at the media and not at the victim, success is defined in terms of media coverage. And there is no way in the West that you could *not* have media coverage because you're dealing in a free society."[2]

In Tanter's comments lie a key to the dilemma regarding the role of the media in terrorism. Censorship in any form is anathema to most free societies. Instead, it has been assumed that the media could be expected to exercise voluntary self-restraints where necessary in reporting such events. But the media is not wholly convinced that restraint is either necessary or desirable. There is still considerable conflict over the extent of the public's "right to know" in the coverage of terrorist events. Executives of most of the major news companies have stated that television's "right to report" is absolute; that, in any case, it is better to report than not report. ABC's William Sheehan has said, "I don't think it's our job to decide what people should not know. The news media are not the reason for terrorism even though they may sometimes become part of the story."[3]

Which is the more accurate picture of the role of the media with respect to terrorism today? Is it the responsible means by which the public is kept informed on events and individuals who are interacting in the international arena? Or is it, as one hijacker said, a "whore" whose "favors" are available to anyone with a pistol?[4] If it is indeed true that the media are responsible for amplifying the effects of guerrilla warfare, to what extent are they responsible for the effects of that amplification? If terrorists have to move to increasingly more spectacular crimes in order to satisfy the increasingly jaded palette of TV audiences sated with violence, to what extent is the media responsible for whetting that appetite?

Some experts have suggested that the media are acting increasingly like a "loose gun," a weapon that terrorists are learning to use with rapidly improving sophistication. It is, moreover, a gun that democratic governments have provided, and continue to provide, essentially without controls, against itself. It would indeed be ironic if one of the fundamental freedoms of the free world—free press—were to be instrumental in its destruction, as the Libyan fable noted in the previous chapter suggests.

LEGAL ISSUE OF THE RIGHT OF ACCESS

The issue of the relationship between terrorism, the media, and the law has received attention from scholars for more than a decade. Legal experts from law enforcement agencies and media services have benefited from the scrutiny of this complex web of relationships. A brief review of a few significant issues raised by experts on this subject may be of value at this point.

Experts on both the law and the media have frequently differed on the nature of the relationships that should exist between law enforcement, the media, and terrorists. Members of the media often claim to have an unlimited right to have access to, and the right to report, all news, including that relating to terrorist events. Those responsible for hostage rescue contend that such rights should not be regarded as unlimited and should never be exercised in ways that might endanger lives. The legal issues inherent in these contrasting viewpoints were explored extensively during the late 1970s and early 1980s. As one researcher succinctly noted, "The media must not be the dupes of the radical scriptwriters, nor should they be the mouthpiece of government. There is a mean. Law enforcement and the media cannot be locked in combat."[5]

The U.S. Supreme Court during Warren Burger's tenure as chief justice did not regard the media's right to access as superior to that of the general public. Abraham Miller created a significant review of case law decisions involving the issue of the press's **right of access** to terrorist events—that is, *the right of the press to get close to the events as they occur*. He noted that, in the *Pell* decision, the Court stated that when the public is excluded from the scene of a crime of disaster, then the media may also be excluded, without violating the First Amendment to the U.S. Constitution.

Miller's study suggests that the Court, under Burger, viewed access by the media to a site where news is being made (as in a terrorist incident) not as a First Amendment right but as a privilege to be granted, or revoked, at the discretion of the law enforcement agency entrusted with ending the breach in the law. Even access to the perimeter between the tactical squad and the public (frequently established by law enforcement units in hostage-taking and siege situations for the purpose of permitting access for the media) is not a right guaranteed to the media by the Constitution but is instead a privilege accorded at the discretion of the government law enforcement agency in charge of the situation. Miller concludes with this observation:

> Access to the site where news is being made cannot be claimed by the press if the general public is also being excluded. Press access, largely a privilege under the most sanguine of circumstances, can be revoked, and where the situation is fraught with imminent danger of people being injured or killed, the media's claim to special access rings especially hollow.[6]

An earlier study by Miller and Juanita Jones reached similar conclusions about the legality of excluding the press from certain areas during hostage situations, particularly those in which law enforcement procedures require secrecy in order to save lives. However, this study also noted that the Supreme Court did not allow blanket denial of access through a set of preconditions. Case law, according to this study, did not support a total or standard ban on news access to terrorist events; only the circumstances surrounding each event could legally justify limitation of access.

Prior restraint, *establishing specific legal limits on the press before the action occurs,* has been a tool used successfully only during times of great national stress, when the security of the state could reasonably be said to be at risk. During the Civil War and both of the world wars, the United States imposed restraints on the press regarding the right of access to events. Fear that an unfettered press might irresponsibly jeopardize the lives of American soldiers or civilians by injudiciously printing too much information about an event led to restrictions on access of the press during time of war.

Even in such extreme circumstances, however, the right of the government to impose such restraints was vociferously challenged, not only by the press itself, but by constitutional scholars who feared the precedent that such rules might set. In the first Gulf War (1990–1991), the press in the United States were permitted to have briefings near the front lines; shown flight recordings and raw data from the advancing armies often before it had been fully analyzed by the military intelligence staff; and allowed to film much of the fighting. Still, the press chafed at the restrictions imposed, sought to get even closer to the fields of battle (to the extent where some media personnel were captured by Iraqi soldiers), and demanded unlimited access to all military information available, to be broadcast live to a worldwide audience.

If the world can watch a war being fought, from start to finish, by 24-hour coverage via Cable News Network (CNN), if the press is allowed to broadcast live footage of Special Forces troops conducting a "stealthy" night landing in Somalia, then it is difficult to imagine the circumstances surrounding a terrorism event that would engender the need to limit the access of the press. If national security was not jeopardized by the filming of the war with Iraq or by the broadcast depicting the landing in Somalia, then it is surely not endangered by filming a hostage-rescue effort or televising the aftermath of a bomb attack.

It could be more effectively argued that self-restraint instead of prior restraint would be in both the press's and the nation's best interest. Few legal scholars have challenged court findings that restrictions on the media comparable to those imposed on the general public do not necessarily contravene the First Amendment's protection of a free press. Differences have arisen over the type of restrictions and the body empowered to impose them. Most recent research has focused on three alternatives: government-directed censorship, self-censorship by the media itself, and restraints imposed by a special commission. All three options have difficulties, and the first two have been seriously discussed for more than a decade.

CENSORSHIP: THE UGLY WORD

No one wants to use the term **censorship,** referring to *efforts by a government to limit and edit what is said by the press about an incident,* in conjunction with the press in its coverage of terrorist events. Yet many democratic states are hard-pressed not to desire to filter what reporters say to a general (and possibly credulous) public about the motives, the lives, the intentions, as well as the actions and individuals involved in perpetrating terrorist events. The power of the press to create heroes is sometimes frightening, and democratic governments are not blind to this danger. But few are willing to sacrifice cherished liberal values in order to keep the press from depicting a person who bombs a supermarket as an heroic "freedom fighter."

As several scholars have pointed out, to impose censorship on the press in a democratic society would be to give to the perpetrators of the terrorist events a significant and unearned victory. When a democratic society, in panic and anger, abandons one of the cherished principles of law that make it democratic, the society has inflicted on itself a greater wound than the terrorists could achieve, were they to bomb a hundred buildings.

Yet anger, frustration, and unrelenting problems have led some democratic systems into just that deplorable situation. The problems in Northern Ireland have taxed the patience and the ingenuity of the British security forces past bearing, time after time. The fabric of democracy has sometimes worn thin in this troubled area, as restrictions have been placed on the press as a kind of "damage control." The damage done by censorship in such situations is difficult to calculate.

This issue has been of serious interest to many Western democracies, because most have been challenged to resolve the tension between a need to guarantee as unfettered a media as possible while maintaining control over terrorist events. Although most of the studies conducted have focused on the ability of the British government to cope with the continuous flow of terrorist events that, until recently, emanated from Northern Ireland, several studies of other Western democracies have also yielded significant insights into this problem.

Miller, a Bradley Resident Scholar at The Heritage Foundation, who conducted the study of the U.S. Supreme Court case law on this issue, expanded his study of this topic in 1990 with research into the struggles of the British government to balance the media's desire to be unfettered against special security needs generated by the struggle in Northern Ireland. As in the study of the U.S. Court decisions, Miller concluded that media access to information was not guaranteed by British law.[7] However, Miller found no evidence to support claims by the government of a need for censorship that extended beyond the limiting of access.

One of the most comprehensive research studies on terrorism and the media was conducted during the 1980s, examining the relationship between terrorist violence, the Western news media, and the political actors.[8] This study is an excellent empirical exercise, including careful scrutiny of terrorist violence, beginning with nineteenth-century anarchists. The study evaluates interaction between terrorists, the media, and political actors in many regions of the world and concludes that much of the blame for the increase in terrorism can be attributed to the media.

Schmid and de Graff summarize the arguments for and against censorship of terrorist news reporting. At the bottom of their list of 11 arguments against censorship is the only one even marginally relevant to the legality of such censorship. This argument is simply that "the assertion of insurgent terrorists that democratic states are not really free would gain credibility if the freedom of the press were suspended."[9] This does not suggest that censorship in such events would be unconstitutional but that it might be counterproductive in constitutional democracies.

Government-directed censorship has been most often studied in the context of Great Britain's efforts to restrain the media on the subject of the conflict in Northern Ireland. Of particular interest in this situation is the legislation banning television and radio broadcasts of interviews or direct statements by members of the outlawed IRA, along with nine other organizations. Two of the organizations are legitimate (or at least not proscribed) groups: Sinn Fein and the Protestant Ulster Defense Association (UDA).

This broadcasting ban was intended, in the words of the prime minister at that time, Margaret Thatcher, to deprive terrorists of "the oxygen of publicity" on which they thrive.[10] Ian Stewart, Minister of State for Northern Ireland when the ban was enacted, stated that it was designed to "put an end to the practice of providing an easy platform for people who represent groups such as Sinn Fein and the UDA in Northern Ireland, who support political action by means of violence."[11]

Although the British legal system does not have a formal written constitution, it does possess a strong legal tradition of protection of civil liberties. There is considerable difference of opinion as to whether such measures are attacks on that legal tradition or simply reasonable precautions taken by a government faced with an extraordinarily difficult situation. As one British commentator noted, "nobody calls it censorship when Mafia spokesmen are not allowed to explain, over the airwaves, why it is advisable to pay protection money."[12]

British governmental restraint of media reporting on terrorism has not been limited to the 1988 ban. Occasionally pressure rather than legislation has enabled the government to limit media coverage of terrorism. In his analysis, *Terrorism and the Liberal State,* Paul Wilkinson noted that the home secretary was able to pressure the British Broadcasting Company into banning the documentary "Real Lives: At the Edge of the Union," which was a portrayal of Northern Ireland extremism.[13]

The controversy in Northern Ireland highlights one dilemma faced by law enforcement officials assigned the task of coping with terrorism. Terrorism is, by definition, a political crime in that it involves political motives. Yet most of the law created by democracies to deal with terrorism have been crafted with a desire to prevent its classification as a political crime, to prevent the use of the "political crime exception" included in most extradition agreements, as discussed in an earlier chapter. Democracies, in general, allow a wide range of political dissent, with political parties and interest groups representing extremes on both the right and the left of the ideological spectrum operating legally within the system. Thus, it is generally not the political motive that is "illegal" but the action taken by the individual or group.

Most formal agreements and legislation concerning terrorism today focus on the illegality of the action taken, not on the group or its motive. Prevention of terrorist acts, not designation of terrorist groups, is the stated focus of law enforcement. The motives of the group may be legal, even laudable; its actions may properly be subject to censure.

It is easier to censure such actions than to censor them. If the motive is not illegal, then it is not reasonable to expect the press not to investigate, evaluate, and report on the motive as it relates to a specific act of terrorist violence. In a system in which the press is allowed to interview perpetrators of violent crime (such as murder, rape, torture, etc.) and to interview their family, friends, coworkers, and any other "relevant" individuals, it seems unlikely that a clear standard could be established for the need to censor stories about individuals and groups involved in terrorist acts.

If terrorist acts are not political crimes, then the press cannot reasonably be censored from reporting information on the individuals and their motivations in such cases, as long as they are permitted to publish similar insights relating to other violent crimes. Such reporting may be in poor taste or reflect bad judgment, but it is scarcely worthy of the serious punishment of censorship.

Broadcasters in the United Kingdom, confronted with the censorship system created by the government to control media coverage of the situation in Northern Ireland, were quick to note the ambiguity of this policy. Certainly it was inconsistent to prohibit Sinn Fein from having access to the broadcast media and to censor news stories about this political group when it was by law allowed to function openly as a political party. If it is legal to report on the activities and the causes espoused by other legal political parties, it is not rational for it to be illegal to report on those same items with regard to Sinn Fein.

Neither the United States nor the United Kingdom has been willing, moreover, to recognize violent acts carried out by radical political groups as acts of war. If they had done so, to justify censoring media reporting that might give "aid or comfort to the enemy during time of war" would have been a fairly simple matter. But if the governments should declare that a state of war exists, then they would also be bound by international law to treat the individuals captured during the commission of those violent acts of terrorism as **prisoners of war,** *combatants actively involved in a war who have been captured by the opposing side.* This would make such prisoners subject to the appropriate Geneva Convention provisions and eligible for exchange.

Governments are certainly aware that such a step would encourage the endless taking of hostages by groups committing acts of terror, to exchange them for the prisoners or war held by the government. This could create an intolerable situation, one certainly not worth the comparatively small advantage that the legitimization of censorship would give.

Although the Northern Ireland situation has received the majority of research attention, other Western democracies also offer interesting viewpoints on the utility and effect of governmental restriction on the media's dissemination of information regarding terrorism. A study by Christopher Kehler, Greg Harvey, and Richard Hall offers interesting perspectives on the delicate balance that democracies are expected to maintain between the need for some form of media regulation and the need for a free press.

Kehler and his associates argue that some form of media regulation is essential simply because media coverage of terrorist events can endanger lives. They cite cases in which the press negotiated with terrorists; where press corps members entered lines of fire and secured zones; and cases in which hostage rescue efforts were endangered by live broadcasts of the rescue forces moving in for assault. Although such cases led these researchers to agree that it would be legally permissible for governments to regulate the media in its access to the scenes of these violent acts, it is interesting to note that these authors concluded that responsible standards created and enforced by the broadcast industry itself would be a preferable solution.

The conclusions of Kehler and his associates are consistent with that of most other researchers on this subject. Although almost all deplore the reckless endangering of lives that sometimes takes place when an unrestricted media abuses its privileges of access, few scholars advocate government censorship as a solution. Most appear to agree with Paul Wilkinson's assessment:

> [A]ny suggestion that any external body is bringing pressure to bear and altering editorial judgement as a result of political considerations undermines not only the credibility of the media, but the credibility of democratic government.[14]

Moreover, the government cannot expect to hold the media to a higher standard than that to which the government itself is able to attain, with regard to the so-called bias in the media toward certain individuals and groups. When the U.S. government refers to one group as freedom fighters and to another, engaged in similar tactics with similar motives, as terrorists, the lack of clarity is both debilitating and deliberate. Although government claims that the press evidences at times too much "sympathy" toward a particular individual, group, or cause may have merit, the standard for clear, precise, and consistent reporting of information about such individuals, groups, and causes must be set first by the government.

Governments must decide the legal status of a terrorist crime before the option of censorship can ever be explored. If it is a political crime, or even a crime of war, then certain restrictions by the government might be applicable. If, however, it is treated by the government as simply a particularly vicious but essentially common crime, then the press should not be prevented from exploring its every facet in the same fashion as it is permitted to explore other violent criminal activity.

COMPLICITY: A VERY SERIOUS CHARGE

The relationship between terrorism and the media does not flow in a single direction; rather, terrorism reacts to and uses the media in a fashion similar to that in which the media reacts to and uses (to sell papers) the terrorist events. This interactive relationship has allowed serious charges of **complicity,** *a legal charge indicating active participation of a primary or secondary nature,* in terrorist events to be leveled at the media by law enforcement and government counterterrorism officials.

Terrorism is a crime of theater. In order for terrorism to be effective, the terrorists need to communicate their actions and threats to their audience as quickly and dramatically as possible.[15] Statistically, terrorist incidents worldwide are insignificant, both in terms of the number of dead and injured and in terms of the number of incidents reported annually. But massive media coverage of individual terrorist attacks reach a vast audience, creating an impact far beyond that which the incident, in the absence of this media, could be expected to effect. Without intensive media coverage, it could be argued that few would know of terrorist actions, motivations, and actors. As Brian Jenkins has noted,

> Terrorism is violence for effect—not primarily, and sometimes not at all for the physical effect on the actual target, but rather for its dramatic impact on an audience. Developments in world communications, particularly the news media, have expanded the potential audience to national and, more recently, to international proportions.[16]

The interaction of the media with terrorists in the Hanafi Muslim siege in Washington, DC, in March 1977 provides evidence of media interference in law enforcement efforts and of the proactive role of some media in terrorist events. Live broadcasts from the scene continued throughout the siege, and overzealous journalists tied up the telephone lines interviewing the terrorists. This constitutes nuisance, perhaps, but not necessarily interference.

However, at least two incidents occurred that highlight the interactive nature of the media and the terrorists in this event. One of the reporters, observing law enforcement officers bringing something [food] to the terrorists, broadcast that the police were preparing for an assault. Eventually, the police were able to convince the Hanafi that the reporter was incorrect, but valuable negotiating time and trust-building efforts were lost. Another reporter called the leaders of the hostage takers, Hamas Abdul Khaalis, and suggested that the police were trying to trick him. Khaalis selected 10 of the older hostages for execution, and police again had to defuse the situation by removing some of their sharpshooters from the area.[17]

This certainly constituted interference in the hostage negotiation process and generated much legitimate criticism of the press. A reporter who was one of the hostages in this siege observed:

> As hostages, many of us felt that the Hanafi takeover was a happening, a guerrilla the-ater, a high impact propaganda exercise programmed for the TV screen, and . . . for the front pages of newspapers around the world. . . . Beneath the resentment and the anger of my fellow hostages toward the press is a conviction gained . . . that the news media and terrorism feed on each other, that the news media and particularly TV, create a thirst for fame and recognition. Reporters do not simply report the news. They help create it. They are not objective observers, but subjective participants.[18]

This charge suggests that the media play an active role in terrorist events, sometimes even impacting the course of the event. Such a claim goes well beyond that commonly made by many who research this issue: that terrorists use the media for their own purposes. Few would argue that terrorists do indeed use the media to reach a large audience and to carry a specific message to that audience as quickly as possible. The hijacking of TWA Flight 847 in 1985 was, as Grant Wardlaw notes "cleverly choreographed to ensure maximum media coverage and maximum expo-sure of [their] propaganda."[19] It remains a disturbing example of the manipulation of the free world's news media by groups involved in terrorist acts.

To propose an interactive relationship suggests that it is possible that the media's impact on terrorism goes beyond that of a reluctant tool, tending instead to-ward that of a generator of action. This does not mean that anyone truly believes that the media plan, or deliberately suggest, terrorist attacks to groups or individuals. But the action of the media has been scrutinized intensely in recent years to deter-mine whether media coverage of terrorist events caused, for instance, terrorists to choose one particular choice of action over another (for example, bombings over hi-jackings).

Schmid offers three hypotheses that attempt to explain the media's effect on terrorism. The first, called the **arousal hypothesis,** *suggests that unusual or unique media content can increase a person's desire to act aggressively; that, in fact, any news story detailing some form of aggressive behavior can increase the potential for more aggressive behavior from members of the media's audience.* The second is termed the **disinhibition hypothesis,** which *suggests that violence portrayed in the media weakens the inhibition of the viewer to engage in similar behavior, which in turn increases the person's readiness to engage in aggressive behavior.*

These are hardly as radical a set of concepts today as they were in 1982 when Schmid suggested them. Indeed, a great deal of time and attention has been devoted to determining whether the media encourage violent behavior in viewers, particularly young people. Results of research into these hypotheses have been mixed, but have generated sufficient concern for the attorney general of the United States to issue a not-too-veiled warning to the television networks, strongly suggesting they initiate self-regulation systems for limiting TV violence before the government decides that it must regulate the industry on this issue.

The third hypothesis suggested by Schmid involves the **social learning theory,** *which is premised on the belief that all behavior is learned by observation.* Thus, if television depicts successful terrorist acts, then viewers will learn all about them; this will in turn increase the likelihood of terrorism. The media would thus be engaged in training individuals in terrorist behavior each time it reported such acts.

Surely this is an extreme assessment of the situation. Live media coverage has, perhaps, given greater importance to events in remote parts of the world, but it seems unlikely that an individual would decide, on the basis of a news report of a terrorist incident, to engage in terrorist activities. Although TV newscasts are more visually exciting than printed news articles, it has been possible to test this hypothesis by tracking the articles generated by terrorist events over a decade to determine whether or not increased coverage of terrorist events actually resulted in an increase in the number of such events.

All that could be determined by such an analysis was that an **interactive relationship** appears to exist; that is, *one of the variables acts upon or influences the other.* It was not possible with this type of data to determine much more than a rough estimate of the strength of the relationship and its apparent direction. Because other variables could also be acting upon the ones being studied, without controlling for all other potential influences on terrorist behavior, it would be difficult to generalize about the results of this research. It did become possible, however, to comment more on the utility of the third hypothesis posited by Schmid, using this limited study.

According to the list generated by the U.S. State Department of terrorist incidents that took place from 1981 to 1989 (this was a time of fairly intense terrorist activity), a total of 119 incidents were recorded involving an American citizen in some respect. Because all of these incidents involved at least one U.S. citizen, it seems logical to assume they would be reported in national newspapers, such as *The Washington Post* and *The New York Times.* Using these two papers, most of whose stories on these incidents were supplied by the Associated Press (thus eliminating the majority of anomalies in the reporting of the data) and categorizing the incidents by type (to discover whether any type of event served better as a "learning tool"), it was possible to note several interesting phenomena:

1. Cumulative regression analysis of the data resulted in a multiple r of 0.843 and a square multiple of r of 0.710. This generally indicates a strong relationship, in this case between the type of event and the amount of coverage.

2. From 1981 to 1989 inclusive, the number of terrorist incidents increased overall while the number of articles generated in response to these incidents actually decreased.

   a. There were exceptions to these trends. The number of bombings resulting in deaths remained relatively constant, actually decreasing toward the end of the period. This occurred in spite of the enormous increase in the number of articles generated by these attacks.

   b. The incidence of assassination (defined, in State Department terms, as any time an American is shot and killed) peaked in 1984, with four incidents that generated a record 14 articles. In spite of the rash of press coverage, however, the number of incidents fell the following year to the 1981 level (one incident), producing only four articles. The following year there were three incidents, clearly not impacted by the previous year's limited press coverage of these types of events. In other words, many articles in one year did not generate many attacks in the following year; nor did a year when the number of articles dropped to only four was there a decrease in the subsequent number of incidents.

c. Hijackings (involving the willful seizure of a means of transportation for a political purpose) occurred only in three years during the decade studied. After three incidents generated a phenomenal 16 articles, there was only one further incident for the remainder of the decade.

d. Kidnappings of Americans actually generated fewer articles than incidents, meaning that some incidents were not even reported in the national news. Nor was there a directional relationship between the number of articles and the number of incidents. Four incidents in 1985 generated only one article, whereas fewer incidents (three) in 1986 evoked seven articles. The same number of incidents (three) in 1987 produced only one article.

This data suggests that, although a relationship appears to exist between the number of terrorist incidents in a given year and the number of articles they generate, this relationship varies with the type of incident. Moreover, even in the same category of incident, there is considerable variation in the number of articles evoked by the same number of incidents. This implies that, as suggested earlier, other factors are at work in this process not accounted for in so simplistic an assumption as the "learned behavior" hypothesis. If all that was necessary for a terrorist to repeat his action, or for another terrorist to attempt a similar action, was news coverage of the event, then all of the types of events should have produced parallel growth lines between incident and article numbers. This was clearly not the case.

Instead, it is obvious that other factors influence the decision of an individual or group to engage in terrorist activities. Although the media may have some impact, it is erroneous to assume the action of the media causes terrorist events to happen merely by the coverage of previous events. Hijacking incidents did not become less frequent because of limited press coverage; instead, press coverage was extensive. However, the enactment of several aerial hijacking conventions, and the subsequent closing of most safe havens for hijackers by the "extradite or prosecute" provisions in international agreements (discussed in the following chapter), may as easily be given credit for reducing the number of hijack incidents.

This limited study of news media in a role of "motivation" for terrorism suggests that, although terrorism and the media show a strong relationship, this does not mean that media coverage results in terrorist acts. Certainly, the mass media do serve to extend experience, present models, stimulate aspirations, and indicate goals for terrorists. But the media are clearly not responsible for terrorist acts occurring.

It is possible to infer from a variety of studies on this issue that the media can impact terrorists by what Schmid terms a **built-in escalation imperative,** *requiring* *that terrorists must commit more and more bizarre and cruel acts to gain media attention.* Because kidnapping failed to generate continued media attention, even though most articles suggested that many times the ransom demands were met, terrorists turned increasingly to the use of assassination. When the shooting of a single American stopped generating many articles (as it did between 1985 and 1989), then bombings resulting in multiple deaths became the weapon of choice.

A relationship certainly exists between terrorists and the media. The strength and direction of that relationship is dependent upon many variables and is thus probably not a suitable target for intervention by the government. Intervention could skew the relationship in an undesirable direction. As Schmid notes, "the assertion of insurgent terrorists that democratic states are not really democratic would gain credibility if the freedom of the press were suspended."[20]

Perhaps it would be more accurate to say that terrorism and the media may share some goals, which impacts the nature of their relationship. An examination of the goals of terrorists, the goals of the media, and the goals of democratic governments reveals some insights into the complex relationship that exists between these three actors.

TERRORIST GOALS REGARDING MEDIA

In the view of several of the experts previously cited, terrorists have goals that the media can help them to achieve. Let us briefly examine a few of these goals to determine more clearly the stakes in this very dangerous game.

Publicity

Because terrorism is an act of theater and requires an audience, most terrorist groups welcome the opportunity to acquire "free" **publicity.** *Getting information out to a large, even global audience* about the cause for which the acts are being committed is a vital part of the act itself. Press coverage that makes the world aware of the problem that the individual or group is seeking to resolve is clearly advantageous. This publicity can offer both **tactical** (*short-term*) and **strategic** (*long-term*) **gains** for the operation itself and in some cases to the cause for which the terrorist act is being committed.

Tactical gains in publicity are usually measured in terms of getting information concerning demands that must be met within a time frame to more than just the law enforcement officers at the scene. If the general public can be made aware of the demands, and the consequences threatened for lack of fulfillment, then pressure may be put on the legal officers to comply by a concerned public. Strategic goals can be met by increasing that large audience's awareness of the "justice" of the cause for which the act is being committed, and the seriousness of the "problem" which the terrorists are trying to rectify.

Favorable Understanding of Their Cause

This is a vitally important goal of most terrorists today. Everyone wants to be understood, and an individual or group that is clearly breaking important laws and norms of behavior has *an intense desire for* **favorable understanding,** *for their audience to understand why they are carrying out these acts.* Sympathy for their suffering, and more importantly, for their cause can be generated by a press willing to convey their message. If, as discussed in a previous chapter, terrorists live with images of their world that are unlike those of most of this audience, then it is critically important to them that they convey to that audience the justice for which they struggle and the reasons that have driven them to carry out acts of terrorism.

As one expert has noted, "good relationships with the press are important here, and they are often cultivated and nurtured over a period of years."[21] Although not all terrorists have access or longevity sufficient to build such "friendly relations" with the press, most individuals and groups carrying out terrorist acts do want the press to share with the public a positive understanding of why the incident is occurring. This leaves the media in an invidious position, determining what is news to be reported and what is rhetoric from the terrorist's pulpit. As Rushworth Kidder suggests, "the decision whether or not to broadcast or publish interviews with admitted terrorists brings journalists to the fine line between news and a forum for propaganda."[22]

Legitimacy and Identity

To recruit effectively, groups must convey **legitimacy and identity,** *a clear sense of purpose and identity to those who might be seeking similar political goals.* Proving to be both committed and effective in kidnaping, bombing, assassination, and other dramatic terrorist events can be a very useful tool in the recruitment of new members to a group's cause. Moreover, if the group needs funding for their operations, as most do, good publicity of a successful operation can be the key to drawing such support from nations and individuals who share a concern for the cause motivating the group.

When numerous groups exist that share a similar general problem focus, then a group may carry out bombings or assassinations simply to establish a separate and credible identity. Certainly in areas such as Northern Ireland and Israel this has been the case, as splinter groups commit acts of terrorism whose tactical goal seems to be establishing a separate identity.

Destabilizing the Enemy

A goal often cited by terrorist groups has been to cause damage to the enemy by **destabilizing the enemy**—that is, *by generating a sense of unrest, enhancing a fear that the government is unable to offer security and stability to its people.* Because terrorism is an act designed to create a mood of fear, the press can be seen by terrorists as a valuable tool in the achievement of this goal. If the media can be used to amplify fear, to spread panic, and to make the population feel insecure, then the terrorists will have won an important goal.

GOVERNMENT GOALS REGARDING MEDIA

In democratic systems, journalists are usually given substantial freedom to report news, including that of terrorist events. But unlimited freedom of the press has led, as noted earlier, to an escalation of events and a loss of life—results that neither the press nor the government desire. In many ways, the goals of the government in terrorist incidents are quite similar to those of the group carrying out the act. (See also Figure 8.1.)

1. *Publicity.* Most governments know that the event will be publicized and therefore will want the press to offer publicity designed to help the government achieve its goal of ending the situation without loss of innocent lives. This means that publicity, from the government's perspective, should be carefully disseminated in a manner that will not endanger lives and that will help the public understand the positive actions undertaken by the government to resolve the situation. This clearly is not compatible with the terrorists' goals, because from the terrorists' perspective publicity should be used to spread fear, not reassurance, about the government's handling of the action. The media is thus left with difficult choices about what news to release and how it should be worded.

2. *Criminality of Act.* Certainly, law enforcement would prefer that the media paint the terrorists as the "bad guys," and the simplest method for achieving that goal is often to stress the illegal nature of the act that is occurring. The terrorists will seek to have the press convey the justice of the cause for which they fight, whereas law enforcement will want to focus on the serious breach of law being perpetrated. Because terrorism is, by definition, carried out against innocent victims, legal authorities will seek to have the media focus on the injustice of the actions being taken by the group, and the criminal nature of the offense will be highlighted by noting the innocence of the victims. If the public can be made to view the terrorists as common criminals of a particularly nasty sort, then the government will clearly be viewed as the "good guys" rescuing the victims and ending the violence. To achieve this goal, the government clearly needs the media's cooperation.

3. *Deny the Terrorist a Platform.* It is certainly in the government's best interest to enforce **denial of a platform**—that is, *not to allow terrorists to use the free press as a "bully pulpit" for their propaganda.* This platform can be used not only to generate understanding and perhaps sympathy for the terrorist's cause, but also to generate tangible support. The 1986 hijacking of TWA Flight 847 in Beirut gave explicit indication of the dangers of this platform. The skyjackers reportedly offered the press tours of the plane for $1,000 and a session with the hostages for $12,500! Although not many situations ever become quite so chaotic, it is in most government's agenda to separate the terrorist from the media as far as possible, so that neither propaganda nor funds can be generated from the event.

4. *Information and Cooperation.* For most law enforcement agencies the optimum solution would be exclusion of the media and other observers from the area in which a terrorist event occurs, but this is seldom an option in democratic systems. Instead, governments may want **information and cooperation,** such as having *the media share information they may have about the individuals involved but be careful not to share information with the hostage takers about data that might be of use to them.* Thus, the media will be asked by governments to be discrete, careful not to reveal how successful operations were performed, and cautious about revealing information about an event that might provoke or enable a **copycat operation,**

one in which a terrorist act is copied by an observer in a subsequent act. In some cases cooperation may even be interpreted by the government as a willingness on the media's part to share **disinformation,** that is, *inaccurate information designed to confuse*—when such cooperation will help in resolving the threat in the terrorist action.

MEDIA GOALS IN TERRORIST EVENTS

Few of these goals held by police and terrorists for working with the media are compatible. Indeed, most are absolutely incompatible, because both sides seek "good" publicity, legitimacy, and cooperation. Before considering methods for resolving this problem in conflicting goals, let us briefly consider the goals of the media in reporting such events. (See also Figure 8.1.)

1. *Getting a Scoop.* In a world with fast-breaking news, 24 hours a day, **getting a scoop,** *being the first to report the news,* is a crucial goal. High-tech communications make it possible, and increase the pressure, to transmit news stories in "real time"—that is, as the event actually happens. This leaves little option for editing or carefully evaluating the impact of such a news release on the situation. In such cases, this may mean that discussing the impact of their reporting with public safety officers, noted as part of several goals of the law enforcement community, may be costly to the journalists, who stand to lose that scoop to a less scrupulous reporter.

2. *Dramatic Presentation of News.* The media, in this fierce competition for public attention, clearly *need to create a* **dramatic presentation** *of the event as well as a timely one.* During the hijacking of TWA Flight 847 in June 1985, ABC broadcasted extensive interviews with the hijackers and the hostages. Indeed, in one dramatic reel, a pistol was aimed at the pilot's head in a staged photo-op for the interviewers.[23] The media argue that the intense scrutiny they give to each aspect of the event actually protects the hostages. This assumes that the primary goal of the act is to communicate a cause, drawing support from this explication. If drama is needed to demonstrate the seriousness of the cause, however, then the lives of hostages could be jeopardized by a media demand for drama. If killing a hostage or a planeload of hostages becomes the price of drama, then the media may be held responsible for raising the stakes in the hostage "game."

3. *Protection of Rights.* The media have a strong commitment to **protection of rights,** *specifically the public's "right to know" about events as they occur.* Usually, this does not mean that the media see their role in opposition to law enforcement. Most media seek to be professional and accurate, careful not to give out disinformation, and playing as constructive a role as possible in the event. Freedom of speech is not an absolute and inviolable value; most democracies have experienced times when civil liberties, including free speech, have had to be curtailed in the interests of national security. As one scholar notes, the conflict discussed here between the media and law enforcement "is between our commitment to unhindered public discourse and the need for public security."[24] Censorship of the press in most democracies in unacceptable; voluntary restraints by the press on itself is advocated, but difficult to evoke in a form flexible yet effective enough to satisfy all concerned. If democracies give up free speech to stop terrorism, then regardless of the "success" of this effort, the terrorists win, because the government and its citizens lose a fundamental part of their system. But an absolutely free press can cost lives. In the hijacking of TWA Flight 847 mentioned earlier, radio broadcasts alerted the hijackers aboard the Lufthansa jet that the captain of the plane was

transmitting information to authorities on the ground. The hijackers then killed the captain. The press was free and the cost was the life of the pilot.

4. *Personal Security.* The Committee to Protect Journalists, based in New York, notes that more than 300 journalists have been murdered since 1986 as a result of their work. In 1995 alone, according to this group's records, 45 were assassinated.[25] Thus, one of the goals of the media is increasingly **personal security,** *to be able to protect themselves, both during and after terrorist operations.* Journalists who interview terrorists are at risk and those who fail to satisfy terrorists' goals of favorable understanding and publicity may be vulnerable to attack by the terrorists and their sympathizers. On January 23, 2002, *Wall Street Journal* reporter Daniel Pearl was kidnapped in Karachi, Pakistan, by members of a Pakistani organization with links to al-Qaeda. Its members beheaded him.

Terrorists	Government	Media
1. Publicity	1. Publicity	1. Getting a scoop
2. Favorable understanding of their cause	2. Criminality of the act	2. Dramatic presentation of news
3. Legitimacy and identity	3. Deny terrorists a platform	3. Protection of rights
4. Destabilizing the enemy	4. Information and cooperation	4. Personal security

FIGURE 8.1   Comparison of Goals

CASE STUDY   **Bin Laden's Tapes**

A brief look at the skillful use of the media by one of the world's best-known terrorists, Osama bin Laden, makes many of the preceding goals clear. It also raises interesting questions about the impact of the media on events during a terrorist crisis.

As Judith Miller so aptly put it, "With his turban and camouflage jacket, his ornate Arabic and harsh vows of continued terror against America, Osama bin Laden revealed in his speech the instinctive cunning that has made him such a formidable foe."[26] Referring to one of his taped speeches in which bin Laden articulated once again his call for *jihad,* she noted that the speech gave to this al-Qaeda leader his most visible platform, because it was broadcast over a popular Arabic satellite channel and rebroadcast many times by CNN and many other networks.

Using this platform, bin Laden expressed righteous indignation over the suffering of Iraq and Palestine. With his pledge to end the 80 years of "humiliation and disgrace" that Muslims have endured since the demise of the Ottoman Empire and to recreate the caliphate, the Muslim empire based for about 500 years in Iraq, bin Laden made his appeal for understanding among the common Arab men of the region.

His timing of this platform appearance was excellent. Al Jazeera, the Arabic network, had followed bin Laden's instructions to delay release of the tape until after the start of the American bombing in Afghanistan. Using the West's media weapon very effectively, bin Laden issued his global statement just as President Bush was trying to declare war on terrorism. In his taped address, bin Laden suggested that the world was divided, not by who stood with the United States in rejecting terrorism and those who stood against her, but in terms of people who were faithful to Islam and the infidels who opposed him.

Although this was not the first call by bin Laden to jihad against America—it was in fact the fourth such call—the video shown around the world in early October 2001 was by far the most effective. He used the media to secure a platform with a worldwide audience, to emotionally explain the cause for his anger and his anguish, and to paint the enemies of his jihad in ways that shook the alliance that President Bush was trying to form. Ahmed Abdullah, another of bin Laden's lieutenants and the head of al-Qaeda's media committee, is believed to have arranged the filming and transmission of many of bin Laden's propaganda videos. ❏

CONCLUSIONS

Technological progress in communications systems has made the media a potentially significant weapon in the terrorist arsenal. Whether the media are "the terrorist's best friend," as Walter Lacquer has suggested, or an unwitting ally, as described by Schmid and de Graff's study, it seems clear that the media play a significant role in the "propaganda by the deed" which is modern terrorism.[27] The line between reporter of terrorist events and participant in these events, between impartial journalist and partisan advocate, is often quite thin and easily, if unintentionally, crossed.

Studies suggest that violent behavior can be learned and that copycat behavior among individuals and groups is common. Therefore, it is not unreasonable to assume that portrayal of terrorist events in the news may actually motivate terrorist behavior. This does not suggest that journalists are intentionally involved in the increase in terrorist incidents. Although journalists have, as noted earlier, sometimes interfered in situations to a degree that may have altered the course of the event, this is the exception rather than the rule.

A strong case can be made for the need for media to work with the government to devise workable guidelines in matters of media coverage of terrorism. This should include guidelines for working with law enforcement in setting reasonable limits on access to events, where appropriate, as well as self-regulating rules on the use, nonuse, or delayed use of information, technology, and opportunity in ways that will best protect the lives endangered by the situation and the needs of citizens for a full account of events.

The goals of terrorists, law enforcement, and the media are clearly intensely related and fundamentally incompatible in many respects. There is no greater challenge for democracies in the struggle with terrorism today than that posed by the need to find a policy compatible with the tradition of a free and vigorous press. Democratic governments are confronted with the demand that they be able to reconcile the goals of the media with those of law enforcement in ways that do not satisfy the goals of terrorists. Prior restraints placed on access and censorship of press coverage of terrorist events create too high a price to pay for the dubious value of decreasing press reports of terrorist acts. Terrorists win significant victories against democracies when they force such measures.

This is a formidable but not necessarily an impossible task. The Report of the Task Force on Disorders and Terrorism (1976) made constructive suggestions regarding the synthesizing of the protection of first amendment rights with the need for public security:

1. Limiting interviews during hostage situations
2. Delaying the release of inflammatory or sensitive information
3. Minimizing the intrusiveness of the media in the course of the terrorist events
4. Striving for balanced and noninflammatory coverage of such incidents

The standards suggested by the media during the last decade of the twentieth century often coincide with these recommendations. Most call for balanced coverage, which avoids the use of provocative catchwords and catchphrases. There is agreement, as well, on the need not to offer to terrorists a platform for propaganda. But the media have strongly resisted the concept of government regulation, regarding this as censorship, with the government restricting freedom of speech and the press in ways not compatible with constitutional protections. Although most constitutions have sanctioned powers of emergency that may be invoked, with a consequent limiting of freedom of speech, most democracies are unwilling to concede to terrorists their goal of destabilization by having to invoke such emergency provisions. Deciding which goals must be met and what the acceptable cost will be for meeting them, is a challenge governments in the twenty-first century *must* meet.

One scholar of this thorny issue has stated the essence of this dilemma challenging democracies quite succinctly:

> The potential power of these [terrorist] groups seems to lie not in their threat to overthrow society by force of arms *per se,* but in their ability to symbolize the fragility and vulnerability of the social order and to force that order to subvert itself by eroding the liberal and democratic values upon which its own legitimacy is based.[28]

EVALUATION

1. Ralph Perl suggests several voluntary press coverage guidelines that offer insights on the pattern of self-restriction that may emerge soon. Consider each guideline briefly and decide which goals are placed at risk by each.
   a. Limiting information on hostages that could harm them (e.g., number, nationality, official positions, personal wealth, etc.)
   b. Limiting information of military movements during rescue operations
   c. Limiting or agreeing not to air live interviews with terrorists
   d. Toning down information that may cause widespread panic
   e. Checking sources of information carefully
2. Ted Koppel, anchor of ABC television's *Nightline,* suggested that the U.S. media operate at the outer boundaries of what its European allies would view as acceptable. He notes that "[American television is] particularly vulnerable to misuse. We are vulnerable to misuse by our own leaders. . . . The fact that terrorism by definition tends to be dramatic [and] the fact that by definition it tends to involve acts which are pictorial,

makes us even more vulnerable."[29] How can this "vulnerability" be diminished without allowing terrorists to use media as a weapon—eliminating the former two vulnerabilities by making it subject to a third?

3. David Hubbard, a psychiatrist who has interviewed scores of imprisoned hijackers, contends that TV news broadcasts of ongoing terrorist events is "social pornography" because it "caters to the sick, unmet needs of the public."[30] He is convinced that world terrorism would decrease if television brought its coverage under control. How accurate do you think this assessment is? What kind of controls can a democratic society afford to impose on its media? What are the dangers of such controls? How effective do you think either voluntary or involuntary controls on media coverage of terrorism would be in reducing either the number or the violence of terrorist events?

4. Mary Strep and Ronda Knox, assessing the impact of media portrayals and the events of September 11, 2001, also raise troubling questions.[31] Noting that the media played a central role in the dissemination of information on September 11, 2001, these researchers ask the following: To what extent, then, did the media set the agenda on September 11, 2001? How were the most important stories selected? What images of September 11 do you remember most vividly? How important are those images in shaping your perceptions of what happened that day, what the causes were, and what should have been done about the attacks?

SUGGESTED READINGS

Alali, A. Odasno, and Kenoye K. Eke. "Terrorism, the News Media, and Democratic Political Order." *Current World Leaders* 39, no. 4 (August 1996): 64–72.

Alexander, Yonah, and Robert Patter. *Terrorism and the Media: Dilemma for Government, Journalism, and the Public.* (Washington, DC: Brassey's, 1990).

Finn, John E. "Media Coverage of Political Terrorism and the First Amendment: Reconciling the Public's Right to Know with Public Order." In *Violence and Terrorism: 98/99,* ed. Martin Slann and Bernard Schechterman. New York: Dushkin/McGraw-Hill, 1998.

Kehler, C., G. Harvey, and R. Hall. "Perspectives on Media Control in Terrorist-Related Incidents." *Canadian Police Journal* 6: 225–243.

Kidder, Rushworth M. "Manipulation of the Media." In *Violence and Terrorism 98/99,* ed. Martin Slann and Bernard Schechterman. New York: Dushkin/McGraw-Hill, 1998.

Livingstone, W. D. "Terrorism and the Media Revolution." In *Fighting Back: Winning the War Against Terrorism,* ed. N. C. Livingstone and T. E. Arnold. Lexington, MA: Heath, 1986, 213–227.

Miller, A. H. "Terrorism, the Media, and the Law: A Discussion of the Issues." In *Terrorism, the Media, and the Law,* ed. A. H. Miller. Dobbs Ferry, NY: Transnational Publishers, 1982, 13–50.

———. "Terrorism and the Media: Lessons from the British Experience." In *The Heritage Foundation Lectures.* Washington, DC: Heritage, 1990.

Nacos, Brigitte L. "Accomplice or Witness: The Media's Role in Terrorism." In *Violence and Terrorism 04/05,* ed. Thomas Badey. Guilford, CT: Dushkin/McGraw-Hill, 2004.

Perl, Ralph F. *Terrorism, the Media, and the 21st Century.* Congressional Research Service, 1998.

Schmid, A. P., and J. de Graff. *Violence as Communication: Insurgent Terrorism and the Western News Media.* Beverly Hills, CA: Sage, 1982.

Wilkinson, Paul. *Terrorism and the Liberal State.* New York: University Press, 1986.

NOTES

1. "Terrorism Found Rising, Now Almost Accepted," *Washington Post,* December 3, 1985, A4.
2. These quotes were gathered by Neil Hickey in "Gaining the Media's Attention," *The Struggle Against Terrorism* (New York: Wilson, 1977), 113–114.
3. Ibid., 117.
4. Ibid., 112.
5. T. K. Fitzpatrick, "The Semantics of Terror," *Security Register* 1, no. 14 (November 4, 1974): 23.
6. A. H. Miller, "Terrorism, the Media, and the Law: A Discussion of the Issues," in *Terrorism, the Media, and the Law*, ed. A. H. Miller (Dobbs Ferry, NY: Transnational Publishers, 1980), 43.
7. Abraham J. Miller, "Terrorism and the Media: Lessons from the British Experience," in *The Heritage Foundation Lectures* (Washington, DC, 1990), 1–9.
8. Alex P. Schmid and Janny F. A. DeGraff, *Violence as Communication* (Newbury Park, CA: Sage, 1982).
9. Ibid., 172.
10. Rushworth M. Kidder, "Manipulation of the Media," in *Violence and Terrorism 91/92,* ed. Martin Slann and Bernard Schechterman (New York: Dushkin, 1991), 118.
11. Henrik Bering-Jensen, "The Silent Treatment for Terrorists," *Insight* (November 21, 1988), 34.
12. Ibid., 35.
13. Paul Wilkinson, *Terrorism and the Liberal State* (New York: New York University Press, 1986).
14. Abraham H. Miller, "Terrorism and the Media," 8.
15. Billy M. Turner, "America: Bull's Eye for Terrorists?" *Security Management* (June 1987), 45.
16. Brian M. Jenkins, "High Technology Terrorism and Surrogate War: The Impact of New Technology on Low-Level Violence," in *Contemporary Terrorism: Selected Readings,* ed. J. D. Elliott and L. K. Gibson (Gaithersburg, MD: International Association of Chiefs of Police, 1978), 101.
17. Schmid and de Graff, *Violence as Communication,* 77.
18. Ibid., 42.
19. Grant Wardlaw, "State Response to International Terrorism: Some Cautionary Comments," paper presented to the Symposium on International Terrorism, Defense Intelligence Agency, Washington, DC, 1985, 8.
20. Schmid and de Graff, *Violence as Communication,* 172.
21. Rushworth Kidder, "Manipulation of the Media," 151.
22. Ibid., 152.
23. On June 13, 1985, two Hezbollah gunmen hijacked this flight en route from Athens to Rome and murdered U.S. Navy diver Robert Stethem after the plane landed in Beirut for a second time. The U.S. State Department was highly critical of the impact of the media on this event.
24. John E. Finn, "Media Coverage of Political Terrorism and the First Amendment: Reconciling the Public's Right to Know with Public Order," in *Terrorism and the Media: Dilemma for Government, Journalism and the Public,* ed. Yonah Alexander and Robert Latter (Washington, DC: Brassey's, 1990).
25. See Web site http://www.cpj.org/
26. Judith, Miller, "Bin Laden's Media Savvy: Expert Timing of Threats," *The New York Times,* October 9, 2001, A1.
27. Schmid and de Graff, *Violence as Communication,* 172.
28. Ralph Perl, *Terrorism, the Media, and the 21st Century* (Washington, DC: Congressional Research Service, 1998), 2.
29. Kidder, "Manipulation of the Media," 53.
30. David Hubbard, *Skyjacker: His Flights of Fancy* (New York: Wilson, 1997), 134.
31. Mary Strep and Rhonda Knox, "Terrorism and the Media," *Council on Foreign Relations* (August 5, 2004), 1.

9
Domestic Terrorism in the United States

Key Concepts

genocide	Animal Liberation Front
slavery	Aryan Nations
vigilante terrorism	Christian Identity Movement
right-wing extremism	Montana Freemen
insurgent terrorism	Christian Patriots
transnational terrorism	1993 World Trade Center bombing
Johan Most	cyberterrorism
Earth Liberation Front	Waco, Texas, incident

Terrorism is neither unique nor new to the United States. Nationalist terrorism began during frontier wars in the seventeenth century and has continued to the present day.

Jonathan A. White

To apply some of the concepts and definitions discussed thus far, study of terrorism as it has developed in one country may be helpful. Although the United States has been slower than some other Western democracies in developing definitions and coping strategies for domestic terrorism, the pattern observed may help to clarify the strengths and weaknesses of the profiles of terrorists, their patterns of training, and the philosophies that motivate them.

HISTORICAL ROOTS IN THE UNITED STATES

This nation was, as one historian noted, "conceived and born in violence,"[1] from early settlers and their wars with the Native American populations, to the Sons of Liberty and the patriots of the port cities during the 1760s and 1770s to the vigilante groups who enforced justice as the settlers moved West. Much of the violence of the nineteenth and twentieth centuries was rooted in these early patterns, making a quick look at these early patterns of terrorism useful in understanding and predicting terrorism in the twenty-first century.

     Terrorism certainly occurred during the early years of colonial settlement in North America. The efforts of the British, and then the young American leaders, to eliminate the threat from the indigenous populations certainly became **genocide,** because, by definition, it evolved into *efforts to reduce in size (to facilitate control of) or to destroy ethnic groups.* This included massacres of men, women, and children, decimating whole villages or forcing the inhabitants of those villages on what became "death marches" to distant locations, as records of the treatment of the Cherokee of western North Carolina indicate.

Not all deaths of Native Americans at the hands of British or Americans were done by open violence; instead, evidence exists that some died from weapons of bioterror. Although diseases have historically killed large numbers of indigenous peoples as colonial intrusions brought diseases for which native populations had no resistance, the diseases were also used as weapons. There are accounts, for example, suggesting that certain local British commanders in 1769 planned to give to the Native Americans, as a peace offering, blankets from military hospitals that had been infected by smallpox. Although a smallpox epidemic did break out among the Native Americans in Pennsylvania, it is uncertain from historical records whether the blankets played any role in this outbreak.

Violence during the Revolution has often been justified by the Machiavellian philosophy of the ends justifying the means, an operational philosophy frequently claimed by modern revolutionary groups. Thus, the tarring and feathering of Tories in the seaport cities during the 1770s, a brutal act involving pouring tar over a victim and then dumping feathers over him or her (or rolling the person in a pile of feathers), was treated as a patriotic act of violence that helped to win the Revolutionary War.

The guerrilla warfare that encompassed the colonies from New York to Georgia was also marred by terrorism. Rival parties of Whigs and Tories bushwhacked houses and travelers, burning homes and often killing innocent family members. Neither Whigs nor Tories showed any mercy, and prisoners were frequently tortured and then hanged. Terrorism perpetrated against members of a family on one side often made the surviving members of that family willing to carry out equally atrocious acts of terror in revenge.

Although most of the Revolutionary War was no doubt fought according to the rules, at least in the sense that targets were primarily military rather than civilian and terrorism was the exception rather than the rule, it is evident from historical accounts that terrorism did take place. This pattern makes it clear, though, why nation-states such as the United States today are hesitant to condemn revolutionary violence in emerging states, even when such violence involves occasional acts of terrorism. Most states, in their own history, have seen similar acts of terrorism, sometimes carried out by historically venerated "patriots," for reasons that touch cords of sympathy in modern times.

Like many modern nation-states, the United States also experienced a violent civil war. Although the practice of slavery, in the twentieth century, was declared an international crime, it was widely practiced in the United States until the mid-1860s and was a major contributing factor in generating the conflict. **Slavery,** which involves *the holding of a person as the property of, and completely subject to, another* *person,* was a violent act carried out legally at that time by thousands of families and businesses throughout the world. The practice of slavery and the violent conflict that tore the nation during efforts to end the practice left legacies of violence that endured through the twentieth century and are still inherent in many right-wing groups active today.

In the U.S. slave trade, individuals and families were captured and carried from one continent (usually Africa) against their will, in appalling conditions, to another continent (North America), and sold to U.S. citizens and businesses. This violent up-rooting, brutal treatment, and degradation of an ethnic community would unques-tionably today be classified as terrorism if it were carried out for political motives rather than economic ends. Regardless of its motives, its legacy has been both bitter and violent in the United States, contributing significantly to the right-wing terror-ism currently emerging.

White supremacist groups that operate in the United States today trace their roots to the group that emerged after the Civil War, during the period of Southern re-construction, known as the Ku Klux Klan (KKK). This name has been applied to ei-ther of two distinct secret terrorist organizations in the United States. *One of these is the organization founded just after the Civil War lasting until the 1870s. The other KKK began in 1915 and continued through the end of the century.* The first Klan was originally founded as a social club for Confederate veterans in Pulaski, Tennessee, in 1866. They apparently derived the name from the Greek word *kyklos,* from which comes the English term *circle,* the Klan part of the name came from an effort at allit-eration. Rapidly becoming a vehicle for Southern White underground resistance, its members sought to restore White supremacy to the South through intimidation and violence aimed at the newly enfranchised black freedmen.

This Klan reached its peak between 1868 and 1870, dressing in white robes and sheets to intimidate the freedmen and to avoid being recognized. Klansmen beat and killed freedmen and their White supporters in nighttime attacks. The violence of this group caused its founders to order it to disband and the U.S. Congress to pass the Ku Klux Klan Act in 1871, which imposed heavy penalties on this terrorist organization. This Klan essentially disappeared in the following years, largely because its goal of restoring White supremacy had been largely achieved and the need for such an orga-nization was no longer felt.

The new Klan, which emerged in 1915, added a hatred of Roman Catholics, Jews, foreigners, and organized labor to its hostility toward Blacks. A burning cross became the symbol of this new organization. It peaked in membership in the 1920s, dropped drastically in activity in the Great Depression of the 1930s, and experienced a resurgence in membership and activities with the civil rights movement of the 1960s. Bombings, whippings, shootings, and lynchings were again committed by members of this group against innocent people.

By the end of the twentieth century, Klan membership was again fragmentary and dispersed. Many became members instead of White supremacist groups active throughout the country. According to Bill Stanton, the Klan broke with the past in 1979 and emerged in North Carolina and Georgia as a paramilitary organization.[2]

This emergence of a new form of right-wing extremism will be examined in more depth later in this chapter. It is sufficient to note here that the practice of slavery and the subsequent growth of racist groups carrying out violence against the newly freed slaves created a legacy of violence still generating terrorist acts today.

While the colonial period produced acts of genocide and slavery generated much of modern right-wing terrorism, one form of this, **vigilante terrorism,** in which *individuals or groups seek to defend the status quo or return to that of an earlier period by using terrorist tactics on a population without legitimate authority to do so,* grew as the frontier of the new nation expanded. Settlers developed their own form of justice, with vigilante groups often comprised of leading citizens holding moot, illegal, "courts" to try and often execute those disrupting civil society.

This trend toward vigilante violence helps to explain the growth in the western United States of modern vigilante groups, such as The Order, the Christian Identity Movement, and many of the militia organizations that exist nationwide. These groups tend to be based on the assumption that the current system of justice is inadequate and that vigilante action, often of a terrorist nature, is required to restore order to the system.

Several of these groups will be examined in more depth in the discussion of contemporary terrorism. At this point it is sufficient to conclude that most modern terrorist acts taking place in the United States have roots in its history.

CONCEPTUALIZING DOMESTIC TERRORISM IN THE UNITED STATES

Political violence in America has a long history; therefore, establishing categories for the types of domestic terrorism will make analysis more coherent. Most of those who have researched violence in the United States have suggested three categories of terrorist types, although they differ somewhat in the naming of those types. Ted Gurr suggested that the categories be called vigilante terrorism, insurgent terrorism, and transnational terrorism.[3] This is very similar to that suggested by Brent Smith in 1994, who grouped terrorism by motivation as well, but called the categories right-wing extremism; left-wing extremism, nationalist terrorism, and single-issue violence; and international terrorism.[4]

Vigilante terrorism, mentioned earlier, is simply a form of **right-wing extremism,** in which individuals or groups *seek to retain or to reestablish an earlier status quo by use of terrorist acts.* While the second category seems quite broad (including left-wing, nationalists, and single-issue extremists), most could fit comfortably in the category Gurr suggests of **insurgent terrorism,** since all of these do *seek to rebel against or radically change the political system through the use of terrorist tactics.* The inclusion of single-issue violence in this category may be somewhat confusing, but most proponents of this type of action do also seek to change (by violent challenge) the current status quo. Those who bomb abortion clinics, for example, seek to create a mood of fear in those who would use or operate such clinics, in an effort to change the current status quo that allows such clinics to operate. Finally, **transnational terrorism** is the same as international terrorism, as both terms indicate *terrorism that involves two or more countries.*

Insurgent Terrorism

Because this is, as Smith's work makes clear, a very broad category, it will be useful to examine its different manifestations separately. Movements from the extreme left (such as anarchism), the more moderate left (nationalism), and issue-specific insurgency will be explored separately, with conclusions offered linking these "insurgent" movements in the context of U.S. terrorism.

Left-Wing Extremism

One of the early forms of insurgent terrorism to reach the United States was anarchism, which was imported from Europe during the late nineteenth and early twentieth century. Where Russia and parts of Europe experienced anarchists like Mikhail Bakunin and Sergey Nechayev, discussed in earlier chapters, America had **Johan Most,** *an anarchist who immigrated from Germany to the United States in 1882,* after serving a jail sentence in London for praising the assassination of the Russian czar.[5]

Most was the first U.S. citizen to provide a philosophical rationale for terrorism, advocating the linkage of anarchism to the labor movement and arguing that violence was the only method available for overcoming the tyranny of the wealth and power of the state. In his revolutionary newspaper, *Freiheit* (which means "freedom" in German), Most discussed the value of organized violence in labor struggles, seeking to incite members of the labor movement to violence. In this newspaper, Most advocated a bombing campaign against the U.S. government and industry. He also developed plans for a letter bomb, which become a "unique American contribution to the terrorist arsenal."[6]

Most, like his occasional companion Emma Goldman, who emigrated from Russia to the United States in 1885, spent most of his time trying to incite others to violence. Both were closely linked to the labor movement, strongly advocated social change and the use of violence to achieve those changes. Like many of their European counterparts, Most and Goldman were violent in words but not in deeds for the most part, limiting the extent to which they could accurately be accused of terrorism.

Like Europe, too, the United States experienced a surge of left-wing terrorism in the mid-to-late twentieth century, much of it initially on its college campuses rather than among its working poor in labor movements. Within the category of insurgent terrorism that flourished in the latter part of the twentieth century would fall the Puerto Rican nationalists who carried out terrorist acts, student-based revolutionary groups, and single-issue groups, according to Smith's analysis. These disparate left-wing groups tended to espouse Marxist philosophy, to be violently opposed to the economic "status quo," to seek to create bases for their movements in urban rather than rural areas, and like most other groups engaging in terrorism, chose symbolic rather than strategically important targets for their attacks.

Unlike much of Europe, however, the U.S. left-wing revolutionary movements did not generate widespread public support, nor were most groups long-lived or successful in efforts toward carrying out acts of violence. In 1967, several protest groups began to coalesce around the Students for a Democratic Society (SDS). The Weather Underground, the Symbionese Liberation Army (infamous for its kidnapping of heiress Patty Hearst) were active in the 1960s and 1970s. Many in these groups linked with Puerto Rican nationalist groups, like the Macheteros. Fortunately for the United States, most of the student-based groups were active in ideological rhetoric but not skilled in violence. Many of the bombing attempts killed more of the student activists than they did the intended targets.

By the 1980s, however, a group with elements of many of these earlier groups had emerged. The May 19 Communist Organization (M19CO) brought together members of the SDS, the Black Panther Party, and several other groups. This new group was racially mixed, about half of its members were women, and it spawned numerous splinter groups. M19CO's violence tended to take the form of robbery and subsequent shootings involving police. By the end of the 1980s, this group was largely dispersed or jailed by coordinated police efforts, because many members had been involved in a wide variety of common crimes.

Nationalist Groups

Puerto Rican nationalists have been active for more than four decades, because the U.S. government has had difficulty deciding the ultimate status of this territory. In addition to the very violent Macheteros, the Armed Forces of National Liberation (FALN), the Volunteers for the Puerto Rican Revolution (OVRP), the Armed Forces of Liberation (FARP), the Guerrilla Forces of Liberation (GEL), and Omega 7 operated in the United States. Many routinely joined other left-wing organizations, such as M19CO. In addition to conducting one of the largest armored car robberies in U.S. history, Puerto Rican groups carried out several bombings, assassinations, and one rocket attack (on FBI headquarters in San Juan).

Although most of the left-wing revolutionary violence of the 1960s and 1970s has diminished substantially, but not entirely vanished, from the United States, the problem of violence erupting from Puerto Rico's status is likely to remain. Among Puerto Ricans, there is considerable division of opinion as to what is best for the islands: some want statehood within the United States; others would like to have an independent country; and some are satisfied with its current commonwealth status. This ambivalence is compounded by the strategic importance placed on Puerto Rico by the U. S. military, which continues to use portions of the territory for target practice and military maneuvers. Regardless of which solution for its future status is adopted, at least one or two groups will be angry and may well carry on the violent attacks on U.S. targets.

Single-Issue Groups

Within the category of insurgent terrorism are included, by Smith's categorization, groups and individuals motivated by a single issue, such as protection of the environment or animal rights. These groups, according to Smith, are like the left-wing revolutionaries in their ideologies, their views of human nature, their economic views, and their fanatic devotion to their cause. Brief case studies of two of these types of groups will illustrate these points.

CASE STUDY   Earth Liberation Front

The **Earth Liberation Front** (ELF), *a violent environmental activist group,* is believed to have splintered off from the Earth First movement at a meeting in Brighton, England, in 1994. The notable difference between the Earth First movement and the Earth Liberation Front is that the ELF advocates the destruction of property against corporations that it believes are hurting the environment.

The FBI upgraded the ELF to a terrorist organization in January 2001. This upgraded status was due to an incendiary attack on a ski resort under construction, as well as other destructive attacks. During the attack on the Vail Mountain ski resort in Colorado, the ELF burned three buildings and caused a partial destruction of four ski lifts. The estimated cost of the damage exceeded $12 million. The ELF immediately claimed responsibility for the attack via an e-mail sent from Denver, Colorado. The reason for the attack, according to the e-mail, was that the Vail resort was planning an expansion of the ski resort that would encroach on the best lynx habitat in the state.

The FBI was unable to make immediate arrests or to uncover the identity of the group's members. One of the main reasons contributing to this sluggish legal response is the lack of a central hierarchy in the organization. The FBI believes members of the ELF work in small groups composed of members who know each other extensively and do not keep membership lists or release their identities outside the organization. Because the ELF formed from a grassroots movement, the members are likely to remain in small groups and continue to lack a central government or leader.[7]

Individuals, however, have been apprehended for less dramatic but still violent acts. One member of the original Earth First organization placed spikes in mountain trails to discourage the destruction of natural habitats by bikers. Unfortunately, a student who was part of a track team ran those trails and virtually destroyed his foot on one of the stakes. In a similar action, spikes were placed in trees to protest or prevent the logging of the trees, and a 65-year-old man's saw exploded in his face on contact with a spike. In both cases, individuals responsible were apprehended and charged with the crimes; neither expressed regret at the injuries to the innocent victims. One even stated that, given the choice between saving people and saving trees, he would save the trees. ❏

CASE STUDY   Animal Liberation Front

The **Animal Liberation Front** (ALF), *unlike the more peaceful animal rights group PETA, chose violent paths to reach similar goals.* The ALF open their homepage with a quote by Utah Phillips, which states, "The earth is not dying, it is being killed. Those who are killing it have names and addresses." The group's press office, The North American Press Office, is the principal resource for all actions by this group that take place in the United States, which describes its role as that of explaining the actions of the ALF but not explaining the ALF itself. This office is also a mailbox for ALF members throughout North America, to which supporters can send their reports of their actions on behalf of animal rights. Because there is no central headquarters and no actual membership in the ALF, all members are referred to as supporters. The press office encourages supporters to send taped news coverage, gather newspaper articles, recorded radio shows, and any other form of documentation so that the world can be made aware of their actions. However, the use of pseudonyms, encryption devices, and similar security techniques are encouraged for members when writing. Potential supporters are informed they need to assume the authorities are reading all e-mail and regular mail.

The ALF grew substantially in the 1990s. With this growth came the use of new techniques for destroying those enemies who, in their view, were abusing animals. Instead of only rescuing animals, the ALF began to use economic sabotage and property destruction as new forms of violence to encourage compliance with their demands. One example of such an action performed by the ALF took place on May 30, 1997, when a record number of mink were "liberated" from the Arritola Mink Farm in Mt. Angel, Oregon. Timed incendiary devices were left on the farm, which, when they ignited in the morning, caused over $1 million in damages. The farm was closed as a result of this action, for which the ALF was proud to take credit.

The ALF seeks to create a mood of fear through its propaganda as well as its actions. Through its Web site as well as statements sent to newpapers, it has tried to make its audience fear that someone will come after them for treating any animal in a "wrong" way, to avenge the deaths of animals. On the ALF's Web page, one threatening sentence asserts,

> anyone could be a part of the ALF, without you knowing. This includes your PTA parents, church volunteers, your spouse, your neighbor, or your mayor. No one is immune to the ALF.[8]

ALF supporters have attacked the same business repeatedly, as many as 13 times in one week, as they did to a Kenny Rogers Rotisserie in New York. They attacked the place with such persistence that it was unable to change its methods of operations quickly to suit their demands and instead had to close. At a large university campus in California, the ALF set explosives off in a laboratory, killing all of the animals and destroying the information that had been obtained from the lab's research. The animals in the labs were killed in the fire, but the ALF reasoned that these deaths were necessary so that no other animal could ever be harmed again at that location.[9] ❏

These single-issue organizations do not exist only in the United States; indeed, many were formed first in Europe and have created cells in America, in a pattern similar to that of most other types of terrorism. This kind of terrorism appears to be increasingly prevalent and spans a wide range of issues, from abortion-clinic bombings to the destruction of laboratories where cosmetics are tested on animals.

Conclusion: Revolutionary and Nationalist Terrorism in the United States

Although revolutionary and nationalist violence were fairly strong in the 1960s through the mid-1980s, the predominant type of insurgent terrorism in the United States in this new century appears issue oriented, lacking in clear organizational structure and membership rolls and often carried out by individuals acting on their own rather than as a part of a planned group effort. This type of terrorist organization fits the category of an all-channel network, with each cell or individual operating separately, focused against a common enemy or toward a common goal. This is the most difficult structure of network to combat, because it lacks a hub or chain, linking the pieces, making prediction of movement, membership, and resources difficult to make with any accuracy.

Right-Wing Extremism: From Militia Groups to Religious Fanatics

Abortion clinic bombings are at least ideologically linked to groups engaged in right-wing extremism in the United States, although they are also clearly a form of single-issue terrorism. Unlike the objective of vigilante groups prevalent during the early years of nationhood, the White supremacist groups and the militias that have been a part of the American landscape for much of the country's history share with those carrying out the bombing of abortion clinics a desire to return to the status quo of an earlier period. Individuals in right-wing terrorism have tended to be, in the United States as in Europe, those who either want to protect the system as it currently exists (against revolutionaries or forces of change they perceive as harmful) or to help the system return to an earlier status from which, in their view, it has mistakenly wandered.

Right-wing terrorism, unlike that of the left, *is* strong in the United States, both in historical and contemporary times. In the last two decades of the twentieth century, in fact, there was an upsurge of right-wing groups, in membership and in activity. Just as the left-wing movements began to diminish in the mid-1980s, organizations like The Order, the Aryan Nations, the Christian Identity Movement, and hundreds of militia groups began to gain strength.

Militia Movements

Numerous local or state militias are in the forefront of the antigovernment movement in the United States. Some militias are very well armed and have assumed that they need to be for the ultimate conflict with federal authority they believe will inevitably occur. They have adopted April 19, the anniversary date of the Battle of Lexington in 1775 that launched the American Revolution, as a special date, since militia personnel consider themselves as instrumental in restoring the pristine values that the Revolution fought to protect.

At a gathering now known as the Rocky Mountain Rendezvous, held on October 23–25, 1992, at a YMCA in Estes Park, Colorado, plans were developed for a citizens' militia movement that exceeded anything the United States had yet experienced. The group of 160 White men who gathered there were White supremacists and progun extremists meeting at an invitation-only gathering two months after FBI attempts to arrest Randy Weaver resulted in the deaths of Weaver's wife and son on April 19 at Ruby Ridge in Idaho. This group meeting led, only three years to the day later, to the most destructive act of domestic terrorism in U.S. history: the bombing of the federal building in Oklahoma City.

The bombing of the Alfred P. Murrah Federal Building in Oklahoma City on April 19, 1995, is the most violent expression of antigovernment sentiment by a member of a militia group. This was the most lethal terrorist attack ever perpetrated on American soil, until the September 11, 2001, attacks on New York and Washington. One hundred sixty-eight people were killed and 850 others were injured.

A year later on April 19, 1996, after a 51-day siege by the FBI and the ATF, a fire broke out at Mount Carmel in Waco, Texas, where David Koresh and his followers had stockpiled a large supply of illegal weapons. All these events have provided the militia movement with inspiration and martyrs.

Most of the militias firmly believe that the federal government is an aggressive force intent on undermining liberty in the United States and that they are only preparing to defend themselves against unconstitutional authority. However, not all militia members are advocates of violence or desirous of committing violent acts. The Constitution protects free speech, even if it is offensive or extremist. Only those militia members accumulating arsenals composed of illegal weapons have been targeted by government agencies.

The armed right-wing groups offer a significantly different challenge to government efforts to provide security than that offered by the left-wing college radicals of the 1960s and 1970s. Unlike the isolated, crudely unsophisticated pipe-bomb manufacturers who dominated most of the U.S.-based terrorist groups for at least two decades, members of right-wing groups are often well trained in the use of arms and explosives. They generally have skilled armorers and bomb makers and many who are adept at guerrilla-warfare techniques and outdoor survival skills. Usually coupled with racial and religious intolerance, and even an apocalyptic vision of imminent war, these groups have more potential to engage in lethal and increasingly sophisticated terrorist operations, as the Oklahoma City bombing demonstrated.

This form of right-wing activity has wide-ranging geographical dimensions, a diversity of causes its adherents espouse, and overlapping agendas among its member groups. There are militia groups from Idaho to California, Arizona to North Carolina, Georgia to Michigan, Texas to Canada. Almost every state has at least one such group, and most have several. These groups share motivations spanning a broad spectrum: antifederalist, seditious, racial hatred, and religious hatred. Most have masked these unpleasant-sounding motives under a rather transparent veneer of religious precepts.

Writing generated by these groups indicates they are bound together by a number of factors, including a shared hostility to any form of government above the county level and even an advocacy of the overthrow of the U.S. government (or the Zionist Occupation Government, as some of them call it). Vilification of Jews and non-Whites as children of Satan is coupled with an obsession for achieving the religious and racial purification of the United States and a belief in a conspiracy theory of powerful Jewish interests controlling the government, banks, and the media.

These facets of right-wing ideology give interesting insights, in light of the images that terrorists have of their world, their victims, and themselves. To view the enemy as "Children of Satan" is to dehumanize them, as terrorists must in order to kill. To view the struggle of the group as an effort to purify the nation is to view it as a battle between good and evil, as terrorists must. The view of a coming racial war fits the millenial view that many terrorists maintain. A warrior fighting in a cause to purify a state from the children of Satan will have little problem in justifying the use of lethal force.

Right-wing groups capable of terrorism in the United States are widespread, intricately linked by many overlapping memberships and bound together in a political and religious doctrine that defines the world in terms that make the use of violence not just acceptable, but necessary. Because many of the members of these groups are skilled in the use of weapons and use survival training in camps throughout the country, planning for an "inevitable" racial war, the impact of these groups may well be formidable in the twenty-first century.

Although the United States has produced many different types of right-wing extremist groups, particularly in the last two decades of the twentieth century, the striking similarities in ideology and overlapping membership help to explain several important factors: the broad popular base enjoyed by militia groups; the assumption on the part of the general public and much of the law enforcement community, until the Oklahoma City bombing, that such groups are nonthreatening as a whole; and the festering of support for hatred that such groups provide to individuals seeking someone or something to blame for the loss of jobs, income, family farms, and so on. A quick look at one umbrella group, one religious movement, and one militia organization may offer examples of these factors.

CASE STUDY   Aryan Nations

The **Aryan Nations,** *a white supremacist group,* traces its origins back to the 1950s and early 1960s. Its current structure was organized in 1970 under the leadership of Richard Butler, with headquarters in Hayden Lake, Idaho. Its ideology is a mixture of theology and racism, being anti-Semitic and anti-Black. The literature of this group indicates that its beliefs are couched under a religious doctrine of "identity," which holds that Jesus Christ was not a Jew but an Aryan, that the Lost Tribes of Israel were in fact Anglo-Saxon and not Semitic, and that Jews are the children of Satan.

The operational profile for this group derives from a book written by an American neo-Nazi, William Pierce. This book, *Turner's Diaries,* offers a blueprint for revolution in the United States based on a race war. It is a disturbing book, freely available on the market and used by many groups that have splintered from the Aryan Nations for tactical reasons, focusing on certain elements of the doctrine. Pierce calls his book the "Handbook for White Victory," and says that it has been "effective in educating and inspiring a substantial portion of the people who have read it."[10] These groups include but are certainly not limited to The Order; the Silent Brotherhood; the White American Bastion; The Covenant, the Sword, and the Arm of the Lord; Posse Comitatus; the Arizona Patriots; and the White Patriot Party.

These groups have been linked to armored car and bank robberies, counterfeiting, assassinations, and assaults on federal, state, and local law enforcement personnel and facilities. One leader in the Aryan Nations, who was also the head of the Texas Ku Klux Klan, proposed a point system to achieve "Aryan Warrior" status. One could achieve this status (which required achieving a whole point) by killing:

Members of Congress = 1/5 point

Judges and FBI director = 1/6 point

FBI agents and U.S. marshalls = 1/10 point

Journalists and local politicians = 1/12 point

President of the United States = 1 point (Warrior status)

The Aryan Nations is regarded as an umbrella group for many factions involved in violent, often terrorist, activity. ❏

CASE STUDY   Christian Identity Movement

The **Christian Identity Movement** (CIM) in the United States *links individuals by opposition to gun control, the federal government, taxes, environmental regulations, homosexuality, racial integration, abortion, and by support for home-schooling, states' rights, and a shared belief in an international one-world conspiracy that is about to take over the United States and the world.* Christian Identity teaches that Aryans are God's chosen people, that Jews are the offspring of Satan, and that minorities are not human. Many Identity adherents are driving forces in the militia movement and believe the system no longer works, because it has been taken over by the New World Order, a secret group that actually runs the world. The membership of this secret group is less clearly defined; for some it is the Jews, for others, the United Nations.

Many Identity members, particularly those in militias, define the enemy as the U.S. government, which is recast into the role of King George III, with members of the movement defining themselves as true patriots. They reject the normal democratic processes of change, including election, petition, assembly, and constitutional amendment, believing instead that they alone are the defenders of freedom in their country.

The Identity theology permeates many of the right-wing groups, militias, and their proponents. William Porter Gale, a former aide to General Douglas MacArthur and Robert DePugh, millionaire founder of the ultrarightist Minutemen, were fervent Identity believers, as were Glenn and Stephen Miller, organizers of the White Patriot Party; Jim Ellison, founder of the Covenant, Sword, and Arm of the Lord; and James Wickstrom, former Posse Comitatus leader.

Norman Olson, a militia movement leader in Michigan, suggested that

> the militia is the militant or the right wing, if you will, the front line, of the patriot community. The patriot community is a broad spectrum . . . involving the militia all the way down to the Religious Right and the political action groups and jury reform legislative action groups.[11]

It is important to distinguish between the Christian Identity Movement and the Christian Patriots, even though there is considerable overlap in membership and philosophy. Christian Identity came from a nineteenth-century belief called British Israelism. A person can be an Identity member in Australia, Canada, and other former British colonial territories. Christian Patriots, in contrast, are only found in the United States. One could be a Christian Patriot without subscribing to Identity religious ideology.

It would be a large step for those who would go from the Christian Coalition—which from its position on the religious right of the political spectrum wants to impose its ways on American society within the rules, not by breaking them—to a militia movement, which rejects the rules and flouts them with enthusiasm to "save" America. It is a much smaller step to go to the militias from the CIM, since CIM also despises much of what comprises the system today and can rationalize, by religious doctrine, the death and destruction of children of Satan and other non-Aryan types. It is as unlikely that a militia leader will be elected to the U.S. Congress as it is that a Christian Coalition leader will consider poisoning a town's water supply. The CIM members could do either.

The Religious Right and the Christian Identity were, for a long time, separated by many theological gaps. The cross-fertilization of these movements began occurring in the 1990s, sparked in part by the collapse of the Soviet Union. Although the Christian Identity religion, with its focus on hatred of certain peoples and its distortion of biblical texts, has been an anathema to legitimate Christian groups, this began to change as the uncertainty of the 1990s engendered a fear that American society was "under attack," not from without but from within. Instead of an "evil empire" upon which both the Religious Right and the Christian Identity could project its worst fears and personify as Satan, the enemy became internal: the U.S. government. It became easier to bridge the theological gaps when a common enemy was perceived at home.

The CIM has links in many directions, including groups that focus on issues like gun control and abortion. Larry Pratt, an activist in the antiabortion movement and head of the 100,000-member Gun Owners of America, attended that meeting in 1972 convened by Christian Identity leader Peter Peters in Estes Park, Colorado. Held shortly after the surrender of Randy Weaver at Ruby Ridge, the meeting attracted a vast array of leaders from the White supremacist world. Researchers believe this 1992 meeting was the "birthplace" of the militia movement. ❏

CASE STUDY   Montana Freemen

The **Montana Freemen** is the name taken by a *right-wing extremist group located in eastern Montana*. In March 1996, the FBI initiated a siege of the Clark Ranch near Jordan, Montana, headquarters of the Freemen, for outstanding warrants. The siege ended peacefully with no gunfire or loss of life.

The Clark Ranch is also known as the Justus Township to Freemen members and is considered by them to be their sovereign territory. The Freemen's doctrine is a mixture of the British Magna Carta, the U.S. Constitution (including the first

10 amendments), and Biblical law (the parts that emphasize the sovereignty of its members). From this doctrine, Freemen state that the U.S. government has no authority to govern and that federal laws and tax codes are not binding upon them.

Led by LeRoy Schweitzer, the group showed its people how to manipulate the U.S. tax codes to make an (illegal) profit. Liens against the federal government were accepted as collateral to purchase money orders, and debtors printed fake money orders. Money order amounts were written larger than the amount owed and the overpayment was returned to the sender. In addition to money fraud, Freemen members also threatened and harassed local government officials.

Local government agents and law enforcement officials of Garfield County asked the FBI to assume the investigation of this group and to detain Freemen members, primarily because these actions would require a large amount of resources. In late March 1996, FBI agents lured Schweitzer and other members out from the Justus Township/Clark Ranch and placed them under arrest. The remaining members barricaded themselves inside the ranch and refused to surrender. The FBI encircled the Freemen enclave and prepared to wait, deciding not to use force, as in the Waco and Ruby Ridge incidents. Mediators, including Bo Gritz and Gerry Spence, were called in but provided few results. Electricity and water was shut off and all cell-phone use was blocked. After several weeks of negotiations, the remaining Freemen members surrendered on June 13, 1996, and were taken into federal custody.[12]

The Montana Freemen militia group received considerable national attention after the Oklahoma City bombing attack by Timothy McVeigh, who had been a member of this group. The man convicted of conspiring with him in this attack, Terry Nichols, was also involved with the **Christian Patriots** (CP). This group *shares key ideological and theological tenets of many in the militia movement and the CIM in the United States, teaching that the United States is the biblical promised land, promised to White/Aryan/Nordic types.* Members of this movement hold that the Constitution and the Bill of Rights are divinely inspired and should be treated like scripture, while the amendments to the Constitution which follow the first 10 (like those guaranteeing equality under the law, votes for women and those of non-White races, and freeing the slaves) are regarded as "human-made" and hence flawed "derogations" of the original Constitution.

Christian Patriots frequently file documents announcing that they are sovereign citizens with no link to the "corporate entity" known as the United States of America, which they regard as an evil government that pays attention to those derogating post-Bill of Rights amendments. Terry Nichols, involved in the Oklahoma City bombing and Militia of Montana leader John Trochmann have made such pronouncements.

The members of the Montana Freemen were advocates of Christian Patriotism and shared many overlapping memberships. The Freemen's refusal to pay their taxes was defended in terms of CP belief that America is promised to the White race, and by opposing and even severing ties to an evil government that tolerates and even advocates equal rights for minorities, White Americans can "reclaim their birthright." Rodney Skurdal, a Freeman, stated that he based his belief that he owed no taxes

> on the theological premise that . . . we the white race are God's chosen people . . . and our Lord God stated that "the earth is Mine," so there is no reason for us to be paying taxes on His land.[13]

Christian Patriots have links with other militia groups, the CIM, and the Christian Coalition, but there are significant differences between each. Transition from a member of the nonviolent Christian Coalition to the militia groups, Christian Patriots, or the CIM is often a large step. James Nichols, brother of Terry Nichols (mentioned earlier as being involved in the Oklahoma City bombing), was a Christian Patriot who considered, but was convinced not to accept, Identity theology by a Christian friend. For him, as for many others, the theology rather than the willingness to commit violence was a critical factor for such a transition.

Networking of such groups does occur in the United States. Christian Patriots exist only in the United States, because their ideology focuses only on the U.S. government, its history, and related documents. CIM adherents and militia groups, however, have appeared in other countries and network with members of CP in the United States. Networking also occurs inside the country based on common positions on issues such as gun control and abortion.

The networks for most of the religious right are hub or spoke networks, focused on and led by strong central figures and linked by common doctrines and belief systems. Militia groups in the United States, however, fit more easily into the all-channel pattern, with no specific group leader or hub; instead, each cell is capable of acting independently, with varying degrees of skill and success, against a common target, frequently a government individual or facility. When an individual such as Timothy McVeigh has membership in both the religious right (in the form of the CIM) and a militia group, his ability to act independently is enhanced but it is more likely that he would be see himself as a "holy warrior" in a good cause supported by his religious beliefs. This combination of independence, military expertise, and religious zeal can be clearly quite lethal.   ❑

Transnational Terrorism

Although right-wing terrorism flourished in the United States during much of its history, and left-wing extremists made some impact on the system during the 1960s and 1970s, the United States was aware of very little transnational terrorism—other than the connections of the Puerto Rican nationalists and some of the left-wing extremists to groups from Cuba and other socialist states—until the 1990s. Most of the efforts of the government agencies charged with domestic security from terrorist threats were focused on campus radicals, antiwar protesters, and groups with socialist or communist philosophies. The assumption was that most of the danger to the nation lay from these elements within the system, possibly supported by outside agents seeking to foment revolution rather than from external groups with cells operating within the U.S. system.

The networking of terrorists across national boundaries, in fact, was not researched with as much intensity in this country as it was in Europe and the Middle East. Since the country is bordered on two sides by oceans, and on the north and south by friendly governments, the likelihood of a transnational attack seemed remote. The technology that made such linkage easier and transportation across oceans simple and convenient was not factored as thoroughly into the assessment of homeland security as it would be during the last decade of the twentieth century.

The first bombing of the WTC in 1993 made the nation aware, for the first time, of its vulnerability to attacks from transnational terrorist agents. According to the research of Steven Emerson, a network news correspondent who created a Public Broadcasting System (PBS) program entitled *Jihad in America* after this incident, the United States had long been a target of hatred from groups in the Middle East who linked the United States with Israel and with European colonial policies. Until the 1990s, most such groups had lacked the infrastructure to provide support for an attack on Americans *in* the United States.

That infrastructure clearly existed by 1993, however, as this attack on the WTC was carried out by a network of internal and external individuals who shared this common hatred of the United States. A brief account of this event, from news reports, highlights several key points: the extent of the network of internal infrastructure uncovered, the obvious capability of transnational groups to carry out devastating terrorist acts, and the growing U.S. intelligence capabilities for information gathering and analysis of such incidents.

CASE STUDY   1993 World Trade Center Bombing

On February 26, 1993, at approximately 12:18 p.m., an improvised explosive device detonated on the second level of the WTC parking basement. The resulting blast produced a crater approximately 150 feet in diameter and five floors deep in the parking basement.

The main explosive charge consisted primarily of approximately 1,200 to 1,500 pounds of a homemade fertilizer-based explosive, urea nitrate. The fusing system consisted of two 20-minute lengths of a nonelectric burning-type fuse such as green hobby fuse. The hobby fuse terminated in the lead azide as the initiator.

Also incorporated in the device and placed under the main explosive charge were three large metal cylinders (tare weight 126 pounds) of compressed hydrogen gas. The resulting explosion killed 6 people and injured more than a 1,000. More than 50,000 people were evacuated from the WTC complex during the hours immediately following the blast.

The initial inspection on February 27 was a scene of massive devastation, almost like walking into a cave, with no lights other than flashlights flickering across the crater. There were small pockets of fire, electrical arcing from damaged wiring, and automobile alarms whistling, howling, and honking. The explosion ruptured two of the main sewage lines from both WTC towers and the Vista Hotel as well as several water mains from the air conditioning system. In all, more than 2 million gallons of water and sewage were pumped out of the crime scene.

On February 28, four FBI forensic chemists and four ATF chemists arrived to begin explosive residue collection. A transient chemistry explosive residue laboratory was put together in the already existing New York City Police Department Laboratory. Later that evening, six forensic chemists, two from each agency (FBI, ATF, NYPD) were dispatched to the crater area to collect explosive residues. A bomb technician from the NYPD and an ATF agent were also assigned to provide safety support for the chemists.

During the early morning hours of this residue collection, the bomb technician discovered a fragment from a vehicle frame that displayed massive explosive damage. The ATF agent and bomb technician placed the 300-pound fragment on a litter and carried it to a police vehicle. The fragment was transported to the laboratory for analysis. Due to sewage contamination, the piece was of no value for explosive residue analyses. A closer inspection of the fragment displayed a dot matrix number. The number was identified as the confidential vehicle identification number of a van reported stolen the day before the bombing. The vehicle was a 1990 Ford F-350 Econoline van owned by the Ryder Rental Agency, rented in New Jersey and reported stolen in New Jersey. The frame fragment displayed explosive damage consistent with damage from a device exploding inside the vehicle.

By Tuesday, four assistant U.S. attorneys were assigned to the prosecution. It was fortunate that the attorneys were assigned at that time because late on Monday night the vehicle fragment was identified by the FBI laboratory as having been a portion of the vehicle that contained the device and as having been reported stolen on February 25, 1993. FBI agents traveled to the Ryder Rental Agency in Jersey City, New Jersey, which had rented out the vehicle, and began an interview of the station manager.

While the interview was under way, an individual by the name of Mohammad Salameh telephoned Ryder and wanted his security deposit returned. A meeting was arranged so that Salameh would return to the Ryder Agency on March 4. When he returned for the $400 deposit, FBI agents were on hand to place him under surveillance. As Salameh was leaving, numerous media personnel were observed outside, setting up their photography equipment. It was then decided that Salameh would be arrested on the spot.

His arrest and the subsequent search of his personal property led to Nidel Ayyad, a chemist working for the Allied Signal Corporation in New Jersey. Ayyad was connected to Salameh through telephone toll records and joint bank accounts. At the time of Ayyad's arrest his personal computer was seized from his office. Also through toll records and receipts, a safe house or bomb factory was located on Pamrappo Avenue, in Jersey City. A search of this bomb factory revealed that acids and other chemicals had been used at that apartment to manufacture explosives. Traces of nitroglycerine and urea nitrate were found on the carpet and embedded in the ceiling. It appeared that a chemical reaction involving acid had occurred in the apartment. At the same time, telephone toll records from Salameh and Ayyad showed that calls had been made to a self-storage center not too far from the bomb factory.

An interview with the manager of the self-storage center indicated that Salameh had rented a space and that four "Arab-looking" individuals had been observed using a Ryder van several days before the bombing. The manager also said that the day before the bombing, AGL Welding Supply from Clifton, New Jersey, had delivered three large tanks of compressed hydrogen gas. The storage manager had told Salameh to remove them that day. During the search of the storage room rented by Salameh, many chemicals and items of laboratory equipment were located. Among the items seized was 300 pounds of urea, 250 pounds of sulfuric acid, numerous one-gallon containers, both empty and containing nitric acid and sodium cyanide, two 50-foot lengths of hobby fuse, a blue plastic trash can, and a bilge pump. While examining the trash can and bilge pump, a white crystalline substance was found. A chemical analysis identified urea nitrate.

On March 3, a typewritten communication was received at the *New York Times*. The communiqué claimed responsibility for the bombing of the World Trade Center in the name of Allah. The letter was composed on a personal computer and printed on a laser printer. Very little could be identified as to the origin of the printer, but a search of the hidden files in Ayyad's computer revealed wording identical to that of the text of the communiqué. Saliva samples from Salameh, Ayyad, and a third man, Mahmud Abouhalima, were obtained and compared with the saliva on the envelope flap. A DNA Q Alpha examination concluded that Ayyad had licked the envelope on the communiqué received by the *Times*. Abouhalima, who was an integral part of the conspiracy, had fled the United States the day after the bombing and had later been arrested in Egypt and extradited to the United States.

In September 1992, a man named Ahmad M. Ajaj had entered the United States from Pakistan at New York's JFK airport. He was arrested on a passport violation. In his checked luggage, Ajaj had numerous manuals and videocassette tapes. These tapes and manuals described methods of manufacturing explosives, including urea nitrate, nitroglycerine, lead azide, TNT, and other high explosives.

Interviews and latent fingerprint examinations identified two other individuals who were an integral part of the bombing conspiracy. The first, Ramzi Yousef, had entered the United States on the same flight as Ajaj, but had been deported immediately. Yousef was identified through fingerprints and photos as having been associating with Salameh immediately prior to the bombing. His fingerprints were also found on the explosive manuals located in Ajaj's checked luggage. The second individual, known only as "Yassin," was identified in much the same manner and was probably involved in the packaging and delivery of the bomb on the morning of February 26.

The FBI laboratory was under orders to complete all scientific examinations by July 7, 1993, in compliance with the Speedy Trial Act. A trial date was established for September 6, 1993. During the examination of evidence in the laboratory, the remains of three high-pressure gas cylinders belonging to the AGL Welding Company were identified. A small fragment of red paint with a gray primer was located on one of the metal fragments of the gas cylinder. This paint fragment was compared with the red paint used by AGL on their hydrogen tanks and was found to be the same. On one portion of a fragment of the Ryder truck bed, several fragments of blue plastic, the size of a pinhead, were located. These fragments were compared with the plastic from the trash container at the self-storage center premises Salameh had rented and were found to be alike. Fragments of all four tires were found at the crime scene and compared with the data on the maintenance scheduled at Ryder. All four tires were accounted for in the research.

Prior to the trial, the FBI laboratory's Special Project Section constructed a scale model of the portion of the WTC that was damaged by the blast. The model incorporated push-button fiber optic lighting to depict the location at the crime scene where pertinent items of evidence were found. Once illuminated and described to the jury during the trial, the lights and the model told a very clear and precise story.

During the six-month trial, more than 200 witnesses introduced over 1,000 exhibits. On March 4, 1994, exactly one year after Salameh's arrest, the jury found Salameh, Ajaj, Abouhalima, and Ayyad guilty on all 38 counts.[14] ❑

The impact of this event on U.S. response to terrorism cannot be overstated. U.S. citizens began to assume that *any* large-scale terrorist attack would be carried out by foreigners, probably from the Middle East. Ironically, when the Oklahoma City bombing occurred a few years later, the immediate assumption on the part of the press and the public was that the perpetrator was Middle Eastern. The actual perpetrator, Timothy McVeigh, did not fit this profile at all.

Information gathered in the hunt for the individuals responsible led the United States to a better understanding of the networking of terrorism which existed. When Ramzi Yousef's safehouse in the Philippines was raided, information was discovered linking him to al-Qaeda (which would later be responsible for the 2001 bombing attacks on the WTC) and to Abu Sayyaf, the indigenous groups carrying out attacks in the Philippines. Intelligence agencies began to seriously investigate al-Qaeda, and its leader Osama bin Laden, linking him to the bombing attacks on the U.S. embassies in Kenya and Tanzania in 1998, the attack on the U.S. *Cole* in Yemen's harbor, and the events of September 11, 2001.

An Egyptian-born Muslim and peace activist, Seifeldin Ashmawy, editor of the magazine *Voice of Peace,* testified before the U.S. Senate in 1997 about the spread of transnational terrorism into America. He warned that

> the heart, if not the soul, of the extremists is in fact largely in the United States, where these radicals have set up many of their fund-raising and political headquarters. These people have literally hijacked the mainstream Islamic organizations in the United States.[15]

The investigations by law enforcement and intelligence agencies since the events of September 11, 2001, revealed the existence of many organized cells of groups like al-Qaeda, HAMAS, and Islamic Jihad throughout America. From Santa Clara, California, to Tuscon, Arizona, from Detroit, Michigan, to Springfield, Virginia, these groups have organized membership cells, utilizing the Internet to connect across state lines and to facilitate the transfer of funds. Although most of the activities of these cells have been nonviolent, the radical theology shared is in many respects similar to the radical form of Christianity shared by Identity members and militia groups. Such theology is not illegal, but it is troubling as the world slides closer to engagement in a holy war in which terrorism is justified by faith.

CYBERTERRORISM

One of the areas of concern in terms of domestic security from terrorist attacks that has emerged in recent years is the threat of what is called "cyberterror." **Cyberterrorism** is a difficult term to define. Using the operational definition adopted in this text, it could include *cyberspace activities organized by individuals or groups pursuing political or systemic objectives to destroy or violently disrupt persons or patterns of activity vital to the survival of the person(s) or system under attack.*

This definition draws several distinct lines to differentiate cyberterrorism from other types of cyber crime. Like all forms of terrorism, cyberterror must have a political motive, not simply a desire to disrupt, destroy, or simply annoy. Thus, not all computer hackers who send worms into an e-mail system to destroy or disrupt other users are committing cyberterror, although their acts may well be cyber crimes under both state and national law.

Actions intended to destroy innocent persons, when motivated by political objectives and designed to create a mood of fear in an audience, can readily be called terrorism, even if the attack is made in cyberspace. For example, an attack on a computer system that routes airlines or passenger trains would clearly fit the parameters for this text of "terrorism." So cyberterror must involve destructive acts against innocent persons or on the systems vital to their survival and must be motivated by political goals.

But most of what is called cyberterror today is plagued by very fuzzy definitional boundaries. Would, for instance, a cyber attack on the stock market of a country be a form of cyberterror, because it could involve no immediate, tangible violence, nor would there be universal agreement on the essential nature of the stock market to the survival of those living in the system? What about an attempt to corrupt information within a system, such as that pertaining to blood types in a hospital? If the only result is additional costs in terms of time delay and effort, not lives lost or medical emergencies, is this still terrorism?

Technology in the last two decades has radically altered the patterns of organization and interaction of individuals, groups, and governments. As one scholar noted,

> The headlong rush of the U.S. and other advanced nations into the information age involves new risks. The information systems central to national security, the conduct of government and commerce have significant weaknesses that can be attacked.[16]

Thus far, attacks on such systems have achieved only limited impacts, but the potential for such attacks and the clarity with which the definitional line can be drawn to separate ordinary cyber crime from cyberterror must be the subjects for careful study.

CONCLUSIONS

Clearly, terrorism escalated in the United States in the last decade of the twentieth century and during the first decade of the new century. Although many other developed countries, particularly in Europe, had dealt with a much higher level of terrorism for decades than that which afflicted the United States, the basic types of terrorism were approximately the same. The mistake, perhaps, by the United States was in its assumption that its physical isolation would make it less vulnerable to terrorism, since its democratic system tolerated a wide range of divergent views, multiple options for open disagreement without recourse to violence, and a general tolerance for many cultural and ethnic differences.

Blindness to the impact of globalization to the peoples and the economies of many in the developing world, ignorance of the anger felt against the United States for its policies in the Middle East, and a lambent isolationism that has colored U.S. domestic life since its birth have all contributed to its tardy awareness of the threat of domestic terrorism. The events of September 11 were a wake-up call, offering an opportunity to carefully assess the strengths and weaknesses of U.S. counterterrorism policy.

As analysis continues to be generated in the wake of the September 11 events, interesting insights can be seen on the differences between terrorists in the United States and those in other countries.

> *Age.* Terrorists born in the United States tend to be older than terrorists indigenous to other countries. Foreign operatives carrying out operations in the United States appear to follow this trend. In recent years, most domestic terrorists have tended to be over 30—old, compared to the profile of terrorists noted in an earlier chapter.
>
> *Infrequent Occurrence.* As noted earlier, the United States has had a relatively low incidence of terrorism compared to other developed countries. This has made tracking of terrorist patterns and data analysis of terrorist incidents difficult, because the base of data is relatively small.
>
> *Ordinary Criminal Act.* most terrorist activities, until the September 11 attacks, were treated under domestic law as violations of criminal laws. Criminal law enforcement agencies have normally been charged with responding to terrorism, unlike the apparatus and laws applied in Western Europe to this crime. Efforts to address this problem in the PATRIOT Act have met with mixed success and much criticism.

These three differences are significant. Older individuals tend to plan with more patience, waiting years if necessary to complete plans to carry out attacks; better trained, if only because they have had more years to complete their training; and overall, more formidable enemies. Infrequency of events, while not a bad situation, does make it difficult to generate either funds or support for counterterrorism training, laws, or equipment. Until the events of the fall of 2001, the United States did not place a high priority on combating domestic terrorism, not even on tracking transnational terrorism that might emerge domestically. This lack of incidence led to a complacency in the security of the country, which was clearly misplaced.

Finally, because domestic terrorism until the fall of 2001 had been primarily handled as an ordinary criminal offense, there was little coordinated interagency preparation for dealing with terrorist events, insufficient training in the differences between terrorists and ordinary criminals for the law enforcement units responsible, and a meager legal framework for the prosecution of terrorism as a unique form of criminal activity.

In the wake of the bombing attacks that occurred on September 11, 2001, the links between the attacks on the WTC in 1993, the bombings at the U.S. embassies in Kenya and Tanzania, and the September 11 attacks became clear, focusing the attention of authorities on the specific threat of the al-Qaeda network and on transnational terrorism. The magnitude of the September 11 attacks fully captured the attention of the U.S. government and of its citizens, who experienced a strong upsurge of nationalism as the president sought a response to this dramatic evidence of the damage that transnational terrorism could inflict.

As intelligence agencies scrambled to secure information about those involved in the attacks, hundreds of people were taken into custody and questioned. Gradually, the links to bin Laden became sufficiently convincing for the administration to designate him as the prime suspect as leader of the al-Qaeda network. On September 27, President George W. Bush addressed a joint chamber of the House and Senate to pledge a war on terrorism, which he said would be a "lengthy campaign," committed to "find, stop, and defeat every terrorist group of global reach." In this speech, Bush demanded that the Taliban, leaders of the (unrecognized) government of Afghanistan, where bin Laden had made his headquarters for several years, hand over all terrorist leaders to U.S. authorities.

The U.S. sought support and assistance from allies and from states bordering Afghanistan in this war on terrorism. Support from the North Atlantic Treaty Organization (NATO), in terms of invoking a crucial article of the organization's charter regarding collective self-defense in general and British military planes, ships, and missiles in particular, were offered. Some degree of consent, but less tangible support was built, through the efforts of Secretary of State Colin Powell, among nations near Afghanistan, including Pakistan, Iran, Saudi Arabia, and Uzbekistan. The ensuing bombing campaign initiated with British and U.S. missiles and followed by waves of U.S. bombers, stressed this uneasy alliance against terrorism.

Efforts to track the money that supported the terrorist attacks were less dramatic but seemed productive, as were efforts to engage nations within the international community to support the UN treaty on the financing of terrorism, which was by this time operative. Securing cooperation from international banking communities to track terrorist support funds through private accounts was somewhat difficult, because banking secrecy laws in many countries are designed to provide maximum anonymity for customers. However, this front of the war on terrorism generated peaceful results and useful evidence of links between terrorist cells in various countries.

The effort by the U.S. administration to lead a global effort to rid the world of a shameful practice—terrorism—has involved economic, financial, political, and religious elements. It has stretched to include many countries as well, and its initiators assume it will take years to successfully conclude. In the early nineteenth century, it took the British Royal navy almost 50 years to close down the Atlantic slave trade; the effort to eradicate terrorism is a task that may require at least that much time and much more military as well as political effort on the part of many nations.

Subsequent attacks in the United States in the form of anthrax in the mail system led to further measures to alter legal restrictions on intelligence operations and to the more rapid creation of the Homeland Security Department given the responsibility of improving domestic security against terrorist attacks. Responsibility for these anthrax attacks has not yet been determined.

EVALUATION

Domestic terrorism in the United States highlights the weaknesses of many democracies in dealing with the problem of terrorism. Inadequate structure for coordinating response efforts, a lack of clear guidelines for law enforcement personnel for the successful resolution of terrorist situations, and complacency in security has marred much of counterterrorism efforts in the United States. Some of the more dramatic missteps by government agencies have actually fueled further terrorist events, as the evidence from the Oklahoma City bombing clearly indicated. Noted Chris Temple, writing in *The Jubilee,* a major CIM newspaper, about the events in Ruby Ridge, when an FBI standoff resulted in the shooting of Randy Weaver's wife while she was holding their child:

> All of us in our groups . . . could not have done in the next twenty years what the federals did for our cause in eleven days in Naples, Idaho.[17]

Read carefully the following case study and evaluate U.S. preparedness and response to such attacks. Examine each incident for the *type* of group perpetrating the incident (right-wing, left-wing, or transnational), and for the extent to which the perpetrators fit the unusual profile of terrorists in the United States suggested earlier.

CASE STUDY   Waco, Texas, Incident

On February 28, 1993, the ATF attempted to serve arrest and search warrants for Vernon Howell at the Mount Carmel compound of the Branch Davidians. Vernon Howell, also known as David Koresh, was the leader of the Branch Davidians, an apocalyptic religious group. Their compound, located just northeast of Waco, Texas, off route 7, sat on 70 acres of land.

Seventy-six ATF officers attempted to enter the compound. The ensuing melee of gunfire, in which an estimated 6,000 to 10,000 rounds were fired, left both sides reeling. Four ATF agents died and another 20 were injured along with an unknown number of Branch Davidians in the 45-minute confrontation. Local media personnel had been alerted and had positioned themselves to watch the raid.

Following the failure of the initial raid, the ATF withdrew to a safe position and alerted the FBI. The FBI allocated its Hostage Rescue Team, Critical Incident Negotiations Team, and other experts while securing a perimeter around the Mount Carmel compound. A 51-day standoff began.

David Koresh considered himself the second coming of Christ and a messenger of God. After the raid, Koresh and his followers were waiting for a sign from God to leave their Mount Carmel compound. Koresh was also writing his interpretation of the Seven Seals found in the Christian Bible's book of Revelations. Until both the sign from God was received and Koresh's interpretation of Revelations was completed, the Branch Davidians were at an impasse with the FBI.

Throughout the standoff, constant telephone negotiations between senior members of the FBI and the Davidians occurred. Overall, a total of 21 children and 14 adults left Mount Carmel during the standoff. In FBI attempts to coerce the Branch Davidian members to leave the compound, varied tactics were used, including cutting off electricity and water, use of high-power halogen lamps to illuminate the compound at night, and broadcasting loud music. Negotiations were fruitful early in the standoff for both sides. Fourteen children were released after a recorded tape was aired on a local radio station. However, by the end of March progress slowed and negotiations began to stall.

After FBI officials decided that negotiations could not resolve the standoff, a plan to use CS gas—a form of tear gas—became a viable option. The plan to introduce CS gas was finalized on April 17. Senior FBI officials conferred with Delta Force, the Army's antiterrorist group on the plan's formulation and feasibility, but Delta Force was prohibited by law from participating in the resolution of a domestic terrorism incident.

Early on the morning of April 19, 1993, Combat Engineer Vehicles (CEVs) began pumping CS gas into certain areas of the compound, coupled with another 300 rounds of CS canisters. Fires erupted at multiple points within the compound by noon. Not long after the fires began, explosions from ammunition and other combustibles totally engulfed the Branch Davidian structure. Nine people survived the blaze and 75 bodies were recovered, many of them women and children.

As a result of the standoff, changes were made in the way federal law enforcement agencies dealt with future crises. The FBI was finally designated as the lead agency in hostage and barricade situations and incidents of domestic terrorism. Greater resources were allocated to the FBI to deal with high-risk operations and raids, and funds were increased for research operations.[18]   ❏

SUGGESTED READINGS

Sargent, Lyman Towed, ed. *Extremism in America*. New York: New York University Press, 1995.

Segaller, Stephen. *Invisible Armies: Terrorism into the 1990s*. San Diego: Harcourt Brace Janovich, 1987.

Smith, Brent L. *Terrorism in America: Pipe Bombs and Pipe Dreams*. Albany: State University of New York Press, 1994.

Stern, Kenneth S. *A Force on the Plain: The American Militia Movement and the Politics of Hate*. New York: Simon & Schuster, 1996.

_____. "Militias and the Religious Right." *Freedom Writer* (October 1996).

White, Jonathan R. *Terrorism: An Introduction* (2nd ed.). Belmont, CA: West/Wadsworth Publishers, 1998.

NOTES

1. Richard Maxwell Brown, "Historical Patterns of American Violence," in *Violence in America: Historical and Comparative Perspective,* ed. Hugh Davis Graham and Ted Robert Gurr (London: Sage, 1979).

2. Bill Stanton, *Klanwatch: Bringing the Ku Klux Klan to Justice.* (New York: Grove Weidenfield, 1991).

3. Ted Robert Gurr, "Political Terrorism in the United States: Historical Antecedents and Contemporary Trends," in *The Politics of Terrorism,* ed. Michael Stohl (New York: Dekker, 1988).

4. Brent L. Smith, *Terrorism in America: Pipe Bombs and Pipe Dreams* (Albany: State University of New York Press, 1994).

5. Bernard K. Johnpoll, "Perspectives on Political Terrorism in the United States," in *International Terrorism,* ed. Yonah Alexander (New York: Praeger, 1976), 32–33.

6. Jonathan R. White, *Terrorism: An Introduction.* (Belmont, CA: West/Wadsworth, 1998), 161.

7. Ivan Blackwell, "Earth Liberation Front," in *Encyclopedia of Terrorism,* ed. Cindy Combs and Martin Slann (New York: Facts On File, 2002), 59.

8. The Animal Liberation Front Homepage, 1999, http://www.animalliberation.net.

9. Erin Graves, "Animal Rights Groups as Terrorists," in *Encyclopedia of Terrorism,* ed. Cindy Combs and Martin Slann (New York: Facts, On File, 2002), 8–11.

10. Morris Dees, *Gathering Storm: America's Militia Threat* (New York: Harper Collins, 1997), 205.

11. Ibid., p. 25.

12. Tim Linker, "Montana Freemen," in *Encyclopedia of Terrorism,* ed. Cindy Combs and Martin Slann (New York: Facts On File, 2002), 122.

13. Kenneth S. Stern, "Militias and the Religious Right," http://apocalypse.berkshire.net (10/24/99).

14. Anthony Spotti, "World Trade Center Bombing, 1993," in *Encyclopedia of Terrorism,* ed. Cindy Combs and Martin Slann (New York: Facts On File, 2002), 236–240.

15. Steven Emerson, *American Jihad* (New York: Simon & Schuster, 2002), 168.

16. Gregory J. Rattray, "The Cyberterrorism Threat," in *Terrorism and Counterterrorism,* ed. Russell D. Howard and Reid L. Sawyer (Guilford, CT: Dushkin/McGraw-Hill, 2002), 227.

17. Dees, *Gathering Storm,* 33.

18. Tim Linker, "Waco Texas Incident," in *Encyclopedia of Terrorism,* ed. Cindy Combs and Martin Slann (New York: Facts On File, 2002), 231–232.

10

Legal Perspectives
on Terrorism

Key Concepts

innocent persons	extradite
innocence	universal jurisdiction
special provisions in the Geneva	attentat clause
Convention	judicial delegations
protected persons	technological terrorism
rule of proportionality	political crime
hostis humanis generis	political offenders
skyjacking	loophole in the law
novation	signatories
jurisdiction	parties
provisions for jurisdiction	Terrorism Prevention Branch

> *International and transnational terrorism are nothing more nor less than the wanton
> and willful taking of human lives, the purposeful commission of bodily harm, and the
> intentional infliction of severe mental distress by force or threat of force.*

Robert Friedlander

TERRORISM IS A CRIME

If Friedlander's assessment of the nature of terrorism is correct, then one would assume that such acts would already be designated as common crimes in the legal
codes of most countries today. One could also be forgiven for assuming that international law, if it truly reflects the laws and mores of the international community,
would reflect a similar tendency to declare such acts illegal.

That this is not the case is perhaps due less to a lack of consensus about the de-
sirability of such a law or even the criminality of "a willful and wanton taking of
human life" than to two critical factors: the nature of the international system itself
and the political problems in defining an act as "terrorism." The latter factor has already been discussed in an earlier chapter and the problems involved with defining
terrorism are clear. Examining the international community's legal response to terrorism, however, offers insights into how the internal difficulties in defining terrorism translates into a global inability to create clear legal parameters for terrorist acts.

In the international community, although there may well be general agreement
on the undesirability of such things as war, racial discrimination, genocide, and other

violations of basic human rights, there has been a significant reluctance to translate that agreement into workable treaties with enforcement powers. Why, if nations generally agree with the idea of reducing the incidence of such "evils," cannot workable methods of getting rid of these evils be constructed?

The answer to this question must be the same as that given by municipal leaders when confronted with a question as to why a society's evils (such as poverty, unemployment, and discrimination) are not being effectively eliminated. Unfortunately, consensus about the undesirability of these evils at any level is often difficult to translate into acceptable, enforceable rules and regulations that might remedy the situation. General policy directions are always easier to formulate than specific legislation.

Moreover, the constraints that make progress in creating such legislation difficult at the local and national levels are magnified many times at the international level. An examination of at least a few of these constraints may help us to understand the dearth of international law on terrorism.

The first problem involves a lack of legislative authority. However inept one may consider state and national legislators to be, at least lawmaking bodies can be said to exist at such levels. But on the international level, there is no body invested with such authority. The United Nations was certainly never designed to "rule" the nations of the world or to create rules for its governance.[1] The United Nations offers a forum for discussion, for cooperation and consensus building on issues. It does not make laws in the sense that governing bodies make laws for subordinate individuals and groups in the national arena.

There is, too, a distinct lack of central authority in the international community. To describe it even as a confederation is to invest it with properties that it does not really possess. A confederal system has mechanisms for governing at the top level, whereas no such governing system exists in any real sense at the international level. Not only is there no legislative body empowered to make laws within the international community, there is also neither an autocratic nor a democratic chief executive who is able to speak with authority for, and issue commands to, the community of nations.

Moreover, there is no judicial system to which all have recourse and whose decisions are binding at the international level. The International Court of Justice's decision-making authority depends for the most part on the willingness of states to amicably resolve a difficulty and on their willingness to submit their disputes to the court for adjudication.[2]

So the most serious infractions of international law often go untouched by the court, because many states are not willing to submit their disputes for adjudication. A voluntary judicial system that can neither hail an offender to the bar of justice nor enforce compliance with its judgments, and that has no provisions by which entities other than states (such as individuals, groups, or corporations) can seek recourse for injustice, seems to be sadly lacking in judicial accouterments.

The international system governing states, then, has no central authority figure or figures, provides only a forum for debate rather than lawmaking, and possesses only a voluntary (and frequently ineffective) judiciary. It is thus even less able than municipal governments to deal with the difficulties inherent in enacting and enforcing laws designed to eliminate societal problems. The political and enforcement problems that hamper the making of effective laws within nations are even more capable of preventing the successful completion of treaties designed for dealing with sensitive issues in the international community.

This incapacity is complicated by the absence of law enforcement officers. With the possible exception of INTERPOL (which is strictly charged to stay out of political problems), there does not appear to be anyone at the international level with the authority to act in this capacity. Just as there are few procedures for bringing a miscreant to justice, there is no one authorized to physically do so.

The absence of such international legal enforcement mechanisms is not universally regarded as a handicap for the community of nations. While it is true that law, at the state level of analysis, does require enforcement apparatus, it is also true that most obedience to the law is dependent upon habits of compliance rather than the presence of a policeman at every intersection. At the international level, this is even more clearly true. Certainly, the laws are agreements that states make between themselves to establish guidelines for acceptable behavior, but the states in the international community have expressed little consistent interest in creating enforcement units to patrol the international community. Such a force, in the views of some legal experts, might threaten state sovereignty and exercise power in ways that might be detrimental to international peace and security.

Lacking these instruments of governance most commonly found at the national level, however, the construction of rules at the international level has become an extremely delicate and difficult task. Political considerations of the nations in the international community are usually accommodated as fully as possible, because compliance with any rules is largely voluntary.

The more highly politicized the issue and the greater the perception of national interests involved, the more difficult it becomes to construct an effective treaty—that is, one both strong and acceptable. This may derive, as one scholar suggests, from the nature and scope of national interests' inevitable tension with political reality. When diverse national interests appear to oppose perceived common goals, as they often do in discussions on terrorism, then this "tension" becomes heightened to unworkable levels, according to this scholar.[3]

Recent history provides lots of examples of the hazards that abound when international law extends itself further than the limits of assured compliance within the community of nations. The most striking instance of such overextension may be the attempts to outlaw war, notably through the Kellogg-Briand pact.[4] Despite the majority consensus that may exist on the undesirability of war, it is not within the power of international law to enforce a prohibition of war.

More successful, perhaps, have been efforts within the international community to restrict certain highly undesirable practices during times of war. This was partially accomplished by putting together "rules of conduct" for times of war. Conventions about the treatment of prisoners of war and innocent civilian personnel, as well as some involving prohibitions of certain methods of warfare and weapons of war, have been more effective, in terms of compliance, than the ill-judged and altruistic Kellogg-Briand pact.

This success in creating laws to deal with specific aspects of generally undesirable behavior has important implications in terms of understanding the attempts by the international community to deal with the politically sensitive issue of terrorism. Attempts by the international community to construct general treaties dealing with terrorism were largely unsuccessful until the events of 2001. But on treaties or conventions that deal instead with specific aspects of terrorism, greater progress has been made. A quick review of the provisions and "success" record in preventing or punishing terrorism could make it easier to decide on the most effective ways for handling the problem of current and future terrorism.

First, let us examine portions of international law that do not deal specifically with terrorism, but from which laws and regulations on terrorism have evolved. Three areas of international law come immediately to mind in this regard: laws of war, laws on piracy, and laws concerning the protection of diplomatic personnel and heads of state.

LAWS OF WAR

International law has been divided by some scholars into laws of war and laws of peace. This can be a somewhat confusing dichotomy, because some peacetime laws continue to apply even during times of war. However, it is true that the rules of behavior change in many respects during wartime. This change is usually in the direction of allowing greater latitude for suppressing or eliminating ordinary protections and courtesies. It is fair to say that, during times of war, more types of violence may be employed against a wider range of targets with far fewer safeguards for human rights than are permissible during times of peace.

This is not a tautological statement. It is instead an important point when one considers that it is the laws of war most often invoked by terrorists to justify their acts. If, even under the rules that permit a broader range of acceptable actions there are certain significant prohibited actions, then those actions could be said to be always prohibited, regardless of the provocation. If the laxity of safeguards that exists during times of war still does not allow certain actions the semblance of legality, then those actions could be regarded as unacceptable to the international community, both in times of war and in times of peace.

Although the mass of rules and laws that govern warfare today has grown to immense proportions, a number of fundamental rules meet the criteria described above, in that they involve the establishment of minimum standards of behavior, even for parties engaged in hostilities. Of these rules of war, perhaps the most significant for this study are those that affect the treatment of **innocent persons.**

This category of persons is an extremely important one for students of terrorism. It is crucial to establish a clear understanding of what is meant by the term *innocent*. Terrorists have asserted that "there is no such thing as an innocent person,"[5] yet the Geneva Convention extends special protections to *"persons taking no active part in the hostilities."*[6]

Innocence, as used by the laws of war, has much the same meaning as that found in any expanded international dictionary definition of the term. In both cases, **innocence** signifies *freedom from guilt for a particular act,* even when the total character may be evil. It is in one sense a negative term, implying as it does something less than righteous, upright, or virtuous. Legally, it is used to specify a *lack of guilt for a particular act or crime, denoting a nonculpability.*[7]

Innocence is thus imputed to a thief found innocent of the crime of murder. By this logic, even a government official guilty only of indifference can still be said to be "innocent" of any crime committed by his or her government. That official, in other words, has been guilty of nothing that would justify his or her summary execution or injury by terrorists having a grievance with his or her government.

This concept of a lack of guilt for a specific act is particularly appropriate in examining the random selection of "any Englishman, any Israeli" by terrorists as acceptable targets.[8] If "innocent person" status can only be removed by guilt for a specific act or crime committed by the person (not by others of the same age group, nationality, race, religion, or other similar categories), then there can be no legal justification for such a random selection of targets.

International law, like that of most civilized nations, neither recognizes nor punishes guilt by association. The Nuremberg trials records give credence to this point, in terms of the efforts made to establish personal guilt for specific criminal acts (such as murder or torture), instead of prosecuting simply on the basis of membership in the Nazi Party or Hitler's SS troops.[9] In refusing to punish all Germans or even all Nazi Party members for crimes against humanity and crimes of war, the precedent was established for differentiating between a person guilty of committing a crime during time of war and those innocent of actual wrongdoing.

The importance of this legal concept of innocence as an absence of guilt for a particular act cannot be overstated. The reason for its significance lies in the justification set forth by modern terrorists for their selection of victims. Many organizations that commit terrorist acts today do so on the premise that they are legitimately engaged in seeking to overthrow an existing government or to radically change existing conditions and are thus engaged in warfare.

Accepting, for the moment, this claim to revolutionary action, it is logical to assume the actions of these groups should still conform to the rules of warfare. Terrorists have rejected the laws of peace as too restrictive for their revolutionary efforts.

Table 10.1 offers a brief overview of the primary provisions in the laws of war that would apply to acts of terrorism, which should help to clarify whether terrorism is legal under the laws of war.

The Geneva Convention on the Treatment of Civilians During Times of War demands special protections for "persons taking no active part in the hostilities." Nonactive status, like innocence, does not imply that the person is good, virtuous, or even disinterested in the outcome of the conflict. A person need only be innocent of participation in the hostilities to be protected by the convention.

TABLE 10.1   Protection for Civilians During Time of War

Treaty	Property	People
Geneva Convention Relative to the Protection of Civilian Persons in Time of War (1949)	**Prohibits** Pillage Reprisal	**Prohibits** Mutilation Torture Violence to life Punishment for offense not personally committed Hostage taking
Protocols I and II of convention listed above (1976)		**Prohibits** Acts or threats of violence to spread terror No indiscriminate bombing of towns Rule of proportionality (loss of civilian life to be minimal compared with military advantage gained) Objective is always military, never civilian target (death of civilian incidental, not intentional)

This means that membership in the civilian population of a nation against which a group is waging war is insufficient reason for according a "guilty" status to a person, thereby removing those special protections. Thus, the waging of war against "any Israeli" or "any Englishman" is not acceptable behavior under the laws of war.

What are, then, the **special provisions in the Geneva Convention** relating to the treatment of civilians?

> Article 3 of this document lists actions which are prohibited "at any time and in any place whatsoever with respect to such persons." These prohibited acts include
>
> > violence to life and person, in particular murder of all kinds;
> >
> > mutilations, cruel treatment and torture;
> >
> > taking of hostages;
> >
> > outrages upon the personal dignity, in particular humiliating and degrading treatment.[10]
>
> Article 27 emphasizes the degree of legal protection afforded to these noncombatants, stating that they are
>
> > entitled, in all circumstances, to respect for their persons, their honor, their family rights, their religious convictions and practices, and their manners and customs;
> >
> > at all times to be treated humanely;
> >
> > to be protected especially against all acts of violence or threats thereof.[11]
>
> Article 33 of the Geneva Convention for the Protection of Civilian Persons (1949) provides that
>
> > No protected person may be punished for an offense he or she has not personally committed.

Collective penalties and likewise all measures of intimidation or terrorism are prohibited.

Pillage is prohibited.

Reprisals against protected persons and their property are prohibited.

"Protected persons" in this convention are *civilians who have the misfortune to be living in a combat zone or occupied territory*. Not only does this convention specifically prohibit the use of terrorism against this civilian population, but it also, in Article 34, prohibits the taking of hostages of any sort. Such rules make it clear that the kidnapping or murder of any civilian, even during times of war, to exact punishment for an injustice real or imagined, is not legal, unless the victim was directly responsible for the injustice.

This prohibition against collective punishment applies to states as well as to revolutionary organizations. Control Council Law No. 10, used in the trials of war criminals before the Nuremberg Tribunals, makes this clear.[12] Neither side in an armed conflict, whether involved in the "liberation" of a country or in the efforts of the state to maintain itself while under attack, may engage in warfare against the civilian population.

Terrorist acts against innocent persons by the state, as well as acts of terrorism by nonstate groups, are as illegal in time of war as they are in time of peace. The laws of war offer neither justification nor protection for the willful and wanton taking of innocent life. If terrorism by its very nature involves victimizing an innocent third party to achieve a political goal and to evoke a particular emotional response in an audience, then it seems reasonable to say that terrorism is illegal under the laws of war.

Although this convention was drafted with the protection of civilians in occupied territories in mind, Protocols I and II to the convention, drafted in 1976, extend these protections to civilians in nonoccupied territories. Article 46 of Protocol I codifies the customary international law doctrine that the civilian population as such, as well as individual citizens, may not be made the object of direct military attack. One significant provision in this article states, "Acts or threats of violence which have the primary object of spreading terror among the civilian population are prohibited."

This article goes on to prohibit indiscriminate attacks that are "of a nature to strike military objectives and civilians or civilian objectives without distinction." It further states that "a bombardment that treats as a single military objective a number of clearly separated and distinct military objectives located within a city, town or village, or other area which has a concentration of civilians is considered to be indiscriminate and is therefore prohibited."

What does this mean, in terms of legal restraints on terrorism? It means, for one thing, that a state may not commit an attack on a city or town as a whole, just on the basis of information that insurgents or combatants may be making a base in that area. To do so would be to commit an act of terrorism under international law. These conventions, in other words, make it clear that states as well as groups are prohibited from punishing the innocent in efforts to stop the insurgents in guerrilla warfare. To do so would be to commit acts of terrorism.

Article 50 of Protocol I clarifies the precautions that a state and a revolutionary army must make in conducting attacks. This article also codifies customary international law concerning what is called the **rule of proportionality.** Generally speaking, this refers to *the need for the loss of civilian life to be minimal compared to the military advantage gained.* It states specifically that those who plan or decide upon an attack must

> refrain from deciding to launch any attack which may be expected to cause incidental loss of civilian life . . . which would be excessive in relation to the concrete and direct military advantage anticipated.

In simple terms, this provision, along with other provisions in the article, means that those launching or planning to launch an attack are legally responsible for making sure that the military objectives they expect to gain justify the minimal loss of civilian life that may occur. This provision is extremely practical. It recognizes a basic fact of life during war: There are inevitably civilians on and around military targets who will no doubt be injured or killed during an attack on those targets.

There are two important points here. One is that the objective is assumed a military, never a civilian, target. The law makes it clear that, whereas legitimate attacks may be expected against military targets, there is no legal expectation or right to launch attacks against civilian targets. On the contrary, the civilians within the target zone are to be protected against the effects of that attack, as far as it is militarily possible.

The other point is that, although military reality makes note of the fact that some civilian injury may occur during an attack, the injury or deaths of civilians should be incidental to the operations, on a scale proportionate to the military objective sought. If civilian casualties are expected to be high, then the attack cannot be justified under international law.

Two thoughts come to mind with respect to these provisions. One is that guerrilla or revolutionary groups who select predominantly civilian targets are in violation of international law, even if there is a military target that may also be hit. Thus, the fact that a cafe is frequented by members of an enemy military does not make it a legitimate target, because there would be a great likelihood of many civilian casualties in such an attack. If the target area is populated predominantly with civilians, then it cannot be a justifiable military target.

The other thought that this provision evokes is that states may not strike civilian settlements, even if there are guerrilla soldiers taking refuge or making their headquarters in such settlements. To attack such places would mean inflicting unacceptably high levels of civilian casualties in proportion to the military objective sought. Thus, those who seek to destroy Palestinian revolutionaries may not, under international law, drop bombs on Palestinian refugee camps or in residential sections of the West Bank or Gaza, because such areas have large civilian populations, including women and children, the sick and the infirm.

It is true that those revolutionaries who make their headquarters in the midst of civilian encampments are deliberately placing those civilians at risk in the ensuing war. But this does not legally justify the attacking of such settlements by the enemy. The civilians, for the most part, have no choice but to be there, in their own homes or shelters. The state seeking to destroy the revolutionaries cannot take advantage of their vulnerable state to make war on the insurgents at the cost of countless civilian lives. Even when seeking to destroy an enemy who takes refuge among protected persons, a state may not deliberately wage war on those protected persons.

PIRACY OF AIR AND SEA

If, during times of war, terrorist acts against innocent persons are illegal, then it seems logical to assume that such acts are also illegal during times of peace. Indeed, the term *crimes against humanity,* which was used to describe war crimes at Nuremberg, did not originate with laws of war, but with laws of peace. The term was used in international legal writings to describe acts of piracy. The famous English jurist, Sir Edward Coke, in the time of James I, described pirates as **hostis humanis generis,** meaning *"common enemies of mankind."*[13]

National case law confirms this view of piracy as an international crime. The U.S. Supreme Court, in the case of *U.S. v. Smith* (1820), went on record through Justice Joseph Story as declaring piracy to be "an offense against the law of nations" and a pirate to be "an enemy of the human race."[14] Judge John Bassett Moore of the World Court reaffirmed this assessment in his opinion in the famous *Lotus* case (1927).[15]

In fact, from the Paris Declaration of 1856 to the Geneva Convention of 1958, the proliferation of treaties dealing with aspects of terror-violence on the high seas has helped to codify international law with regard to piracy.[16] Piracy—of the sea, at least—is one of the first and most universally recognized "international crimes."

Nations have not been so willing, through international law, to deal with modern **skyjacking,** which some legal experts termed *air piracy.* One legal expert suggested that "the legal status of aerial hijackers could become the same as sea pirates through the process of novation wherein the former would be presumed to stand in the shoes of the latter."[17] Theoretically, this would provide a way to bring perpetrators of the modern crime of skyjacking under the existing legal restrictions and penalties imposed on crimes of a similar nature, that is, of sea piracy, which were more common at an earlier date.

Novation is not a complicated process. Legally, it refers to *the substitution of a new indebtedness or obligation, creditor or debtor, for an existing one.* In other words, aerial hijackers would assume the legal "indebtedness" of sea pirates under international law. Thus, it would not be necessary to create new international law to deal with what is, in many respects, a very old form of criminal activity.

But modern nations have not seen such a process as an adequate or acceptable solution. Instead, three major agreements on aircraft hijacking have evolved in recent years, as well as a number of smaller agreements between nations concerned with this crime. A short review of these agreements sheds some light on the state of the law with regard to this modern form of piracy.

One of the more successful bilateral antihijacking agreements was the Memorandum of Understanding on Hijacking of Aircraft and Vessels and Other Offenses signed between the United States and Cuba on February 15, 1973.[18] In spite of a denunciation of the agreement by Cuba in October 1976, there has been a rather impressive record of interstate cooperation in combating aerial hijacking between the two countries. Many of the hijacking attempts that occurred between the United States and Cuba after 1978 resulted in the prompt return of the hijacked aircraft and the somewhat less prompt seizure of the hijackers for prosecution.

But treaties of a broader nature have met with less success. Three issues that need to be addressed in any successful hijacking convention have not been adequately resolved. These are the problems of determining who has jurisdiction, of establishing a prosecutable offense, and of providing for prompt processing of extradition requests.

The Convention on Offenses and Certain Other Acts Committed on Board Aircraft, signed in Tokyo on September 14, 1963, provided a general basis for the establishment of **jurisdiction,** that is, *legal authority to exercise control.* The hijacking of an aircraft is an act that often takes place in flight between countries. Such planes are often registered to yet another country and carry citizens of many countries. So a decision as to who has the right to bring a hijacker to justice is often a difficult one.

Article 3 of the Tokyo Convention provides that the state of registration is the one that has the first and primary right to exercise jurisdiction.[19] But this convention does not place the responsibility on any signatory nation to ensure that all alleged offenders be prosecuted. Thus, a nation may accept jurisdiction and then refuse or neglect to bring the offenders to justice.

The subsequent Convention for the Suppression of Unlawful Seizure of Aircraft, signed at The Hague on December 16, 1970, deals more specifically with the issues of extradition and prosecution. This convention obliges contracting states to make the offense of unlawful seizure of aircraft punishable by severe penalties.

This convention offers a definition for the actions that constitute the offense of skyjacking, in Article 1, which states that any person commits an offense while on board an aircraft in flight

1. unlawfully, by force or threat thereof, or by any other means of intimidation, seizes, or exercises control of, that aircraft, or attempts to perform any such act; or,
2. is an accomplice of a person who performs or attempts to perform any such act.

Although not as explicit as a later convention drawn up at Montreal, this convention does provide an important legal framework for prosecution of an offense, reasonably and clearly defined in legal terms directly applicable in the legal systems of many states (meaning the states are thus not given the sticky political task of creating laws to make such acts a legal offense).

Under this convention, too, **provisions for jurisdiction** were extended. Three states were legally given the responsibility for jurisdiction, in the following order of precedence: (1) the State of registration; (2) the State of first landing; and, (3) the State in which the lessee has its principal place of business or permanent residence. Moreover, this convention requires each contracting state to take measures to establish jurisdiction, if the offender is within its territory and is not to be extradited.

This convention also addresses the issue of prosecution, obligating each contracting state to either **extradite**—that is, *to send the person to another state seeking to prosecute*—an alleged offender, or to submit the case "without exception whatsoever to its competent authorities for the purpose of prosecution." Although it does not create an absolute obligation to extradite, the convention states that the offense referred to is deemed to be included as an extraditable offense in any existing extradition treaties between contracting states, and is to be included in every future extradition treaty concluded between such states.

The Convention for the Suppression of Unlawful Acts Against the Safety of Civil Aviation signed in Montreal on September 23, 1971, adds more detail to the description of the offenses affecting aircraft and air navigation. It includes

1. acts of violence against a person on board an aircraft in flight if that act is likely to endanger the safety of that aircraft; or
2. destruction of an aircraft in service or damage to such an aircraft which renders it incapable of flight or which is likely to endanger its safety in flight; or,
3. placing or causing to be placed on an aircraft in service, by any means whatsoever, a device or substance which is likely to destroy that aircraft, or to cause damage to it which is likely to endanger its safety in flight; or,
4. destruction or damage of air navigation facilities or interference with their operation, if any such act is likely to endanger the safety of the aircraft in flight; or,
5. communication of information which is known to be false, thereby endangering the safety of the aircraft in flight.[20]

The Montreal convention also articulated what has come to be called the concept of **universal jurisdiction** for crimes of aerial hijacking. Building on the agreement included in the convention of the previous year, the signatories in Montreal made it clear that *aerial hijacking is an international crime, for which every nation party to the convention has jurisdiction.* This means that, regardless of where the crime is initiated or concluded, on whose territory it is committed, every state party to this convention agrees to treat the act as a crime under their jurisdiction. Thus, each state either extradites or prosecutes the person accused of this crime, under the laws of the state.

Table 10.2 offers a simple comparison of these three important treaty efforts to create international agreement on this type of terrorist activity. Although other

TABLE 10.2   Key Legal Issues in Hijacking Conventions

Treaty	*Significant Legal Points*
Convention on Offenses and Certain Other Acts Committed on Board Aircraft (Tokyo, September 14, 1963)	**Jurisdiction** given to state of registration
Convention for the Suppression of Unlawful Seizure of Aircraft (The Hague, December 18, 1970)	**Jurisdiction** State of registration has first claim State of landing is given second claim State in which lessee has principal place of business or primary residence has third claim
Convention for the Suppression of Unlawful Acts Against the Safety of Civil Aviation (Montreal, September 23, 1971)	**Definition of aerial hijacking jurisdiction** Universal jurisdiction—obligation to extradite or prosecute

agreements have emerged to deal with alternative acts of terrorism impacting aerial safety, such as bombing, these three conventions provide a relatively firm agreement on the part of states about this one type of terrorist crime.

In the succeeding decades, other protocols and conventions focusing on "the suppression of unlawful acts" that endangered civil aviation continued to be debated, rewritten, and occasionally accepted as law. The 1988 Protocol for the Suppression of Unlawful Acts of Violence at Airports Serving International Civil Aviation, supplementary to the Convention for the Suppression of Unlawful Acts against the Safety of Civil Aviation (Montreal), attempts to clarify the nature of the offense. In the Montreal convention, the crime being described only included

an act of violence against a person on board an aircraft in flight;

destruction or incapacitation of an aircraft in flight;

placing (or causing to be placed) of a bomb aboard an aircraft in service;

destroying or damaging navigation facilities;

communication of false information to endanger flight.

The Protocol expands the crimes treated by this convention to include acts of violence against a person at an airport serving international civil aviation and damages to facilities at such an airport. This legal change reflected a change in the patterns of terrorist attacks, which had by the mid-1980s begun to include attacks in the airport in addition to aircraft bombings or hijackings.

In 1988 the laws of the sea, which had been the basis from which the laws of air piracy were drawn, were amended to include some of the new piracy laws just described in the context of similar acts at sea. The Convention for the Suppression of Unlawful Acts against the Safety of Maritime Navigation, written in 1988, and the Protocol for the Suppression of Unlawful Acts against the Safety of Fixed Platforms Located on the Continental Shelf were both in many respects a reflection of the earlier conventions relating to the safety of civil aviation described earlier. Terrorism became a recognized crime against both fixed and moving targets in the air and sea, at least in terms of specific types of acts.

PROTECTION OF DIPLOMATIC PERSONNEL AND HEADS OF STATE

Similar difficulties have hindered efforts to create effective protections against attacks on diplomatic personnel and heads of state. In light of the seizure of American diplomatic personnel in Iran, which was never formally "punished" as a crime under international law, it could be argued that there still exists no effective international law concerning such acts. However, laws do exist (despite the fact that they are broken without punishment) on this politically sensitive subject. Since these laws concern terrorism of a specific sort, they deserve consideration here.

Perhaps the unwillingness to punish or even to condemn those guilty of attacks on these "protected persons" has its roots in the venerable Western tradition of granting political asylum to offenders who have committed "political" crimes. Although concern for the preservation of societal order influenced some Western European governments to modify their positions on granting asylum for "political" crimes, political asylum remains the primary focus in extradition questions in many modern states.

In 1833, Belgium enacted a law providing for nonextradition of political offenders, a principle incorporated into a Franco-Belgium treaty in 1834.[21] Following attempts, both successful and unsuccessful, on the lives of heads of state in subsequent years, however, an **attentat clause** began to be incorporated into successive treaties. *This clause made the murder or attempted murder of any head of state or his immediate family a common (not political) crime.* These clauses stated essentially that such attempts "shall not be considered a political offense or an act connected with such an offense."[22]

In 1957, the European Convention on Extradition invoked the principle of the attentat clause by making assaults on heads of state and their immediate families nonpolitical offenses.[23] The Vienna Convention on Diplomatic Relations gave evidence of a broadening concern for diplomats as well as heads of state. Under this Convention, it is made "the responsibility of the States" to prevent attacks on a diplomatic agent's person, freedom, or dignity."[24] The Convention on the Prevention and Punishment of Crimes against Internationally Protected Persons including Diplomatic Agents, which came into force in February 1977, declared it the responsibility of all states party to this convention to take all practicable measures to prevent, and to either extradite or punish those committing "crimes against diplomatic agents and other internationally protected persons." This convention declared acts which jeopardized the safety of such persons "are of grave concern to the international community."[25]

This broadly stated concern and general delegation of authority, however, has failed to secure significant enforceable protections for diplomats. As one expert expressed it, "what was needed, beyond the incidental tightening of police measures, is a constant vigilance on the part of states, acting individually and collectively in an organized way, to prevent the occurrence of incidents."[26]

But while subsequent treaties on this subject have attempted to make clear the specific acts prohibited and the states that have a right to claim jurisdiction over the crime, there remain serious flaws in the protection afforded to diplomatic agents today. No "collective, organized" approach to the problem has evolved.

Furthermore, the delegation of responsibility for protecting and punishing in the event of attacks on diplomats creates serious problems when the government of a state is itself a party or a tacit accessory to the taking of diplomatic hostages. It is clearly useless to expect a government that actively or tacitly approves of such a crime to prosecute the perpetrators of the crime. Such a requirement could mean that the government must at some point prosecute itself for committing what it obviously did not regard as an illegal act—a most unlikely scenario!

One further development in the law regarding the protection of diplomatic personnel should be noted. The Venice Statement on Taking of Diplomatic Hostages, issued by the Heads of State and Government of the Seven Summit Countries during their meeting in Venice in 1980, not only expressed grave concern about the Iranian hostage situation, but also called on nations to ratify the recently completed Convention Against the Taking of Hostages, adopted by the UN General Assembly on December 17, 1979. Thirty-nine states were signatories, and 96 states were parties to this convention as of October 2001.[27]

Completed shortly after the seizure of the American Embassy in Tehran, this convention effectively makes it a crime to take *any* person as a hostage. Through this convention, the protection of international law is extended to every individual, regardless of his or her position (or lack of one), with the exception of those in armed forces engaged in armed conflict.

This broadening of the law in this respect suggests that nations consider certain actions unacceptable to the community of nations. Just as in laws of war, we noted that certain actions were prohibited at all times, whether at war or at peace, so we note that there are some actions that the international community has come to believe are unacceptable, regardless of the cause.

REGIONAL LEGAL EFFORTS TO PREVENT OR PUNISH TERRORISM

Although it is true that most regions have drafted and ratified a treaty to "prevent and punish" acts of terrorism, most of these conventions are no more specific than the international instruments in place today. The Organization of American States was the first region to draft such a treaty, creating the instrument in 1971. However, like the efforts by the international community at that time, it was vague and lacked a definition of terrorism or even a specification of types of terrorist acts. Instead, all member states simply agree to prevent and punish acts of terrorism, "especially kidnapping, murder, and other assaults against the life or physical integrity of those persons to whom the state has the duty according to international law to give special protection."[28]

Each regional convention, while fundamentally similar, has at least a few unusual qualities. The European Convention on the Suppression of Terrorism (1977), for instance, invokes the use of existing regional instruments, such as the European Court of Human Rights, to resolve disputes between states over the interpretation or application of the convention. No other regional instrument suggests such a yielding of sovereignty to a nonstate body in reference to the politically sensitive crime of "terrorism."

However, the Arab Convention on the Suppression of Terrorism, completed two decades later, offers in Articles 9–38 provisions for the arrest, extradition, or prosecution of individuals accused of terrorist acts, including the use of **judicial delegations,** *specially appointed delegations instructed to hear the testimony of witnesses and take depositions as evidence, examine and inspect evidence, and obtain relevant documents and records relating to the actionable offense.* Although each contracting state has a right to refuse to allow such a delegation, it must put into writing the reasons for its refusal. Thus, although the obligation to "extradite or prosecute" is similar to that in earlier conventions, this regional instrument creates the process for establishing a special tribunal with the authority to investigate charges of terrorism. This is a step that the international community has not yet taken.

More recent regional conventions, such as the Treaty on Cooperation among the States Members of the Commonwealth of Independent States in Combating Terrorism (1999) and the Convention of the Organization of the Islamic Conference on Combating Terrorism (1999), make extensive reference to all the existing international documents on terrorism. Each of these, however, also include types of terrorism not included in international conventions. In the Commonwealth of Independent States convention, Article 1 incorporates **technological terrorism**—*the threat or use of nuclear, radiological, chemical, or bacteriological weapons or their components, including the seizure, disruption, or destruction of nuclear, chemical, or other facilities posing an increased technological and environmental danger*—a type of terrorism not yet incorporated in any international instrument on terrorism. The Islamic Conference's convention adds to the category of terrorist crimes those that endanger the environment or other national resources, again a type of action not legally described as terrorism in any international convention to date.

Regions, then, although not necessarily moving a great deal faster than the international community in defining or creating a legal framework for terrorist crimes, have begun to offer new directions for international legal cooperation. Some of these new directions are ones that the international community, in the context of debate at the United Nations and related international organizations, is exploring with increasing vigor, particularly that of "technological terror," the financing of terror (mentioned in Article 3 of the Islamic Conference convention in terms of measures to prevent terrorism), and the need to halt the flow of arms to groups engaged in terror (discussed at length in the Islamic Conference convention). Each of these new directions is now, or will soon be, the subject of a new international convention.

SUMMARY: INTERNATIONAL PROTECTION OF THE INNOCENT AGAINST SPECIFIC CRIMES

Although limitations persist on the extent of the protection provided by the conventions reviewed thus far, several significant points illustrate the strengths—and weaknesses—of international law on terrorism contained in these examples. Certainly, the two international crimes already reviewed—air piracy and hostage taking—offer several interesting points that could be briefly recapitulated and summarized to good effect at this point.

Innocence, as noted earlier, connotes not virtue but an absence of guilt for a particular act. The international laws governing piracy protect those considered innocent in the most common meaning of the word, those whose only "crime" was to be in the wrong place at the wrong time. Similarly, the expanded law on hostage taking propounded by the 1979 convention offers legal protection to a similarly innocent person.

However, the laws on the protection of diplomatic personnel, including the 1979 convention, offer a broader concept of the innocent person and of his or her right to the protection of the law. Diplomats, consular agents, and similar governmental agents are precisely that: agents who carry out the policies of a government. As the Nuremberg trials demonstrated, it is possible to hold such persons legally responsible if their actions transgress the laws of nations.

That is the crucial point, though: it must be their *own* actions, not merely any of a variety of actions of the government they represent, which transgress the law. It is not enough that their government adheres to unacceptable or illegal policies. If the agent is to be punished for those policies, then personal guilt (in terms perhaps of carrying out of illegal policies, such as genocide) must be established before the agent can be punished. Thus, although such persons are perhaps less innocent than, for example, the tourist who boards an airplane that is subsequently hijacked, government agents cannot legally be "punished" (taken hostage or executed) unless they can be proven guilty of a specific illegal action.

Similarly, the representative of a multinational corporation must be considered legally innocent unless proven guilty of a specific crime. Thus, the kidnapping of a multinational corporation employee for ransom, to redress perceived exploitation by the company of a nation's resources, would be without legal justification.

International law, it appears, extends its protection to those truly innocent of any crime as well as those who could only be considered guilty of association with a government or corporation whose actions may be unjust. Both types of persons are regarded under the law as being sufficiently innocent to merit protection. Indeed, as the Nuremberg Tribunals demonstrated, even individual governmental agents thought guilty of heinous "crimes against humanity" were nevertheless given a trial by law rather than a summary execution.

This presumption of innocence, which precludes summary judgment, is a major stumbling block to the justification of terrorism. The taking of any innocent life, however meritorious the cause to which the act is designed to call attention, cannot be justified under international law. No wrong can justify, or require, the commission of another wrong to rectify it. To accept such a premise would be to agree that the end for which one strives serves to justify the means that one employs to attain it.

This does not leave revolutionary groups with no legitimate targets. The range of innocent persons protected by international law is fairly broad, but it is not absolutely inclusive. Military and police officials, for example, are far less clearly "innocent" in any sense of the term, particularly in regimes that practice forms of state terrorism. International law prohibits the summary taking of innocent life. The extent to which terrorism violates this prohibition is a measure of its transgression of the law.

IS TERRORISM A POLITICAL CRIME?

The definition of what constitutes a "political" crime has become a crucial part of the modern legal debate concerning terrorism. The crux of the problem appears to be in deciding how one determines what is and what is not a political crime. It is a problem that is far from solved and one whose political ramifications may well make it, for the present, insoluble.

For centuries, the nature of a **political crime** *rested largely upon the intended victim of the crime.* That is, the assassination of a head of state or of a diplomat was regarded as political in nature and therefore to be handled differently—more leniently or more severely, depending upon the state's system of laws—than an ordinary, nonpolitical offense, such as the murder of an ordinary citizen.

If such a criteria were applied to many terrorist acts today, such as the hijacking of an airplane or the bombing of a cafe, then such acts would not, on the surface, qualify as being political. The argument could be (and indeed has been) made that the real intended "victims" of such crimes are the governments forced to helplessly watch and perhaps ultimately capitulate as the events unfold.

But to assume there is a victim involved beyond the obvious captives or casualties, one is forced to rely upon knowledge or inference about the motives of the perpetrators. In other words, the action would be described as a political crime, not specifically by its intended victim but by the motives that prompted the commission of the crime.

There are at least two problems with this reasoning. The first is that, to make such a determination concerning a motive for an action, the person rendering the judgment would need a knowledge of why the terrorists committed the crime. How is such knowledge to be obtained? Does it come from propaganda put out by the terrorists, which is designed to persuade but is not necessarily truthful? Does it come from interviews with the perpetrators or their allies, assuming such interviews could be arranged?

Is there any way, indeed, to discover the facts concerning the motive for a crime? To search for a factual basis is not useless by any means, but the attribution of a motive for any crime, political or common, is essentially a judgment call. In the courts of most civilized nations, assessment of motivation may affect the degree of severity with regard to the prosecution or sentencing but has little effect on the decision as to whether or not a crime has been committed.

Yet if one allows motivation to be the determinant for delineating political from common crimes, there is reason to suspect that, for crimes judged political in motivation, there would in fact be neither prosecution nor sentencing. This is the second problem in allowing motivation to be the guiding factor in determining what constitutes a political crime. For under the laws of many nations, **political offenders** are accorded special status. *Those believed guilty of political offenses are eligible for the granting of political asylum by friendly states.* States granting such asylum are under no legal obligation to prosecute the perpetrator for the crime.

Even those who are prosecuted are afforded special treatment. Seldom are political criminals jailed with those who have committed common crimes. To be a political prisoner confers, in many nations, a unique status on the offender. There is nothing wrong with this: political crimes are not the same as common crimes. Their perpetrators are often regarded as motivated by high ideals for political change for which they are willing to pay a high personal price, often imprisonment or even death.

That is another important point, however. Just like the perpetrator of any other crime, the political offender does so with the knowledge, even the acceptance, of the penalty that must be paid for the crime. Perpetrators of political crimes in earlier centuries committed their offenses in the full expectation of being required to pay the legal penalty for their crimes. Those who would classify terrorism as a political crime do so to enable its perpetrators to evade the payment of those penalties. The concept of political offense has become a loophole through which terrorists try to avoid having to pay the just penalty for their crimes.

This **loophole in the law,** *which allows political offenders to escape extradition or even punishment,* has worried international legal experts for years. Attempts have been made to advocate the creation of an international criminal code and an international criminal court. Under these innovations, terrorism could be specified as an international crime, punishable in international court. But although the efforts to create an international criminal court has progressed dramatically in recent years, with the convention establishing such a court now open for signatures, the leaders working in Italy to construct the code for this court were unable to resolve both practical legal and political problems relating to international terrorism. Indeed, it is interesting and discouraging to note that the issue of terrorism was removed early in the conference as a crime for which this international criminal court would be expected to adjudicate. So the loophole of political offender still allows terrorists to commit heinous crimes for political purposes and escape the hand of justice.

UNITED NATIONS AND THE WAR ON TERRORISM

The issue of terrorism was brought before the UN General Assembly in 1972, after the massacre of Israeli athletes at Munich by a Palestinian group. Sporadically since that time, the United Nations has worked on measures to combat the global problem. In the 1970s, the Ad Hoc Committee tasked with generating consensus for action on the issue deadlocked in a struggle to define the term *terrorism.*

After a decade of effort, the committee reported that the issue was "too politically difficult" to define, making consensus on appropriate actions in response not possible. The problem in the General Assembly (GA) lay in differentiating between the legitimate struggles of peoples under colonial rule or alien domination and foreign occupation and terrorism. Self-determination and national liberation were processes that many member states had experienced, and most were reluctant to create law that could impinge on these fundamental rights.

The GA, in December 1985, passed a resolution containing these ambivalent feelings about causes as well as the effects of terrorism, but with sufficient strength to generate a new convention. Although GA Resolution 40/61 urged all states "to contribute to the progressive elimination of causes underlying international terrorism," it also unequivocally condemned "as criminal, all acts, methods, and practices of terrorism wherever and by whomever committed." In response to some of the explicit challenges of this resolution, and quoting it as the reason for the drafting of the treaty, the Convention for the Suppression of Unlawful Acts against the Safety of Maritime Navigation was drafted in Rome on March 10, 1988.[29]

Similarly, the Convention on the Marking of Plastic Explosives for the Purpose of Detection states, in its preamble, that it was written in response to UN Security Council Resolution 635 of June 14, 1989, and UN General Assembly Resolution 44/29 of December 4, 1989. These two resolutions urged the International Civil Aviation Organization to "intensify its work on devising an international regime for the marking of plastic or sheet explosives for the purpose of detection."[30] This convention carefully defines the relevant terms, such as "explosives" and "detection agent" and "marking," and delineates a careful system by which such marking would be administered and monitored, making the detection of the source of explosives on board aircraft more technologically possible.

On November 26, 1997, the GA Third Committee condemned terrorism. The committee drafted a resolution condemning violations of the rights to life, liberty, and security, reiterating its condemnation of terrorism. Provisions of this resolution, approved by a recorded vote of 97 in favor to none against, with 57 abstentions, called on states to take all necessary and effective measures to prevent, combat, and eliminate terrorism. It also urged the international community to enhance regional and international cooperation for fighting against terrorism and to condemn incitement of ethnic hatred, violence, and terrorism.

Less than a month later, the GA adopted an International Convention for the Suppression of Terrorist Bombings. This convention referred to earlier UN action, notably the Declaration on Measures to Eliminate International Terrorism, annexed to

General Assembly resolution 49/60 of December 9, 1994, as part of the reason for the drafting of the convention. This convention was drafted, according to it preamble, because of the increasingly widespread use of explosives in terrorist attacks and because of a perceived gap in existing multilateral treaties in the context of such attacks.

Using the General Assembly Plenary Declaration in 1994, which stated that acts of terrorism could also threaten international peace and security, the Security Council (SC) became more involved in the struggle to deal with this issue. Unanimously adopting resolution 1269 (1999), the council stressed the vital role of the UN in strengthening international cooperation in combating terrorism and emphasized the importance of enhanced coordination among states and international and regional organizations. It called upon all states to take steps to cooperate with each other through bilateral and multilateral agreements and arrangements; prevent and suppress terrorist acts; protect their nationals and other persons against terrorist attacks; and bring to justice the perpetrators of such acts. The SC continues to advocate exchanging information in accordance with international and domestic law, cooperating on administrative and judicial matters to prevent the commission of terrorist acts, and using all lawful means to prevent and suppress the preparation and financing of any such acts in member states' territories.

In other resolutions passed in the 1990s, the council called on all states to deny safe havens for those who planned, financed, or committed terrorist acts by ensuring their apprehension and prosecution or extradition. These resolutions also stressed that, before granting refugee status, states should take appropriate measures in conformity with national and international law, including international standards of human rights, to ensure that the asylum seeker had not participated in terrorist acts.

The SC has been careful not to take actions on this issue that would replace the efforts of the GA but sought to interact with it on the basis of its competence within the charter. Noting that the degree of sophistication of terrorist acts and the increasingly globalized nature of those acts were new trends and that the extensive international networks of organized criminals were creating an infrastructure of catastrophic terrorism, the SC resolved that terrorism posed a serious threat to international peace and security, making it an issue that needed SC action as well as that of GA and Economic and Social Council (ECOSOC).

In the wake of the attacks on September 11, 2001, the SC passed Resolution 1368, condemning the attacks and obliging states to "combat by all means threats to international peace and security caused by terrorist attacks." Two weeks later, on September 28, the council passed Resolution 1373, which called on states to control "the financing and preparation of any acts of terrorism" and to ratify and implement all relevant UN protocols and conventions.[31]

To date 12 major conventions and protocols designed to combat terrorism have been adopted by the UN General Assembly and have been ratified by a sufficient number of states to become international law. These conventions require states to cooperate on issues such as the suppression of unlawful seizure of aircraft (in the two conventions and protocol mentioned earlier in this chapter), the physical protection of nuclear materials, and the marking of plastic explosives for detection.

The International Convention for the Suppression of the Financing of Terrorism obliges states to freeze assets flowing to terrorist networks was adopted by the GA of the United Nations on December 9, 1999, and remains open for signatories. The preamble to this convention highlighted a growing conviction that "the financing of terrorism is a matter of grave concern to the international community as a whole" and focused on "the urgent need to enhance international cooperation among States in devising and adopting effective measures for the prevention of the financing of terrorism." It is interesting to note that this convention does not seek to create a new definition of terrorism; instead, it includes a list of treaties on terrorist acts in its annex and states, in Article 2, that a terrorist act "constitutes an offense within the scope of and as defined in one of the treaties listed in the annex." The annex includes all of the treaties discussed thus far in this chapter, including those dealing with maritime acts and the International Convention for the Suppression of Terrorist Bombings.

This approach, including a list of all treaties dealing with the issue of terrorist acts rather than redefining the problem is an apparently successful effort *not* to have to struggle once again with the political problems of definition but instead to concentrate efforts on preventive action and punishment. This convention on financing terrorism had, as of October 5, 2001, 57 signatories and four parties (**signatories** are *states that have signed the convention*, and **parties** are *states that have both signed and ratified the convention, making it law within these states*).

The UN has created a **Terrorism Prevention Branch** (TPB), which *researches terrorism trends, assists countries in upgrading their capacity to investigate and prevent terrorist acts, and fosters international cooperation based on best practices and lessons learned from previous events.* This department works with the UN Drug Control Program (which promotes the adoption and implementation of major drug control treaties and assists governments with research, analysis, and information sharing on the illicit drug trade, believed a major source of funds for terrorist activities) and the International Center for Crime Prevention (which works, among other things, on combating money laundering, also a key aspect of terrorist financing) to coordinate the efforts of states and organizations within the international community in preventing, inhibiting, and punishing terrorist acts.

The United Nations and its related agencies have been active in creating a framework of international law to define acts of terrorism. The resolutions, conventions, and protocols generated by this body also serve to articulate international concern and to generate cooperation in efforts to prevent terrorist acts and to bring perpetrators to justice. Although much clearly remains to be done in this arena, the generation of consensus by this body on this politically hot issue has increased markedly in the past decade, particularly in the wake of the September 11 attacks.

CONCLUSIONS

International law is perhaps most useful as a measure of international concern and opinion on an issue such as terrorism. Lacking methods and mechanisms for enforcement, it cannot be said to be an effective deterrent to terrorism, either on the national or the international level. Because its formulation is so ad hoc, relying on loose associations of states rather than any legislative body to draft conventions, it is somewhat less than coherent and often indecisive. Political considerations often weaken the resolve of nations to deal with politically sensitive subjects.

In the absence of a judiciary empowered to adjudicate without the consent of all parties, and lacking an executive or police force to enforce the laws, international law on terrorism has evolved as a patchwork of treaties. Among the most successful of these treaties have been those relating to specific types of terrorism and the most recent conventions on terrorist bombings and the financing of terrorism. Even these treaties, however, have been seriously hampered by political concerns relating to issues of jurisdiction, prosecution, extradition, and political asylum. Nor will the new international criminal court, as it comes into fruition, be of significant help in filling this absence of international legal authority.

As a means for combating terrorism, then, international law appears a somewhat dubious tool. When agreements are entered into that have enforcement capabilities, then such laws can be used to curb terrorism. But to date, only a few such agreements are in force within the international community.

EVALUATION

There are, however, two other types of international legal agreements on terrorism that have been attempted, and one serious international legal question generated by individuals captured or arrested during the war on terrorism declared by the United States. Consider each of the following descriptions of international legal efforts to deal with terrorism. Decide which, if any, have a reasonable chance of success, given what you now know about the problems of enforcement and adjudication.

1. A Convention for the Suppression of Terrorist Bombings was adopted by the General Assembly of the United Nations on December 15, 1997. This convention, in Article 2, stated that "any person commits an offense within the meaning of this Convention if that person unlawfully and intentionally delivers, places, discharges or detonates an explosive or other lethal device in, into or against a place of public use, a State or government facility, a public transportation system or an infrastructure facility." After defining each of the key terms (such as "place of public use" and "explosive or other lethal device," this convention makes it clear that it is the responsibility of every state party to the convention to apprehend, investigate, report, and either extradite or prosecute any alleged offenders. Because the international community has not yet created an international criminal court that can try cases of terrorism, is this a viable solution?

2. The creation of an international criminal court could have offered a solution to the politicization of the crime of terrorism. If the new court could include in its code laws on terrorism, its impact might be dramatic. Some who have advocated such a system suggest that it include such things as an international prison, to allow states to rid themselves of terrorist prisoners whom the states may be under pressure by other terrorists to release. On whose territory should this international prison be located? Who would supply the maintenance of such a prison? Who would have the right to release a prisoner

from that prison on parole? Would anyone have the right to grant clemency to a prisoner? Would, in fact, placing a prisoner in the hands of the international criminal court create as many problems as it would solve, even with respect to the crime of terrorism?

3. Several hundred people were captured by U.S.-led forces in Afghanistan after the attacks of September 2001 resulted in a declared "war on terrorism." Hundreds remain detained at the U.S. base in Guantanamo Bay, Cuba. The United States has called these individuals "enemy combatants" rather than prisoners of war, and argues that they have no right to legal counsel and may be held indefinitely without being charged with an offense. Is this a legitimate use of legal authority to combat terrorism or a violation of the rights of "protected persons" during times of war?

SUGGESTED READINGS

Arab Convention on the Suppression of Terrorism (signed at a meeting held at the General Secretariat of the League of Arab States in Cairo on April 22, 1998, deposited with the Secretary General of the League of Arab States).

Bremer, L. Paul, III. "Terrorism and the Rule of Law." U.S. State Department, Bureau of Public Affairs, Current Policy No. 847, April 23, 1987.

Convention for the Suppression of Unlawful Acts against the Safety of Civil Aviation (signed at Montreal on September 23, 1971, deposited with the governments of the Russian Federation, the United Kingdom, and the United States of America).

Convention for the Suppression of Unlawful Acts against the Safety of Maritime Navigation (signed in Rome on March 10, 1988, deposited with the Secretary General of the International Maritime Organization).

Convention for the Suppression of Unlawful Seizure of Aircraft (signed at The Hague on December 16, 1970, deposited with the governments of the Russian Federation, the United Kingdom, and the United States of America).

Convention on Offenses and Certain Other Acts Committed on Board Aircraft (signed at Tokyo on September 14, 1963, deposited with the Secretary General of the International Civil Aviation Organization).

Convention on the Marking of Plastic Explosives for the Purpose of Detection (signed at Montreal on March 1, 1991, deposited with the Secretary General of the International Civil Aviation Organization).

Convention on the Organization of the Islamic Conference on Combating International Terrorism (adopted at Ouagadougou on July 1, 1999, deposited with the Secretary General of the Organization of the Islamic Conference).

Convention on the Prevention and Punishment of Crimes against Internationally Protected Persons, including Diplomatic Agents (adopted by the General Assembly of the United Nations on December 14, 1973).

European Convention on the Suppression of Terrorism (concluded at Strasbourg on January 27, 1977, deposited with the Secretary General of the Council of Europe).

Friedlander, Robert A. *Terrorism: Documents of International and Local Control.* Dobbs Ferry, NJ: Oceana, 1979.

International Convention against the Taking of Hostages (adopted by the General Assembly of the United Nations on December 17, 1979).

International Convention for the Suppression of Terrorist Bombings (adopted by the General Assembly of the United Nations on December 15, 1997).

International Convention for the Suppression of the Financing of Terrorism (adopted by the General Assembly of the United Nations on December 9, 1999).

International Instruments related to the Prevention and Suppression of International Terrorism. New York: United Nations Press, 2001.

Joyner, Nancy D. *Aerial Hijacking as an International Crime.* Dobbs Ferry, NJ: Oceana, 1974.

OAS Convention to Prevent and Punish Acts of Terrorism Taking the Form of Crimes against Persons and Related Extortion that are of International Significance (concluded at Washington, DC on February 2, 1971, deposited with the Secretary General of the Organization of American States).

OAU Convention on the Prevention and Combating of Terrorism (adopted at Algiers on July 14, 1999, deposited with the Secretary General of the Organization of African Unity).

Protocol for the Suppression of Unlawful Acts against the Safety of Fixed Platforms Located on the Continental Shelf (done at Rome on March 10, 1988, deposited with the Secretary General of the International Maritime Organization).

Protocol on the Suppression of Unlawful Acts of Violence at Airports Serving International Civil Aviation, supplementary to the Convention for the Suppression of Unlawful Acts against the Safety of Civil Aviation (signed at Montreal on February 24, 1988, deposited with the Secretary General of the International Civil Aviation Organization).

SAARC Regional Convention on Suppression of Terrorism (signed at Kathmandu on November 4, 1987, deposited with the Secretary General of the South Asian Association for Regional Cooperation).

Treaty on Cooperation among State Members of the Commonwealth of Independent States in Combating Terrorism (done at Minsk on June 4, 1999, deposited with the Secretariat of the Commonwealth of Independent States).

Tucker, David. "Responding to Terrorism," *21 Debated Issues in World Politics.* Upper Saddle River, NJ: Prentice Hall, 2000.

NOTES

1. As Werner Levi points out in his text, *Contemporary International Law: A Concise Introduction* (Boulder, CO: Westview Press, 1979), a degree of political cooperation is only implied, not stated, in the UN Charter (P. 265–268). Considerable difference of opinion as to a legal obligation for political cooperation by member states continues to exist today.

2. See the Statute of the International Court of Justice, 6 U.S.T. 3517, T.I.A.S. No. 3043, 74 U.N.T.S. 244 (1944).

3. Stanley Hoffman, in his article, "International Law and the Control of Force" (*International and Comparative Law Quarterly* 32 [June 1995]: 22) suggests, for example, that "peace" as a common goal is a weak tool. He asserts that many states embrace doctrines that have stated goals of protracted confrontation and ultimate conquest—goals incompatible with this "common" goal of peace.

4. See the Treaty for the Renunciation of War (Paris: August 27, 1928), 46 Stat. 2343, 94 L.N.T.S., 57.

5. Statement credited to Emile Henry, a nineteenth-century French anarchist who bombed a crowded Paris cafe, killing one customer and wounding 20 others. At his trial Henry is reported to have said that his only regret was that more people had not been killed. Henry's reply to the judge's exclamations that "those were innocent victims that you struck" has formed the dogma of "collective guilt" that is often invoked to justify indiscriminate acts of terror.

6. Convention Relative to the Protection of Civilian Persons in Time of War, U.S.T. 3516, T.I.A.S. No. 3365, 75, U.N.T.S. 287 (1949).

7. See Funk and Wagnall's *Standard Comprehensive International Dictionary* (Chicago: Ferguson, 1987), vol. 1, 653.

8. Irving Howe, "The Ultimate Price of Random Terror," *Skeptic: Forum for Contemporary History,* 11, no. 58 (January–February 1976).

9. See the Judgment of the International Military Tribunal, Nuremberg, September 30, 1946, vol. 22, Trial of the Major War Criminals before the International Military Tribunal Proceedings, 411, 427, 459, 461, and 463 (1948).

10. Marjorie M. Whiteman, *Digest of International Law* (Washington, DC: Department of State, 1968), vol. 11, chap. 35, Article 2, 3518–3520.

11. Ibid., Article 32, 3528.

12. This law defines as criminal "atrocities and offenses, including but not limited to murder, extermination, enslavement, deportation, imprisonment, torture, rape or other inhuman acts committed against any civilian population . . . whether or not in violation of the domestic laws of the country where perpetrated."

13. Quoted by Robert Friedlander, *Terrorism: Documents of International and Local Control* (Dobbs Ferry, NJ: Oceana, 1979), 18.

14. *U.S. v. Smith,* 18 U.S. (5 Wheat.) P. 71, 73–75 (1820).

15. The case of the *S.S. Lotus,* P.C.I.J., Series A, No. 10 (1927), 2 Hudson, World Court Rep., 20.

16. See "Harvard Research in International Law: Piracy," *American Journal of International Law,* 26 (1932), 739, 754, 759–760. See also text of Geneva Convention on the High Seas, 13 U.S.T., 2312, T.I.A.S. No. 5200, 450 U.N.T.S. 82, and Article 100 of the Third United Nations Conference on the Law of the Sea, A/Conf. 62/WP. 10/Rev. 1 (April 28, 979).

17. Friedlander, *Terrorism Documents,* 13. For further insights on this subject, see Nancy Joyner, *Aerial Hijacking as an International Crime* (Dobbs Ferry, NJ: Oceana, 1974).

18. 24 U.S.T. 737, T.I.A.S. No. 7579 (1973); *International Legal Materials* (1973), vol. 12, 370.

19. Tokyo Convention on Offenses and Certain Other Acts Committed on Board Aircraft, signed September 14, 1963.

20. Convention for the Suppression of Unlawful Acts against the Safety of Civil Aviation, signed in Montreal on September 23, 1971.

21. Extradition Treaty, November 22, 1834, France-Belgium, Articles 5 and 6, *Recueil des Traites* (France) 278, 84 Perry's T.S. 456.

22. See, for example, the Treaty of Extradition between the United States and Venezuela, January 19, 1922, Article 3, 43 Stat. 1698, T.S. 675, 49 L.N.T.S. 435.

23. Convention of Extradition, Dec. 13, 1957, 24 Europe T.S., 173–175.

24. Signed April 18, 1961, 500 U.N.T.S. 95.

25. Convention to the Prevention and Punishment of Crimes against Internationally Protected Persons, Including Diplomatic Agents. *United Nations Treaty Series,* vol. 1035, no. 15410 (1977).

26. See comments by Christos L. Rozakis in, "Terrorism and the Internationally Protected Person in Light of the ILC's Draft Articles," *International and Comparative Law Quarterly,* 23 (January 1974): 72.

27. International Convention against the Taking of Hostages. Adopted by the General Assembly of the United Nations on November 17, 1979. Entered into force on June 3, 1983. *United Nations Treaty Series,* vol. 1316, no. 21931.

28. Article 1, OAS Convention to Prevent and Punish the Acts of Terrorism Taking the Form of Crimes against Persons and Related Extortion that are of International Significance. Concluded in Washington, DC on February 2, 1971. In force on October 16, 1973. *United Nations Treaty Series,* vol. 1438, no. 24381.

29. *International Instruments Related to the Protection and Suppression of International Terrorism.* New York: United Nations Press, 2001, 25.

30. Ibid., 42.

31. Ibid., 105.

11

Counterterrorism: The Use of Special Forces

Key Concepts

Munich massacre
strike forces
Sayaret Mat'kal
Special Night Squads
Irgun
King David Hotel
Entebbe raid
Operation Nimrod

secrecy and surprise
killer course
GSG-9
Mogadishu
U.S. Special Operations
  Command
U.S. Army Special Forces
  Command

Delta Force
Ranger
Air Force Special
  Operations Command
SEALs
Operation Eagle's Claw
Operation Chavin de
  Huantar

> *As soon as men decide that all means are permitted to fight an evil, then their good becomes indistinguishable from the evil that they set out to destroy.*
>
> Christopher Dawson

Although international laws of war and peace make it clear that terrorist acts have begun to be regarded as illegal, there does not yet exist a cohesive framework capable of guiding the actions of nations confronted with, or perpetrating, terrorism. In the absence of such a framework, the burden of regulating the acts has fallen upon individual nation-states. The review of U.S. efforts in this direction revealed some of the flaws that exist in national responses to terrorism.

Recent history abounds with examples of individual state efforts to combat the problem of international terrorism, highlighting both the dangers and the degree of success they have achieved. The success and failure of the efforts, and an assessment of the price paid for both success and failure, provide interesting insights into the strengths and limitations of nations engaged in waging single-handed war on terrorism.

Moreover, if international law truly grows or evolves from international norms, then it may be that strategy for dealing with international terrorism internationally will strongly resemble those strategies found successful among nations individually. Thus a review of the responses of nations to terrorism today may provide some clues as to the shape of international responses in the future.

NATIONS WITHOUT DEFENSES

It has been said that the **Munich massacre** *of Israeli athletes by Black September terrorists at the Olympic games in 1972* marked the turning point in the Western world's indifference toward terrorism.[1] Until that event, few of the nations most frequently the victims of terrorist attacks had made any coherent policy for combating terrorism. Although CIA analysts concluded that "terrorists continue to prefer operations in the industrialized democracies of Western Europe and North America,"[2] the very characteristics that cause nations to be included in this category also make it difficult for them to organize defenses against terrorist attacks.

In liberal democracies, dissent is part of the very fabric of the social and political milieu. This adherence to an almost absolute right to disagree sometimes creates conditions that allow radical dissent to become violent opposition before governments are able to prepare for this transformation. In West Germany, for example, before the publicized exploits of the Baader-Meinhof gang, any hint of the formation of an elite army or police unit to combat terrorism would have provoked a storm of protest inside (and outside) of the country.

Similarly, the United States, where both the army and the public bore scars from the traumas of Vietnam and Watergate, was in no condition to prepare for terrorist threats. This was partly due to the demoralizing effect of the Vietnam conflict on the army's special units and partly to the perceived need to curtail (rather than expand) domestic surveillance operations.

Nor were these nations alone in their lack of preparedness. France (in the wake of their protracted Algerian war) shared Germany's abhorrence of secret or special armies, while the British, with their problems in Northern Ireland, were perhaps too confident in their assumption that their anti-IRA network would also deal effectively with any international terrorist. Italy, at this time, was oblivious to the growing potential for terrorism within its borders, misled by a belief that most contemporary terrorism was confined to participants in the Arab-Israeli conflict. In fact, virtually every Western nation, except Israel, lacked the equipment and staff to combat the growing terrorist threat; they also lacked a realization of the impending danger.

At Munich, this complacency and inattention was effectively shattered. When a group of Black September terrorists, with logistical support from German and French sympathizers, captured the Israeli athlete's dormitory in the Olympic village in Munich in 1972, West Germany's response was firm, but it failed to prevent disaster. As the world watched transfixed in helpless terror, the Germans set up an ambush at Furstenfeldbruck Airport. Five sharpshooters succeeded in killing five of the terrorists, but not before the terrorists had killed all nine hostages.[3]

STRIKE FORCES: A FIRST LINE OF DEFENSE?

This spectacular attack and the equally spectacular failure of the government troops to secure the hostages' safety prompted several Western governments to reevaluate the quality of their counterterrorism strike forces. Since 1972, the creation of effective **strike forces,** *military or police units specially trained, equipped, and organized to combat terrorism*, has become a fairly common practice—with varying degrees of success and divergent degrees of legality. A review of the strike forces created by a few nations, their methods of operation, and their patterns of success and failure may help us understand the problems and pitfalls of the use of such forces.

Israel's Sayaret Mat'kal

Israel has been engaged in antiterrorism warfare for perhaps longer than any other nation. It has, as a result, a more extensive history in the use of strike teams. As such, it serves as an interesting case to study to determine the strengths and weaknesses of this tactic for combating terrorism.

In Israel, the Talmudic injunction, "If someone comes to kill you, rise and kill him first," has become the slogan of the **Sayaret Mat'kal.** This *specialized Israeli antiterrorist strike force* is so secretive that the Israelis rarely even mention it by name. It is this unit that was responsible for raids into Beirut to murder Palestinian leaders and for the Entebbe rescue operation in 1976.

Founded nearly a decade after Israel's establishment in 1948, the Sayaret Mat'kal was one of the country's early elite antiterrorist military formations. The application process is severe and only a tiny percentage of applicants are admitted to the training program. The Sayaret Mat'kal specializes in hostage rescue operations in Israel. However, the unit also engages in foreign activities and is understood to have been involved in the 1976 Entebbe operation. Sayaret Mat'kal frequently cooperates with other Israeli counterterrorist organizations such as Sayaret Tzanhanim, the elite paratroop unit.

This unit has both successfully thwarted terrorist attacks, and in its zeal to "strike before being struck" and to punish terrorists, has also been guilty of the murder of innocent persons. When Prime Minister Golda Meir unleashed "hit teams" the day after the Munich massacre, with orders to roam the world seeking out and summarily executing those responsible for the attack, the results were neither entirely legal nor wholly desirable.

One of these "hit teams" assassinated the wrong man. At Lillehammer, Norway, in 1973, an innocent Morrocan waiter was gunned down by a hit team in front of his pregnant Norwegian wife. The team had mistaken the waiter for the architect of the Munich massacre, Ali Hassan Salameh. International indignation forced Israel to temporarily restrain the hit squads.

This was, however, only a brief setback in Israel's use of strike forces in its war on terrorism. In January 1979, one of Israel's hit teams succeeded in killing Salameh with a radio-controlled car bomb in Beirut. This bomb also killed his four bodyguards and five innocent people who happened to be passing by at the time. The Israeli hit team may also have been responsible for the assassination in Tunis on April 16, 1988, of Khalil al-Wazir, the PLO's mastermind of terrorist strategy against Israel.

One of the ironies of Israel's response to this incident is that, as an excusatory footnote to their (unofficial) admission of regret at the loss of innocent lives, the

Israelis suggested that these people were just "in the wrong place at the wrong time."[4] This has unfortunate echoes of the "justification" offered by terrorists of harm to innocent people caused by their bombs.

The innocent persons killed, like Susan Wareham, a British woman working as a secretary for a construction company in Beirut, committed only the mistake (crime?) of being too near Salameh's car when it exploded. Although counterterrorist attacks like this may not deliberately take innocent life, they are undoubtedly culpable of a wanton disregard for the safety of innocent persons. Callous uncaring or deliberate disregard for the safety of innocent persons—the difference may be in the degree of disregard for the sanctity of human life. The net result for the innocent bystander is unhappily the same.

Not all of Israel's counterattacks on terrorism have been so counterproductive. Indeed, the Sayaret Mat'kal is one of the best-trained and equipped special forces units in operation today, with an impressive record of successful missions as well.

This unit is not part of the regular army and reports only to the chief of intelligence. Its members, however, do wear uniforms. This unit does not rely on trained volunteers but instead draws on raw recruits from the Kelet (the recruit depot). Usually an officer of the Sayaret Mat'kal will go to the Kelet to select about 15–20 recruits to form a team.

This team does much of its training in enemy territory, where the bullets are as real as the enemy. Recruits who survive this basic training become permanent members of a squad. Such squads are trained in the use of the .22 Beretta pistol as well as the Uzi, the Israeli-invented machine pistol, and the Kalashnikov, the Russian assault rifle.

The willingness of such teams to commit acts of terrorism in order to counter terrorism may perhaps lie in the very roots of Israel's history. The joint British-Jewish **Special Night Squads,** of which Moshe Dayan was a member, operated during the 1930s. These squads *were trained by their leader,* Orde Wingate, *to kill rather than wait to be killed.*

The **Irgun,** *a successor to these squads in the increasing spiral of violence in the region of Palestine,* boasted Menachem Begin as a member. This organization was responsible for the *bombing at the* **King David Hotel** *on July 22, 1946, which took 91 lives—British, Jewish, and Arab.* The terrorists of the Irgun who perpetrated this violence still meet annually to observe the anniversary of this bombing—at the King David Hotel. Thurston Clarke's account, *By Blood and Fire: The Attack on the King David Hotel,* is detailed and well-documented in a publication by G. P. Putnam's Sons (1981), for those interested in a further review of this incident.

Given this concept that it is better to kill than to wait to be killed, which seems to have pervaded Israel's brief and bloody history, it is perhaps easier to understand both the brilliant successes that reflect the intense training and dedication and the disasters that have occasionally resulted because of the ruthless determination of these special strike force teams.

The Sayaret Mat'kal conducted a raid inside Lebanon in December 1968 that was described as an attempt to force the Lebanese to prevent Palestinian terrorists from mounting their attacks from Lebanon. Earlier that year, the Palestinians had carried out a successful hijacking, taking over an El Al airliner en route from Rome to

Tel Aviv. They had also attacked another El Al plane at Athens airport in Greece, damaging it with automatic fire and grenades. Israeli intelligence reports showed that both terrorist incidents originated in Beirut.

So a commando raid, carried out by the Sayaret Mat'kal, was launched against Beirut International Airport. Thirteen Arab aircraft, including nine jetliners, were destroyed. There were no casualties, because all of the airplanes were cleared of passengers and crew first.

Although the raid was a tactical success, its long-term effects were less rewarding. President De Gaulle condemned the raid as a violation of the sovereignty of a nation-state and used it as a reason for cutting off all arms shipments to Israel. This cutoff came at a time when the Israeli Defense Forces were relying heavily on French equipment. Moreover, the other major supplier of Israeli arms, the United States, expressed its displeasure over the raid but stopped short of cutting off arms shipments.

Furthermore, the Palestinians acquired both publicity and a certain amount of public sympathy for their cause, two of the primary goals of terrorists, with respect to the media. Finally, the airline company that owned and operated the planes, Middle East Airlines, was able to purchase a whole new fleet of jetliners—with the insurance money from the destroyed planes!

Other assault operations were equally "successful" but had perhaps less negative impacts. It was the Sayaret Mat'kal that in 1972 successfully ended the hijacking of a Sabena Boeing 707 jetliner, Flight 517 from Brussels to Tel Aviv. When four members of the Black September Palestinian group hijacked the plane and forced it to land at Lod airport, they announced that they intended to blow up the plane, with its 90 passengers and 10 crew members, unless the Israeli government met their demands for the release of over 300 Arab prisoners.

The Sayaret Mat'kal assault force succeeded in storming the plane and freeing the passengers and crew members. Although one passenger and two of the hijackers were killed, this minimal loss of life became the standard for similar feats, such as that carried out by Germany's GSG-9 at Mogadishu.

When the Palestinians struck again, it was at the Olympic Games in Munich, only months after the Lod Airport rescue. Israeli athletes were the target, and the Sayaret Mat'kal was excluded from the attempts to free those hostages.

This unit also was responsible for the successful **Entebbe raid** in *June 1976 when an Air France Airbus, Flight 139 en route from Tel Aviv to Paris was hijacked after a stop at Athens airport and Israel responded by organizing a brilliant and successful military rescue operation.* The plane, which landed at Entebbe airport in Uganda, carried 248 passengers and crew members. All but 106 of these hostages were released by the terrorists before the Israeli raid. Only the Israeli citizens and Jews of other nationalities were kept hostage, to increase pressure on Israel to agree to the release of 53 "freedom fighters" imprisoned in Israeli prisons.

The military incursion mounted by Israel succeeded in freeing all of the hostages held at the airport, with the exception of three who either misunderstood or did not hear orders by the commandos to lie down as they opened fire on the terrorists. All seven of the terrorists (two of whom were German and five of whom were Palestinian members of the PFLP) were killed, along with a number of Ugandan soldiers, who tried to prevent the Israeli commandos from escaping with the hostages.[5]

International opinion, for the most part, supported Israel, in spite of the fact that Israel militarily invaded Uganda. Part of this approbation derives, no doubt, from a common love for a "winner." But part is due to the perceived legal right of a nation to intervene for "humanitarian" purposes in another country. Although this right of humanitarian intervention is limited, it seemed to most of the community of nations to be acceptable in this case.

Thus, Israel had the first and arguably the most highly trained of the strike forces. Their greatest liability may lie in the fervor with which they pursue their enemies. This zeal has caused them to cross not only national boundaries in their quest for vengeance, but also international law.

The British Special Air Services

On May 5, 1980, a clear crisp Monday morning, Britain's 22nd SAS, the Special Air Service Regiment, supported by special police units, carried out **Operation Nimrod,** *an assault on the Iranian Embassy in the heart of downtown London.* As thousands of people on the streets of London watched, black-clad SAS members swung down from ropes and burst into the building through windows. Wearing gas masks, the assault force moved from room to room throwing stun grenades mixed with CS gas. As they moved through the building, they identified the terrorists, shot them with their Heckler & Koch MP5s or Browning automatic pistols, and bundled the hostages out of the burning building.

This was not the only successful counterterrorist attack carried out by Britain's SAS, but it was unique in at least one sense. Most citizens do not have the opportunity to see their special strike forces in operation on their home soil. Most operations of such forces take place on foreign soil, far from home and the attention of citizens.

Even in Operation Nimrod, however, Britain worked very hard to preserve the speed and secrecy that have become the hallmark of SAS operations. The assault team wore hoods, which served to hide their identities as well as to frighten the terrorists. When the incident was over, the unit handed authority back to the police and quietly made its way to the St. John's Wood barracks for a small celebration before returning to their permanent station at Bradbury Lines in Hereford.

Secrecy and surprise have been *the watchwords of this regiment* ever since it was formed over 40 years ago. Lieutenant David Stirling, of the Scots Guard, is credited with creating this special unit. Under his plan, the SAS was designed to operate in units of five (later reduced to four) men, which continues to be the standard SAS stick.

The units have tended to be made up of a high percentage of Scottish Roman Catholics, perhaps because its founder Stirling was himself a Scots Catholic, and perhaps because the Catholics of Scotland have had a history for generations of guerrilla warfare and traditions of secrecy. All of its members are volunteers, mostly from the Parachute Regiment. It is not a "young" regiment; the average age is about 27.

Each recruit is required to give up his rank and pay (most have already reached the rank of corporal or sergeant before attempting to join) and go back to the rank of trooper. Training in the Welsh countryside is rigorous, literally a killer. Three men died on Brecon Beacons during solo treks in 1979 and 1980, in terrible weather through the Welsh mountains.

Recruits are trained in combat survival, survival in Arctic conditions, and swimming fully clothed. They also receive special parachute training, including night jumps from extraordinary heights. Emphasis is placed on weapons training, using the SAS weapons, the aforementioned Heckler & Koch submachine gun, the Browning .45 automatic pistol, the pump action shotgun, and the Sterling submachine gun fitted with a silencer. In addition, they are given training in foreign weapons, so that they can both use captured weapons and be familiar with weapons that their enemies may use on them.

Out of every 100 men who apply, only about 19 will meet the physical and mental requirements. The initial tests include a series of treks across the Welsh hills, carrying weighted packs. *The final trek covers 37 miles while carrying a 55-pound pack, over some of the toughest country in the Brecon Beacons. It must be covered in 20 hours, and it is literally a* **killer course.** As noted earlier, men have died trying to complete it.

Once they have passed these initial courses, they continue to receive specialized training in such subjects as explosives, battlefield medicine, and the operation of communication equipment. They train in the use of various personal weapons, knives and crossbows for "silent" killing, and submachine guns fitted with silencers. They learn about desert and jungle warfare, and wilderness survival.

After this, they continue to specialize. Their specialties may be in such fields as medicine, languages, skiing, mountaineering, or underwater warfare. Individual skill development is encouraged at all times.

The SAS finds itself operating more often than most other national strike forces, with the possible exception of the Sayaret Mat'kal. This is due to the decades of violence in Northern Ireland. Although the SAS rarely figures in press reports on antiterrorist activities in that region, many operations have been carried out by this unit in cooperation with the British occupying forces. The SAS has also seen overseas service in Aden, Oman, and Borneo. Indeed, much of its training for the guerrilla warfare that it has faced in Northern Ireland finds its origins in the SAS experience in Aden in the mid-1960s.

In Northern Ireland, the SAS served as a backup for the regular army units and the Royal Ulster Constabulary. It was a largely thankless and often a very dangerous job. As members have somewhat cynically noted, if the "Sassmen" (as the Irish have called them) were killed or injured in an ambush, little public mention was made of the incident. But if the SAS was responsible, even indirectly, for the injury or death of any civilians, then public indignation was quite vocal.

Britain, unlike Israel, has indeed been willing to criticize its own strike forces when their actions have resulted in needless injury or loss of life. One judge, in whose court two Sassmen were on trial for responsibility in the death of a civilian in a stakeout of an arms cache, stated that although terrorists might consider themselves outside the rule of law, the army could not.

Forty years of experience as a special forces regiment has made the SAS into one of the best counterterrorist strike forces in the world today. Many nations' own strike forces benefit from training and assistance offered by this unit. Relations between the SAS and Germany's GSG–9 are quite cordial and have resulted in considerable mutual training and assistance efforts.

Relations between the SAS and Israel's Sayaret Mat'kal, however, are far less amiable. Both units can remember a time when the British, under the Palestine Mandate, formed Q Squads to hunt down Jewish terrorists, particularly those of the infamous Stern Gang. In one particularly nasty incident, Roy Farran, responsible for the formation of the Q Squads on SAS principles, was acquitted in a court martial of the murder of a suspected member of the Stern Gang. Israeli terrorists, not satisfied with the verdict, sent a book bomb to Farran's home in England. Roy's brother, Rex, opened the package and was killed as the bomb exploded in his face. The memory of such tragedies and the vindictiveness that caused them, has historically made the relations between these two special forces units strained, although relations improved in the late 1990s.

Moreover, the Sassmen are frequently called upon by their government to protect the leaders of various Arab states. Because many of these states and their leaders were regarded by some in Israel as natural enemies, the SAS and the Sayaret Mat'kal often found themselves on opposite sides of these security situations.

Germany's GSG-9

Grenzschutzgruppe 9 (called **GSG-9**) makes no claim to being a "killer troop" or "hit squad." This group, *formed when the Bavarian State police were unable to deal adequately with the Munich situation in September 1972*, has made a point of being less dependent upon weapons than upon the talents, discipline, and training of its men.

The Federal Border Guard became the parent unit for this special unit, which works out well since it is the only force in Germany directly under the control of the central government. GSG-9 became the ninth unit of the Border Guard, making its headquarters at St. Augustin just outside of Bonn. It was formed very much along the same lines as the SAS, operating with five-man sticks.

Within GSG-9 there is a headquarters unit, a communications and documentation unit, and three fighting units. Its three technical units deal with weapons, research, equipment, backup supply, and maintenance services. Each of its three strike forces has 30 men, comprising a Command Section and five Special Tactical Sections (composed of four men and an officer)—the five-man stick.[6]

This group differs from the Sayaret Mat'kal and the SAS in that it is a civilian police force. Although much of the training given to its members is similar to that of the SAS, it is unique in the training its members receive in knowledge of the law, particularly the law applying to counterterrorism operations. Members of this special force are more conscious of the law, and of their need to stay as far as possible within its bounds, than are other similar strike forces.

This does not mean that GSG-9 does not train its personnel in active counter-terrorism techniques. In fact, Germany's elite force has one of the most sophisticated arsenals in the world. Because the deplorable shooting at Furstenfeldbruck Airport demonstrated the need for marksmanship training, every man of GSG-9 is taught to be an expert marksman, using weapons such as the Mausser 66 sniper's rifle, equipped with infrared sights and light intensifiers for night shooting. Like the SAS, they favor the Heckler & Koch MP5s for their routine work, but they are also armed with .357 Magnum revolvers.

Because they are required to reach any part of Germany within two hours ready for action, units are supplied with Mercedes-Benz autos of special design, and BO 105 type helicopters. They are trained to descend via special ropes from hovering copters.

But these units are trained in more than just combat. They spend a great deal of time studying the origins and tactics of known terrorists, to determine how best to defeat them. Every member of a team learns such useful tricks as how to pick locks and how to handle airport equipment, to facilitate efforts to mount successful attacks against terrorists who have hijacked an airplane.

GSG-9 practices assaults on hijacked airliners, training on mock-ups of aircraft and sometimes on aircraft on loan from Lufthansa. Such training placed them in good stead in **Mogadishu** in 1977. In October of that year, *Zohair Akache's terrorist team hijacked a Lufthansa Boeing 737 with 82 passengers, in support of the Baader-Meinhof gang.* After touring the Middle East in search of an airport willing to let them land, they finally landed at Mogadishu in Somalia.

Unlike the situation in Uganda faced by the Israelis, the Germans found Somalia more than willing to cooperate with them in their efforts to end the hostage situation. Twenty-eight handpicked men stormed the airliner, rescuing all hostages without harm. It was, if not a perfect raid of its kind (the original assault ladders were too short), a very good example of careful planning and execution. No laws were broken, no unnecessary injuries to innocent persons occurred, and both hostages and plane were recovered.

TOO MANY U.S. OPTIONS?

American counterterrorist forces are based in the United States, far from the Middle East where the current war on terrorism is focused. The Joint Special Operations Agency, headed by a two-star general, is charged with preparing guidelines and plans to guide counterterrorist forces during their formation, training, and operations. But this agency has no command authority over the forces.

The **U.S. Special Operations Command** (USSOCOM) *was established by the Department of Defense, under congressional orders, on June 1, 1987, as a single command for all of the special operations units.* This command is located at MacDill Air Force Base, Florida, and commands the following units: the Special Operations

Command (SOCOM) unit based at Fort Bragg, North Carolina; the Naval Warfare Special Operations Command, and the Joint Special Operations Command. The Air Force Special Operations Command is located at Hurlbert Field, Florida. At present, the U.S. Army maintains the highest number of special operations units, with three distinct parts. The U.S. Air Force and the Navy each have one unit, and the U.S. Marines also have one unit, arguably the largest special operations unit, dedicated to amphibious beachfront assaults. The U.S. Navy's SEAL teams are under the command of the Naval Special Warfare Group, headquartered in San Diego, California.

A brief look at some of these units will help make understanding the whole collection a little easier. It may also make clear the problems faced in successful use of such forces.

Special Forces, U.S. Army

The Joint Special Operations Command (JSOC) and the U.S. Army Special Operations Command (USASOC) are both headquartered at Fort Bragg, North Carolina, under SOCOM. JSOC is a multiservice and interdepartmental command, with antiterrorism its primary job. It includes a command staff that overseas the training and operations of Army's Delta Force, the Navy's SEAL Team Six, and in times of national emergency, the FBI's Hostage Rescue Team.

USASOC has more that 25,000 personnel and includes the **U.S. Army Special Forces Command** (SFC), the 75th Ranger Regiment, the 180th Special Operations Aviation Regiment (SOAR), the JFK Special Warfare Center and School, the U.S. Army Civil Affairs and Psychological Operations Command, the U.S. Army Special Operations Support Command, and various chemical reconnaissance units. Each of these "communities" has special roles and missions. For example, SOAR, often referred to as the "Nightstalkers," is the most secret and technologically advanced unit in USASOC, while the SFC is home of the more widely known Green Berets and is regarded as the "brains" portion of the USASOC; the Rangers are referred to as the "muscle" of the SOCOM.

SFC has the highest operations tempo of any community within SOCOM, because the average SF soldier generally spends more than half of every year in the field. These are the *"trained professionals," who with high levels of technical, cultural, and combat skills, trained to work together to solve problems.* In this sense, they are more like a Peace Corps team with guns than a counterterror unit. Yet they continue to be used in areas where terrorism is a serious threat, as in Iraq and Afghanistan during the early part of the war on terrorism. Thus, this community deserves a quick look.

Although a special forces unit has three types of teams, (A, B, and C), the latter two teams are generally not deployable, since they consist of staff and support personnel. Usually, an A-Team consists of 12 men, including a captain, a warrant officer, and ten men who all are at least sergeants. All candidates for such a team must pass a very rigorous training course, much like the SAS. This training includes a "selection" session, with intense physical and mental training, and a Qualification Class (or Q-School). The 25-week process creates candidates who are experts in a variety of tasks, including but not limited to land navigation, basic weapons and demolition, water navigation, intelligence, and reconnaissance. Upon completing Q-School successfully, the candidate must then continue training in his chosen area of specialty, which can take from 6 to 56 weeks to complete.

1st Special Forces Operational Detachment—Delta (Delta Force), U.S. Army

Delta Force *was commissioned under the command of Colonel Charles Beckwith on November 19, 1977, to be primarily a hostage-rescue and counterterrorism force.* Most of its people are drawn from the Ranger units or the Special Forces units by a desire to serve in this very secret unit. Like the SAS, Delta Force is built on the premise of a critical need for secrecy and its training is in many ways similar to that of the SAS.

Very little public information is available about this unit, except in very general terms. It is designed to rapidly resolve hostage or hijacking incidents involving U.S. citizens abroad or on planes traveling beyond U.S. territory. Consequently, its members have a wide range of skills, from rappelling (as the SAS did in London) to parachuting (into hostile territory) to rapid repair of a wide range of vehicles. Most of the training is altered regularly to be certain the men are able to respond to current world situations.

Ranger, U.S. Army

Drawn usually from the Airborne Infantry units, candidates for **Ranger** units must be extremely physically fit initially, since training involves intense physical challenges. The first stage involves successful completion of the Ranger Indoctrination Program (RIP), a three-week course of physical and mental training, including building strengths in swimming, land navigation, and endurance as well as classroom instruction.

The next nine weeks, if one successfully completes RIP, has four phases, each of which presents a different type of challenge. The first phase is another week of RIP, designed to weed out those not completely motivated or physically able to continue. The second phase training takes place in the swamps and forests near Eglin Air Force base in Florida, where the candidates stay "continuously wet, continuously moving, continuously hungry."[7]

During the third phase of Ranger training, candidates operate in a mountainous terrain near Dahlonega, Georgia, again with little sleep or food, learning to rappel down cliffs and to navigate through difficult valleys. Finally, the training groups are sent to the desert near Dugway, Utah, to learn how to navigate without many discernable landmarks and to conduct patrols and ambushes without cover or concealment. The objective for such a multifaceted form of training is to create *a highly mobile infantry unit able to deploy quickly anywhere in the world and to lead through any terrain ground forces that will be deployed to follow.*

Air Force Special Operations Command

The Air Force Special Operations Command (AFSOC) is based at Eglin Air Force Base in Florida. Although the **Air Force Special Operations Command** units cover four different types of mission areas, only one, the Special Operations Forces Mobility, is usually associated with counterterrorism. *This unit consists of numerous fixed- and rotary-winged aircraft, with the pilots and support crews used to insert and recover soldiers of other special ops units of every service branch.* The AFSOC currently has units located strategically throughout the world which are ready to deploy with little advance warning to facilitate counterterrorism efforts by the other branches.

Naval Special Warfare Command

Although it has units stationed around the world, the NAVSPECWARCOM has its home base in Coronado, California. A part of the Naval Special Warfare Groups, the **SEALs** (Sea, Air and Land) *are made up of highly trained and intensely motivated seamen, who have successfully completed 25 weeks of difficult training.* If the volunteer candidates make it through the first five weeks of Basic Underwater Demolition training (the "toughening up" phase), they must then spend a week pushed to the limits of their physical endurance (called "hell week" by the men). Those who successfully complete this will then spend the next 19 weeks learning to navigate great distances underwater, become proficient at underwater demolition, reconnaissance and navigation, and a variety of other skills essential for combat diving, including how to enter and exit a wide range of vehicles to carry out operations at sea.

These seamen also receive jungle, desert, and arctic training, as well as training at Fort Benning and the U.S. Army Parachute School. The final five weeks of their training is in simulations in which they are required to use their new skills to resolve real-world situations they might encounter.

Clearly, the United States has a wide range of military units that could be utilized in counterterrorism efforts. The problems with U.S. counterterrorism forces are equally obvious, particularly those brought on by the lack of cohesive command illustrated by *the abortive attempt to send a strike team into Iran to free Americans held hostage in the U.S. Embassy in Tehran.* **Operation Eagle's Claw,** as this mission was called, was characterized by a confusion of command, insufficient training, and critical equipment failure.

Cloaked in so much secrecy that even some of the military officers involved were not told the aim of the mission for which they were preparing, this operation became a model for what can go wrong in a strike force maneuver. In addition to too much secrecy, there were too many "chiefs" and not enough cooperation between military units. An army officer, Major General James Vaught, was in command overall; Colonel James Kyle of the Air Force had responsibility for fixed-wing aircraft, while Colonel Charles Pitman of the Marines also had command responsibility and Colonel Beckwith controlled the Delta Force unit.

The Delta Force squad lacked sufficient training and experience for such an operation. It had been created by Colonel Beckwith only two years earlier in 1987, and its training program was incomplete and not designed for the type of situation that evolved. Delta Force was underfunded and ill-equipped to handle the hostage raid, having trained primarily in guerrilla warfare and low-intensity conflict.

Today, the United States has taken steps, outlined above, to create a command unit in which to vest coordination for this specialized training and command. However, within the armed services there remain strong rivalries, making it difficult for one branch to create and receive support needed for each of these separate specialized units. In the wake of Operation Eagle's Claw's disaster a call was made for a new special counterterrorism unit, with personnel drawn from all of the armed services, but there has been little success in creating such a unit. Interservice rivalries make its creation very unlikely in the near future.

According to government reports, the Delta Force unit has been deployed several times, other than the highly publicized Operation Eagle's Claw fiasco and the *Achille Lauro* incident. It was, for instance, sent to Venezuela to advise the armed forces there on the ways to retake a hijacked aircraft. It was sent on a similar mission to Oman, to prepare to retake a hijacked plane in nearby Kuwait. At the time of the TWA hijacking, Delta Force was deployed to the Mediterranean. But in each of these cases, its activities stopped short of assault; it simply made preparations for, or advised in preparations for, the assault.

Some have argued this has had a detrimental effect on the morale of the individuals in Delta Force. To always be preparing for but never performing counterterrorist activities is infinitely frustrating, as the men in GSG-9 and SAS could attest. But the United States has been reluctant to field a strike force against the terrorists, until a war on terrorism was declared in 2001. The role that Delta Force plays in this war will remain secret for the foreseeable future, and hence its effectiveness today is impossible to gauge.

Delta Force remains one of the best that the United States has to offer in terms of a strike force. Since the Iranian fiasco, it has proved itself capable of successful missions. The "skyjacking" of the *Achille Lauro* hijackers was an outstandingly successful operation, whose questionable legality has been overshadowed by its brilliant execution, giving a much-needed boost to Delta Force's morale.

Because the United States did not have many indigenous groups engaging in domestic terrorism until the 1990s, unlike Germany and Great Britain who were challenged by events in the 1970s to create units to deal with terrorism domestically, it was able to focus its attentions on training its special forces to operate overseas. Emphasis was placed less on secrecy of identity than on rapid-response capabilities and combat training. If coordination of command problems can be surmounted, these forces may develop into units as efficient and respected as the SAS and GSG-9.

New Units—and New Technologies

In the wake of the Operation Eagle's Claw debacle, the Pentagon began to establish the closest thing this nation has ever had to a secret army. Small, specially trained units were developed that were designed to operate much more covertly than some of the older military units, such as the Navy SEALs. In addition to being given rather exotic code names, such as Yellow Fruit and Seaspray, these units were armed with newer, more sophisticated types of equipment. These included such items as the small, high-tech helicopters with which Task Force 160, operating out of Fort Campbell, train.

These new units were also given more sophisticated communications gear. This gear includes, for example, the one-man satellite-communications radios and dishes.

More important than these technological "toys," however, was the creation of the Intelligence Support Activity (ISA), a far-ranging intelligence organization that gave the Army, for the first time, the ability to engage in full-fledged espionage, fielding its own agents. Through this organization the strike forces were able to gather the information they needed to plan their counterterrorist activities. They were no longer dependent upon the CIA or other intelligence services for vital data, which was too often not available or kept classified at a critical juncture in the planning process. Indeed, their intelligence and reconnaissance efforts in the early stages of the war on terrorism in 2001 facilitated U.S. military response options at this critical juncture.

Even with these innovations, however, these units have had difficulty in rising above the bureaucratic infighting and bungling that has for so long plagued U.S. strike forces. Although the units still exist, their morale, and even their preparedness, is too often in disarray. Seaspray, Yellow Fruit, and the ISA became involved in clandestine operations in Central America, which seriously impaired their credibility with Congress and within the military and intelligence units of the United States. The use (or misuse) of counterterrorism forces in this area has jeopardized America's efforts to develop a credible and respected strike force, respected by and capable of working with units such as the SAS and GSG-9. The struggle in Afghanistan has offered U.S. special forces units and the SAS opportunities for joint operations that, when they are more clearly evaluated after the war, may improve the international perspective of these forces.

A quick look at three different efforts by governments to use special forces to resolve situations involving terrorism may help to illustrate both the strengths and the weaknesses discussed thus far in using special forces to resolve terrorism.

CASE STUDY   Operation Chavin de Huantar

On December 17, 1996, rebels from the Tupac Amaru seized the Japanese Embassy residence in Lima, Peru, during a festive cocktail reception. Demanding the release of 400 of their comrades who were in Peru's prison at the time, the 14 Tupac Amaru guerrillas gradually released hundreds of the hostages, retaining only 72 for the entire seige. Alberto Fujimori, Peru's president, saw little chance for resolving the situation peacefully, because he was determined not to release the prisoners. But he gave the negotiators an opportunity to try. Attempting to alleviate the tension, he arranged the safe passage to Cuba for the rebels if they wished (which they did not choose to accept, as most wanted to remain in Peru). He also appointed Archbishop Luis Cipriani to be the special negotiator.

The 72 hostages who were held for the whole 126-day siege included senior Peruvian officials, Fujimori's brother Pedro, foreign diplomats, and the Japanese ambassador. Britain, Germany, Israel, and the United States all offered to help in the rescue attempt, but were all officially turned down. Fujimori, however, was under intense pressure to resolve the situation as quickly and peacefully as possible.

But he resisted all calls for a quick solution, choosing instead to allow time for his military and intelligence units to create and implement **Operation Chavin de Huantar** (named in honor of a pre-Incan archaeological site that was honeycombed with underground passages), *the rescue mission, using 140 Peruvian special forces troops and professional miners.* During the seemingly endless weeks of the standoff, while negotiations continued, the professional miners were brought into the area near the residence to build large, ventilated and lighted tunnels through which the troops could reach the inside of the compound.

The outstanding success of the operation (with only one of the 72 hostages being killed) can be attributed to split-second timing, well-planned diversions, and superb intelligence. During the months of the incident, listening devices were smuggled into the residence. Some were hidden in a guitar and thermos bottle that the Red Cross workers were given to deliver; others were placed in buttons on clothing brought to the hostages as changes of clothes were needed. During the final four days, intelligence agents posed as doctors and were allowed to enter the compound to check on the health of the hostages, implanting while they were there matchstick-sized two-way microphones that helped intelligence officers on the outside to communicate with the military and police commanders being held among the hostages within.

With this intelligence access, those planning the operation were able to monitor the movements of the guerrillas and hostages each day, noting patterns of behavior. This information made a carefully timed assault possible, because the intelligence officers were able to learn that the Tupac Amaru guards played a game of soccer at about 3 p.m. in the ground-floor living room each day. Prior to this game, the 14 guards stacked their rifles in a corner of the room.

Because the building plans were readily available to government forces, the special forces team had plenty of time to train on mock-ups of the building. Construction of the tunnels, if detected by the hostage takers, could have triggered a violent battle and possibly a massacre of the hostages. To prevent this, Peru's leaders played blaring martial music day and night outside the embassy compound to mask the noise. This diversion also served to deny rest to the hostage takers, demoralizing or at least weakening their resistance and stamina. Moreover, the tunnels were built to offer as many as six different accesses to the compound, which would increase the rebels' confusion when the assault began, thus providing another strategic advantage to the rescue teams.

At 3:10 p.m., the listening devices indicated that the afternoon soccer game had begun, with at least half of the guards participating. By 3:17 p.m., the hostages, who were being held upstairs during the game as usual, were alerted by a hidden receiver held by a military officer who was among the hostages. They moved a desk to block the second-floor entrance and took cover. Three minutes later, nine pounds of explosives were detonated in the tunnel directly under the reception room, where the soccer game was in progress. This explosion killed four of the eight guards and opened a hole through which troops began to pour.

The patience exercised by the Peruvian government in talking with the terrorists through extensive negotiations, using the time to gather intelligence, to build tunnels, and practice the assault, was amply rewarded when the hostages were successfully rescued with the loss of only one hostage's life. Peru presented to the international community an example of the value of careful intelligence and planning in such hostage-rescue situations. The rescue efforts broke no laws, it wasted no civilian or innocent lives (except for the one, who was shot by a guard as the attack began), and the rescue team was given plenty of time to plan a successful final act. Patience and careful planning, based on timely intelligence information, were keys to the success of Operation Chavin de Huantar.[8]   ❏

CASE STUDY   Mogadishu

Germany's newly created GSG-9, with only about 180 total personnel who had undergone a few years of counterterrorism-specific training, was nevertheless one of the best units of its kind in the world in 1977. GSG-9 was confronted early in its career with a challenging hostage-rescue operation involving an airline hijacking, which tested the group's ability to operate successfully within the law, without loss of life.

In September and October 1997, shortly after the unit was formed, the RAF took German businessman Hans-Martin Schleyer hostage. The RAF immediately demanded the release of 11 of their comrades-in-arms who were being held in prison in [West] Germany. In spite of attempts by the German government to find a nation willing to take the terrorists, a whole month passed without resolution of the situation. At last, on October 13, French authorities reported that a Lufthansa had been hijacked en route from the Balearic Islands to Germany. The Boeing 737 jet, with 85 passengers and 5 crew members, had been hijacked by an individual calling himself "Captain Mahmoud" (later identified as known terrorist Zohair Youssef Akache) and forced to change course toward Rome.

Landing in Rome, the plane refueled after the hijackers threatened to blow up the plane with all aboard. It flew to Cyprus, where Mahmoud demanded another refueling—then a new problem arose. Word about the hijacking had spread, and many governments publicly resolved not to allow Flight LH 181 to land on their territory. Indeed, in Beirut, the runways were physically blocked with equipment to prevent an unauthorized landing. The pilot eventually landed in Dubai, despite government denial of landing privileges.

At Dubai, the crew was able to communicate with ground officials, telling them there were in fact four terrorists aboard. The long ordeal began to have an effect on terrorists as well as hostages, to the extent that later that same day Mahmoud killed the pilot. He also postponed his original deadline (for the release of the 11 held in prison in Germany) from 4 p.m. to 2:45 a.m. the next day, as he accepted a promise from the [West] German minister of state (who was acting as chief negotiator).

Having changed the deadline, Mahmoud ordered the plane to be flown to Mogadishu, Somalia, where it landed on October 17.

One of GSG-9's 30-man groups had been following the aircraft since its landing in Cyprus, in a modified Lufthansa 707. This group was airborne soon after the German government learned of the plane's Mogadishu destination, having flown from Bonn to Cyprus, to Ankara, and back to Germany before learning of its final destination. A second 30-man unit, including commander Ulrich Wegener, had flown in the mean time from Germany to Dubai, and was thus in a better position to attempt hostage rescue operations.

The Somali government was cooperative and permitted Wegener's group to land. The government also set up a security perimeter of Somali commandos around the airport before their arrival. This enabled the GSG-9 unit to receive vital intelligence about the plane from the security forces. GSG-9 deployed sniper and reconnaissance teams and prepared to carry out an immediate assault on the plane, if the need for such an event arose. An assault was not required, and with the arrival of the second GSG-9 unit, intense planning for hostage rescue began.

As the night progressed, officials concluded that, because Mahmoud was growing increasingly unstable and had already demonstrated a willingness to execute hostages (e.g., the pilot), a rescue operation would be necessary. At 11:15 p.m., sections of the assault team began a covert approach to the plane, accompanied by two SAS men who were skilled in the use of "flash-bang" grenades. In an attempt to draw at least some of the terrorists to the cockpit (to establish their location), Somali commandos at 2:05 a.m. lit a bright signal fire a few hundred feet from the front of the plane. GSG-9 reconnaissance reported that Mahmoud and another terrorist had gone to the cockpit and appeared confused by the fire.

Simultaneously, GSG-9 commandos made entry through the airplane's doors, using special rubber-coated ladders to muffle the sound of their approach. The emergency doors were blown open at 2:07 a.m., with explosive charges. The two SAS men, who had managed to slip undetected onto the plane's wings, tossed their grenades inside, and the GSG-9 teams entered the plane, ordering the hostages to get down. In just a few seconds, three of the terrorists were killed, the fourth severely wounded, with all of the hostages unharmed and one GSG-9 man slightly wounded. The operation was officially over by 2:12 a.m., October 18.

Three days later, the body of Schleyer, the German businessman, kidnapped about a month earlier, was recovered.[9] ❑

CONCLUSIONS

The use of special forces to combat terrorism has both assets and liabilities. Too little commitment can result in an insufficiently trained and equipped force, as happened to the U.S. forces in the Operation Eagle's Claw disaster. Too zealous a desire to use such forces can result in the loss of innocent lives, as Israel has discovered.

Determination, unsupported by sufficient training or equipment, is also a recipe for disaster, as became evident in November 1985. An Egyptian airliner en route to Cairo from Athens was hijacked and diverted to Malta. Egyptian troops stormed the plane the next day, after the hijackers began to kill some of the hostages on board. As the troops rushed onto the plane, the hijackers tossed grenades at passengers. The death toll was put at 60, 57 of whom died in the rescue attempt.

It is not enough just to have such a force. Nations must train and equip them with adequate information and weaponry to meet an increasingly sophisticated terrorist threat. Nations need also to instill in its strike forces, as Germany has sought to do, a respect for the law and its restraints on strike force activities. So equipped and so trained, such forces can operate to significantly reduce not necessarily the number but the success of terrorist attacks worldwide.

EVALUATION

There are many conflicting views on whether strike forces are legitimate and useful tools in combating terrorism. Some view such strike teams as potential threats to democracy, creating elite troops that could be used to quell demonstrations as well as to stop terrorist attacks. Others view them as essential to a nation's security, operating in ways not open to a large military unit to safeguard a nation's citizens, both at home and abroad.

Below are two quotations that reflect, in part, this divergence of view. Each viewpoint expressed is a bit extreme, tending toward opposite ends of the spectrum of opinion. Read each, and decide which more accurately reflects the appropriate assessment of the need and use for such forces in today's world.

1. "The Israeli argue the case for pre-emptive strikes: it is better to kill their enemies in their own bases and so prevent them mounting their operations, rather than conduct elegant sieges inside Israel. While appreciating the excellence of other forces' pieces of electronic wizardry and the skill of the talk-out experts, their aim is to prevent the need for such expertise arising. Such a policy has its attractions, especially for a beleaguered, small nation like Israel under continual attack from enemies based round its borders. When national survival is at stake all manner of actions become permissable that would not be countenanced in more secure societies."[10]

2. "The danger inherent in the war against terrorism is, of course, the prospect of desperate societies willing to substitute state terror for (non-state) terrorism, to trade individual rights and freedoms for relief from chaos and violence, reconstituting what were once relatively benign governments into coldly efficient, centralized tyrannies, whose populations are held in close check by armies of secret police and informers, widespread electronic eavesdropping, and a constant deluge of propaganda."[11]

SUGGESTED READINGS

Clancy, Tom. *Special Forces: A Guided Tour of U.S. Army Special Forces.* New York: Berkley Books, 2001.

Dobson, Christopher, and Ronald Payne. *Counterattack: The West's Battle Against the Terrorists.* New York: Facts On File, 1982.

"Patterns of Global Terrorism." U.S. Department of State Publications (annual publication— available on the World Wide Web).

Rivers, Gayle. *The Specialists: Revelations of a Counter-terrorist.* New York: Stein and Day, 1985.

Strategic Assessment 1999: Priorities for a Turbulent World. Washington, DC: National Defense University's Institute for National Strategic Studies, 1999, http://specialforces.com

NOTES

1. Christopher Dobson and Ronald Payne, *Counterattack: The West's Battle Against the Terrorists* New York: Facts On File, 1982, xvi.

2. *Patterns of International Terrorism in 1980: A Research Paper* (Washington, DC: National Foreign Assessment Center, 1980), 1–6.

3. "International Terrorism: Issue Brief No. 1874042" (Washington, DC: Congressional Research Service, 1978), 41–42.

4. Dobson and Payne, *Counterattack*, 84.

5. Seventy-four year old Dora Bloch was not being held with the hostages at the airport. She had been transferred to a Ugandan hospital. After the raid, she disappeared, amid reports that she was dragged screaming from her hospital bed and murdered, on Ugandan President Idi Amin's orders. She has never been seen or heard from since that time.

6. Dobson and Payne, *Counterattack*, 96.

7. Gary Mitchell, "Special Operations Units of the United States Government," in *The Encyclopedia of Terrorism,* ed. Cindy Combs and Martin Slann (New York: Facts On File, 2002).

8. Cindy Combs and Martin Slann, "Operation Chavin de Huantar," in *The Encyclopedia of Terrorism* (New York: Facts On File, 2002), 135–137.

9. Ibid., 121–122.

10. N. C. Livingstone, "Taming Terrorism: In Search of a New U.S. Policy," *International Security Review: Terrorism Report*, 7, no. 1 (Spring 1982): 20.

11. Dobson and Payne, *Counterattack*, 83.

CHAPTER 12

Terrorism, Intelligence, and the Law

Key Concepts

Red Brigade	lone-wolf terrorists	Operation Chavin de
FLQ	national security	Huantar
War Measures Act	letters	Osama bin Laden
Northern Ireland Act	Department of Homeland	phases of modern
Prevention of Terrorism	Security	terrorist incidents
Act	INTERPOL	Ottawa Ministerial
Irish Republican Army	"the Kommissar"	Declaration on
ETA	PIOS	Countering Terrorism
penititi	target searches	Terrorist Threat Integration
U.S.A. PATRIOT Act	TREVI	Center

The greatest threat posed by terrorists now lies in the atmosphere of alarm they create, which corrodes democracy and breeds repression. . . . If the government appears incompetent, public alarm will increase and so will the clamor for draconian measures.

Brian Jenkins

LEGAL INITIATIVES TO COUNTER TERRORISM

Politicians and scholars have expressed grave doubts about whether any government can remain strong, but not oppressive, in the face of severe emergencies. If a government is to make a measured but effective response to the great emergencies generated by terrorist acts today, then coping strategies other than sole reliance on the use of strike forces must be considered.

It is not feasible to evaluate all of the options available to nations today in their efforts to deal with terrorism, both as an internal and an external threat. Various nations have experimented with a wide range of policy options in their attempts to deal with this recalcitrant problem. Some have tried to fashion a broad spectrum of legislative initiatives designed to make it clear that terrorists and groups resorting to terrorism operate outside the law of the land and can expect neither sanctuary nor quarter to be given them at the hands of the law.

These efforts have met with mixed success, depending in large measure on the determination of the government to enforce the laws that it creates and on the degree of entrenchment that the terrorists enjoy within the society. Canada's efforts to curtail the activities of the FLQ, for example, met with considerable success. Italy's offer of pardon to "penitent" terrorists, combined with its efforts to close all havens in which those engaged in terrorism might hide, also enjoyed some measure of success. It is difficult to gauge the success, yet, of the legislative initiatives undertaken in the United States after the events of September 11, including the passage and utilization of the PATRIOT Act and the creation of the Department of Homeland Security. Examining its initital steps in comparison to the approaches by other countries sharing a similar commitment to democracy and the rule of law, however, may offer useful insights.

In the cases of Canada and Italy, legal initiatives were combined with efforts at social reform designed to reduce the grievances that terrorists voiced with the existing system. Italy's success in its efforts is less clear than Canada's, due in part to Italy's geographic location. Canada, with the help of a friendly nation on its only border, was able to keep terrorists from either escaping across its border or receiving help from other similar groups. Italy had to contend with both indigenous and imported terrorism. Middle Eastern terrorists, as well as terrorists from several other European nations, have been able to offer support in the form of training, arms, personnel, and safe haven to Italy's indigenous terrorists. Thus, *Italy's strongest indigenous terrorist group,* the **Red Brigade,** was able to survive several intensive police crackdowns. Its ability to revive after each of these efforts is perhaps due less to Italy's lack of diligence in its efforts to eradicate the group than to the inability of the Italian government to effectively shut its borders to other terrorist support groups.

A quick look at the cases of Canada, the United Kingdom, and Italy offer insights into the effectiveness—and the lack thereof—of legal initiatives in coping with terrorism. These cases were chosen to illustrate two crucial points:

1. Legal initiatives alone are insufficient to eliminate a terrorist problem.
2. The use of extraordinary legal measures is not without risk, particularly to democracies.

Canada's Legal War with the FLQ

Canada offers an instructive example of emergency legislation, enacted and applied on a limited scale, in terms of both scope and time. As the first North American nation to face a vigorous and violent native terrorist campaign, Canada from the late 1960s throughout the early 1970s was forced to create its own answer to terrorism. Faced with a series of violent attacks by the **Front de Liberation du Quebec (FLQ)** in early 1970, culminating in the kidnapping of James Cross (British trade commissioner for Quebec) and Pierre Laporte (minister of labor in the Quebec provincial government), Prime Minister Pierre Elliott Trudeau decided to take firm, but extraordinary, measures.[1]

In 1970, Trudeau invoked the **War Measures Act,** *which empowered him to call in the army to enforce his refusal to be coerced by terrorists.* Although Trudeau agreed to deal with the kidnappers, allowing them to be flown to Cuba in return for Cross's release, he was determined to rid Canada of the FLQ terrorists.

He was willing to use any means at his disposal to accomplish this aim. He was willing to subordinate civil rights to the preservation of public order. As he noted:

> When terrorists and urban guerrillas were trying to provoke the secession of Quebec, I made it clear that I wouldn't hesitate to send in the army and I did, despite the anguished cries of civil libertarians.[2]

To a large extent Trudeau succeeded in ridding Canada of its indigenous terrorist organization. To do so, he saturated the Montreal area with troops, who acted to pin down terrorist cells, and used the Royal Canadian Mounted Police to concentrate on locating the cells that had organized the terrorist attacks. Using broad local powers of search and arrest, more than 300 suspects were apprehended.[3]

Excesses were no doubt committed during the course of this crisis. Nevertheless, the crisis had an end, with civil liberties restored, the army withdrawn, and local police once again constrained by strict laws on search and seizure operations. It may be true, as David Barrett, head of the opposition New Democratic Party once stated, that

> the scar on Canada's record of civil liberties which occurred [at that time] is a classic illustration of how the state, in an attempt to combat terrorism, overstepped its boundaries and actually threatened its own citizens.[4]

But it is also true that after Trudeau's crackdown, Canada enjoyed a decade relatively free of terrorism, with civil rights and liberties fully restored. It is also worth noting that Trudeau was astute enough to accompany the repression of this period with political measures designed to end some of the grievances that may have contributed to the terrorism. These political initiatives included creating compulsory French courses for English-speaking persons in Quebec and heavy government investment in the French-speaking minority areas. Such measures helped to deprive those advocating terrorist actions of the support of the moderates among the French community.

The problems, ironically, that Canada faced in the 1990s over the efforts of Quebec to secede stem at least in part from the success of the government in "co-opting" the frustrated French-speaking population that had offered some support to the FLQ. By making the option of "working with the system" to achieve their objectives more attractive, Canada diminished its terrorism problems, but may well have enhanced the probability of secession in the first decade of the twenty-first century.

The "Temporary" British Problem in Northern Ireland

At what point should the general welfare of a nation take precedence over the rights of its citizens in a democratic society? How long and to what extent can those rights be reduced or taken away to secure that "general welfare" without doing irreparable damage to the fabric of democracy within that society?

Totalitarian and authoritarian states often justify the suspension or severe curtailment of civil and political liberties based on a "need to secure the general welfare." But it is not only undemocratic states who have been guilty of repressing civil rights for this reason. This very issue has confronted the United Kingdom during the last three decades of the twentieth century in its struggle with terrorism in Northern Ireland.

The periodic outbreaks of violence in Northern Ireland prompted the British Parliament to enact the **Northern Ireland (Emergency Provisions) Act** in 1973. Parliament renewed this act each year for the next two decades, retaining in its title the term *emergency,* even though it had been in effect for more than a decade. This draconian measure

1. allows suspects to be detained by the executive authority,
2. gives police powers of arrest without warrant for up to 72 hours,
3. gives security forces broad authority for search and seizure, and
4. makes it possible for those charged with terrorism to be tried by a judge, without benefit of a jury.

This extraordinary legislation was followed in 1974 by an act called the **Prevention of Terrorism (Temporary Provisions) Act.** Under this act, the home secretary was given special powers

1. to exclude from the United Kingdom, without court proceedings, persons "concerned with the commission, preparation, or instigation of acts of terrorism," and
2. to detain a suspect for up to seven days without bringing him or her to court (after arrest by police officers without a warrant, as allowed under the Emergency Provisions Act).

The Temporary Provisions Act also allowed the prohibition in the United Kingdom of organizations considered to be connected with terrorism.[5]

Both acts were renewed annually by Parliament, though often after heated debates. So, although they carried the titles of "Temporary" and "Emergency," such terms are not really appropriate. *Emergency,* by definition, refers to a "sudden condition or state of affairs calling for immediate action."[6] Used in reference to a state of affairs that has persisted for more than a decade, it is meaningless.

These two legislative acts clearly demonstrate the extent to which a democratic state is willing to compromise on civil rights to combat terrorism within its borders. The prolonged curtailment of fundamental civil rights (such as the right to a trial by jury, the right to be charged with a crime when arrested, the right to be free to associate with organizations of one's choosing) and the granting of extraordinary powers to police (allowing them to violate certain rights in the process of search and seizure) surely diminish the democratic ideals of a state, even one that has been as committed to democracy as has the United Kingdom.

To create some measure of social order, Great Britain gave away some rights and freedoms of its Northern Ireland citizens. Unlike Canada, whose restriction of liberties was of relatively brief duration, the United Kingdom faced a restrictive situation that, because it showed only sporadic signs of improvement, seemed likely to assume an indefinite, if not permanent, position in the governing of this nation. Only the agreement reached in 1998 has offered substantive commitment to a change in this governing position.

In Canada's case, the terrorists were not well organized or well armed, and they lacked substantive support from either other terrorist groups or supporters in other nations, particularly from the nation with which it shares a border. So a determined effort by the Canadian government succeeded fairly well in wiping out the terrorist threat. Given these conditions, the curtailment of rights and liberties was of short duration.

The situation that the United Kingdom faces is very different. The **Irish Republican Army (IRA)** is *a well-organized, heavily armed, and well-funded resistance group in this region.* It received both training and weapons from supporters in many places. Other terrorist organizations contributed to the arms and training of IRA operatives, and supporters and sympathizers from several nations, particularly the United States and the Republic of Ireland, have given this group, and many of its splinter organizations, resources including money, arms, and logistical support.

There are many difficulties in fighting on one's home soil an entrenched and heavily supported organization committing terrorist acts. As Spain found in dealing with the **ETA,** *Spain's militant Basque separatists,* the presence of a friendly or neutral border over which terrorists can escape and find safe havens makes counterterror operations almost impossible for a nation to carry out on its own.[7] Cooperation between nations to thwart terrorists (as between Canada and the United States) can help make counterterror legislation unnecessary or at least short term; the absence of such cooperation, particularly when linked with transnational support for the group engaged in terrorist acts, makes it very difficult for national "emergency" legislation to be effective in eliminating the terrorism.

Italy and the "Penititi"

Italy has experimented with a unique legal strategy, with considerable success. In June 1983, Italians voted for the first time in more than a decade without an array of urban guerrilla groups holding the nation's political system at gunpoint. Long regarded as the Western European country most vulnerable during the general upsurge of terrorism in the 1970s, many of Italy's politicians and media experts hoped their country was finally beginning to emerge from its terrorist nightmare.

The man credited with a large share in Italy's success in its war on internal terrorism was Interior Minister **Virginio Rognoni,** who assumed his office in the wake of the kidnap-murder of former prime minister Aldo Moro. At the time he took office, the Red Brigade terrorists appeared to be acting with impunity.

Statistics issued by the Interior Ministry indicated that, in 1978, there were 2,498 terrorist attacks within Italy. Between 1968 and 1982, 403 people were killed in terrorist incidents in Italy and another 1,347 were injured. These people came from all walks of life. One out of every four was a police officer. Apart from politicians like Moro, businesspeople and journalists were favorite targets. But the bulk of the dead and injured were ordinary citizens unlucky enough to be on a train or in a piazza when it was blown up.

After 1980, Italy's internal terrorist activity dropped significantly, apparently because of a combination of legal initiatives and coordinated police efforts. Nearly 2,000 convicted urban guerrillas, including most of the leading members of the Red Brigade, were imprisoned. The Italians gave the task of hunting down these persons to a portly general of the Carabinieri named Carlo Alberto Della Chiesa. Armed with about 150 carefully chosen men, his antiterrorist cadre, he was responsible only to the minister of the interior, Rognoni, and to the prime minister.

With his support, the government enacted a number of decrees: strengthening sentences for convicted terrorists, widening police powers (allowing police to hold suspects longer for questioning and to search without a warrant), and making abetting terrorism a crime. Increased powers were also given to the police in matters of detention, interrogation, and wiretapping.

Rognoni, during this increased police activity, began to exploit what he saw as a growing disillusionment with the efficacy of terrorism as a problem-solving instrument. He helped to have enacted in 1982 a law that promised the ***penititi,*** *"repentant"* terrorists, lighter sentences if they confessed. Beset by gathering doubts, large numbers of the *brigadisti* began to confess. One of the most prominent of the *penititi* was Patrizio Peci, a former Red Brigade commander from Turin. He commented that, while he had been driven to become an urban guerrilla by police harassment for bomb outrages (which were later discovered to have been committed instead by neofascists), he no longer believed the Red Brigades could create, through terrorism, a better society in Italy.

Terrorism has not, in any sense, been eliminated in Italy. Both left- and right-wing terror continues to destroy individuals and property. Right-wing terrorists were responsible, in 1981, for an explosion in the Bologna train station that killed 85 people. But for a time, terrorism was significantly reduced. Consider the following facts:

During 1980, deaths from terrorism occurred every 3 days on the average.

In the first 6 months of 1983, in the wake of the government's police and legislative initiatives, only one terrorist-related death was reported.

The cost to Italy's democracy was, arguably, substantial—due process was certainly impaired by the expanded police powers, for instance. But it is also possible that Italy's democracy could not have lasted much longer as a democracy under the barrage of terrorist attacks. Citizens' right to vote, to security of person, as well as to life and liberty were under constant, serious threat of attack by terrorists. To have stabilized the situation without a civil war and without transforming Italy into an authoritarian regime is quite an accomplishment.

Much could be learned from Italy's experience. The judicious blending of strong police investigative and arrest action, coupled with the offer of a government pardon for "penitent" transgressors, proved a potent and effective mixture. By closing most of the places to hide while holding open a friendly government door to pardon, Italy has made serious efforts to resocialize a large number of its disaffected youth without unnecessary violence.

That Italy remains under attack by terrorists is due, in large measure, to its ties in the Arab world, and its position in the Mediterranean make it a natural staging ground or pathway for terrorism from the region. Most of Italy's terrorist activities in the late 1980s were conducted by foreign terrorists, primarily Middle Eastern, who were easily able to enter and exit this democratic nation.

Thus, general legislative initiatives, as well as emergency legislation, can be effective in reducing the threat of terrorism within a nation, without undue damage to democratic institutions. As one government publication noted:

> There is an almost irresistible tendency to react to terrorism by enacting laws and practices that diminish the rights of the accused or increase the authority of the state. The adverse consequences of that reaction are magnified by the equally predictable tendency to apply these specialized laws and mechanisms to an ever-increasing class of investigations. While the facts may justify certain changes, we must guard against overboard, non-productive, or counter-productive changes.[8]

Clearly, Italy and the United Kingdom have sought to deal with terrorism by an integrated use of law enforcement and legislative action, with mixed results. Since the events in the United States during the fall of 2001, this country has created similar legal and legislative efforts to reduce the threat of terrorism domestically. A brief analysis of these efforts may be useful in this comparative context.

CASE STUDY   The PATRIOT Act and the Department of Homeland Security

In the immediate wake of the terrorist attacks on September 11, 2001, the federal government of the United States of America rushed to create new measures to protect the nation from future terrorist events. President George W. Bush, only six weeks after the attacks, signed into law legislation called the **U.S.A. PATRIOT** (*Provide Appropriate Tools Required to Intercept and Obstruct Terrorism*) **Act.** Supporters of this new law claim it was designed to help law enforcement detect and disrupt terrorist plots; critics contend that its provisions can be used to infringe the rights of U.S. citizens and immigrants. There is some truth in both assessments, unsurprising since the law was created very quickly in the emotional wake of devastating events.

A brief look at this act offers some insights into its strengths—and weaknesses. Essentially, the PATRIOT Act

> enhances electronic surveillance authority for law enforcement, enabling greater access to communication by e-mail, telephones, and other electronic devices;
>
> permits the government to arbitrarily detain or deport individuals suspected of connection with terrorism;
>
> allows law enforcement to clandestinely survey records of political and religious organizations (whose privacy rights have usually been upheld in the courts);

monitors financial transactions;

expands the monitoring of foreign students;

makes possession of any biological agent or toxin (except for bona fide research or a peaceful project) a criminal act.

The expanded authority to tap phones or computer links given to local as well as national law enforcement authorities is a two-edged sword. Although the absence of this type of intelligence-gathering mechanism has been cited as one of the critical weaknesses that might have contributed to the nation's vulnerability to the September 11 attacks, these tools in the hands of law enforcement also offer serious potential for abuse of civil liberties, as does the ability of law enforcement to hold for extended periods of time persons not charged with any crime.

Both areas of expanded law enforcement capabilities are described by their advocates as vital in the effort to secure sufficient intelligence in a timely fashion to prevent future attacks like those of September 11. Ironically, these tools judged by some to be vital to ensure U.S. security may also be dangerous to the liberties of the system they are being employed to secure. As Benjamin Franklin noted in his *Historical Review of Pennsylvania* (1759), "Those who would give up essential liberty to obtain a little temporary safety deserve neither liberty nor safety."[9]

Several of the provisions of the PATRIOT Act threaten a loss of protection for civil rights (to privacy of mail and phone contacts) as well as civil liberties (to be considered innocent until proven guilty, not held indefinitely without being charged with a crime). A short-term loss of rights and liberties, such as that experienced in one region of Canada, may be tolerable in a free society for a short period of time, to permit the system to resolve a problem. But the continuation of the loss of rights and liberties is less easily justified, as noted in the case of the British in Northern Ireland.

Moreover, although the PATRIOT Act has a so-called sunset provision, limiting its lifetime to five years unless it is renewed, additional legislation expanding law enforcement capabilities have been drafted and are moving through the Congress. The U.S. House of Representatives is considering legislation that would allow the government to conduct secret surveillance on *suspected terrorists or spies not affiliated with a foreign government or terrorist organization,* the so-called **lone-wolf terrorists.** The legislation also strengthens **national security letters,** *tools used by the FBI in counterterrorism cases to obtain business and financial records and electronic communications from third parties with no judicial oversight.*

The PATRIOT Act is only one of the initiatives undertaken by the Bush administration in the wake of the September 11 attacks. In a broad sweep of arrrests similar to that carried out by Italy under Della Chiesa, U.S. Attorney General John Ashcroft announced in the fall of 2001 that 5,000 men between the ages of 18 and 33 were being "picked up and detained" indefinitely for questioning by the FBI. These young men were ones who had been in the United States for two years and were from "suspect" countries. According to Ashcroft, the objective of this arbitrary detention was to obtain information that these individuals might have regarding terrorist elements at home or abroad.

This form of arbitrary arrest based on a type of "profiling," rather than on any known connection to a crime is a serious violation of the civil rights and liberties on which this country was founded and was denounced by many groups monitoring the protection of these rights, including the Center for Constitutional Rights, Amnesty International, and the American Civil Liberties Union. It is unclear at this point whether these detentions resulted in a diminishing of terrorist threats domestically, and few of the individuals picked up in this sweep were ever charged with crimes and brought to trial. Many remain in detention, unable to obtain either freedom or the right to a trial.

The PATRIOT Act was rushed through Congress so quickly after September 11 that many members were unable to read it before the vote to approve the legislation, as one of the few Republicans to vote against it noted. Subsequent executive orders from the White House and rules from the Attorney General's office—including the rule permitting eavesdropping by the Justice Department on the confidential conversations of inmates and uncharged detainees with their lawyers and the executive order directing Defense Secretary Rumsfeld to establish military tribunals to try noncitizens charged with terrorism—have been drafted with equal swiftness and have evoked similar outcries of dismay. Like the emergency and the temporary legislations created by the United Kingdom to deal with terrorism in Northern Ireland, these legislative and executive office efforts are not intended to be permanent, but their incorporation into the legal system of this country diminishes its credibility as a democracy where civil rights and liberties are cherished. Given the historical record of such an approach in a similar cradle of democracy, it appears unlikely that these measures will effectively resolve the problem of terrorism in the United States.

Unlike Italy in its efforts to control the actions of the Red Brigade, President Bush also created a *special administrative unit to deal with all security issues, including terrorism,* an agency called the **Department of Homeland Security (DHS).** This new department, headed in its first years by Tom Ridge, was created by combining parts of at least nine different agencies, including the Customs Service and the Secret Service from the Treasury Department, Federal Emergency Management Agency (FEMA), the Coast Guard and the Transportation Security Agency from the Department of Transportation (DOT), the Immigration and Naturalization Service (INS), and the National Communications System from the Defense Department.

The structure of DHS and its turf are evolving slowly as the diverse parts of these agencies are brought together under one leadership. This new agency has established a Web site from which to disseminate information to the general public as well as to offer the public opportunities to be involved as citizens in the efforts to prevent domestic terror. Borrowing from the military, one of its first efforts was to establish a color-coded "terror alert" system, by which the public could be kept aware of the threat level the department believed the counry to be facing at any given time. Although not a particularly clearly delineated tool, it was at least psychologically useful in maintaining public awareness of the potential for terrorist attacks, an awareness that, until the events of September 11, most of the country had not experienced.

Unfortunately, a total of 88 congressional committees and subcommittees originally had jurisdiction over issues relating to homeland security, giving the new department a large number of "bosses" to work with and to satisfy as the new department seeks to create a "safer" United States. Turf war with agencies who have lost programs, and hence personnel and funding, have also cost the new department time and attention it can ill-afford, if it is to successfully increase domestic security.

Italy's leadership took an existing agency, provided it with additional powers and resources, and committed it to the task of reducing the threat of terrorism by the Red Brigade. The United States, instead, has created a new agency, pulling expertise from existing programs and providing separate funding. This suggests a more long-term bureaucratic commitment to the administration of counterterrorism efforts, which may be beneficial, since terrorism is unlikely to cease any time in the near future. It has also clearly taken more time to simply complete the establishment of the agency, which only moved into its formal headquarters (using a building in the northwest corner of the capital city) in January 2004. Thus, it is too new a project to evaluate success or failure yet—unless another large terrorist attack occurs before the agency has completed its "birthing" process. ❏

INVESTIGATION: THE INTELLIGENCE INITIATIVE

There is at least one other coping strategy that nations have used with some degree of success that merits further attention. Because most nations, and many terrorist groups, are currently engaged in the use of this strategy, an examination of the promises and pitfalls offered by such a strategy provides some interesting insights into the way in which nations can, and cannot, cope with the rising threat of terrorism today.

Investigation is an initial and certainly the most universal technique used by governments in their efforts to combat terrorism. Its potential as an antiterrorism tool is enormous. It has been effectively used to both prevent and punish terrorism. At the same time, its potential for abuse has been all too evident in recent years. Indeed, investigation has shown itself to be a powerful two-edged sword, capable, when improperly applied, of resulting in serious loss of civil rights, though seldom of human life.

The successful use of investigative techniques to counter terrorism is of relatively recent vintage. Although for decades Israel has had an intelligence operation that accumulates vast amounts of information about Arab terrorists, even Israel has been unable to keep pace with the internationalization of terrorism, particularly of the Palestinian movement.

However, until West Germany turned its attention in the 1970s toward intelligence gathering, Israel had the most active antiterrorist information system. In fact, they flooded Western European governments and police forces with information about terrorists, their movements, and planned actions. In fact, the French complained at one point that the mass of information gathered by Israeli agents (who had infiltrated Arab groups in France) was just too much for them to manage.

An international body has been in existence for some time that would seem useful to national governments trying to cope with the investigation of international terrorism. **INTERPOL,** *the international police organization,* with its data banks on criminal activity worldwide, would appear to have many of the resources necessary for such investigations.

Under its charter, however, this organization was restricted, until fairly recently, to investigations of ordinary crimes. Because not all of its charter members are as yet clear on what constitutes the crime of "terrorism," INTERPOL has been hampered in offering substantive assistance in intelligence research. In October 1984, changes in the rules governing this organization were made, broadening its ability to assist nations in investigation of terrorism. It is today an active participant in the gathering of intelligence information about terrorist activity.

Germany's Intelligence Gathering

However, Germany developed and has shared what is doubtless one of the most sophisticated antiterrorist intelligence operations in existence today. In Weisbaden, *a computer nicknamed* **"the Kommissar"** plays a vital role in that country's battle against terrorism. It is controlled by the Federal Criminal Investigation Department (the BKA). During the 1980s and early 1990s, it experienced an enormous growth in the federal resources put at its disposal.[10]

The heart of this computer system is an index of information called **PIOS** (*Personnen, Institutionen, Objekte, Sachen*), in which is stored every clue (such as addresses, contacts, movements) about known and suspected terrorists. Every address found in a suspect's possession, every telephone number, and the name of every person who writes to him or her in prison is stored in this system. Information about every object found at the scene of a terrorist attack or in a place where terrorists have been becomes a part of this computer's data sheets.

This information has been effectively used by another German intelligence investigative tool—a special unit of investigators operating in small teams on *Ziefahndung* **(target searches).** Target searches are instituted, according to German officials, for the apprehension of terrorists wanted under an arrest warrant, with priority given to a "hard core" of about 15 violent offenders. Every police officer in Germany carries at all times a set of cards bearing the photographs and identification data on all of these "targeted" persons. This is perhaps comparable to the U.S. FBI's Ten Most Wanted list, except that this list, coming out of Weisbaden, focuses on terrorists.

When in operation, a target search team focuses on one terrorist and immerses itself in his or her life, using the Weisbaden computer. All of the information about a suspect, however trivial it may seem, can be useful to the search team. If the information suggests, for instance, that a suspect always telephones his or her mother on her birthday, then the mother's phone can be wiretapped. Support indicated by the subject for a certain soccer team can lead investigators to attend that team's matches.

These intensive search methods have had documented success. Using such methods, 15 terrorists were tracked down in one six-week period in 1978. After that point, however, the success rate becomes somewhat less impressive. Having tracked the terrorists to other countries, the difficulty became one of securing their arrest and return for trial.

Four of the previously mentioned 15 terrorists sought in 1978 were traced to Bulgaria. According to the lawyer for Till Meyer, Gabrielle Rollnick, Gudrun Sturmer, and Angelika Loder (the four suspected terrorists), four hired cars containing heavily armed German police drew up outside a cafe in Sonnenstrand (a Bulgarian resort). Meyer and the three women were overpowered, taken to a nearby bungalow, and tied up. At 2:00 a.m., they were taken to Bourgas Airport in a minibus with German customs license plates and put on a plane with 25 other armed German police. The cooperation of the Bulgarian authorities in this "kidnapping" of terrorists makes this a remarkable instance of cooperation between a communist and a non-communist state in the apprehension of terrorists.[11]

Similar success was achieved in a cooperative effort with France in May 1980, when five women wanted on terrorism charges by Germany were arrested in a flat in the Rue Flatters on the Left Bank of Paris. Again, no complicated extradition procedures hampered the operation. France simply sent the five to Germany.[12]

This does not mean that cooperation on all such intelligence ventures is guaranteed. Indeed, the French, in another famous case, refused to extradite Abu Daoud, one of Black September's commanders, to either Germany or Israel. Daoud had arrived in Paris (under an assumed name) for the funeral of the PLO's representative. The French, who had photographed the funeral party, circulated the pictures to friendly governments, asking for information in their efforts to solve the murder of the representative.

When British intelligence identified Daoud from a photograph, French police promptly arrested him, much to the French government's embarrassment. Israel and West Germany immediately requested his extradition, but the French government quietly set him free—outside of their borders.

Daoud had been formally introduced, in fact, to senior government officials and had been entertained at the Quai d'Orsay. France's decision not to extradite or prosecute was partly due to the embarrassment of having officially entertained Daoud, but more a result of the French government's ties to Arab states, whose sympathies lay with the PLO. Because these ties were attributable in part to France's dependency on Arab oil, the decision not to extradite was the result of both political and economic factors.[13]

Similarly, France arrested the German terrorist Wilfred Bose (whose connection with Carlos the Jackal was known to them) but released him. In this case, an extradition request was made, based on intelligence information on the crimes committed by this man. Although this intelligence information was made available to France, the French government decided to neither extradite nor punish this offender. Lacking a treaty or convention that could create a legal obligation to do one or the other, France was free to act, as it did, in what it perceived to be its best national interest.

Nor is France the only nation to refuse to either extradite or prosecute when given intelligence information about suspected terrorists. The former Yugoslavia, for example, refused to arrest Carlos when informed (in detail in an intelligence report) of his presence and his crimes by a German target search team. Yugoslav officials did arrest four of West Germany's most wanted terrorists (Rolf-Clemens Wagner, Brigitte

Mohnhaupt, Sieglinde Hofmann, and Peter Boock) on information given by a German target search team. Subsequently, however, these suspects were released without either a trial or extradition proceedings.[14]

The point is that intelligence gathering as a weapon against terrorism is often of erratic value in the absence of either a legal system with established guidelines for the treatment of terrorist suspects or an alternative method of compelling cooperation among nations in the prosecution or extradition of such persons. Today, if a government thinks that its national interests will be best served by letting a known terrorist go free, it can (and will) usually do so. Where no overriding national interests are involved, cross-national intelligence gathering and arrest operations are feasible; where such interests are perceived to be at stake, they are far less likely to succeed.

Today, some international police cooperation structures do exist that facilitate sharing intelligence concerning terrorism. In Europe there is a permanent, though comparatively secret, structure, code named **TREVI** for *terrorism, radicalism, and violence international.* This is a formalization of the "old boy" police network, which regularly brings together police chiefs from European Union countries. It also engages in day-to-day consultations through national bureaus. Furthermore, NATO has an antiterrorist network that allies Canadians and Americans with Europe. This system facilitates the exchange of information on terrorists, their organizations, techniques, and weapons.

Computers as Tools of Investigation

The Internet and, with it, the new abilities of intelligence officials to eavesdrop on e-mail and phone calls became primary tools in the efforts to track down the perpetrators of the September 11 attacks. Several Internet tools offer interesting options for investigators.

Surveillance. The use of an inexpensive computer that can be plugged into an Internet service provider's network to monitor the communications of suspects has become one of the most important tools for the FBI. The system, called Carnivore, is a version of a common technology that system administrators use to maintain networks. Carnivore was designed to help law enforcement officers determine who receives a suspect's e-mail and who sends e-mail to the suspect. It can be programmed, however, to capture whole messages. It does not, unfortunately, interpret encrypted messages.

Cooperation. A system for listening in on conversations, developed by the United States, Britain, Canada, Australia, and New Zealand, consists of a network of satellite dishes known as Echelon. This cooperative effort to create a shared information system has at times been criticized by privacy activists. Nor does it solve the problem of the reluctance of law enforcement officials to jeopardize a source or an investigation by sharing the information with others.

Searching. Information that can be digitally scanned can be electronically searched by law enforcement. Digitalized fingerprints, pictures of suspects, even passport stamps that have been scanned, can be searched by computers utilizing software designed to rapidly sift through large amounts of information. The possibility of using retinal scans as a part of airport security is also being considered in the United States.

None of these computer tools will make the investigation or prevention of terrorist acts simple, of course, and all have been challenged by those concerned that civil rights may be violated by the intrusion of electronic surveillance. But such tools may well be crucial for future investigations of terrorist acts, and perhaps even for the prevention of terrorism through enhanced security measures.

GOVERNMENTS USE INVESTIGATION AND INTELLIGENCE

Two interesting cases of the use of intelligence and investigation as tools in counter-terrorism offer useful contrasts in the use of these techniques in the late 1990s. Both involve the use of violent force rather than legal initiatives to resolve the situation, but both also are critically dependent for success on intelligence gathering and investigation efforts by law enforcement agencies.

CASE STUDY   **Peru's Rescue of Diplomats: A Model of Patient Intelligence Gathering**

This first case is one already detailed in the preceding chapter. It involved the Tupac Amaru seizure of the Japanese Embassy in Lima, Peru, in December of 1996. As the details of that incident, dubbed **Operation Chavin de Huantar,** indicate, a successful resolution of a tense hostage situation was achieved in part by the patient collection of information about the patterns of activity, resources, personnel, and other useful data about both the hostage takers and the hostages.

Although the hostages were held for 126 days, and hence there was intense pressure to use force in a rescue attempt, Peru's president remained determined to resolve the situation with a minimum amount of violence.

The spectacular success of the rescue mission (only one of the 72 hostages was killed) can be attributed in large measure to superb intelligence. During the months of the incident, listening devices were smuggled into the residence, concealed in items that the Red Cross workers were allowed to deliver, including being placed in buttons on clothing brought to the hostages as changes of clothing were needed. Using every opportunity to gather intelligence, during the final four days intelligence agents posed as doctors and were allowed to enter to check on the health of the hostages, implanting matchstick-size two-way microphones while they were there that allowed intelligence officers on the outside to communicate with the military and police commanders being held inside.

With this intelligence access, those planning the operation were able to monitor the movements of the guerrillas and the hostages each day, making a carefully timed assault possible. For example, intelligence officers were able to learn that the

14 Tupac Amaru regularly had a makeshift game of soccer each afternoon at about 3:00 p.m. in the ground-floor living room and that prior to beginning this recreation, they stacked their rifles in a corner of the room.

Thus, when the listening devices indicated, at 3:10 p.m. on the day planned for the assault, that the regular afternoon soccer game had begun, with at least eight of the rebels participating, the hostages, who were being held upstairs, were alerted to move a desk blocking the second-floor entrance and take cover. The assault, initiated minutes later, began with the detonation of nine pounds of explosives in the tunnel directly under the room where the rebels were playing soccer, killing four of them and opening a hole through which troops began to pour, without injuring the hostages.

Peru, in this case, offered the international community an excellent example of the value of careful intelligence and planning in such terrorist attacks. The rescue efforts broke no laws, wasted no innocent lives (except for one who was shot by a rebel as the attack commenced). Patience and careful planning based on up-to-the-minute intelligence were rewarded.

This success, when compared with the botched U.S. 1993 assault on the Branch Davidian compound in Waco, Texas, offers dramatic evidence of the importance of accurate and current intelligence. At Waco, as one analyst noted, "the assault went disastrously wrong in part because agents relied on months-old intelligence that those in the compound were always separated from their weapons at 10:00 a.m."[15] The inaccuracy of this information contributed to the loss of four agents. Clearly, intelligence is a critical factor in counterterrorism exercises. ❑

CASE STUDY   U.S. Strikes in Afghanistan and the Sudan: On the Edge of the Law

Bombings devastated U.S. embassies in Kenya and Tanzania on August 7, 1998. More than 250 people, including 12 Americans, were killed. Intense investigation by federal officials from the United States, working with officials from Kenya and Tanzania, identified several suspects, including Khalid Salim (a Yemeni citizen) and Mohammed Saddiq Odeh. Salim was sent to the United States to stand trial less than three weeks after the bombing, and Odeh was arrested by Pakistani authorities on a flight from Nairobi the day of the bombing. He reportedly confessed under interrogation in Pakistan to a role in the bombings.

Although continuing to seek evidence and to bring suspects in the bombing incident to trial in this country, the United States did not wait to complete the investigation. Instead, on August 20, it carried out a missile strike against two targets: camps in Afghanistan used by **Osama bin Laden,** *leader of the al-Qaeda organization* and the man believed responsible for orchestrating and funding the embassy attacks; and a pharmaceutical plant in Khartoum, linked by intelligence information to bin Laden's operations.

Investigators at the time stated that gathering information admissible as evidence of bin Laden's connection to the embassy bombings would take at least weeks, perhaps months. The circumstantial evidence seemed clear, but was insufficient to warrant an indictment in early August. Political pressure at home to take action, however, was intense and unlikely to accept the need to exercise patience while intelligence was accumulated. Hence, the bombings were ordered, although intelligence on the targets of the missile attacks was not clear, in that it lacked information about whether the camps in Afghanistan were in use by bin Laden or his leaders at the time.

The links of bin Laden to the embassy bombings were numerous and dated back at least five years, to the first bombing attempt on the World Trade Center in New York in 1993. By 1996, the United States was pressuring Sudan to cut its ties to the multimillionaire, indicating that the United States considered him to be masterminding and funding terrorism in the region. While bin Laden did subsequently leave Sudan, the resulting threats to the United States from bin Laden and his organization led to a removal of most U.S. embassy personnel in Kenya and Egypt, without, it should be noted, increasing embassy security in Kenya, where it was fairly "soft." Thus, the ties of Salim and Saddiq to bin Laden were not surprising to those tracking the actions of this dissident leader. But the gathering of sufficient admissible evidence to substantiate guilt is a very time-consuming operation.

The cruise missiles inflicted serious damage on the physical facilities at both targets, with minimal loss of life. This effort to prevent civilian casualties in Sudan was important, because the United States gave Sudan no warning of the attack or of its concern with the facility itself. This unprovoked attack, as Sudan and many of its neighbors viewed the bombings, was both illegal and unjustified. Had the attack resulted in a high civilian casualty count, the anger of the international community might well have been formidable. Instead, the small amounts of evidence that the United States was willing to offer to public scrutiny concerning the alleged use of the facility frustrated many allies, who deplored the lack of firm intelligence prior to the attack and the lack of diplomatic interaction between Sudan and the United States that might have prevented its necessity.

The attack on Afghanistan in 1998, although it provoked less concern in the international community in terms of the legality of the action (because most of the evidence clearly indicated its use as a training facility for rebellious groups), was less clearly effective because there was little evidence gathered before the attack to indicate that bin Laden or any of his people were at the site when attacked. Destroying empty, relatively inexpensive shacks used for mercenary training may have satisfied domestic desire for "action" but did not eliminate the threat of bin Laden. Indeed, it may well have offered him further reason to hate the United States and to lead further actions of vengeance against its citizens.

The lack of intelligence concerning the presence of bin Laden at his headquarters and the lack of admissible evidence against the Sudanese factory diminished the value of the American actions in August 1998. While the productivity of both actions, in terms of counterterrorism, cannot yet be determined, both were impugned by the lack of up-to-date intelligence. ❏

INTELLIGENCE GATHERING AND
COUNTERINTELLIGENCE BY TERRORISTS

The use of intelligence gathering and counterintelligence is not limited to those opposing terrorism. These have long been tools of terrorists, as well. Indeed, the better organized and funded of the terrorist organizations could probably give lessons on the techniques of such operations to many governments today.

Study of the **phases of modern terrorist incidents,** discussed in Chapter Seven, indicates that considerable attention is given by the terrorists to the function of intelligence gathering. In most terrorist incidents, there is both a preincident phase and a postincident phase. Essentially, this means that before and after the incident actually occurs, the terrorists are involved in gathering and evaluating intelligence information.

In the preincident phase, terrorists are concerned with planning, reconnaissance, and usually a rehearsal of the event. To effectively carry out the planning necessary to launch an event in a country perhaps hundreds of miles from the group's home territory, considerable intelligence gathering is clearly essential. Much of this is done not by members of the group itself, but by members of an indigenous group sympathetic to the terrorist's cause. In incidents in which timing is crucial, intelligence information is also essential information that will allow for a realistic rehearsal according to a carefully constructed plan.

This concept of planning for a well-orchestrated terrorist event is neither new nor radical. What many observers do not realize, however, is that today terrorists also have an extensive postincident phase to most events. In this phase, the terrorists (the ones who survive the event) usually regroup and critique the event. They learn from their mistakes, far more rapidly, it sometimes appears, than do the police forces charged with combating them. Those lessons learned from past mistakes are shared, becoming a part of the intelligence information available to terrorists in many areas of the world.

This does not mean that there exists a network of terrorists who share intelligence information globally on a regular basis. But information and incidents have led many observers to conclude that such sharing does in fact exist on a regular but not always an organized basis, among many terrorists. This seems particularly true in the Middle East, where anti-U.S. feelings have served to unite several diverse groups in a common cause.

Like TREVI, however, the links in intelligence gathering and sharing between terrorists appears rather loosely organized and based more on informal contacts than on regular channels for the dissemination of information. As long as terrorists are no more organized than the law enforcement organizations that seek to combat them, then neither side can effectively win. That is a situation that neither side may be willing to tolerate indefinitely. The 1998 U.S. attack on the training camps in Afghanistan may have been most significant if it had destroyed the base of such a network of intelligence sharing for terrorists. But the events of September 11 made clear this was not the case.

CONCLUSIONS

> For a democratic society, the issue is not merely survival, but the way in which society chooses to survive.
>
> Robert Friedlander

Just as terrorism is essentially a war against both the state and all of civilized society, so the struggle to eliminate, or at least to restrict, terrorism is also war of a sort. The cost of this war on terrorism, if carried by each state alone, can be quite high. Each of the strategies used by countries to combat terrorism has potentially high costs, both politically and economically. Moreover, as noted earlier, when a state tries to pursue a strategy unilaterally, its effectiveness can be quite limited.

Furthermore, the value of strategy's effectiveness in eradicating terrorism must be balanced against the too-frequent concomitant loss of other democratic values and civil liberties when a nation decides to wage war on terrorism. Terrorists can be said to have "won" in some respects when emergency measures are enacted: seeds of doubt and dissension about the government's commitment to democracy are sown and the government might have been forced to take distasteful measures that could serve to reduce both its legitimacy and its stability. The first steps on a very dangerous slide toward repression and state terrorism are indeed "victories" of one sort for terrorists.

However, the heads of state and government for the seven most industrialized nations and Russia, meeting in December 1995 at Ottawa, discussed countering terrorism by collective effort. The **Ottawa Ministerial Declaration on Countering Terrorism** stated that these nations

> are determined as a group to continue to provide leadership on this issue to the international community, using bilateral and multilateral measures and agreements to counter terrorism. We will continue to develop specific, cooperative measures to deter, prevent, and investigate terrorist acts and to bring terrorists to justice.[16]

Collectively, these nations pledged to strengthen the sharing of intelligence and information on terrorism and to promote mutual legal assistance and extradition. Six years later, this network of shared intelligence and cooperative effort was unable to successfully cooperate and prevent the attacks of September 11. Ironically, several of those who carried out or supported this attack as part of a network came across the border from Canada or came from airports of group members signing this cooperation agreement. This does not mean that such agreements are without merit. This one is, in fact, of such recent vintage that the mechanisms for such cooperation were clearly not in place. If similar agreements and resolutions signed in the wake of September 11 are more swiftly implemented, states may well begin to win the war on terrorism declared by the United States through the United Nations.

EVALUATION

The international community, after the September 11 attacks in the United States, initiated efforts to strengthen international cooperation to combat terrorism. The United

Nations became the forum in which nations came together to denounce terrorism and to pledge support in an international effort to combat this problem. On September 28, 2001, the Security Council of the United Nations unanimously adopted Resolution 1373, proposed by the United States, which established a body of legally binding obligations on all UN member states. Its provisions required, among other things, that all member states prevent the financing of terrorism, deny safe havens to terrorists, and review and strengthen their border security operations, banking practices, customs and immigration procedures, law enforcement and intelligence cooperation, and arms transfer controls. This resolution also mandated that each state report on the steps it had taken, and it established a committee of the Security Council to monitor implementation.

Unilateral efforts to combat terrorism continue to evolve as well. Based on the information in this chapter about efforts made by other governments to combat and control terrorism through legal and administrative initiatives, evaluate a few of these initiatives, which have received much less press coverage than the more dramatic war in Iraq, in terms of how effective you think such measures will be, how much cooperation will really evolve to make the initiatives work, and the ability of this state to use intelligence gathering to provide security against terrorism in the future.

1. On September 23, 2001, President Bush issued an executive order freezing all assets of 27 foreign individuals, groups, and entities linked to terrorist acts or supporting terrorism and authorized the freezing of assets of those who commit, or pose a significant threat of committing, acts of terrorism.

2. On October 29, 2001, the United States created the Foreign Terrorist Tracking Task Force, aimed at denying entry into the United States of persons suspected of being terrorists and locating, detaining, prosecuting, and deporting terrorists already in the United States. The profiling of people from the Middle East as suspected terrorists or supporters came at a time when racial profiling was being designated as a prosecutable crime when committed by law enforcement officers in several cities.

3. On May 1, 2003, the **Terrorist Threat Integration Center** (TTIC) was established by the Bush administration. The purpose of this center was to ensure that the many government agencies and departments involved in the war on terrorism work closely together and share threat information and analysis that could be used to prevent terrorist attacks. The TTIC is *a multiagency joint venture that integrates and analyzes terrorist-threat related information, collected domestically or abroad, and disseminates information and analysis to appropriate recipients.* This center does not collect information; rather, it integrates and analyzes information in cooperation with the Department of Justice/Federal Bureau of Investigation, Homeland Security, Defense and State departments, and the Central Intelligence Agency. It would, in theory, be the central data bank and analysis center for all terrorism-related intelligence gathered by any government source.

The need for cooperation is real; securing it on an organized basis is very difficult. Similarly, strong intelligence efforts can help to prevent or resolve criminal activity but can also be the source of significant government abuse of civil rights. The choices that governments must make are critical in the use of the vital set of tools that intelligence can provide.

Preserving our freedoms is one of the main reasons that we are now engaged in this new war on terrorism. We will lose that war without firing a shot if we sacrifice the liberties of the American people.

Russ Feingold, Senator from Wisconsin

SUGGESTED READINGS

Baden, Thomas, ed. *Annual Editions: Homeland Security 04/05*. Guilford, CT: McGraw-Hill, 2004.

Dobson, Christopher, and Ronald Payne. *Counterattack: The West's Battle against the Terrorists*. New York: Facts On File, 1982.

Howard, Russell D., and Reid L. Sawyer, eds. *Terrorism and Counterterrorism: Understanding the New Security Environment*. Guilford, CT: Dushkin, 2001.

Jenkins, Roy. *England: Prevention of Terrorism (Temporary Provisions)—A Bill*. London: Her Majesty's Stationery Office, 1974.

Moore, Brian. *The Revolutionary Script*. New York: Holt, Rinehart, and Winston, 1971.

"Ottawa Ministerial Declaration on Countering Terrorism." Released at the Ottawa Ministerial on December 12, 1995.

"U.S. Report to the Counterterrorism Committee." *Patterns of Global Terrorism*, U.S. Department of State. December 27, 2001.

Weinberg, Leonard B., and Paul B. Davis. *Introduction to Political Terrorism*. New York: McGraw-Hill, 1989.

NOTES

1. See Brian Moore's *The Revolution Script* (New York: Holt, Rinehart, and Winston, 1971), for an account of these kidnappings; see also Leonard Beaton, "Crisis in Quebec," *Round Table* 241 (1971): 147–152.

2. Quoted by Robert Friedlander, *Terrorism: Documents of International and Local Control* (New York: Oceana, 1979), vol. 1, 113.

3. Christopher Dobson and Ronald Payne, *Counterattack: The West's Battle against the Terrorists* (New York: Facts on File, 1982), 113. For six months, Trudeau flooded the Montreal area with troops. It took nine weeks to track down those responsible for Laporte's murder.

4. Dobson and Payne, *Counterattack*, 113. It was Barrett's contention that "democratic governments cannot legitimately establish consent by the use of force."

5. For information on these two acts, see Great Britain, "Report to the Commission to Consider Legal Procedures to Deal with Terrorist Activities in Northern Ireland" (London: Her Majesty's Stationery Office, 1972). For analysis of the Temporary Provisions Act, see Roy Jenkins, *England: Prevention of Terrorism (Temporary Provisions)—A Bill* (London: Her Majesty's Stationery Office, 1974).

6. See Funk and Wagnall's *Standard Dictionary of the English Language,* international edition (Chicago: J. G. Ferguson, 1977), vol. 1, 413.

7. French Basques are living north of the Pyrenees, and there is little doubt that they give help to people they consider to be compatriots in Spain. ETA men on the run frequently cross the border to find refuge in safe houses in France. In 1979, the French government finally removed the political refugee status of ETA members.

8. "Report on Domestic and International Terrorism," Subcommittee on Civil Rights of the Committee on the Judiciary (First Session, April 1981) (Washington, DC: U.S. Government Printing Office, 1981), 4.

9. www.worldofquotes.com/author/Benjamin-Franklin/.

10. Ibid., 18. This report includes an evaluation of German officials on the effectiveness of this intelligence system. The officials included Siegfried Froelich, state secretary; Gerhard Siegle, administrative head of the terrorism office; Dieter Osterle, deputy head of the Director's Office of the Police Superior Commission; and Captain Ulrich Grieve, representative of GSG-9.

11. Dobson and Payne, *Counterattack*, 101.

12. Bundeskriminalant (BKA) men stripped the apartment where the five women lived and carried railway timetables, cigarette stubs, and fingerprints back to Weisbaden. Even information on kitchen utensils was "fed" into the Kommissar.

13. See the *New York Times*, January 12, 1977, sec. 1, 1, for a concise recounting of this incident. This was not, of course, the only time that France refused to extradite known terrorists. However, recent French efforts to capture and prosecute Carlos indicate a significant change in French attitude toward the problem.

14. In this case, the reasons were both legal and political. The Yugoslavs demanded that the Germans give them in return a number of anti-Tito Croatian nationalists, some of whom were in German jails serving sentences for acts of terrorism against Yugoslav property and officials inside Germany. Germany could not, it decided, overcome the legal and moral complexities of meeting this demand.

15. "Peru Takes No Prisoners," *U.S. News & World Report,* May 5, 1997, 38.

16. "Ottawa Ministerial Declaration on Countering Terrorism," released at the Ottawa Ministerial on December 12, 1995.

Security Measures: A Frail Defense

Key Concepts

physical security

penetration teams

operational security

personnel security

Operation Eligible Receiver

infowar

hardening the target

training programs

taggants

trace detectors

general threat indicators

local threat indicators

specific threat indicators

shoot-ats

Power, in its most primitive sense, can be defined as the capacity to disrupt or destroy. Terrorists through the use of selective, yet often indiscriminate, violence have been able to force governments to negotiate and often grant concessions to their demands. They have been able to attract worldwide attention to themselves and their goals. Terrorism has forced governments to expend vast amounts of time and resources on security.

M. K. Pilgrim

Confronted with a growing tide of terrorist destruction, governments have indeed been forced to spend increasing amounts of time and money on the problems related to security. Modern society is both fragile and complex, with much interdependence within the systems. As such, the possibilities for interference by terrorism are almost infinite.

Some aspects of security have received more attention than others, due to their spectacular selection as targets of terrorism. It is more than possible that this focus will shift, as new technologies make current security measures obsolete and as successful security systems harden certain targets against attack.

Technological developments during the past few decades have increased dramatically the potential targets and weapons available to persons committing terrorist acts. While the technology accessible to governments has also grown, governments are to some extent more hampered than helped by the technology boom. Governments are simultaneously confronted with a rapidly growing number of targets that must be secured and constrained by democratic principles from utilizing many technological devices to secure those targets. Creating an effective security system that protects against a wide range of terrorist attacks while it continues to afford a maximum exercise of democratic freedoms and privileges is a formidable task indeed.

THREE FACETS OF SECURITY

Security is not a one-dimensional issue. Instead, those confronting security problems are faced with at least three aspects of the situation that must be considered: physical security, operational security, and personnel security. Each of these facets of security is closely related to the others and cannot be easily differentiated in an analysis of counterterrorism security efforts.

But certain features of each aspect can, if explained, offer a better understanding of the security measures that nations and businesses are, even now, taking against terrorist incidents and threats. Let us examine each of these aspects of security briefly.

Physical security has, as its objective, *the hardening of the target against which an attack may be made.* Although no blueprint for successful physical security measures against terrorist attack has been in any sense adopted, there are certain considerations and countermeasures that have begun to achieve acceptance in both the government and the business community.

Both these communities are slowly recognizing that security measures against terrorism must go beyond the level of normal crime prevention. These are not "normal" criminals: their goals, their willingness to sacrifice innocent lives, and their willingness to die in their attacks make them extraordinary criminals, against whom extraordinary measures must be taken if security is to be achieved and maintained.

In order to determine what, if any, extraordinary security measures are needed to protect against a terrorist attack, government and business have employed a number of relatively ordinary tactics. A physical security survey by professionals who are aware of the dangers in a particular area or to a particular business or region is standard procedure. This has, in recent years, begun to include the use of **penetration teams,** *whose job it is to discover holes in security systems through which other teams, such as terrorist attack teams, could presumably penetrate and sabotage or destroy the target.*

The penetration team, or the organization conducting the physical security survey, may suggest in its report that the business utilize certain devices that have proven useful in guarding against attack or sabotage. For example, a variety of intrusion detection devices are available on the market today.

Or such an evaluation may emphasize the importance of such factors as lighting, access control, or physical security and access control codes. Organizations may be advised to inhibit surreptitious approaches by increasing lighting of entryways, fences, hallways, and other points of access. Greater access control is often recommended, usually in the form of limitations on the numbers of individuals cleared to work in the facility as a whole, or in specific, sensitive parts of the operation. One of the more common recommendations for improved physical security is that security and access codes be changed fairly frequently, to make penetration of the operation more difficult.

Some operations, where security has been a relatively minor problem until recently, are being urged to consider the use of personnel, such as guards, whose specific duty it is to ensure physical security. Others, who have already taken this step, have discovered from security surveys that they have need of additional guards or specially trained counterterrorist guards.

Physical security is clearly dependent upon other types of security—operational security and personnel security. Fortress walls, barbed fences, and barred gates are not, in modern times, either reasonable or sufficient protection against determined terrorist fanatics. The operation of the facility itself must be secure, and its personnel well trained in security procedures, to circumvent modern terrorist attacks.

Operational security *has as its objective the denial of opportunity for terrorists to collect such information on either the facility or its activities as might enable it to predict those activities.* To be able to predict those activities would help the terrorist to successfully penetrate the facility or activity and disrupt or destroy it. By denying that information to terrorists, the risk to terrorists carrying out an attack against the activity or facility significantly increases.

Prediction of operational activities usually relies on discerning patterns of behavior, so operational security analysis focuses on identifying those patterns and how they are communicated to personnel. Emphasis is placed on making such patterns less predictable, randomizing activities as far as possible without creating chaos within the organization. Too often, repeated activities create in the minds of the individuals responsible for security a lack of alertness to small differences that may be crucial. The arrival of a particular car at the same time every morning, the use of a van of a specific color and model delivering goods at the same place and time—these routines can deaden the alertness of personnel to such factors as the identity of the driver or the presence of an authorized person in the vehicle. Such a failure to notice, to carry out a thorough security check, can prove fatal to the organization or to some of its personnel.

The training of personnel in operational security measures is also important. Organizations are advised to train personnel in the recognition of intelligence-gathering activities, so that they can more readily spot individuals engaged in such activities. Screening of both employees and casual but regular contacts—such as vendors—is also a major focus of operational security efforts, as all such individuals can constitute a threat to the operation.

Moreover, the organization as a whole is often encouraged to improve its own operational security by a variety of fairly obvious, but essential, measures. These include, but are not limited to

1. maintaining a low profile, so that the organization does not become an attractive, publicity-provoking target;
2. improving communications security, so that it is less possible to penetrate the flow of commands or patterns of communications; and
3. developing counterintelligence capabilities, within both management and security-related personnel, so that the organization need not always be on the defensive in this struggle against terrorism.

Neither operational nor physical security can function effectively without the third crucial type of security: personnel security. **Personnel security** focuses on *the training of personnel to take responsibility on their own for security,* by teaching them to know how to recognize and respond to a potential terrorist threat. For many years, this type of security was directed toward high-threat individuals, those whom the organization regarded as being at a greater risk of attack than most of the rank-and-file personnel.

Many organizations have developed individual crisis management files, which help management to decide which individuals need special security training and protection. Using those files, these at-risk individuals are often advised on how to randomize travel routes and maintain a low profile. Training is also given to certain individuals in special antiterrorism devices, such as bulletproof clothing.

But today, personnel security has taken on added dimensions. Organizations routinely schedule periodic training for all personnel in counterterrorism procedures. Such training is usually designed to heighten awareness among employees of the potential for terrorist attacks, and the preincident phases—particularly intelligence gathering—which may alert personnel to a terrorist attack in progress. The proper use of security measures at all times is stressed, so that employees are less likely to be lulled by a sense of routine into a possibly fatal breach of security procedures.

Most of all, the need to tell someone about suspicious or threatening behavior, to alert the proper authorities to potential threats, has become a major focus in the training of personnel in many organizations. The alertness of personnel to security breaches may well mean the difference between a successful terrorist attack and the failure of such an attempt.

CASE STUDY   NSA's Operation Eligible Receiver

Using a "penetration team" comprised of a group from within the National Security Agency (NSA) in 1998 and software easily obtained from hacker sites on the Internet, **Operation Eligible Receiver** *demonstrated how easy it would be for computer-efficient cyberterrorists to cripple U.S. military and civilian computer networks.* The simulated attack was run during a two-week period, and the results were "frightening," according to a defense official involved in the simulation. This official noted that this attack "run by a set of people using standard Internet techniques, would have basically shut down the command-and-control capability in the Pacific theater for some considerable period of time."[1]

The "game" played by the penetration team was simple: they conducted *information warfare attacks,* or **infowar,** on the Pacific Command (and ultimately on the United States) to soften its policies toward the communist regime in North Korea, with the hackers posing as paid agents for North Korea. The "Red Team" of NSA surrogate hackers, using computers, modems, and software technology easily accessible on what is often called the "dark side of the Internet" (network-scanning software, intrusion tools, and password-breaking "log-in scripts"), were able to inflict crippling damage. According to news reports, they were able to break into computer networks and gain access to the systems that control the electrical power grid for the United States, giving them the power, if they had so desired, to disable the power grid and leave the country in darkness.

This power knock-out option was only a sideshow: the primary target of the attack was the U.S. Pacific Command, which is in charge of the troops (about 100,000) who would be called on to respond to wars in Korea or China. According to one defense official involved in the exercise,

> The most telling thing for the Department of Defense, when all was said and done is that basically for a two-week period the command-and-control capability in the Pacific theater would have been denied by the "infowar" attacks, and that was the period of the exercise.[2]

The attacks were not, of course, run against the infrastructure components, since there was no desire to actually shut down a power grid or disable Pacific Command. But the referees monitoring the simulation were shown the attacks and the structures under attack, and they concluded that the attacks would be successful. Moreover, the pseudo-attackers foiled essentially all efforts to trace them, even though the FBI joined the Pentagon in trying to locate them. Only one of the numerous units of NSA groups (one based in the United States) was uncovered. The others operated without being located or identified.

These attacks, run by "friendly" agents working as teams of hackers to penetrate "secure" computer networks, offered useful insights to government officials in Defense and Justice responsible for the security of such systems. This operation also makes clear the response of the U.S. government in 2003 to a massive power failure in the northeast section of the country, including New York City. Federal agencies were able to announce fairly quickly that this power failure was *not* a terrorist attack, because the parameters for such an attack had already been studied in this operation and did not fit the pattern of the 2003 grid failure. Being able to eliminate the possibility of a security breach as the root of the failure no doubt enabled a more rapid assessment of the real cause and the initiation of appropriate measures to resolve the problem. Thus, security tests cannot only indicate weaknesses in a system; they may also make evaluation of disaster situations at least one step easier.   ❑

AIRPORT SECURITY IN THE UNITED STATES

Nations such as the United States have tried to institute some security measures at one of terrorism's favorite targets: airports. Travelers of commercial airlines in this country were, even before the September 11 attacks, routinely subjected to electronic or manual luggage inspection and to electronic or physical body searches—a practice virtually unknown only a few years ago. In airports in the United States, too, individuals without purchased airline tickets can no longer meet incoming plane guests at the arrival gates, nor can they take their friends or relatives to the departure gates after the security rules were changed in the wake of the attacks.

These are potentially controversial measures, involving some invasion of privacy and some searches without a warrant of persons not accused of any crime. Yet few citizens today have serious objections to these measures. Even the presence of air marshals on randomly selected flights and the use of National Guard troops for airport security were accepted with complacence by most citizens, perhaps in recognition of the fact that threat to their lives and property created by a terrorist is greater than that incurred in airline security measures.

Such security measures, of course, only offer a measure of protection, in one country, against only one type of terrorism. If such measures are not universally applied by all nations, then the potential for skyjacking or bombing remains substantial, even for citizens of countries having such security systems.[3] Moreover, even U.S. measures until late in 2001 focused primarily on the hijacking of airlines with the use of conventional weapons, most of which was clearly inappropriate in terms of security preparations for the events of September 11.

Most of the security measures against hijacking with conventional weapons were enforced by measures that were incomplete and poorly enforced. Consider the results of investigations of airport security in several major U.S. airports. Federal auditors, testing X-ray procedures for carry-on luggage, reported recently that major airports missed, on the average, about 20 percent of the auditors' dummy weapons. One airport missed 66 percent of these weapons! This is clearly a breakdown in both physical and operational security.

Other surveys suggest that the problem does not lie exclusively with laxity in X-ray procedures. One audit, for instance, found that Los Angeles International Airport could not account for 6,000 employee identification badges. Two thousand were missing at Dulles International Airport near Washington, DC. Obviously, personnel security is also somewhat lax in this industry, contributing to a breach in operational security.

Consider the results of the informal "penetration team" of *U.S. News & World Report* reporters who checked several U.S. airports:

1. At Washington National, a reporter with a suitcase walked right past a security checkpoint on the side where arriving passengers walk out of the arrival gate. The reporter pretended to make a call at a row of pay phones near the checkpoint, then slipped by when the guards' backs were turned. What if his suitcase had contained a bomb?

2. At Chicago's O'Hare International Airport, a visitor found a baggage-room security door open. He walked through with his briefcase into the baggage-truck passageway, onto the tarmac where planes fuel and load, and up a jetway staircase. He then entered the terminal as if deplaning and caught another flight—without ever going through security. He could have sabotaged either luggage or a plane, without any contact with security.

3. A reporter watched in amazement as janitors at Midway airport in Chicago pushed large trash cans up to the passenger checkpoint. The janitors went through metal detectors, but they pulled the cans through on the unscreened side. Guards neither inspected the trash cans—a serious security breach—nor did they check parcels brought into the same area by food vendors.

4. A reporter at Atlanta's Hartsfield Airport watched as an employee punched a code into a security door's lock. She then tried the same code on several other doors in the concourse. It opened them all! These doors led, among other things, to the planes on the tarmac.[4]

Such lapses in airport security must frighten and worry both those responsible for such security and the passengers and crew whom such security is designed to protect. The lapses are clearly both in personnel and operational security. The argument is made that security personnel operate under the disadvantage of a mandate by their employers to make air travel as pleasant as possible. In other words, we want airport employees to be both unfailingly courteous and unrelentingly suspicious—of everyone. They are trained to put the comfort and convenience of the passengers first—but also to regard all individuals, including those same passengers, as potential threats to the airline's peace and security. It would appear, on the surface, to be an almost impossible task.

Weaknesses in the Security System

It has been suggested by several experts that commercial aviation was used as the "weapon" in the September 11 attacks precisely because of convenient flaws that existed within the security system of this industry. A quick look at a few of these weaknesses will illuminate the logic of this claim.

Ease of Access to the Cockpit

Because none of the September 11 pilots had the pilots or copilots informing air traffic controllers that they were being hijacked, and because the planes were turned into "missiles" flown deliberately into facilities on the ground, it seems reasonable to assume the terrorists were able to take over the cockpits. This was probably done in one of three patterns: by stealth, by the use of sudden overwhelming force, or by creating a disturbance drawing one of the crew to exit the cockpit and thereby create access to the flight deck for the hijackers.

Taking the cockpit by stealth would require access to a key to the cockpit of the plane. Unfortunately, prior to September 11, every flight attendant was required by the standards of the Federal Aviation Authority (FAA) to carry such a key at all times. On American Flight 11 (the first plane to fly into the World Trade Center), one of the flight attendants reported that two flight attendants had been stabbed. The second plane to fly into the WTC, United Flight 175, also reported that one flight attendant had been stabbed and two had been killed. Since each of these attendants had a key to the cockpit, it is reasonable to assume that the terrorists were able to take the cockpit by stealth.[5]

As one expert notes, prior to the events of September 11, "a normal-sized man with a karate kick or a shoulder shove could have broken down a cockpit door without too much exertion."[6] Numerous examples of this weakness were reported by news agencies, including attacks by a passenger on a Boeing 747-400 British Airways flight from London to Nairobi in December 2000 and by a young couple on a flight in February 2001 from Miami to New York. In these as in so many other cases, the passengers were able to breech the cockpit by force—and neither incident involved a large or well-trained attacker.

Finally, it was possible to take the cockpit by creating a distracting disturbance in the passenger area. This security weakness was possible because pilots were instructed, in the event of a disruptive incident in the passenger cabin, to intervene personally by leaving the cockpit and confronting the disruptive passenger. This instruction may have led to access for the terrorists on September 11. After the United flight crashed into the WTC, the operations center in Chicago sent an electronic text message to the airliners (including United Flight 93) that read: "Beware, cockpit intrusion." This message could have been interpreted by the flight crew as an air rage incident, requiring that the pilot exit the cabin to confront the problem. The pilots responded to confirm receipt of the message, and a few minutes later the plane was taken over by four terrorists. The policy of having the pilot exit the cockpit to confront may have facilitated the seizure of the aircraft.

Inadequate Screening Processes

As noted in the account of earlier penetration teams at airports, the screening process for passengers and luggage prior to the events of September 11 were seriously flawed. Perhaps the most obvious evidence of the flaws in this process lies in the handling of at least half of the 19 hijackers. Consider this:

> Nine of the hijackers were selected for special security screenings on the morning of September 11.
>
> Of these, six were chosen for extra security by a computerized screening system.
>
> Two others were singled out because of irregularities in their documents.
>
> One was listed on ticket documents as the travel companion to one who had questionable identification.

Yet they were all, in the end, allowed to board their flights, since on September 11, FAA security regulations required that passengers selected for further screening were only required to have their *checked* baggage further evaluated for possible weapons. Because only one or two of the terrorists actually checked any luggage, there would be no reason for the security process in place at that time to detect the weapons in the carry-on luggage of the terrorists.[7] Clearly, the process needed refining.

IMPACT OF SEPTEMBER 11 ATTACKS ON AIRPORT SECURITY

Although airport security clearly had flaws prior to these attacks, this demonstration of the dreadful consequences of airline hijacking dramatized the issue and forced the government and the industry to rapidly reassess and reorganize to reassure the public. The attacks, as noted earlier, caused airports across the country to be shut down in an effort to prevent further hijackings to occur. It took several days before the airports could be fully reopened, leaving thousands of passengers stranded at airports to which their flights had been diverted when the closings were ordered.

Moreover, we learned that the September 11 hijackers cased airports in the weeks prior to the attacks, taking test runs on flights to identify weaknesses within the system.

Confronted with the task of both reassuring the public that it was safe to fly and immediately taking effective measures to ensure (as far as possible) that such hijackings did not occur again, government and industry took several rapid steps:

1. Banning curbside check-in of luggage.
2. Severely limiting the use of e-tickets.
3. Restricting access to areas beyond the security scanning checkpoints to ticketed passengers only.
4. Assigning members of the National Guard to offer visible security at the check points.

Not all of these initial steps remained permanent or even universally applied at all airports, but they represented a significant effort to improve airport security and the public's perception of that security. At some airports, scrutiny of handbags and carry-on luggage was intense and resulted in the confiscation of fingernail files, pocket knives, letter openers, and a variety of other potential "weapons." Because those who carried out the hijackings in September apparently did not use guns or other conventional weapons for which baggage handlers had been trained to scan, this represented a serious change in the perception of dangerous personal items on the part of airport personnel.

Moreover, new potential threats continued to emerge, challenging previous patterns of security operations at airports. The potential of explosives in shoes became evident with the attempt of an individual to "light" what appeared to be a fuse attached to his shoes on a flight from Paris. Subsequently, airports at several major points around the country began to require passengers to submit to a scanning of their shoes for explosives.

That the people who seized control of the airplanes were not initiating a conventional hijacking situation also demonstrated a need to change security patterns. Pilots had been trained to cooperate, if possible, with hijackers, in efforts to get them to allow the plane to land, to offer opportunities for negotiation or hostage-rescue operations. The cockpits of the planes were seldom equipped with locking systems that would prevent such a takeover of the plane by skilled pilots. Thus, the pilots' training had to be revised, and mechanisms have now been added to most passenger planes that enable the cockpit to be secured from the inside against passengers, if necessary.

The United States struggled with the question as to who should have the task of maintaining internal airport security: private industry (in the form of security personnel businesses) or the federal government. Because the attacks on September 11 were made when airports contracted for their own security personnel with private agencies, the assumption was made that this process was flawed. But both the cost and the practical problems of making airport security a government enterprise are staggering, although it is the route currently being mandated. The hiring and training—including the setting of qualification standards for employment, training regimens, and quality enforcement—have become the responsibility of the federal government, which must also try not to create unemployment problems with its new rules.

In addition, physical security is still not completely effective. Weapons experts have testified before Congress about the possibility of smuggling guns through metal detectors by carrying them on certain spots on the body. Nor are these metal detectors, on which much airline physical security relies, effective at all heights. Although some airports now have technology to detect explosive materials, it is expensive and therefore will not be used in all airports. Training in the search for explosive materials, too, is not yet effective. A gentleman whose shoes showed evidence of explosive materials was stopped in January 2002 at the San Francisco airport and then allowed to walk away before security personnel could check it out, resulting in a shutdown of flights for several hours as airport security tried to locate the individual, without success.

Until after the events in September, no system was in place to X-ray check baggage on domestic flights, according to the FAA. The argument was made that the volume of such baggage was too high and that many weapons forbidden in carry-on baggage (for which the current detectors are designed) were still permitted on checked baggage. After those events, a program to match luggage with passenger flight manifests has been instituted, but only for the first check-in point. Unless all checked baggage is tested for weapons and explosives, a person could still get a bomb into a plane in checked luggage if his or her flight had at least one stop where the passenger could disembark, leaving the luggage (and the bomb) on the next leg of the flight. The argument against the more comprehensive scanning and baggage matching scheme continues to be that it is too expensive in terms of time and money, but the Transportation Safety Administration is beginning to draft and implement rules to make more comprehensive scanning and matching mandatory.

So what are airports to do to harden themselves as targets against terrorism? They could insist on training for security personnel to make them more security conscious, but it might well be at the cost of a loss of the "friendly" image with which airlines have sought to market their services. They could install more detection devices, for weapons as well as explosives, but again unless the laws regarding the type of weapons that may be carried in checked luggage change and the public becomes more reconciled to delays in flights due to essential security checks, then the cost of such measures to the airline industry may seem prohibitive.

THE COSTS OF SECURITY

The costs of such antiterrorism measures are high, materially as well as politically. Unfortunately, a great deal more money is required to erect defenses against terrorist attacks than to commit such acts.

If the cost of defending just one type of industry against attack is so high, then the cost of erecting coordinated international defenses against a multitude of types of terrorist attacks may well be prohibitive. The protection of specific targets against terrorists, including air transport facilities, would be a mammoth task. It is also a task which would not in itself be sufficient to secure entire nations and persons against terrorist attacks of all kinds.

The difficulty, as Robert Kupperman noted, is that potential targets for terrorist attacks are not limited to airports. As he has pointed out, there are numerous vulnerable targets in our sophisticated society. Electrical power systems, for example, are very tempting as accessible targets. A well-placed bomb or shots from a high-powered rifle could conceivably cause a blackout in an entire city. The same is true about the potential for destructive attacks on telephone systems, gas pipelines, dams, water systems, and nuclear power plants.

Kupperman also noted that, with the extensive reliance on computer information systems—for banking, credit cards, real estate, and so forth—that now characterizes industrial societies, the potential for economic disruption by terrorist attacks on those systems may also be substantial, as noted in a preceding chapter. As any computer hacker knows, no matter how carefully a computer system's security may be designed, a blend of time, patience, knowledge, and a little bit of luck will usually suffice to break into it. The potential of cyberterror, discussed in an earlier chapter, in which computers are used to destroy banking systems, public records, even water purification systems, presents a serious threat to many industries in the twenty-first century.

Concern has surfaced, too, over the protection of oil rigs in international waters. There are by now hundreds of oil rigs in the Gulf of Mexico and a rapidly growing number in the North Sea, all of which are vulnerable to terrorist attacks. Recent movies and novels depicting attacks on such rigs serve to highlight the plausibility of this potential disaster.

This industry, so vital to modern economies, is particularly open to attack, according to some experts, not only at its drilling operations, but also at a variety of other points. Although established petroleum and natural gas operations, their pipeline interties, and associated tankage and storage facilities have been the most attractive targets to date, there are many other points at which this industry is vulnerable, as events in the recent war in Iraq and subsequent attacks in Saudi Arabia have demonstrated.

The point is that the list of potential targets that could require security measures is extensive and growing rapidly with the development of modern technological interdependence. It might be possible, although incredibly expensive, for a nation to undertake to protect its own citizens and structures, but destructive attacks in another nation can have a substantial impact on the economy and lifestyle of the "protected" nation.

An attack on a North Sea oil rig, for example, would not only affect the cost of oil in Britain (and any nations that Britain supplies), but it could damage the North Sea countries' fishing industries as well. A successful attack on the computerized international banking system could have serious consequences for many national economies. The poisoning of a water supply in one nation could affect all of the other nations who share the use of that poisoned river or lake.

Just as no nation can entirely protect itself from terrorism by securing all potential terrorist targets, it is probably impossible for any nation, acting alone, to prevent or control the flow of weapons to terrorists. If targets cannot be fully protected, the next security step logically would appear to be an effort to curb the number and types of instruments of destruction available to terrorists. But again, the vast array of security measures required are staggering.

Some of the security measures in place or under consideration involve what is called **hardening the target,** which *involves efforts to make targets less accessible*. As noted earlier, these include the installation of metal detectors and X-ray machines at points of entry, the use of sensor or closed-circuit television to monitor accessways, and other similar technical devices. Such measures also can include the erection of fences, vision barriers, and heavy barriers around the perimeters of the installation. Related security measures can involve increased use of such items as armored cars, security guard forces, and bulletproof vests. An increasing number of executives are enrolling employees in expensive **training programs** designed *to teach skills in such things as high-speed car chases, surviving a kidnapping, and how not to look like a businessman traveling abroad.*

Indeed, companies offering to help make a business or a businessman more secure from terrorism have proliferated. One enterprising woman launched a business in 1987 that offered fake passports from nonexistent countries. Most of her clients were military men and businessmen traveling in the Middle East, South America, and Europe. Donna Walker, president of International Documents Service, pointed out, "When you're up against a bunch of gun-waving crazies, you should have an option"—such as a passport that does not label you as an American.[8]

Whether such exercises in protecting the target are useful or not, they continue to generate both interest and money for the companies providing them. What is not clear is the extent to which they offer real protection against a terrorist attack that is commensurate with the money expended on them.

Nor is it clear whether such measures are either legal or acceptable in a democratic society. Fake passports could well be used by criminals to baffle legitimate customs officials. The erection of heavy barriers and guards around public buildings, although perhaps necessary to protect them from attack, are still unpopular with a democratic public, accustomed to easy access to, for example, their nation's capitol buildings. It is, as the United States found in the wake of the Oklahoma City bombing, neither popular nor practical to harden all buildings that have federal offices against the public that they serve. Similarly, even though the general public supports, as a whole, the *idea* of strengthening airport security in the wake of September 11, individuals still do not want to wait longer or pay more for tickets in order to achieve that enhanced security.

PROTECTING PUBLIC TRANSPORTATION

Public transportation networks in large cities are enticing targets for terrorists because

1. they typically carry large numbers of people;
2. they move in concentrated, predictable geographic areas under routine time frames.
3. they are highly accessible, since they are "public service" operations, and cannot be hardened easily against their primary users—the general public.

Thus, in terms of physical, personnel, and operational security, they are attractive targets for those seeking to reach a large audience and disrupt a system with little effort. The U.S. State Department, in its record of international terrorist attacks in 1996, noted that 92 of these—almost a third—were against transportation and transportation infrastructures. While European, Middle Eastern, and Asian countries rely on their public transit systems much more heavily than the United States and have consequently developed more expertise in protecting these systems, officials were unable to prevent the sarin gas attack on the Tokyo subway in 1995 or the bombings of trains in Madrid in 2004.

Attempts to share learning experiences and technologies have evolved among some of the nations with a shared interest in this security threat. The advanced industrial nations (Canada, France, Germany, Great Britain, Italy, Japan, and the United States—the G-7) plus Russia have met several times in recent years to discuss the need for cooperation. On July 30, 1996, these nations met at the Lyons Summit in France, adopting a 25-point plan for international cooperation to combat terrorist acts. This plan included several significant points:

1. Tightened control on firearms and explosives
2. Improved bomb detection methods
3. Prevention of terrorist communications on the Internet
4. Faster exchange of information on terrorist activities, including those involving chemical, biological, and nuclear materials

Based on the progress made at this summit, two further meetings focusing on land transportation security were held in Washington, DC, in 1996 and 1997. In April 1998, domestic and international presenters (primarily from the G-7 plus Russia) met in Atlanta, Georgia, to discuss current and emerging terrorist threats, results from case studies, lessons learned and techniques developed due to terrorist actions, and new technologies useful in protecting land transportation systems. Some of the developing technologies discussed at this meeting, which may be of particular service in this target area, include weapons detection systems that can identify a weapon containing little or no metal at a distance of 30 feet, less-than-lethal incapacitation technologies that are both legal and socially acceptable (such as laser dazzlers, pyrotechnic devices, enhanced pepper spray delivery systems, and net devices), and sniper fire identification systems, capable of detecting and locating a sniper within a 10- by 10-foot area of an urban environment.[9]

Cooperation with other states is indispensable in the effort to provide security for land transportation systems. The techniques and equipment developed by other nations, if shared, may make future attacks on these vulnerable targets more difficult. But, as the officials at these meetings noted more than once, security for such accessible targets is not possible without a loss of freedom unacceptable to democracies. Furthermore, the events of September 11 demonstrated that the cooperation came *after* the terrorist event, not before, and thus did not prevent the attack but made capture of others involved possible.

PREVENTIVE SECURITY

Security has not been exclusively concerned with the hardening of targets that terrorists may—or may not—select today. Some efforts are also being directed at what has been termed "preventive security," meaning the making of terrorist attacks themselves less likely.

One such security technique in use today involves efforts to tag and trace various weapon components. There exist **taggants**—*chemically identifiable trace agents*—for many types of explosives today. It is also possible, although not as easy, to use **trace detectors** *for chemical agents*, which would enable security agents *to detect the presence of dangerous or hazardous chemicals in innocuous-looking containers.*

The use of tagging devices and trace elements for portable rocket security, in addition to more complete inventory control measures, is also under advisement. The advantage in the use of taggants, in addition to an ability to detect certain substances, is an ability to determine the country, and sometimes even the company, of origin. Although this would not necessarily be of immediate use in preventing terrorist attacks, it would be of considerable use in determining responsibility, perhaps thereby making future such attacks less likely.

However, companies and countries manufacturing such materials, from explosives to handguns, from nuclear to chemical and biological weapons, have resisted many attempts to institute a comprehensive tagging effort. Most have argued that laws requiring such security measures violate the rights of businesses engaged in lawful enterprises.

Political reality has made it clear that nations cherish their right to sell arms to whomever they please, under whatever conditions they deem advisable. Even nations that have made no secret of the fact that they sponsor, with arms and war matériel, terrorist groups have little difficulty securing those arms on the world arms market.

Regardless of the motivation, arms are increasingly available to anyone with the money (or a moneyed sponsor) to pay for them. This makes the efforts to limit terrorist access to weapons, as a form of preventive terrorism, largely futile. What terrorists cannot purchase legally on the open arms market they can surely procure illegally on the black market. Fake end-user certificates are readily available from several countries, such as Nigeria.

Moreover, it is difficult, in the shadow world of illegal arms sales, to use most preventive measures effectively. Shell companies, Swiss bank accounts, and the routing of weapons from country to country three or four times to hide the country of origin make the labyrinth of arms deals difficult to penetrate with regulation or preventive action.

The use of taggants might make tracing the country of origin feasible (even through this maze of sale and resale), but it is also highly probable that nations winking at such sales by their industries are going to be unwilling to force those industries to institute measures that might make it easier for a finger to be pointed accurately at violators of arms agreements. For monetary reasons they may have tacitly agreed to the sales; for political reasons they do not want such arms sales easily traced home.

Preventing terrorism becomes, in such cases, less crucial than being held accountable for violation of arms control laws and agreements.

The issue of arms sales becomes particularly critical when the arms being sold are nonconventional weapons. The growing threat of chemical, biological, and nuclear weapons in the hands of terrorists willing and able to use them will be discussed in the next chapter.

THREAT ASSESSMENT: HOW DO YOU KNOW WHEN YOU ARE AT RISK?

How do nations or businesses decide which of their operations or activities are likely to be victims of terrorist attacks? Nations and individuals use three types of indicators to assess the potential threat of terrorism. These can be described as general threat indicators, local threat indicators, and specific threat indicators. Let us look briefly at each of these types of indicators.

General threat indicators are used to *determine whether, within the nation or state, there exist conditions that might stimulate or provoke terrorism.* Such indicators are extremely general and are consequently of little use in predicting the likelihood of a specific terrorist attack. Instead, they are used to assess the climate—political, ideological, religious, and so on—that might influence the willingness of a portion of the population to resort to terrorism. Politically, for example, the presence of an unpopular, repressive, or corrupt government is considered a positive indicator of the probability of terrorism. Similarly, an economic climate that includes extreme poverty and/or high unemployment is regarded as conducive to terrorism.

This does not mean that any nation or region possessing these political or economic conditions will necessarily have a large degree of terrorism. It simply means that the presence of such conditions makes the likelihood of terrorism greater in such places than it might be in areas that do not have similar political or economic climates. These are indicators only, not predictors of terrorism. For instance, one geopolitical indicator has been the concentration of large foreign populations within a nation. In the United States, many such concentrations exist in major cities without outbreaks of terrorism, but they may provide terrorism support networks for future terrorist attacks. In occupied territories or in nations involved in border disputes, such populations have been useful indicators of the probability of terrorism.

Local threat indicators are used *to assess more specific and localized possibilities for terrorism.* Usually, such indicators focus on the forms that dissent tends to take on the local level and the degree of violence involved in the expression of such dissent. The formation of radical groups; reports of stolen firearms, ammunition, and explosives; violence against local property, including looting and arson; violence against individuals, including murders, beatings, threats, and abductions; and the discovery of weapon, ammunition, and explosives caches are all considered local threat indicators. Again, this does not mean that any radical group that forms must necessarily be a terrorist threat, nor that any demonstration against a government or a company must be the prelude to a terrorist attack. These are just some indicators of the possibility of terrorism in a particular location.

Specific threat indicators are used *to evaluate the vulnerability of a particular target to terrorism,* not the likelihood of terrorism in a nation or neighborhood. These indicators include such things as the history of attacks on similar targets, the publicity value of the target, the target's access to infiltration, its counterterror capability and its communications capability, the tactical attractiveness of the target, and the availability of the police or other security personnel.

Some of these indicators are essentially judgment calls, such as the determination as to whether the industry involves a "sensitive" installation, which is generally used to refer to a nuclear, chemical, or other similar facility. Others are very easily quantified, such as the population density in the immediate area.

None of the three types of indicators can be said to predict the probability of a terrorist attack. Nevertheless, government and industry are beginning to rely increasingly on such indicators to help them decide what, if any, terrorist threat exists and what direction such attacks may take. With the cost of installing, staffing, and maintaining security systems spiraling, no one is anxious to spend more than is warranted on protection against a threat that may never materialize. But few are willing, either, to risk remaining unsecured where strong indications exist that terrorist attacks may cripple or destroy costly facilities and irreplaceable lives.

CONCLUSIONS

The question is how much a company, a government, or a people are willing to sacrifice in order to achieve greater security from terrorist attacks. For some, as long as the attack happens to "somebody else," the sacrifice of rights to prevent terrorism will always seem too high a price. To others, the prevention of terrorism will justify the loss of precious rights and freedoms. Governments, trying to strike a delicate balance between the need for its citizens to be secure and the need to protect its citizens' rights, have an increasingly difficult task.

Terrorism is fundamentally an attack on the state. Just as offshore maritime terrorism is a crime waiting to happen, terrorism with nuclear, biological, or chemical weapons is an international disaster waiting to occur. Neither national nor international security measures have proved adequate in terms of either protecting targets or preventing the dissemination of such agents of mass destruction.

As governments and industries come to grips with the rocketing costs of securing themselves against terrorism, serious questions continue to be raised concerning the priority that security should have in the allocation of resources. However real the terrorist threat may be, few are willing as yet to meet the exorbitant costs, both political and economic, of providing adequate security against that threat. The costs that the United States is incurring in the wake of September 11 are enormous; to date it is not clear how long the general public will support the continued use of finite government resources, in a time of recession, to meet the threat of terrorism.

Unlike the issues raised with intelligence-gathering and investigative counter-terrorism measures, in the United States security measures costs were reckoned less in terms of political ideals such as civil liberties than in terms of convenience, and more importantly, money. Until terrorism was perceived to be enough of a threat to the economic well-being of the nation, its citizens, and its industries to justify the expenditure of countless millions of dollars, security remained a weak weapon in the arsenal against terrorism. Until terrorism seriously pinches the pocketbook of nations and businesses, that pocketbook will be slow to open to defeat or prevent that "pinch." Once that pinch is felt, however, the willingness to pay may allow significant steps in security at airports, water systems, nuclear power plants, and many other vulnerable points to evolve.

EVALUATION

Making a decision to take on the cost—in economic, political, and public relations terms—of installing and enforcing security systems is seldom easy. Rarely is there a clear indicator that makes such a decision effortless or obvious. Governments and industries continue to wrestle with the problems, and while their solutions seldom satisfy everyone, it is often difficult to state, unequivocally, what they should do in a given situation.

Consider the following cases, and try to formulate an appropriate response. Remember to take into account both the monetary and political costs of any decision. Could you justify your decision to a corporate board or an irate citizen in terms of cost-effectiveness? That is, does the security measure that you may recommend pay for itself in terms of the security gained, in a way that would recommend itself to a stockholder or taxpayer?

1. In spite of the events of September 11, many airports are reluctant to maintain the initial limits imposed on passengers in terms of curbside baggage check-in, e-ticketing, and allowing friends and relatives to accompany passengers to the boarding areas. Should the FAA require these increased measures, as well as the installation of more and better screening devices for all check-in baggage on all domestic as well as international flights? Could you justify spending large sums for increased security? As a citizen, passenger, and potential target of aircraft terrorism, do you want better security systems in place? Are you willing to pay for them, in higher-priced airline tickets, longer lines, and more flight delays?

2. The 2004 bombings of the trains in Madrid, Spain, were clearly timed to impact the upcoming national elections, which they clearly did. As other nations approach similarly critical transition points in their national government, should additional security be taken to prevent such incidents, or should the events be postponed or cancelled? What types of targets should be protected? Will any type of security really be effective, if individuals or groups engaged in a crusade are determined to carry out such attacks? Should public events, like the Olympics or other types of international sports competitions, be restricted, postponed, or cancelled out of security concerns?

3. Technology now exists, and is used in some airports, that can detect plastic explosives. The equipment is based on the detection of plastic and is similar to a metal detector but much more expensive (about $1 million per unit). Because it was a plastic explosive that caused the destruction of the flight over Lockerbie, Scotland in 1989, this seems an important technological breakthrough. But in order to detect the amount of plastic material used in the Lockerbie bombing, the machine's calibrations would have to be set so low (since it was a small amount) that the machine would detect every credit card that passengers had in their wallets. Setting it high enough not to set off an alarm for every credit card and driver's license (with the ensuing passenger frustration and endless delays) would mean that the Lockerbie bomb would not have been detected by the machine. Should airports be required to have such devices, even though they are very expensive, to prevent the bombing of an airplane? How low should the calibrations on the machines be set—low enough to detect the Lockerbie-type bomb, even though to set it that low would mean long lines and much passenger frustration at having to surrender, even for a moment, credit cards? What if the airport cannot afford the machines? Should the government provide them, as well as training for the security personnel to use them? How real does the threat of a bomb on a plane have to be before the security devices and the ensuing hassles are worth the trouble and the cost?

4. **Shoot-ats** are *incidents in which in-flight aircraft (commercial and general or charter planes) are fired at from the ground (generally by SAMs, antiaircraft artillery, or small arms fire), or from the air.* In November 2002, an Israeli charter jet was shot at by two SA-7s (SAMs) as it was traversing over Mombasa, Kenya. In May 2002, a U.S. military aircraft experienced a shoot-at by an al-Qaeda member also using a SA-7. Can commercial passenger aircraft be secured against this type of attack? What would it cost? Should such protection be mandatory for all civilian aircraft? Who would pay for it?

SUGGESTED READINGS

Aberlin, Mary Beth. "Trace Elements: Taggants Can Help Finger Terrorists and Counterfeiters." *The Sciences* 36, no. 6 (November/December 1996): 8–10.

"Corporate Security: Risk Returns." *The Economist* (U.S.), 353, November 20, 1999, 78.

Gleick, Elizabeth. "No Barrier to Mayhem." *Time* 148, July 29, 1996, 42ff.

Hahn, Robert W. "The Cost of Airport Security Measures." *Consumer's Research Magazine,* 80, July 1997, 15ff.

Jain, Vinod K. "Thwarting Terrorism With Technology." *The World & I,* 11, no. 11 (November 1996): 149–155.

Laqueur, Walter. "Postmodern Terrorism." *Foreign Affairs* 75, no. 5 (September/October 1996): 24–36.

Thomas, Andrew R. *Aviation Insecurity: The New Challenges of Air Travel.* Amherst, NY: Prometheus Books, 2003.

Wallis, Rodney. *Combatting Air Terrorism.* Dulles, VA: Potomac Books, 1998.

NOTES

1. Bill Gertz, "NSA's Operation Eligible Receiver," *The Washington Times,* April 17, 1998. http://www.landfield.com/isn/mail-archive/1998/Apr/0089.html.
2. Ibid., 2.

3. One CIA official (who requested anonymity) noted that in many less developed nations, the lack of any real security at airports constitutes "a terrorist attack waiting to happen."

4. "The Next Bomb," *Life,* (March 1989): 130–138.

5. Andrew R. Thomas, *Aviation Insecurity: The New Challenges of Air Travel* (Amherst, New York: Prometheus Books, 2003), 33.

6. Ibid., 37.

7. Ibid., 38–39.

8. Walter Laqueur, "Postmodern Terrorism," *Foreign Affairs* 75, no. 5 (September/October 1996), 24.

9. "Protecting Public Transportation From Terrorists," *National Institute of Justice Journal* (March 1998): 17–24.

14

The New Terrorist Threat: Weapons of Mass Destruction

Key Concepts

fanatics	biotoxins	nerve gases
biological weapons	botulinum toxin	ricin
chemical weapons	tularemia	small plutonium device
plague	smallpox	dirty bombs
unit 731	anthrax	agroterrorism
bacteria	viral hemorrhagic fever	Operation Silent Prairie
viruses	choking agents	suicide carrier
rickettsiae	blistering agents	
fungi	blood agents	

Science and technology have made enormous progress, but human, alas, has not changed. There is as much fanaticism and madness as there ever was, and there are now very powerful weapons of mass destruction available to the terrorist.

Walter Laqueur

CONTEXT OF THE THREAT

As noted earlier, terrorism is not a new phenomenon; instead, it is a pattern of behavior with deep roots in the history of most modern nation-states and peoples. Nor are all weapons of mass destruction new; biological and even chemical agents have been used in conflicts for centuries. But most analysts of contemporary terrorism assumed, until recently, that the costs—financial and political—were too high for modern terrorists to seriously attempt the use of such weapons today.

This reasoning contained several errors. The first is that the financial costs of all forms of weapons of mass destruction (WMDs) are too high today to be paid by individuals or groups willing to commit acts of terrorism. Although the cost of building a nuclear bomb is still quite high, access to nuclear material and the technological skills to develop such weapons have become much less restricted since the fall of the Soviet Union. So-called backpack nukes and other small-scale tactical nuclear weapons have made it to the black market in arms sales fueled by the Soviet collapse. Nuclear waste material, too, continues to be generated at an alarming rate, although secure storage of a permanent nature for such material remains a serious problem, making the possibility of a nuclear dirty bomb as a terrorist weapon quite feasible.

The second flaw in the logic lies in the insistence that terrorists would not use nonconventional weapons today, because the use of such weapons would carry too high a political or support network cost. Groups supported by states would, it was reasoned, be unlikely to use WMDs, because to do so would bring down attacks using similar weapons on the sponsor state. To deliberately jeopardize the patron state, thus perhaps causing the cutting off of all lines of support, would be an irrational move. Nor, it was reasoned, would patron states be willing to put such weapons in the hands of groups carrying out terrorist acts, because such retribution would surely fall on the state if the group used the weapon.

This reasoning is based on the assumptions that terrorists are rational actors and that all terrorists' groups are supported by states and would thus be unwilling to damage that relationship by the use of such weapons. As the September 11 attacks demonstrated, terrorist groups today are not necessarily funded by or networked with any particular state, and so cannot be assumed unwilling to use such weapons for this reason. As noted in the chapter discussing the motivations of terrorists, it is also probably erroneous to assume that terrorists are rational actors in the commonly accepted sense. Because they define their world in ways that often make little sense to those who do not see the struggle or the enemy as they do (as discussed in Chapter 4), then to assume their rationale for the use or nonuse of WMDs would meet the world's criteria for logic is itself irrational.

Furthermore, as Walter Lacqueur discusses in his book, *The New Terrorists: Fanaticism and the Arms of Mass Destruction,* there are now many terrorists who are **fanatics,** *individuals who are overenthusiastic, zealous beyond the bounds of reason.* Because reason is clearly not, by definition, going to be a factor in the decision-making process of a fanatic terrorist, then to assume he or she would not use WMDs is a forlorn hope, indeed, an irrational act on our part. To know that such weapons exist, to be aware they are much more accessible now to potentially fanatical users, and *not* to attempt to assess the potential for such destructive attacks and their probable consequences, would be irrational—as illogical as the fanatic who may well seek to use such weapons today.

The greater the understanding of the reality of the threat, the potential for destruction of these weapons, and the capability of groups to utilize such weapons, the better will be our ability to deal with the current world situation without either paranoia or desperate security measures. This chapter, then, will deal with these three aspects of terrorism and WMDs: an historical analysis of the reality of the use of WMDs, the types of such weapons that currently exist and their lethality, and the ability of current groups engaged in terrorism to use such weapons.

HISTORICAL USE OF WEAPONS OF MASS DESTRUCTION

Modern WMDs have one new component—nuclear weapons—but the other two major types of WMDs, biological and chemical, have been part of the arsenal of warriors for much longer. The oldest of these, **biological weapons,** *warfare agents that include living microorganisms and toxins produced by microorganisms, plants, or* *animals,* have the longest history to explore. **Chemical weapons,** *often comprised of binary compounds of chemicals that would not, separately, be lethal,* are not necessarily a completely different category of weapon, since agents like strychnine and ricin (which will be discussed later) are called biotoxins. We will begin with the oldest of these weapons—the biological ones—and progress through chemical to nuclear, taking a quick look at each type.

Brief History of Biological Weapons

During the 1990s, there was a widespread belief that biological and chemical weapons were the greatest danger facing humanity. Biological weapons treaties, including the one signed by the United States and the Soviet Union in 1972, gravely declared that nations would no longer produce such weapons and would destroy their current stocks of these weapons. But the use of such weapons had already been part of the history of conflict throughout the world.

The **plague** of the fourteenth century, *reported to have killed about a third of the population of Europe, was supposedly spread by the Tartars, in their siege of the fortress of Caffa in the Crimea.* According to legendary accounts, the Tartars used catapults to hurl plague-infected corpses into the city, becoming one of the first armies in history to engage in germ warfare. Other plagues were also alleged to be either the result of or to be enhanced by the deliberate use of infected skins and/or corpses by military groups. This includes the account mentioned in the chapter discussing terrorism in the United States of the use of blankets infected with smallpox as "peace offerings" to the Native Americans in Pennsylvania in the 1760s.

During World War I, Germany was accused of trying to spread cholera bacilli in Italy, the plague in St. Petersburg, and anthrax in Mesopotamia and Romania. In 1915, German agents in the United States were believed to have injected horses, mules, and cattle with anthrax on their way to Europe during World War I. The germs were produced in Silver Springs, Maryland, a Washington, DC, suburb, at a small German laboratory headed by Dr. Anton Dilger, who produced a liter of anthrax and glanders. The original seed cultures had reportedly been supplied by Berlin.[1]

In the mid-1930s, *Japan created a special biological warfare force* called **unit 731,** led by General Ishi in Manchuria, and many biological agents were produced in the laboratories of this unit. During the Japanese invasion of China in 1937, fleas were infested with many of these agents, including plague, smallpox, typhus, and gas gangrene. Evidence has emerged that these fleas were put in wheat dropped from Japanese planes over Chinese towns toward the end of the war, resulting in hundreds of deaths.

The United Kingdom and the United States also developed germ warfare capabilities during World War II. The United Kingdom's experiments with anthrax at Gruinard Island off the coast of Scotland resulted in contamination of the island, which was only removed at the end of the 1990s. The U.S. biological warfare program, initiated in 1942, continued after the end of the war, headquartered in Fort Detrick, Maryland, during the 1950s and 1960s.

Germ warfare installations also suffered from problems due to accidents. One of the most famous of these occurred in Sverdlovsk, in the Ural Mountains of the Soviet Union in April 1979. Intelligence assessments, later confirmed by Russian files after the collapse of the USSR, indicated that a large airborne release of anthrax spores used for bacteriological warfare resulted in fatalities. Similar, if smaller, accidents have reportedly occurred at facilities around the world, making the production of such weapons more visibly hazardous.

Brief History of Chemical Weapons

There are today a wide range of potential chemical weapons. Unfortunately, many chemicals used regularly for nonlethal purposes can be easily obtained and used—in combination with other chemicals—as chemical weapons. Chemical agents can be divided into many categories, but at least a cursory look at some of the major types of chemical agents will make a discussion of this type of weapon more easily understood.

Biotoxins, mentioned earlier, are one type of chemical agent. This category includes agents such as ricin, abrin, and strychnine. Another type of agent used by the military in many contexts in the twentieth century are the blister agents, including sulfur mustard, known as mustard gas.

Chemical weapons are a much more recent addition to the arsenal of nations and warriors than are biological agents. For the most part, this type of weapon was not used in conflict until the twentieth century, existing only in the form of plans never carried out in the decades at the end of the nineteenth century. The idea of using poison gas against an enemy has been reported in connection with several groups, including the Finians in the 1870s, who allegedly planned to spray it in the House of Commons in London. Similar plans were apparently made, but not carried out, during the Boer War, and even the Japanese War with the Russians in 1905.

It was not until World War I, by the Germans in 1915 at the battle of Ypres, that a chemical weapon—chlorine gas—was used on a large scale, with shocking success. The gas killed 5,000 Allied troops and injured many more. Five months later, in Loos, Belgium, the Allies used poison gas against German troops, again with dreadful success. The military on both sides continued to use gases as weapons, with varying levels of success. Although chlorine gas continued to be used in gas artillery shelling in a number of battles, including but not limited to the battles of Fey-en-Haye, Verdun, and the Somme, an equally effective mixture of chlorine and phosgene (mustard gas) was also used.

About 25 poison gases were used in World War I. The exact casualty count from this type of weapon is unclear; estimates vary between 500,000 and 1,200,000 total of troops and civilians from both sides. History indicates that the Russians may have suffered the worst losses from this weapon when it was used against them in conflict east of Warsaw in 1915. They reportedly lost about 25,000 soldiers in the first such attack, with countless casualties among civilians in towns near the front line.

Gas attacks, though clearly technologically possible, do not appear to have occurred in World War II. Even the Germans, who had clear technical superiority in the range of chemical weaponry developed, decided for a variety of reasons not to use these weapons. Believing, apparently, that Allied forces had also developed tabun and sarin, toxic gases produced in Germany by 1944, Hitler decided not to use these newest lethal weapons (although it turned out that the Allies had *not* developed these toxins during the war).

The next reported use of chemical weapons occurred when Iraq used them during its war with Iran, against both Iranians and later against members of Iraq's own citizenry. Here are a few of the accounts of the use of these agents in this eight-year conflict:

> *1983.* Mustard gas was used at Haj Umrah.
>
> *1984.* Nerve gases again used, at Al Basra, when Iraqi troops were on the defensive, in retreat.
>
> *1985 and 1986.* Thousands of Iranian soldiers reportedly killed by gas attacks at Um Rashrash, Hawizeh Marsh, and other locations.
>
> *1986 and 1987.* Poison gases used against the Kurds at Panjwin and Halabah. Reports indicate that Saddam Hussein used tabun in these attacks. News reports depicted men, women, and children lying in agonized death sprawls on the streets, after planes passed over the villages spraying the toxins.

Brief History of Nuclear Weapons

History of the actual use of nuclear weapons is quite brief. This relatively recently developed WMD has only been used on the occasion of the bombing attacks, by the United States, on the Japanese cities of Hiroshima and Nagasaki in 1945, bringing about an end to the war in the Pacific during World War II. Although atomic, and later nuclear, weapons were only in the hands of a few nations for several decades, this situation has rapidly changed in recent years.

To date there are at least eight states with openly declared national nuclear weapons capabilities: the United States, the United Kingdom, France, Russia, the People's Republic of China, India, Pakistan, and North Korea. However, many more states have secretly developed, and have arguably tested, nuclear weapons, including such states as Israel, Iran, South Africa, Iraq, and a few others. Moreover, several states that emerged from the former Soviet Union, in addition to Russia, have nuclear weapons still within their arsenals, although most have agreed to turn these over to Russia for the purpose of bilateral United States–Russian disarmament, as initiated in the SALT documents and discussions of the 1980s and 1990s.

Proliferation of nuclear weapons has occurred and is no doubt still occurring. This trend makes it less likely that the history of the use of nuclear weapons has terminated with the two attacks in 1945.

TYPES OF WEAPONS OF MASS DESTRUCTION AVAILABLE TODAY

Clearly, WMDs have been used by groups of warriors and nation-states for many years. The possibility that terrorists today would use such weapons cannot be assessed, because there is no history of previous use by others involved in intense struggles.

Moreover, such weapons have not been used exclusively, or even primarily, by non-democratic states or individuals with a careless disregard for the rules of warfare. Instead, a variety of states, many of them democratic and most of whom would today deplore the use of such weapons as barbaric, have been the major forces employing these weapons. Remember that the *only* use of atomic and/or nuclear weapons was by the United States, against predominantly civilian targets (of military significance but civilian populations).

The next step is to examine the types of WMDs available to terrorists today and the relative capacity of each to create mass destruction. Although many of these weapons have been untested on human populations, estimates can be made as to their relative lethality based on laboratory tests. Such tests cannot be definitive, but information provided about these weapons in such tests offer at least some indication of the toxicity of the substances.

Biological Agents

There are four categories of living microorganisms: bacteria, viruses, rickettsiae, and fungi. **Bacteria** are *small free-living organisms;* they can be grown on solid or liquid media and produce diseases that often respond to specific treatment with antibiotics. A familiar example of a bacteria used recently in a terrorist attack is anthrax, an acute infectious disease caused by the spore-forming bacterium *Bacillus anthracis*. Although anthrax most often occurs in hoofed mammals, it can also infect humans, as the anthrax attack in the mail system of the United States in the fall of 2001 clearly proved.

Viruses are *organisms that require living cells in which to replicate*. This type of organism does not respond to antibiotics, but is sometimes responsive to viral compounds, few of which are available. Again, the most familiar example of viruses as a weapon of terror is smallpox, an infection caused by the *Variola* virus, whose use was mentioned in the chapter on domestic terrorism.

The latter two groups are less familiar to the general public. **Rickettsiae** are *microorganisms that have characteristics of both bacteria and viruses.* Like bacteria, rickettsiae have metabolic enzymes and cell membranes, utilize oxygen, and are susceptible to a broad spectrum of antibiotics. Like viruses, they grow only within living cells. Q-Fever, a zoonotic disease caused by the rickettsiae *Coxiella burnetii*, is a form of rickettsiae. **Fungi,** *primitive plants that do not utilize photosynthesis, are capable of anaerobic growth, and draw nutrition from decaying vegetable matter,* are a little more familiar, but not in terms of a biological weapon. A diverse group of more than 40 compounds produced by fungi *Trichothecene mycotoxins* have been generated in recent years because they can inhibit protein synthesis, impair DNA synthesis, alter cell and membrane structure and function, and inhibit mitochondrial respiration. T-2, as these are called, used as a biological warfare agent aimed at causing acute exposure via inhalation, could result in the onset of illness within hours of exposure, and death within 12 hours.

Biotoxins, *poisonous substances produced naturally by microorganisms, plants, or animals that may be produced or altered by chemical means,* will be discussed later, in the context of chemical weapons. This category would include agents like ricin, abrin, and strychnine.

As one news analyst noted,

> While the list of the most likely weapons in a bioterror attack is short, it includes agents that, if acquired and effectively disseminated, could cause a significant public health risk. The challenge would be to recognize the danger early to limit the number of casualties.[2]

A quick look at five biological agents currently available today illustrates the breadth of the threat of attack from such weapons. A more in-depth case study of one of these— anthrax—will offer further clues as to the danger that such agents pose.

Botulinum toxin *(Clostridium botulinum) is the single most poisonous substance known.* While it is usually food borne, it could be developed as an aerosol weapon. After infection with this biological agent, symptoms generally include blurred vision as well as difficulty swallowing and speaking within 24 to 36 hours. This agent, a nerve toxin, paralyzes muscles, leading to respiratory failure and death. The Aum Shinrikyo cult in Japan was accused of trying to use botulinum toxin sprayed from airplanes over Tokyo, fortunately without success, at least three times in the 1990s.

Plague *(Yersinia pestis) is an incredibly virulent, but not always lethal, biological agent.* If 110 pounds of this agent were released over a city of 5,000,000 people, about 150,000 would contract the disease, but most would survive if treated early in the infection period. Within one to six days after exposure to the plague bacteria, victims would begin to show symptoms of severe respiratory and gastrointestinal distress. Treatment with antibiotics, however, would be effective as long as it was administered within the early stages of infection.

Tularemia *is a potentially lethal infectious organism developed by the United States as a possible weapon in the 1950s and 1960s.* As a weapon, it could be sprayed in an aerosol cloud. Within three to five days of infection, the victims would suffer fever, chills, headaches, and weakness. Subsequent inflammation and hemorrhaging of the airways can be fatal, and no vaccine is currently available.

Smallpox *is an infectious agent that several nations have tried for decades to effectively weaponize,* but which was eradicated in 1980. Some strains of this disease are maintained, however, in only two nations, officially: the United States and Russia. The former Soviet Union reportedly stockpiled large amounts of this virus for use as weapons, and several other nations, such as Iraq and North Korea, may have covert stashes of smallpox today. The smallpox virus is highly contagious and would quickly spread, because even in the United States, vaccinations for this disease stopped more than 25 years ago. An aerosol release of smallpox, infecting only 50 people, could easily unleash an epidemic, killing about 30 percent of those infected with the painful, disfiguring disease.

Anthrax *is an acute infectious disease caused by the spore-forming bacterium* Bacillus anthracis. It most commonly occurs in mammals such as cattle, sheep, goats, camels, and antelopes, but can also occur in humans exposed to infected animals or tissue from infected animals. Anthrax is unusual in that its spores are hardy: they are resistant to sunlight, heat, and disinfectant, and can remain active in soil and water for years. Anthrax spores tend to clump together in humid conditions, making it some-what difficult to spray as an aerosol. Anthrax, unlike smallpox, is not contagious—that is, it is highly unlikely that it could be transmitted from direct person-to-person contact.

Since this particular bacteria was used in 2001 as a biological agent, a closer look at anthrax as a biological weapon would be useful at this point. This case study of anthrax is not an account of the attack, but an evaluation of anthrax as a biological weapon.

CASE STUDY   Anthrax

Anthrax is linked to several devastating plagues that killed both humans and livestock. In 1500 B.C., the fifth Egyptian plague, which affected livestock, and the sixth, known as the plague of boils, were linked to anthrax. The Black Bane of the 1600s A.D. was also thought to be anthrax and killed 60,000 cattle in Europe.

Robert Koch confirmed the bacterial origin of anthrax in 1876. Not long after this discovery, anthrax began to emerge as a biological weapon. The biological weapons programs involving anthrax continued after World War II throughout the 1950s and 1960s at various military bases. In the United States, Fort Detrick in Maryland became the focal point for this program until 1969, when President Richard Nixon formally ended the United States' biological weapons program. In 1972, Nixon signed an international convention outlawing the development or stockpiling of biological weapons.

The ratification of this convention did not end the production, testing, and use of biological agents, including anthrax. From 1978–1980, Zimbabwe experienced an outbreak of human anthrax that infected more than 6,000 people and killed as many as 100. Evidence of continued development of anthrax as a biological weapon emerged in 1979 when aerosolized (weaponized) anthrax spores were accidentally released at Compound 19, a military part of Sverdlovsk in the Soviet Union. An explosion at this secret military base near an industrial complex in the Ural Mountains sent a cloud of deadly microbes over a nearby village. Reputed death tolls from this accident vary, with as few as 68 deaths attributed, and as many as 1,000 dying eventually from this contact with a weaponized form of anthrax.

The group Aum Shinrikyo released anthrax in Tokyo several times between 1990 and 1993, but without any reported deaths or infections. Anthrax, even in weaponized form, is difficult to disseminate over a city, because warm air generated by the traffic and compression of population generally forces the air up, not down, making it difficult to spray above the city with any success. In theory a cloud of anthrax spores inhaled by a city's population would create widespread severe, flu-like symptoms, killing 80 percent of those infected within one or two days after their symptoms appeared. As yet, no successful dissemination of this sort has been recorded. Nevertheless, states continue to seek to produce anthrax as a weapon. In 1995, Iraq admitted to UN inspectors that it produced 8,500 liters of concentrated anthrax as part of its biological weapons program.

In 2001, a letter containing anthrax spores was mailed to NBC offices in New York City, one week after the September 11 attacks on the United States. This was the first of a number of incidents at locations in the eastern part of the country, including letters in Florida and Washington, DC. Five deaths to date have been attributed to anthrax attacks.

Anthrax infection can occur in three forms: cutaneous (skin), inhalation, and gastrointestinal.

> *Cutaneous.* About 95 percent of cutaneous anthrax infections occur from a cut or abrasion on the skin, such as when someone is handling wool, hides, or hair products of infected animals. It begins as a raised itchy bump that resembles an insect bite, but soon turns into a painless ulcer, about one to three centimeters in diameter, with a black center in the middle. About 20 percent of untreated cases of cutaneous anthrax result in death. One employee who contracted anthrax in the U.S. incident had the cutaneous form of anthrax.

> *Inhalation.* Inhalation anthrax occurs when anthrax spores enter the lungs, requiring from 2 to 43 days to incubate. Initial symptoms for this form of anthrax may resemble a common cold but will lead to severe breathing problems and to shock after several days. Inhalation anthrax was thought to be fatal in about 90 percent of the cases, because its symptoms initially appear in a form that does not require a visit to a doctor. This assumption was based on incomplete data, however, from the Russian accident mentioned earlier. The data did not include information on those treated for infection who survived or were not infected. It only identified the deaths from the infection. The employee of the Florida tabloid and four of those handling the mail going through a New Jersey postal service died of inhalation anthrax in the 2001 attack.

> *Intestinal.* Intestinal anthrax generally follows consumption of contaminated meat. It is characterized by an acute inflammation of the intestinal tract, and includes symptoms of nausea, loss of appetite, vomiting, and fever, followed by abdominal pain, vomiting blood, and severe diarrhea. Usually, between 25 and 60 percent of cases of this form of anthrax are fatal. This is the type of anthrax that the Soviet Union initially blamed for the deaths in Sverdlovsk.

Anthrax is not contagious and can be treated with antibiotics. To be effective, the treatments must be initiated early, because if not treated in a timely fashion, the disease can be fatal. A cell-free filtrate vaccine for anthrax exists, which contains no dead or live bacteria in the preparation.

Anthrax is a particularly attractive candidate for a successful bioweapon, because its spores are hardy, as noted earlier. However, manufacturing sufficient quantities of any bacteria in stable form is a technical and scientific challenge, and dissemination of anthrax remains a challenge. The use of crop duster planes, for instance, as a tool for dissemination is difficult, because the planes are designed to spray pesticides in a heavy, concentrated stream. In contrast, anthrax as a bioweapon would perform better if scattered in a fine mist over as large an area as possible. The nozzles of crop dusters are best suited to discharge relatively large particles—100 microns in diameter—not tiny one-micron specks of bacteria.

In its natural state, anthrax has a low rate of infection among people. Experts state that it takes a sophisticated lab and advanced skills to turn the natural anthrax spore into an aerosol that can cause death from lung infection. The organism *Bacillus anthracis* can be grown in a lab to produce a weapons-grade form of the bacteria. Removed from a nutrient-rich environment, the bacteria turn into spores, which naturally clump together. These spores are then purified, separated, and concentrated, then combined with fine dust particles to maintain separation and increase the time that the spores can be suspended in the air.

Used as a weapon in the 2001 attacks, the powdery mixture was apparently put into an envelope. When released into the air, such as during processing of mail at mail centers, a high concentration of spores can be drawn deep into the lungs. The spores return to their bacterial state in the lungs and a rapidly developing anthrax infection releases deadly toxins into the person's system.

In addition to the apparent use of anthrax as a weapon through the mail system in the United States after the September 11 attacks, several other countries reported mail that initially tested positive to anthrax contamination. In Pakistan, at least one of four suspected letters received at three locations in Islamabad contained anthrax; in Lithuania, one mailbag at the U.S. Embassy at the capital tested positive, revealing trace elements of anthrax. Although similarly suspicious letters received in Kenya, Brazil, Argentina, and Germany initially tested positive to anthrax, none resulted in confirmed contamination of workers, and most tested negative in subsequent tests for exposure. Nevertheless, the potency of anthrax as a weapon for disruption and expensive response was clearly demonstrated by the limited attacks occurring in the autumn of 2001. ❑

CASE STUDY   Viral Hemorrhagic Fevers

Although biological agents such as anthrax and smallpox have been used as biological weapons in the past, neither are as potentially lethal as some of the viral hemorrhagic fevers studied at the Centers for Disease Control and Prevention in the United States today. Anthrax is, as noted earlier, a bacterial infection and therefore responsive to antibiotics, reducing its lethality if treated promptly. Although smallpox is a virus, it was eliminated from the natural world in 1977, and exists, officially, only in two laboratory repositories: one in the United States and one in Russia. Moreover, while smallpox is very easy to spread through a population, most patients in modern times infected with smallpox recover, although death would probably occur in up to 30 percent of the cases.

Viral hemorrhagic fever (VHF) is a term used to describe *a syndrome that severely affects multiple organs in the body, caused by several distinct families of viruses.*

Although some of the VHF viruses can cause relatively mild illnesses, many of them cause severe, potentially fatal disease. With a few noteworthy exceptions, there is no cure or established drug treatment for VHFs.

The survival of VHFs is dependent on the animal or insect host, called the natural reservoir, and humans are not the natural reservoir for *any* of the VHFs. But humans may become infected when they come into contact with infected hosts, and in the case of some of the more lethal VHFs such as Ebola and Marburg, may transmit the disease from one human host to another. This type of secondary transmission, from infected human to infected human, can occur directly (through close contact with infected people or their body fluids) or indirectly (through contact with objects contaminated with their body fluids).

VHFs like Ebola and Marburg have terrifying symptoms. Initial signs among persons infected would include marked fever, fatigue, dizziness, muscle aches, loss of strength, and exhaustion. As the diseases progressed, however, the person would exhibit signs of bleeding under the skin, in internal organs, and/or from the mouth, eyes, or ears. Although the loss of this blood externally would appear shocking, the patient would not, in most cases, die from loss of blood. Instead, the patient's body would be assaulted with the collapse of many organs within the system, nervous system malfunction, coma, delirium, seizures—and finally death, which would in many respects be a release.

There is no known cure for Ebola or Marburg VHF. Outbreaks of Marburg and Ebola have occurred through human-to-human transmission. The potential for a crusader willing to be a "suicide patient" rather than a suicide bomber, deliberately infecting himself or herself with one of these lethal VHFs to infect people within an "enemy" nation is still remote, given the fortunate scarcity of the virus. But the possibility exists, and if the virus was obtained and replicated in a lab with deliberate intent to use it as a weapon, the results for humankind might be unthinkable.   ⊔

Chemical Weapons

Although there are potentially thousands of biological agents that terrorists could use, there are, in all probability, even more poisonous chemical agents available. The agents come in a variety of forms, most often as a liquid rather than a gas, usually dispersed as droplets. Biotoxins, mentioned earlier, are one type of chemical agent, which includes agents such as ricin, abrin, and strychnine. *Chlorine* and *phosgene* are **choking agents,** used during World War I, and *causes pulmonary edema. Mustard gas, lewsites, and others that cause chemical burns and destroy lung tissue* are called **blistering agents. Blood agents** include other types of chemicals, such as *hydrogen cyanide* and *cyanogen chloride, that attack the respiratory system and usually result in very rapid coma followed by death.* The *neuromuscular system is attacked* by the **nerve gases**, like *sarin* (used in the Tokyo subway incident), *tabun* (found in Iraq after the Gulf War), *soman,* and *VX.* These agents *block the enzyme cholinesterase, which causes paralysis of the neuromuscular system, resulting in death.*

Most of the substances used to create chemical weapons have a legitimate use. Some, like eserin (a nerve gas), have been used for medicinal purposes. Others are used as cleaning agents, insecticides, herbicides, and rodenticides. This makes many of them available commercially, in some form. As the United States learned in the bombing at Oklahoma City, truckloads of fertilizer can be easily obtained and can be a very lethal weapon in the hands of a terrorist. Evidence of similar efforts by individuals and groups within the United States to secure and even to use chemical agents is a small but growing threat.

Chemical weapons are prolific in number, relatively easy to acquire and stockpile, and not too expensive. They are difficult, however, to manufacture in sufficient quantities for a large-scale attack. More likely, they would be used successfully in isolated attacks of a relatively small nature. Chemical weapons are also difficult to disperse effectively. The attack by the Aum Shinrikyo on the Tokyo subway system in Japan illustrates both the strength, in terms of the psychologically disruptive effects, and the weaknesses, in light of the relative nonlethality of the attack and the problems in dissemination, inherent in the use of chemical weapons by terrorists today.

CASE STUDY   Ricin

Ricin is a *biotoxin found in the bean of the castor plant,* Ricinis communis, and it is one of the most toxic and easily produced plant toxins. Orignially cultivated in ancient Egypt as a lubricant and a laxative, castor beans are today used to produce castor oil, which is a brake and hydraulic fuel component found throughout the world. Ironically, ricin can be made from the waste left over from processing castor beans.

Because it is both highly toxic and easily produced, ricin was studied and developed by the United States during both world wars in the twentieth century. Unfortunately, these same characteristics have made ricin an attractive weapon of interest to radical individuals, groups, and governments in recent years as well.

Like anthrax, ricin may cause toxic reactions in people from three possible routes of exposure: inhalation, injection, and oral ingestion (the least toxic method). Inhaling ricin, according to one group of experts, would produce symptoms within 8 hours, and depending on the dose, death within 36 to 72 hours. There is, unfortunately, no known vaccine for ricin and no antidote to the poison to counter it.[3]

Although ricin poisoning is not contagious (it cannot be spread from person to person from casual contact), it has already been used as a weapon in recent history. In 1978, Georgi Markov, a Bulgarian writer and journalist who was living in London, died after he was attacked by a man with an umbrella—an umbrella that had been fixed to inject a poison ricin pellet under Markov's skin. Reports indicate, too, that ricin was used in the Iran-Iraq conflict in the 1980s. Quantities of ricin were reportedly found in caves in Afghanistan used by al-Qaeda prior to the 2001 attacks, and information about ricin appears in the so-called *Jihad Encyclopedia* discovered after September 11. Ricin is intensely more lethal than sarin, which was used in the Tokyo subway attack. ❏

Nuclear Weapons

Options for nuclear weapons today exceed the prohibitive cost and technological limits inherent in the creation of plutonium-based nuclear missiles. Several types of nuclear weapons may be feasible for use by terrorists in the twenty-first century, although none have yet been used in an attack.

A **small plutonium device,** *requiring at least 2.5 kilograms of plutonium, is constructed with a core made of a sphere of compacted plutonium oxide crystals in the center of a large cube of Semtex (or one of the other new, powerful explosives).* The bomb, when complete, would weigh about a ton and would require at least a van or a truck to get it to the target.

A home-produced or stolen nuclear device of moderate size, about 10–15 kilotons, detonated in a major city would destroy several square miles of territory and could cause up to 100,000 casualties. The bomb would have to be transported and strategically placed for maximum effect. The technical skills required, the facility necessary, and access to a large quantity of plutonium are impediments to the use of such a weapon by a group engaged in terrorism.

Dirty bombs do not require the theft of large amounts of the carefully guarded plutonium, nor does their construction require great technical skills or a well-equipped laboratory. These weapons can be made with *nonfissionable radioactive materials, such as cesium 137, cobalt 60, and strontium, exploded by conventional means.* Even though such a bomb would not cause the vast number of fatalities generated by a nuclear blast, they spread nuclear contaminant over water supplies, crops, and other essential parts of a system. These bombs could be used in shopping malls or train stations to disrupt as well as to destroy.

Attacks on nuclear power facilities would also be a form of nuclear terrorism possible today. This has happened many times, in many countries, but without evidence that such attacks have yet generated a major accident with catastrophic loss of lives. Nevertheless, in the wake of the attacks on September 11, nuclear facilities were recognized as vulnerable to the same type of attack—one using a large, well-fueled plane as a "bomb" flown into the facility.

The black market for weapons has had, since the demise of the Soviet Union, incidents in which small, backpack nuclear devices, and even devices as small as landmines were for sale. Although no records obviously exist of such sales, the leaders of the international community have expressed their concern about the possibility of a group engaged in terrorism, or a "rogue state" willing to operate outside of traditional legal norms, acquiring such fully manufactured devices. This possibility has been the subject of discussion at numerous UN meetings and resulted in resolutions condemning such sales and pledging not to facilitate them, but little documented success in the control of such weapons exists to date.

Terrorists and groups appear more willing to experiment with the use of biological or chemical weapons than nuclear weapons today. If terrorists want biological weapons, they can make potent agents from such substances as isopropyl alcohol (easily available at drug stores and supermarkets), from pesticides and herbicides (available at most home and farm supply stores), and from a host of other equally accessible products.

Most experts also agree that it does not take great skills in chemistry to manufacture many different chemical agents. Some are more difficult than others, of course; but a wide range is possible for someone with perhaps a few graduate courses in chemistry.

Chemical weapons are less attractive to terrorists primarily because of the difficulty in their delivery. As evidenced in the sarin gas attack in Tokyo, if the agent is not administered properly, it may afflict many but kill few. If the desire is for dramatic effect, this may not be a critical factor. But if the desire is to disable as well as frighten an enemy, to punish severely rather than merely inconvenience a target, then this problem in dissemination can be a major stumbling block. Factors such as wind direction, temperature, enclosure of space, and moisture can affect the dissemination process. Nerve gas, for example, rapidly hydrolyzes in water and therefore cannot be put, as many biological agents can, into the water system of a city.

ACCESS TO AND USE OF WEAPONS OF MASS DESTRUCTION

Chemical Agents

As weapons of terrorists chemical agents are relatively easily accessible, potentially very lethal, but are limited in usefulness to date by the difficulty in dissemination, unless the desired effect is primarily psychological rather than physical in nature. Most chemical weapons have been available since World War I, and the processes for manufacturing most usual war gases have been published in open literature. Several nations possess chemical weapons, making it possible for them to supply a group with this type of weapon. Yet only the Aum Shinrikyo cult in Japan has attempted to procure and use a chemical weapon in a large-scale terrorist attack.

The reason for this lack of use may lie simply in practical, rather than political, moral, or monetary terms. Most toxic gases are very difficult to handle, control, and deploy effectively. Even toxic industrial gases, like chlorine and hydrogen cyanide, which are easy to procure, are very volatile. These types of agents could only be used in an attack on a target population in an enclosed area, with limited exits (so that those targeted could not escape, and/or to keep the gases from escaping into the atmosphere outside). As one researcher noted, if a terrorist wanted to use a nerve agent by introducing it into the air-handling system in a building (whose inhabitants are the target population), the device must

1. be of a size and shape that is easily carried by one person;
2. be leakproof; and
3. must have an activation process that will result in the agent being dispersed in a way that will not endanger the terrorist operating the device (unless the terrorist is a crusader,

willing to die in the attack), yet strong enough to reach the population in a sufficiently high concentration to cause a high casualty rate.[4]

Nevertheless, trainees at terrorist camps in Afghanistan learned how to use chemical weapons, according to testimony in U.S. courts in July 2001. Ahmed Ressam told the court that his training for chemical attacks included testing the effect of cyanide and sulfuric acid on a dog. "We wanted to know what is the effect of the gas," Ressam told the court.[5]

Biological Agents

In the early 1990s, perception of the possibility of biological attacks was radically altered due to two dramatic events. The first was the discovery of enormous quantities of such weapons in Iraq after the Gulf War, particularly as there was reason to believe that only a portion of them had been found. Moreover, there was also a growing realization that Iraq and other countries, including but not limited to Iran, were continuing preparations for BC (biological/chemical) warfare. While suspicions had existed before the Gulf War, particularly because Iraq had used chemical weapons against both the Iranians and the Kurds resulting in many thousands of deaths, the realization of the buildup of BC had clearly been enormously underestimated.

At the Al Muthanna laboratories in Iraq, 2,850 tons of mustard gas was found to have been produced, along with 790 tons of sarin and 290 tons of tabun. Iraq was found to have 50 warheads with chemical agents in place at the beginning of the Gulf War. In terms of biological weapons, Iraq had also produced anthrax, botulinum toxin, and other biological agents since 1988, with the result that when inspectors began investigating in 1991, they found that 6,500 liters of anthrax and 10,000 liters of botulinum had been weaponized.

Libya has also engaged in intense production of biological agent capabilities. With help from biological firms from Germany, Switzerland, and several other countries, Libya constructed large underground laboratories at Tarhuna and Rabta. Specialists suggest that such facilities could be transformed in less than one day from weapons factories to peaceful pharmaceutical labs. This makes tracking the production of biological agents difficult, and given Libya's long-term relationships with many groups engaging in terrorist acts, makes the access of terrorists to such weapons potentially feasible, until the recent movement of Libya to distance itself from the creation of WMDs.

The second source of world shock on the issue of biological agents came with the breakup of the Soviet Union. Although Russia promised to destroy its BC weapons, it soon became obvious that it was failing to adhere to its promise and was instead preventing access by foreign inspectors after 1993. Records of the amounts of such weapons in existence, and even of the location of facilities manufacturing or storing them, were lost, destroyed, or hidden, with the result that few are certain of precisely how many BC weapons were produced and who currently possess them.

This type of weapon has been linked to several earlier terrorist groups and activities. It was reported in the late 1970s that the RAF in Germany was training Palestinians in the use of bacteriological warfare. A raid by police in Paris uncovered a laboratory with a culture of botulism. The RAF threatened to poison the water supplies of about 20 German cities unless their demand for special legal defense for three of their imprisoned comrades was met. Microbiologists were believed to have been enlisted in efforts by groups in Italy and Lebanon to generate biological weapons for terrorist use. In the United States, 751 persons in the small town of The Dalles, Oregon, were poisoned by salmonella planted in two restaurants by followers of Bhadwan Shree Rajneesh.

A special issue of the *Journal of the American Medical Association* published the first systematic survey of biological agents in 1997. This survey included brucellosis, the plague, tularemia, Q-fever, smallpox, viral encephalitis, viral hemorrhagic fevers, anthracis, and botulinum. The latter three were described as the greatest potential danger, given their toxicity, contagion rate, and because both were found in large quantities in Iraq, where they had already been weaponized.

Although vaccines could be used to neutralize many of the existing agents, and antibiotics could be used to both treat and prevent most, the weaponizing of these agents presents a problem. Through this process, the agent is changed in ways that could make the majority of the safeguards and remedies ineffective.

It is believed that 30 to 40 countries have the capacity to manufacture biological weapons, because many have a pharmaceutical industry to aid in this production. The greatest concentration of existing weapons is believed to be in the Middle East, including not only Iraq and Iran, but Syria, Libya, and the Sudan. The U.S. bombing of the pharmaceutical factory in the Sudan in 1998 when this laboratory was linked by intelligence information with Osama bin Laden illustrates the rising concern over the possible use of this type of agent by terrorists.

Biological agents have been called "the poor man's nuclear bomb." They are difficult to trace, cheap to manufacture, and potentially incredibly lethal. Botulinum, the most deadly toxin available—100,000 times more poisonous than the sarin gas used in the Tokyo subway attack—is theoretically capable, in a quantity as small as one gram, of killing all the inhabitants of a city the size of Stockholm, Sweden. An aerosol distribution is the ideal method of delivery for such an agent. It has been estimated that botulinum, in optimal weather conditions, could kill all living beings in a 100-square kilometer area. Fortunately, ideal weather conditions seldom last, but many would certainly die from such an attack.

Nuclear Devices

Hundreds of pages of photocopied, handwritten, and printed documents, written in a mixture of Arabic, Urdu, Persian, Mandarin, Russian, and English, were recovered from a number of al-Qaeda houses in the Afghan capital a day after its fall to the Northern Alliance forces in November 2001. These pages confirmed, among other things, that al-Qaeda cells were examining materials to make a low-grade, dirty nuclear device. The pages also indicated that their understanding of bomb-related electronic circuitry at least matched that of the Provisional IRA's experts.

According to John Large, a British nuclear consultant, while the organization would not have been able to make a large-scale missile or nuclear device from the documents found, "it was obviously prepared to consider the use of such weapons, so that if it could not manufacture such for itself then, given the opportunity, it would acquire such for use."[6] Included in the documents acquired by *The Times* relating to nuclear physics was a chart depicting a portion of the periodic table of elements, dealing solely with radioactive materials. This portion, according to Large, contained all of the elements needed if one were constructing a dirty bomb.

Access to nuclear materials is problematic, depending on which type of material is sought. The most carefully guarded, weapons-grade uranium and plutonium is perhaps the least accessible. However, numerous attempts have been made to smuggle nuclear materials out of the former Soviet Union, and there are unconfirmed rumors that nations, and perhaps even a group like al-Qaeda, may have obtained a nuclear warhead. Thus far, police and customs officials in Europe have seized only low-quality nuclear waste that, although it could not be made into a real atomic bomb, it could, in sufficient quantity, be used to build a dirty bomb that would spread nuclear contamination.

The easiest access by which a terrorist group might make a nuclear bomb would be to find a government willing to allow access to its laboratories or its arsenals, but few if any such governments are willing to take such a risk today. UN inspectors after the Gulf War found that Iraq had come within months of building an atomic bomb, but the effort apparently took about a decade and cost nearly $10 billion dollars. There is no evidence that any government today has helped terrorist groups acquire nuclear weapons at such prohibitive costs. The potential cost of being linked to the bomb if the terrorists deploy it successfully has also apparently deterred access to this type of weapons through state conduits.

But the number of potential suppliers of nuclear weapons technology continues to expand. Countries such as North Korea, once dependent on external help from other nations in crafting a nuclear weapons program, now enjoy a vigorous missile- and technology-export business with a number of Middle Eastern countries including Iran, Pakistan, and Syria. Moreover, all technologies become less expensive with the passage of time and proliferate as more begin to utilize them. Although there is no immediate threat of nuclear bombs in the hands of terrorists, the next plane flown into a symbolic target like the World Trade Center may have something more lethal aboard than aviation fuel.

CASE STUDY   Agroterrorism

As concern mounts about the potential for terrorist attacks utilizing WMDs, one of the possibilities receiving special attention is that of agricultural biowarfare, or

agroterrorism, which involves *the deliberate introduction of a disease agent either against livestock or in the food chain for purposes of undermining stability or generating fear.* At least 13 nation-states developed, or are suspected to have developed, biological agents with antilivestock or anticrop properties. Specific, verifiable information on such programs is difficult to access, since most biowarfare programs are (or were) clandestine. The list of diseases developed in these programs by just two countries, the United States and the former USSR, is staggering, including (but definitely not limited to) anthrax, brucellosis, equine encephalitis, foot-and-mouth disease, fowl plague, glanders, African swine fever, avian influenza, contagious bovine pleuropneumonia, Newcastle disease virus, wheat blast fungus, rye blast, and tobacco mosaic.

Concern about the potential for agroterrorism led the United States in February 2003 to conduct a terrorism scenario focused on a domestic agroterror attack, **Operation Silent Prairie,** a *simulation of an attack generating an epidemic of foot-and-mouth disease (FMD).* The national livestock population has had no natural immunity to this disease since 1929, when FMD was eradicated in the United States. Given this lack of immunity, by the conclusion of the exercise, FMD hypothetically had ravaged the livestock herds from North Carolina to the San Joaquin Valley, with what would have been devastating economic consequences.

Organized by the National Strategic Gaming Center and held at the National Defense University, the simulation was designed to give senior government officials (18 members of Congress, the Surgeon General, the deputy secretary of agriculture, the deputy secretary of defense, and representatives from the FBI, FEMA, the North Carolina Department of Agriculture, the National Guard Bureau, the Joint Chiefs of Staff, and others participated), insights into the complexities of the emerging global biosecurity challenges. It certainly served to highlight the devastating potential of the bioterror threat. ❏

CONCLUSIONS

There is growing concern among many who study terrorism that the use of WMDs may become more common in the near future. The legal, political, and financial restraints that have discouraged states from the use of these types of weapons appear less likely to be sufficient to limit the willingness of a group, if it can acquire such a weapon, from its use. Because access to such weapons is clearly growing and groups are already training in the use of the more easily accessed materials, then the likelihood of a threat by terrorists of a WMD seems credible.

Documents obtained from some of the al-Qaeda houses in Afghanistan not only described the organization's efforts to obtain nuclear capabilities, but also outlined this group's plans for chemical weapons. These plans were drawn with large-scale production in mind, with each recipe containing a step-by-step guide explaining how to produce batches that would kill thousands of people. Some of the pages contained photocopies explaining how a device or chemical agent could best be put to devastating effect.

The use of weapons by terrorists, not just al-Qaeda, is clearly not a remote possibility, but an actively sought goal today. Smallpox, which is estimated to have killed 120 million people in the twentieth century alone, offers an incredibly lethal weapon, in weaponized form or in the hands of a **suicide carrier,** *a terrorist willing to be infected with the disease in order to carry it into the target audience to spread it among this group.* If smallpox had not been eradicated, according to the World Health Organization, "the past 20 years would have witnessed some 350 million new victims—roughly the combined populations of the United States and Mexico—and an estimated 40 million deaths—a figure equal to the entire population of Spain or South Africa."[7]

The biological threat is small, in at least two respects: most biological agents are hard to produce and hard to make into weapons. The preparedness of governments to deal with even this small threat, however, was demonstrated in the fall of 2001 by the anthrax attacks in the United States and elsewhere.

In spite of the fact that ordinary airplanes were used as WMDs in the September 11 attacks, the difficulty in generating and appropriately dispersing biological, chemical, and nuclear weapons remains high. But that attack has changed, to some extent, the world's perception of modern terrorists. The suicidal zealotry, the malevolence, and the determination of the individuals who flew the airliners into buildings; their willingness to prepare for the attacks for years; and their clear desire to cause mass casualties have confirmed the possibility that such terrorists would willingly use chemical, biological, or nuclear weapons.

EVALUATION

The attack by the Aum Shinrikyo cult in Japan makes an excellent case study of the use by a modern terrorist organization of a weapon of mass destruction. Carefully study the following account, assessing

indications that such an attack was eminent,

the skill (or lack of it) in the dissemination of the toxin,

the legal response to the attack, and

the impact on the public (that is, the extent to which a terrorist goal of creating a mood of fear was achieved).

CASE STUDY   Aum Attack on the Tokyo Subway

On March 20, 1995, Aum Shinrikyo (Supreme Truth), a Japanese cult, placed containers of sarin gas on five trains of the Tokyo underground subway network, which came together in the Kasumigaseki station, near many government offices. This attack killed 12 people, injured 5,500, and caused serious chaos in the subway system for days afterwards.

The timing of the attack, as well as its focus on trains full of government workers, was significant. Japanese police were actually planning to raid cult leader Shoko Asahara's Tokyo compound on March 22, expecting to find the chemical agents the group possessed. Aum had been able to infiltrate the police department with two sup-porters who warned Asahara of the coming raid. Aum chose to launch the subway attack on March 20 during the police shift change to divert attention from the planned raid.

The subway attack plan had many flaws and consequently left fewer victims than might have been expected. The sarin used was not pure, and the means of distri-bution—polyethylene bags that had been punctured—was primitive and ineffective. The attack was carefully planned, but rushed into place earlier than anticipated, thus relying on improvisation rather than tested techniques.

The Tokyo attack in 1995 was not the cult's first attempt to use a chemical weapon. Aum spent more than $30 million developing poisonous gases, even con-structing a special facility called Satyan 7 to produce sarin gas.[8] In 1994 seven people were killed and another 264 injured at Matsumoto, a resort west of Tokyo. The event was thought to be an accident, although members of this cult later admitted to spray-ing sarin from a van. There had been other minor incidents involving toxic vapors linked to Aum, and anonymous threats referring to coming attacks had been received by the police. Some of these letters even named the Tokyo subway as the probable tar-get, but the authorities took only limited action, until after the March attack.

Because the cult owned a billion-dollar computer empire in Japan, it invested much of its profits in the building of fully equipped laboratories, where it attempted to create or modify deadly chemical and biological toxins. Aum sent scientists in re-search teams worldwide in search of deadly biological agents, even exploring the possibility of securing a culture of the Ebola virus during its outbreak in Zaire.

Evidence gathered after authorities searched the warehouses and labs indicated that Aum had tried to develop weaponized forms of botulinum and anthrax, as well as other toxic agents. In 1993, the cult tried twice to spray what they believed to be a weaponized form of anthrax, in aerosol form, from the top of their compound in Tokyo. After the 1995 attack, they also admitted to spraying botulinum on the walls outside the American Embassy in Tokyo. No injuries or deaths were reported from either of these attempts to use biological agents. The willingness of the group to spend millions to acquire these lethal agents, and its eagerness to use them was bal-anced, apparently, by its inability to produce effective strains or to disseminate them efficiently.

Asahara and the other key leaders in the subway attack were captured by the Japanese government less than two months after the incident.   ❑

Suggested Readings

Butler, Richard. *The Greatest Threat: Iraq, Weapons of Mass Destruction, and the Crisis of Global Security*. New York: Public Affairs, 2000.

Cole, Leonard A. *The Eleventh Plague: The Politics of Biological and Chemical Warfare*. New York: Freeman, 1997.

Falkenrath, Richard A., Robert D. Newman, and Bradley A. Thayer. *America's Achilles' Heel: Nuclear, Biological, and Chemical Terrorism and Covert Attack*. Cambridge, MA: MIT Press, 1998.

Lacqueur, Walter. *The New Terrorism: Fanaticism and the Arms of Mass Destruction.* Oxford: Oxford University Press, 1999.

Miller, Judith, Stephen Engelberg, and William Broad. *Germs: Biological Weapons and America's Secret War.* New York: Simon & Schuster, 2001.

Stern, Jessica. *The Ultimate Terrorists.* Cambridge, MA: Harvard University Press, 1999.

NOTES

1. Walter Lacqueur, *The New Terrorism: Fanaticism and the Arms of Mass Destruction* (Oxford: Oxford University Press, 1999), 61.

2. "Guide to Toxic Terror," *The Charlotte Observer,* September 30, 2001, 11A.

3. "A Focus on Ricin Toxin," *Counter-Terrorism Training and Resources for Law Enforcement,* http://www.counterterrorismtraining.gov/focus/focus.html.

4. Raymond A. Zilinskas, "Aum Shinrikyo's Chemical/Biological Terrorism as a Paradigm?" *Politics and the Life Sciences* (September 1996): 238.

5. Sharon Theimer, "Special Report: Attack on America," *The Washington Post,* September 21, 2001, A27.

6. "Scientists Confirm bin Laden Weapons Tests," *The Sunday Times,* December 30, 2001, 2A.

7. David Ensor, "Biological Attack Threat Real, but Small," *CNN Washington Bureau,* September 24, 2001.

8. Mike Dasher, "AUM Shinri Kyo (Supreme Truth)," in *The Encyclopedia of Terrorism,* ed. Cindy Combs and Martin Slann (New York: Facts-on-File, 2002), 22.

CHAPTER 15

Future Trends

Key Concepts

bureaucratic banality	lethality of attacks
war on terrorism	right-wing terrorism
globalization	generational differences
Dark Winter	HAMAS
volume of terrorist incidents	

The greatest threat posed by terrorists now lies in the atmosphere of alarm they create, which corrodes democracy and breeds repression. . . . If the government appears incompetent, public alarm will increase and so will the clamor for draconian measures.

Brian Jenkins

A "WAR" ON TERRORISM

The late Hannah Arendt, in her controversial book on the trial of Adolf Eichmann, coined the phrase, "the banality of evil." She used this phrase to describe the way in which a "terrifyingly normal" person was able to help turn the murder of a people into an ordinary bureaucratic routine. Eichmann became the quintessential government bureaucrat—highly efficient and mindlessly, remorselessly obedient to orders.

The individuals who carried out the September 11 attacks on the United States were "banal," but in a different manner. Many of the men who hijacked and flew the planes into the targets had come to the United States years earlier to complete the planning and training. They were so "banal," so *ordinary* that none of their neighbors or coworkers noticed anything about them. Yet they were planning to carry out one of the most dramatic and lethal terrorist attacks in modern history.

Until the events of 2001, the suggestion by Brian Jenkins, consultant and author on terrorism, that terrorism had achieved a similar level of **bureaucratic banality** in that *its perpetrators carry out heinous crimes with increasing efficiency, while a* *worldwide audience becomes increasingly "unshockable" when viewing those acts,* seemed an accurate assessment of contemporary terrorism. Statistics appeared to have replaced headlines in referring to the escalation of terrorism. Terrorism had become so much the norm that it was commonplace, not unthinkable.

The events of September 11, 2001, *were* unthinkable, however. The magnitude of the attack; the cost in lives, property, and economic stability; and the multinational network that had worked to carry this out, after several years of planning, staggered the United States and much of the world. For the first time, rapid international action was taken to deal with the problem of terrorism, in the form of UN resolutions, treaties moving toward ratification as well as signatures, and the declaration of a **war on terrorism** *by a coalition of nations from the region involved led by the state that was a victim of the September 11 attacks.* Yet the problem remains unresolved.

The spending and personnel involved both in terrorism itself and in the fight against it have increased exponentially in the last few years. In both 2001 and 2002, the United States designated a dramatically increased portion of its budget to the external and internal efforts to combat terrorism. Establishing a new government office of homeland security, the United States parallels the United Nations, which has created a new office to monitor the agreements nations have now made to control the funding and arming of terrorists. Terrorism has become a bureaucratic reality in a completely new and extremely expensive fashion.

The 1990s were certainly a decade of significant change, with organizations such as the PLO and the IRA, who until the mid-1990s, both engaged in and supported terrorism. They become a more legitimate part of the international community, but the problem of international terrorism clearly remains unresolved and is becoming worse rather than better. For example, although the PLO achieved diplomatic recognition from several states and acted as a major participant in the peace process with Israel in 1994, the creation of a semiautonomous Palestinian system in the Gaza and in parts of the West Bank remains in doubt. Israel has been racked by suicide bombers from these territories, angry and desperate over the stalled process, and the Israeli government has responded with armed incursions and missile attacks into the occupied territories, making further progress in the direction of a Palestinian state less likely. The so-called road map for peace here has stalled in a rising cycle of violence that shows no sign of stopping.

Although we had come, perhaps, to accept the existence of terrorism in our daily lives, the events of September 2001 have made such a tolerant attitude less prevalent. Instead, a "war" on terrorism has been declared and is being fought first in the nation of Afghanistan, home of the Taliban and refuge of Osama bin Laden and his al-Qaeda network, and later, led by the United States, in a war in Iraq to remove a regime that had sponsored terror for decades. Even though society was willing to accept a certain level of violence, the September 11 attacks clearly exceeded those limits. States such as Libya and Syria that had been refuges for, and even supporters of, groups carrying out terrorist acts, were quick to condemn the attacks and offered to work together to end the threat of future attacks.

Efforts are underway to eliminate terrorism now, not only in terms of a successful war on terrorism, but more importantly, perhaps, in terms of working to ensure that such virulent anger does not fester in other places. The developed world today is more conscious that desperate poverty and hunger can provide the breeding grounds for terrorism.

POSITIVE OUTCOMES OF THE SEPTEMBER 11 ATTACKS

In attempts to come to grips with ensuring that such terrorist attacks would not recur, nations not only tried to improve their security measures and to track down and destroy the networks of individuals responsible for those attacks in September, but they also began to try to understand *why* people might feel such hatred toward another country. Understanding the causes of the anger became as important, in many respects, as the ability to punish the perpetrators.

This search for causes has led to an awakening of concerns that may help to ensure such destructive anger does not fester unnoticed. Two important points in this search for factors that may trigger terrorist violence are worth noting: the impact of the widening gap between the rich and the poor nations of the world, highlighted in the movement of globalization; and the lack of understanding between the West and the Middle East, even in terms of religious understanding.

Just as terrorism has become globalized, networking groups and nations in struggles across national boundaries, the economic **globalization**—*the networking of national economies on a global scale*—has come to be recognized as part of the reason for the anger directed at countries such as the United States. Globalization has left at least 20% of the world's population destitute, with little hope for the future. More than 800 million people in the world today are chronically undernourished, a condition with devastating health consequences and community welfare. The poverty and hunger in many developing countries provide fertile soil for those who want to blame the West for these conditions.

Understanding that the economic divide is huge and getting wider did not, of course, lead to a sudden decision on the part of all nations to create some kind of egalitarian communal society. That about 2.8 billion people live on less than $2 per day did not cause workers in developed nations to suddenly give up their high wages. But awareness of the problems created by this divide is growing; with this awareness, a search for solutions of a more realistic and permanent nature are being sought, primarily through the United Nations, but also through religious organizations. The commitment of the United States and its allies to stay and help to rebuild Afghanistan after the war, offering the people hope instead of poverty and despair, suggests that this awareness may indeed produce positive results.

Similarly, the West discovered, in the search for the answers to the *why* questions of the attacks, that most of its people did not understand Islam, nor did most in the Islamic world understand Western culture or religion. The open and concerted effort *not* to make a "war on Islam" in its war on terrorism led the West to host many forums, create many Web sites, and seek out many scholars to better understand Islam, its tenets, and its misuse as a tool by Osama bin Laden. This effort to build cultural bridges of understanding is too new to evaluate for effectiveness in terms of preventing future terrorism, but it clearly offers hope for a lowering of tensions that can make progress toward peace possible.

CASE STUDY Armed Efforts to Eliminate Terror: War in Iraq

From the fall of 2002 through the first three months of 2003, President George W. Bush advocated the use of violent force in Iraq to diminish, in part, the threat of terrorist access to WMDs. Taking his case to the UN Security Council, he sought to convince other nations that Iraq's WMD program had produced weapons not found in the inspections and that the programs were in fact ongoing and constituted a threat to international peace and security because Iraq had sponsored or supported a variety of groups engaging in terrorism.

Unable to secure a vote by the Security Council to affirm that Iraq had failed to comply with the resolutions dismantling such programs under the aegis of a UN inspections apparatus, and determining that a use of force was therefore justified to ensure that WMDs did not become weapons available to terrorists, Bush launched a war on Iraq in the spring of 2003. The United States was joined by the United Kingdom and several other nations, and was able to rapidly overcome Iraq's military and to occupy its capital in a very short time.

However, anger in the Arab world over the non-UN sanctioned invasion, combined with calls from al-Qaeda for followers to engage in a jihad against the troops occupying (or liberating) Iraq, has led to an extended period of conflict in that country. No WMDs have been found to date by the U.S.-led forces, but the daily death toll of both Iraqis, U.S. military, and civilian personnel engaged in the rebuilding process, continues to climb. Although attacks on U.S. military personnel in Iraq do not fit the definition used in this text of "terrorism," attacks on hotels, cafes, and car bombs in the streets do fit the criteria and continue to occur at alarming rates.

The war in Iraq has clearly generated terrorist attacks internationally as well. Madrid, Spain, in April 2003 experienced one of the worst terrorist attacks in recent history in the form of bombs on several commuter trains. Initially blamed by the government on the indigenous separatist Basque ETA, it quickly became clear that Muslim extremists linked to al-Qaeda had carried out the attacks. Perhaps most disturbing was that the events occurred only a few days before the national elections in Spain, with the two leading candidates for president very closely matched in support strength.

The candidate of the party in power—the incumbent—had openly supported the U.S.-led war in Iraq; in fact, Spanish troops were a part of the occupying forces at that point. He was quick to point to the ETA as the group responsible for the attacks when they occurred, because his administration had linked internal terrorism almost exclusively to this group. The opposing candidate openly opposed the war in Iraq equally and had a large popular following on this issue. The statements made by al-Qaeda that all countries should pull out of Iraq and that those who failed to do so would be targets in the jihad made the victory of the opposition candidate appear to be the result of terrorism. Although the outcome of the elections in Spain cannot be wholly attributed to the bombing attacks by al-Qaeda network cells (since the race was too close to call just days before the vote), the timing of the attacks offered a chilling reminder of the ability of terror cells in distant countries to "network" in actions to achieve a common goal.   ❑

DEALING WITH WEAPONS OF MASS DESTRUCTION

Terrorism, in fact, could grow much worse, with access to biological and chemical agents as well as nuclear materials, and the technical skills to effectively construct and utilize such weapons becomes more widespread as the previous chapter on WMDs in the hands of terrorists suggests. The ability of governments to deal with the threat of WMDs is unclear, and events to date suggest that it is also unpromising.

U.S. federal officials found out for themselves in June 2001 how complicated and destructive a bioterrorist attack could be. In *a war game, played at Andrews Air Force base, outside Washington, DC, an exercise code named* **Dark Winter** *began with a report of a single case of smallpox in Oklahoma City*. When the exercise was terminated, after 13 "days" of simulated time, the epidemic had spread to 25 states and 15 other countries, killing over 24 million people. As the exercise unfolded, the government quickly ran out of vaccine, forcing officials to make life-and-death decisions about who should be protected—health workers, soldiers, citizens of Oklahoma only, or in all neighboring states—and whether the military would be needed to quarantine the patients. After the exercise, officials were convinced that the United States was unprepared to deal with bioterrorism.[1]

In the wake of this learning experience and spurred by the events of September 11 and the subsequent anthrax attack, the U.S. Department of Homeland Security planned a third TOPOFF exercise to "improve the nation's ability to prevent, respond to, and recover from terrorist attacks."[2] TOPOFF 3 involved, as did TOPOFF 1 and 2, a series of exercises of increasing complexity, simulating a terrorist WMD campaign. In the third exercise, the simulated attacks occurred in the states of Connecticut and New Jersey, and were intended to enable government officials to respond more efficiently, based on the lessons learned from these earlier scenarios. As noted earlier, terrorist groups practice a postincident phase in which they learn from successes and failures. The U.S. government is attempting to create similar learning patterns in its efforts to cope with terrorists potentially equipped with WMDs.

The Department of Homeland Security (DHS) also has contracts for the development of a variety of technologies for defense against biological and chemical threats. These research teams will seek to develop many new systems, including Bioagent Autonomous Networked Detectors (to detect and treat biological agents in outdoor urban areas) and a Rapid Automated Biological Identification System (a "detect-and-protect" system for round-the-clock, distributed indoor monitoring of buildings and selected outdoor locations for bacteria, viruses, and toxins). Clearly, the DHS considers the potential for use of biological and/or chemical weapons domestically to be strong, since $48 million has already been committed to the first phase of these projects.[3]

The events of September 11 taught us that WMDs need not be biological, chemical, or nuclear. The airplanes flown into the World Trade Center towers were certainly weapons of mass destruction, but did not fall under the parameters of such weapons in most planning scenarios. Today, however, special efforts to secure airports and air transport against use as WMDs, as discussed in Chapter Thirteen, are being made, as the world adjusts to this new type of "weapon."

N. C. Livingstone notes,

> As the nations of the globe learn to live with routine low-level violence, it can be expected that there will be a movement by terrorists toward more dramatic and increasingly destructive acts of terrorism designed to ensure that the public does not forget about them and their cause.[4]

The explosive growth of technology that has brought with it new vulnerabilities to superindustrialized societies will continue to provide incentives for increased destruction.

The 1995 attack on Japanese subways in which sarin gas was used, resulting in numerous casualties although few deaths, indicated that those "unthinkable" weapons—the biological, chemical, and nuclear WMDs—were now not only in the hands of groups capable of violence, but were already in use. Japan was fortunate, in that the group carrying out the attack had ample supply of the toxin but little experience in its effective use; consequently, the death count was low.

Similar "luck" befell the United States in the 1993 bombing of the World Trade Center. Although this sounds like an absurd statement, the court accounts of the incident are interesting. In these records, it was revealed that those organizing the attack had planned to place sodium cyanide in the vehicle as well as the explosive materials. The intent was to create sufficient heat to vaporize the sodium cyanide, creating a lethal cyanide gas, which would have been sucked into the north tower, killing thousands. Although the physical destruction and the injuries caused by the bomb were dramatic, the death toll was very low compared to what was intended, had the materials been correctly utilized.

The United States was similarly fortunate in the anthrax attack it experienced in the fall of 2001. The agent sent through the mail was thought very lethal, but the analysis of its lethality proved false, and only a few died. The attack cost billions of dollars nationwide, created a feeling of paranoia among many U.S. citizens similar to the "fear of flying" experienced after September 11, but the casualty count was small, given the potential for serious casualties in the system's lack of preparedness for such an attack.

Within the United States evidence of efforts by individuals and groups to secure and even to use chemical or biological agents continues to grow. A list of only a few such attempts will make clear the reality of the threat:

a. In 1991, sheriff's deputies in Alexandria, Minnesota, learned of a shadowy group of tax protestors called the Patriots Council. One informant reported discussions of blowing up a federal building. Another turned over a baby food jar containing ricin, one of the most deadly poisons known. In 1995, three of the plotters, whose plans included the assassination of IRS agents, were convicted under the Biological Weapons Anti-Terrorism Act.

b. In December 1995, Thomas Levy, an Arkansas man, with survivalist connections, was arrested by the FBI for possession of a biological agent for unlawful purposes. He had 130 grams of ricin that, used with skill, was enough to kill thousands of people.

c. In May 1995, an Ohio member of the Aryan Nations allegedly ordered bubonic plague bacteria from a Rockville, Maryland, research supplier. He received the bacteria, but the supplier became suspicious over the man's persistent phone calls for delivery of the material and alerted officials. Larry Harris was subsequently arrested.

Terrorists and groups appear more willing to experiment with the use of nonconventional weapons such as these today. Recent alarming developments have occurred, too, concerning the probable access to and use of nuclear weapons by nonstate actors. There is growing evidence of nuclear smuggling from the former Soviet Union, at first across Europe, but later in southerly directions where border controls were less stringent. Although no individual or group has yet used or openly threatened to use such weapons to date, this can no longer be dismissed as an "unthinkable" weapon in this new century.

So our world is, and will for the foreseeable future continue to be, afflicted with the "condition" of terrorism, which in the view of most experts, will probably become worse rather than better. As the public globally becomes inured to low-level violence, that violence has escalated, in very undesirable ways that utilize the incredible innovations in modern technology.

TRENDS IN TERRORISM

The future patterns of terrorism present a grim picture. But it is unfortunately fairly accurate, at least as accurate as any predictions of future events and trends can be. Some specific trends in terrorism in recent years help to bring this view of the future into better focus.

Volume of Incidents

The **volume of terrorist incidents,** *the number occurring annually,* has begun to decrease since the turn of the millennium. After the 1972 attack on Olympic athletes in Munich and continuing through the mid-1980s, the number of terrorist incidents rose at an annual rate of between 12 and 15 percent. This rate of increase was not constant throughout that time frame. In the 1980s, there was a marked acceleration, which brought the average rate up. From 1984 to 1987, for instance, there was a fairly dramatic annual increase. During the period from 1989 to 1991, the escalation recurred, although certain types of incidents became less common (e.g., aerial skyjacking).

In 1992, a total of 363 terrorist incidents were recorded worldwide, a decrease from the 666 recorded in 1987. The rise in the number of incidents in 1993 over those recorded in 1992 was caused by a campaign of 150 attacks carried out by the Kurdistan Workers Party against Turkish interest in Western Europe on two days, one in June and the other in November of that year. In 1994, the number of incidents fell again, this time to 321, according the U.S. State Department statistics.

Although the number of incidents rose again in 1995 to a decade high of 440, the totals declined again until the last two years in the century. Activities by millennial groups, as well as increasing violence in the West Bank and Gaza, contributed to this rise, which peaked in the year 2000. At this point, however, the number of incidents began to fall, to a two-decade low of 190 incidents reported in 2003.

Lethality of Incidents

Unfortunately, although terrorism has decreased in volume, it has increased in **lethality of attacks**—that is, in *the number of people killed.* There is now a tendency toward large-scale indiscriminate terrorist attacks in mundane, everyday locations such as in airplanes or railway stations. In 1993, 109 people were killed and 1,393 were wounded in terrorist incidents around the world, the highest casualty total in five years. The attacks on the World Trade Center and the Pentagon in 2001 killed in excess of 3,000 people.

Religion and Terror Today

Another recent trend has been in the surge in **right-wing terrorism,** *carried out by militant, conservative, and fundamentalist individuals and groups.* If the 1960s can be described in terms of left-wing terrorism, with the 1970s carrying that trend to its logical conclusion by witnessing the involvement of liberation struggles in terrorism, the 1990s and the first few years of the twenty-first century witnessed a resurgence of right-wing terrorism. This was particularly true in Europe and the United States initially, but it is now becoming the norm in Southeast Asia, north Africa, and to a lesser extent Latin America. The activities of such organizations as the neo-Nazi youth groups against refugees from Eastern Europe in Germany provided grim reminders of the existence of right-wing groups increasingly willing to resort to violence. The attacks of September 11 by religious fanatics were poignant examples of right-wing zealotry. Subsequent attacks by cells of al-Qaeda and related groups throughout the world, including the dramatic bombing of the trains in Madrid in 2003, indicate the range and diversity of the threat of right-wing terror today.

The brief examination in Chapter Nine, of the growth of right-wing terror in just one nation offered useful insights into this significant trend. Although the U.S. experience with domestic terrorism from the left in the 1960s was relatively modest compared to the more lethal violence produced by revolutionary and secessionist groups in Europe, its growing pattern of right-wing domestic terror indicates that the ideological pendulum swing may be putting the United States at the apex of this new trend in violence.

IMPACT OF THE GENERATIONAL DIFFERENCE

Generational differences exists *between young militants and older leaders* in the terrorists operating today. Today's terrorists seem less likely to be involved in pickets and demonstrations before resorting to violence. Instead, they seem more willing to throw a bomb first and then talk later (if at all) about their grievances.

This "do something now" mentality has caused some difficulties and even embarrassment for some of the older leaders of established movements. In the PLO, for instance, the decade of the 1990s witnessed a number of splits, frequently between older, more "institutionalized" members of the organization and younger members who want to take violent action now against the existing situation.

HAMAS, *a radical element seeking the establishment of an Islamic state,* which is supported by Iran and active in the West Bank and Gaza, strongly rejected any such renunciation of terrorist tactics. The difficulties experienced by Arafat in governing Gaza during the last decade illustrate the deepening splits between the older leadership, willing to compromise in order to achieve a portion of that for which they fought, and the younger factions, willing to continue the struggle with violence and unwilling to settle for less than full success.

Terrorism has also contributed to changes in the mode of conflict both between and within nations. Conflicts today appear less coherent, at times exhibiting not two clear sides but several confusing and shifting alliances. Such conflicts are also less decisive, with no clear "winner" or "loser." As states use terrorism to engage in irregular warfare against other states, the stakes in the conflict become confused, the rules less clear, and the heroes hard to find.

Most confusing of all, in terms of "who" the enemy is, is the newly declared "war" on terrorism launched in the wake of September 11. The stakes as well as the contestants in this war remain blurred. Moreover, the emergence of "netwar" by terrorist groups linked only by a common cause and separated by great distances and a lack of central leadership, have made the conflict even more chaotic.

TERRORISM AND THE INTERNET

The virtues of the Internet—including but not limited to the ease of access, lack of regulation, large potential audiences, and the rapid flow of information—have begun to be used with increasing skill by groups committed to using terrorism to achieve their goals. Almost all active groups that have engaged in terrorism today have established a presence on the Internet, with hundreds of Web sites now serving terrorists and their support network. The dynamic quality of the Internet enables groups engaging in terrorism to quickly establish their Web site, easily modify their profile, disappear and reappear with startling speed, and evade most efforts by law enforcement to infiltrate or suppress.

Contemporary terrorists use the Internet in a variety of ways. On the Web groups create forums for the less substantive processes of psychological warfare and propaganda dissemination, but they also utilize the Internet for practical purposes like fundraising, recruitment, and coordination of activity.[5] This is clearly a new trend in terrorism and will be of concern to governments and law enforcement agencies as the skill of terrorists increases in this arena.

GRAPHIC EVIDENCE

Ample evidence describes the trends in terrorism in recent years. The U.S. Department of State issues a summary report annually on patterns of global terrorism, in which it reveals not only interesting insights into terrorism during that year, but also

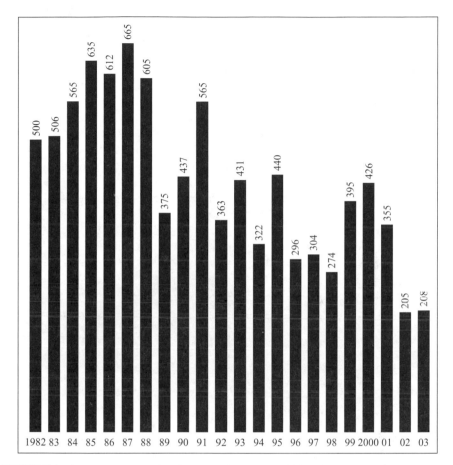

FIGURE 15.1 Total International Terrorist Attacks, 1982–2003

Source: www.state.gov/s/ct/rls/pgtrpt/2003/33777.htm

describes patterns of terrorism over the past several years. A brief look at some of these collective figures on terrorist incidents, locations, and targets may help us to understand both the scope of the problem of terrorism and its probable course in the next century.

Figure 15.1 makes the pattern of increase and decrease in the volume of international terrorist incidents graphically clear.

There is one important caveat to this numeric history, however. In 1982, reports of terrorism were not carefully separated into purely domestic incidents and international incidents, because many incidents by indigenous groups had at least some measure of international flavor, usually in the casualties but also in terms of state sponsorship. Palestinian violence in the occupied territories, for example, was always incorporated in the statistics for international terrorism, because many of the victims were Israelis. Today the U.S. State Department has adjusted its records of international terrorism to exclude intra-Palestinian violence, for example, and thus the figures for the first years of the new millennium may not reflect all of the terrorist incidents that have occurred as not all were, by U.S. measure, "international" terrorism. Because this is one of the few databases of terror incidents openly available to research sources, accuracy of assessment of current trends is potentially biased.

Although Figure 15.1 illustrates that there has been a decline in the number of terrorist incidents, the decline has not been consistent by region in recent years, as Figure 15.2 indicates. Latin America has experienced both a dramatic increase and an equally dramatic decrease in the number of incidents reported within only a six-year period, while the number of incidents reported in North America for all six years only totaled six—four of which occurred in September 2001. So the decrease in number of incidents is not a consistent pattern across regions, nor does it reflect the comparative damage or lethality of the attacks.

The gradual (and somewhat erratic) decrease in number of incidents from the mid-1990s through the early part of the twenty-first century contrasts regularly, in fact,

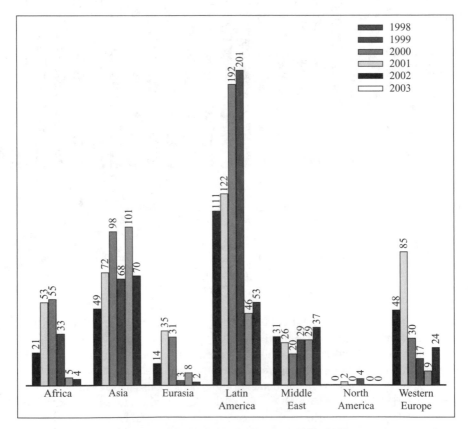

FIGURE 15.2   Total International Attacks by Region, 1998–2003

Source: http://www.state.gov/s/ct/rls/pgtrpt/2003/33777.htm

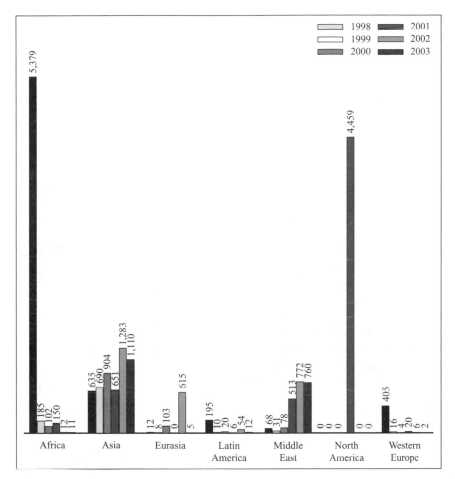

FIGURE 15.3 Total International Casualties by Region, 1998–2003

Source: http://www.state.gov/s/ct/rls/pgtrpt/2003/33777.htm

with the number of casualties inflicted by these incidents. Comparison of the data in Figures 15.2 and 15.3 indicates that the number of casualties actually increased in certain years in some regions, even as the number of incidents in those regions decreased. In Africa, for example, there were only a moderate number of attacks in 1998, but an extraordinary number of casualties—since this was the year of the embassy bombings in Kenya and Tanzania. Similarly, North America only experienced four attacks in 2001, but suffered more than 4,000 casualties. Such data clearly indicates the two trends noted earlier: the decrease in the number of incidents and the increase in the lethality of the incidents. Terrorism is occurring less often, as a whole, but is increasingly deadly.

Figure 15.4 makes the fluctuation in casualty rates even more obvious. It is also clear that single attacks with massive casualty rates, such as the embassy bombings

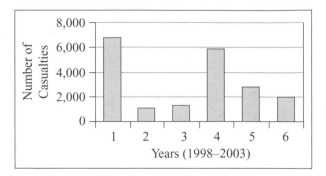

FIGURE 15.4   Total Casualties from International Terrorist Attacks, 1998–2003

Source: www.state.gov/s/ct/rls/

and the World Trade Center attacks, skew the annual casualty rates severely, while only minimally impacting the incidence figures.

Finally, the data presented in Figure 15.5 indicates business personnel remain the favorite target of terrorists as the twenty-first century opens. In spite of rhetoric urging the classification of individuals committing terrorists act as "soldiers" fighting a war of liberation, the military has not been, until the war in Iraq in 2003–2004 (for which data is not yet available), the target of modern terrorist attacks. This move away from the traditional targets in "war" situations to the selection of targets that, by almost any definition, will be considered innocent victims, or at least noncombatants rather than soldiers, indicates a shift that may make the designation of such acts more clearly illegal. It also, however, makes the randomness of the targets to be protected more apparent, making security almost an impossible goal if this pattern continues.

Perhaps this pattern of selecting businesses as targets springs from two sources. One may be the ease of access and the proliferation of these targets in our rapidly globalizing economy. The other reason for this selection, though, may be a negative reaction to this pattern of globalization that, as noted earlier, is regarded by some as widening the gap between the very rich and the very poor. As active participants in this economic pattern, it is possible that businesses make logical targets to those caught in the despair of poverty, malnutrition, and lack of hope for a better future.

These graphs make it easier to examine international terrorist incidents over time, illuminating some interesting trends. Certain generalizations can perhaps be made about these trends.

1. Although the number of terrorist incidents increased at an alarming rate in the 1980s, the number of incidents experienced a gradual, but not consistent, decline in the 1990s and into the early 2000s. The first three years of the twenty-first century clearly indicate a continuing decline of terrorist attacks, but the lethality of those attacks has dramatically, if erratically, increased. So terrorism is not occurring as frequently as it did two decades ago, but the attacks are becoming more lethal.

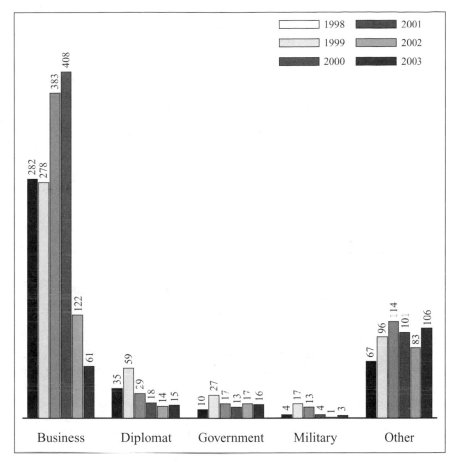

FIGURE 15.5   Total Facilities Struck by International Attacks, 1998–2003

Source: http://www.state.gov/s/ct/rls/pgtrpt/2003/33777.htm

2. The frequency of terrorist attacks varies significantly by region, with some regions continuing to experience a strong pattern of terrorist incidents. The greatest numbers of international terrorist incidents have occurred in Latin America, with surprisingly few incidents reported (in the U.S. Department of State's data) in the Middle East. Again, these statistics do not include the attacks considered by U.S. researchers to be domestic terrorism lacking any international component. Therefore, the data reflects neither the escalating number of suicide bombers in Palestinian territory nor the Israeli attacks on Palestinian communities in the West Bank or the Gaza Strip, because much of this violence did not meet the specified criteria for international terrorism.

3. In terms of the type of facility targeted, business appears to be the target of choice for most terrorist attacks. During the 1990s, terrorists chose businesses and businessmen as targets, rather than the military, government, or diplomatic personnel who had in earlier years been the prime targets. The only other category which indicates a strong position

as the "favorite" for terrorist attacks is "other," which according to the State Department includes grocery stores, restaurants, and other such "civilian" places.

4. Religious extremists have carried out the most lethal attacks in recent history, including the attacks on the U.S. embassies in Kenya and Tanzania, the attacks on September 11, 2001, and the Madrid train bombings. Each peak in Figure 15.3 reflecting a very high number of casualties can be linked to terrorist incidents by religious crusaders. Moreover, such attacks are becoming more frequent, even as WMDs become more available. Religion, then, when it is the motivating force behind a terrorist event, dramatically alters the likelihood of a high casualty rate; because religious zealotry is more and more frequently the motivating force behind modern terrorism, this problem will escalate.

CONCLUSIONS

The world community is now required to deal with unprecedented problems arising from acts of international terrorism. . . . which raise many issues of a humanitarian, moral, legal, and political character for which, at the present time, no commonly agreed rules or solutions exist.[6]

The world community must meet the challenge of terrorism. If it is indeed a condition for which there is no known cure, then we must at least seek to understand the phenomenon in order to better cope with its presence in our midst.

To recognize the existence of terrorism is not to recognize its right to exist or its inevitability. A doctor, faced with an epidemic, must first recognize the problem and then take steps to deal with it, at least in terms of containment and perhaps prevention. Similarly, students of world social, legal, political, and security issues today must study the phenomenon of terrorism in order to better cope with its presence in the world.

Just as that hypothetical doctor facing that epidemic has restraints on what he may do to handle the problem, so nations searching for ways to cope with modern terrorism must exercise restraint in their responses. Nations must weigh the cost, in terms of the loss of liberties and freedoms, against the gains in subduing terrorism, recognizing that to sacrifice too many liberties may well be to give terrorists the victory they seek: the destruction of the democratic systems. The cost of winning some battles against terrorism may be too great.

But to concede there are some ways in which a nation or a people may not combat terrorism is not to concede that terrorism cannot be fought or is in any way acceptable. Regardless of the cause, terrorism is not an acceptable mode of behavior and cannot be permitted to prevail unchecked. The end does not, and can never, justify the means. To attempt to remedy perceived acts of injustice by committing even greater acts of injustice neither solves anything nor excuses anything.

EVALUATION

The on-going insurgency in Iraq has not only escalated the level of violent attacks worldwide, it has also created confusion in the data concerning terrorism today. At the beginning of the insurgency, the US labeled most of the attacks against its "peace-keeping" forces and their civilian support network as "terrorism." This caused the number of terrorist incidents to *increase* rather than decrease, during the "war on terrorism," making policy-makers uncomfortable with the new data. After posting "incorrect" data in 2004 for 2003 events, the US Department of State revised its data on terrorism for 2003, explaining that the lack of consensus about which incidents were truly "terrorist acts" within the insurgency had created problems for data analysis.

This ambivalence about defining "terrorist" events during an insurgency led the State Department to decide *not* to issue data for terrorism in 2004, making it difficult to track trends in terrorism. Thus, trends in terrorism can be accurately and consistently traced through 2003, but have become very difficult to delineate for the following year. Certainly the number of violent incidents in Iraq continues to escalate in 2005; whether the acts are "terrorist" acts cannot be determined by academic research until records of civilian and military casualties are fully released, and the details of the attacks become public record. All that can safely be said, with any accuracy at this point, is that terrorism continues to be a growing threat to global peace and security.

If Iraq is indeed, a "breeding ground" for terrorism, consider the following questions concerning the danger that terrorism presents in the modern world: Has mankind formulated a weapon for its own destruction by fomenting the conditions from which terrorism arises? By putting WMDs in the hands of individuals willing to commit terrorist acts, are we creating the arrow that will destroy our world?

> **So in the Libyan fable it is told**
> **That once an eagle, stricken with a dart,**
> **Said when he saw the fashion of the shaft,**
> **"With our own feathers, not by others' hands**
> **Are we now smitten."**

Aeschylus, Wisdom of the Ages

SUGGESTED READINGS

Friedlander, Robert A. "Terrorism and National Liberation Movements: Can Rights Derive From Wrongs?" *Case Western Reserve Journal of International Law* 13, no. 2 (Spring 1981): 47–69.

Kegley, Charles W., Jr., ed. *The New Global Terrorism: Characteristics, Causes, Controls* (Upper Saddle River, NJ: Pearson Education, 2003).

Livingstone, N. C. "Taming Terrorism: In Search of a New U.S. Policy." *International Security Review* 7, no. 1 (Spring 1992): 12–19.

Nyatepe-Coo, Akorlie A. and Dorothy Zeisler-Vralsted, ed. *Understanding Terrorism: Threats in an Uncertain World* (Upper Saddle River, NJ: Pearson Education, 2004).

"Patterns of Global Terrorism: 2003." U.S. Department of State. Washington, DC: U.S. Government Printing Office, April 2003.

Weimann, Gabriel. *www.terror.net: How Modern Terrorism Uses the Internet* (United States Institute for Peace: Special Report 116, March 2004).

NOTES

1. www.homalandsecurity.org/darkwinter/index.cfm.

2. www.dhs.gov/dhspublic/.

3. www.dhs.gov/dhspublic/display?content=3415.

4. N. C. Livingstone, "Taming Terrorism: In Search of a New U.S. Policy," *International Security Review,* 7, no. 1 (Spring 1992): 17.

5. Gabriel Weimann, *Special Report: www.terror.net: How Modern Terrorism Uses the Internet.* U.S. Institute for Peace. March 2004.

6. Bruce Hoffman, "Defining Terrorism," in *Terrorism and Counterterrorism: Understanding the New Security Environment,* ed. Russell D. Howard and Reid L. Sawyer (Guilford, CT: McGraw-Hill, 2003), 3.

Index